WAITHOOD

Fertility, Reproduction and Sexuality

GENERAL EDITORS:

Soraya Tremayne, Founding Director, Fertility and Reproduction Studies Group and Research Associate, Institute of Social and Cultural Anthropology, University of Oxford.

Marcia C. Inhorn, William K. Lanman, Jr. Professor of Anthropology and International Affairs, Yale University.

Philip Kreager, Director, Fertility and Reproduction Studies Group, and Research Associate, Institute of Social and Cultural Anthropology and Institute of Human Sciences, University of Oxford.

Understanding the complex and multifaceted issue of human reproduction has been, and remains, of great interest both to academics and practitioners. This series includes studies by specialists in the field of social, cultural, medical, and biological anthropology, medical demography, psychology, and development studies. Current debates and issues of global relevance on the changing dynamics of fertility, human reproduction and sexuality are addressed.

Recent volumes:

For a full volume listing, please see the series page on our website:
http://www.berghahnbooks.com/series/fertility-reproduction-and-sexuality

WAITHOOD
GENDER, EDUCATION, AND GLOBAL DELAYS IN MARRIAGE AND CHILDBEARING

Edited by
Marcia C. Inhorn and Nancy J. Smith-Hefner

berghahn
NEW YORK · OXFORD
www.berghahnbooks.com

First published in 2021 by

Berghahn Books

www.berghahnbooks.com

Library of Congress Cataloging-in-Publication Data

A C.I.P. cataloging record is available from the Library of Congress
Library of Congress Cataloging in Publication Control Number:
2020048772

British Library Cataloguing in Publication Data

A catalogue record for this book is available from the British Library.

ISBN 978-1-78920-899-3 hardback
ISBN 978-1-80073-629-0 paperback
ISBN 978-1-78920-900-6 ebook

https://doi.org/10.3167/9781789208993

CONTENTS

ILLUSTRATIONS

Figures

Tables

ACKNOWLEDGMENTS

This book emerged from a meeting that took place at Yale University. For the first time, scholars in anthropology, political science, and religious studies gathered to explore why young people around the world are waiting longer to marry and form families. In these discussions, it became clear that some of this "waithood" is intentional, especially as young women around the world seek higher education. But some of this waithood is unintentional, especially as young men face barriers in an increasingly precarious global labor market. The scholars whose work is included in this volume examine this waithood phenomenon in a variety of different research settings around the world. We are proud of and grateful to these dedicated scholars, beginning with Prof. Diane Singerman of American University, who was the first to forward the "waithood" concept as a way to understand marriage delay in her fieldsite in urban Egypt.

At Yale, our gathering was hosted by The Whitney and Betty Mac-Millan Center for International and Area Studies, the Council on Middle East Studies (CMES), and the Department of Anthropology. Generous support was received from the Edward J. and Dorothy Clark Kempf Memorial Fund and the US Department of Education Title VI National Resource Center, which supports Yale CMES's activities. At CMES, we are particularly grateful for the tireless organizational support of the CMES staff, including Cristin Siebert, CMES Program Director, and Marwa Khaboor, CMES Program Coordinator, who organized many details, from posters to flights to Middle Eastern meals. We also appreciate the support provided by the Yale Department of Anthropology, especially Jennifer DeChello, who was a tremendous facilitator of the meeting that occurred in the Anthropology department's beautiful seminar room.

We are very grateful for the excellent editorial suggestions made by our colleague Lisa L. Wynn of Macquarie University in Sydney,

Australia. The book also benefited from the meticulous professional copyediting services of Bonnie Rose Schulman and the expert indexing services of Larry D. Sweazy. This book's beautiful cover image was provided by Dr. Idris Thaha, State Islamic University Syarif Hidayatullah, Jakarta, Indonesia, and was artistically enhanced by our friend and colleague Mary-Jo DelVecchio Good of Harvard University.

Finally, we thank the dedicated editorial team of the "Fertility, Reproduction, and Sexuality" series at Berghahn Books, especially the founding series editor Soraya Tremayne, assistant editor Tom Bonnington, and publisher Marion Berghahn. We are fortunate to be part of Berghahn Books' efforts to support innovate, cutting-edge anthropological research.

Marcia C. Inhorn and Nancy J. Smith-Hefner
New Haven and Boston, November 2020

Introduction

WAITHOOD

GENDER, EDUCATION, AND GLOBAL DELAYS IN MARRIAGE AND CHILDBEARING

Nancy J. Smith-Hefner and Marcia C. Inhorn

In many societies around the world, young men and women are waiting longer and longer to marry and have children. These delays in marriage and childbearing are growing—and they are global in nature. For instance, in the United States, the Pew Research Center reports that the share of Americans living without a partner has increased, especially among young adults (Fry 2017). Today, about six-in-ten American adults (61 percent) under the age of thirty-five are now living without a spouse or a partner. Of these un-partnered adults, about six-in-ten (58 percent) have never been married. Another Pew Research Center survey shows that about six-in-ten American adults (61 percent) between the ages of eighteen and forty-nine are childless, with about four-in-ten (37 percent) saying that they never expect to have children (Livingston and Horowitz 2018).

Although less pronounced in many other societies, these delays in marriage and childbearing are increasing globally. In a study using a variety of international data sets, demographer Philip N. Cohen (2013) shows that marriage delay, as well as an overall reduction in the marriage rate, is occurring worldwide, particularly in well-to-do countries such as France, Italy, Germany, Japan, and the United States. However, marriage delays and declines are not just found in the Global North. Today, 89 percent of the world's population lives in a country with falling marriage rates. These changes in marriage are part of what Cohen (2013) calls a "package of demographic changes," including higher education, higher incomes, and lower rates of fertility.

Indeed, total fertility rates (TFRs) have plummeted in most countries since the 1980s, including, for example, across the Muslim world, where sharp declines in TFRs since the 1980s have been characterized as a "quiet revolution . . . hiding in plain sight" (Eberstadt and Shah 2012; see also Inhorn 2018 for Arab world trends). Today, roughly half the world's population lives in societies with TFRs below replacement level (Roser 2016). This includes the "ultra-low fertility" societies of East Asia, including China, Hong Kong, Japan, South Korea, Taiwan, and Singapore (Chan, Jones, and Straughan 2008). In these societies, ultra-low birth rates have precipitated a sense of national reproductive crisis, with women potentially blamed for failing to marry and waiting too long to conceive. Yet, these Asia-Pacific nations are emblematic of wider global patterns, whereby the "richest" people have the "lowest" fertility rates, including in much of Western Europe (Roser 2016).

Overall, this global delay and decline in marriage and childbearing has been characterized as "one of the most fundamental social changes that [has] happened in human history" (Roser 2016). But the question is: Why? Why are so many young people around the world waiting to marry and have children—and, in some cases, never marrying at all? Are these delays intentional (e.g., for education) and positive (e.g., for a sense of individual autonomy and personal fulfillment)? Or are there obstacles in the way to marriage and childbearing (e.g., lack of employment opportunities) that lead to prolonged waiting and youth frustration?

In this volume, we examine the multifarious experiences of young people around the world who are living in a state of *waithood*, which, in the most general sense, refers to an extended period of young adulthood in which young men and women are waiting to marry and have children, sometimes delaying indefinitely, and sometimes opting out altogether. Waithood may be intentional, unintentional, or some combination of both. From the standpoint of intentionality, waithood may be planned and experienced in aspirational terms, as when young women put off marriage and childbearing to pursue their educations and careers. But waithood, in its original meaning, refers to unintentional delays in marriage and childbearing due to political and economic realities that force young people into a state of deferred adulthood.

This latter meaning of waithood was first forwarded by the political scientist and ethnographer Diane Singerman, who originally coined the term. Viewing the rates of education and marriage across the Middle East and North Africa (MENA) region, Singerman (2007, 2013) used the term "waithood" to refer to a widespread pattern of delayed marriage and—because marriage is culturally linked to social adulthood—delayed adulthood. As Singerman argued, the pattern is not socially or affectively neutral: it has resulted in considerable youth frustration and societal concern across much of the MENA region. In her foundational work, Singerman observed that in countries like Egypt, Iran, Syria, and Morocco, young people are obtaining higher levels of education than ever before, but that education is not leading to higher levels of employment.

While her research focuses on youth in general, Singerman emphasizes the experiences of young men, highlighting the failures both of national governments to supply sufficiently remunerative employment opportunities and educational systems to adequately prepare young men for the jobs that exist (see also Dhillon and Yousef 2011; Honwana 2014). Across the Middle East and North Africa, the skyrocketing expense of marriage and housing has combined with cultural norms enjoining young people to live at home until they marry. The effect is a situation of prolonged dependence on parents as young people are forced to wait—for jobs, for housing, for marriage, and for families of their own (Singerman and Ibrahim 2003). It is not surprising that at least some young men find this liminal period between adolescence and adulthood a time of boredom and despair (see Schielke 2008, 2015). No less seriously, political observers voice concern that this shift in patterns of marriage and social adulthood creates dangerous possibilities for youth unrest and even radicalization (Khosravi 2017).

As depicted in several chapters in this volume, particularly those from sub-Saharan Africa, young men's marriage delay is often a by-product of an economic and political situation that makes finding work and saving for marriage difficult, if not impossible. While a pattern of later age of marriage for men is nothing new, neoliberal policies of economic restructuring in many societies within the Global South have pushed young men into a position of unintended, unwelcome, and extended waithood—or a prolongation of the period of time between adolescence and the achievement of full adulthood, which is typically associated with marriage and the establishment of a family of one's own.

At the same time, and sometimes even in the same cultural context, there are young men who view this waithood period more productively—as a space for personal exploration and self-improvement. Writing on waithood in Africa, anthropologist Alcinda Honwana (2014: 20) has astutely observed that the waithood phenomenon represents "the contradictions of modernity, in which young people's opportunities and expectations are simultaneously broadened and constrained." As shown in this volume, young men in Africa may use the waithood period to pursue education, employment opportunities, friendship, and self-development, thereby clarifying their future aspirations and formulating new self-identifications. Indeed, this combination of social disappointment and aspirational achievement may characterize waithood in many late-modern contexts, particularly for young men.

However, one of the key insights of this volume is that the waithood period may be experienced quite differently by women, which, in turn, has broader social, cultural, and affective consequences and significance. One of the "quiet revolutions" occurring in the world today for women is their educational achievement, with women students outperforming their male peers in higher education in more than one-third of the world's nations (Inhorn et al. 2018; Inhorn, Chapter 15, this volume). As educational opportunities have become more widely available, young men and especially young women have taken advantage of these opportunities, with concomitant delays in marriage and childbearing as a result (cf. Goldstein and Kenney 2001; Jones 2005).

The most striking consequence of women's educational achievement is the later age for women at first marriage—or, more consequentially, no marriage at all. During the three-decade period from the 1980s through the 2000s, marriage rates among educated women between the ages of thirty and thirty-four plummeted around the world. As demographer Philip Cohen (2013) puts it simply, "Women with more education are less likely to be married."

What many of the chapters in this volume demonstrate, however, is that the "higher education means lower marriage" equation for women has not come without significant social and cultural consequences. An unanticipated and often worrying effect of women's educational achievements—which is often coupled with men's waning educational achievements in many societies, including in the United States (Autor and Wasserman 2013)—is that many well-educated women who would like to be married face a smaller pool of well-educated men. The result is that the identification of an appropriate marital partner—namely, one who shares a vision of marriage as a joint project and is willing to accept a more equitable household arrangement—has become increasingly difficult for educated women around the globe. The fact that "older" educated women in countries such as China are deemed unmarriageable—and referred to in such callous terms as "surplus women," "unmarketable women," "leftover women," or, if they have PhDs, the "third gender"—bespeaks the often significant social and personal challenges that educated women face in their efforts to marry (Lake 2018).

Today, long-standing patterns of hypergamy (or women marrying "up") in most societies are being challenged by a pattern of hypogamy (or women marrying "down"). New patterns of hypogamy most often involve a woman marrying a man who has less education; however, in some cases, they may also involve a man who is younger or less economically secure. In yet other cultural contexts, the pattern involves women reaching across previously circumscribed ethnic, racial, or religious divides for possible marriage partners (Ortega and Hergovich 2017).

Having said this, in many countries of the world, women's educational achievements have also gone hand-in-hand with new visions of conjugality and shifting marital arrangements. In many societies today, parentally arranged marriages are giving way to self-choice of partner and the "modern" desire among many youth for a romantic, companionate marital relationship (Ahearn 2001; Hirsch and Wardlow 2006; Inhorn 2012). These aspirations are often buttressed by other social changes, including access to new social media technologies and the development of consumer cultures including Western-style cafés, shopping malls, and multiplex movie theaters that facilitate intimate encounters.

The postponement of marriage and the prolongation of unmarried singlehood have also led to a noticeable reconfiguration of courtship and dating practices and the emergence of new types of partnerships. This trend assumes multiple forms, and can be seen in, among other things, the growth of online dating and matchmaking services, multiple romantic/sexual partners, unmarried cohabitation, polyamory (i.e., multiple committed relationships), and both temporary and unofficial marriage. At times, these emergent forms of partnership and conjugality—with or without legal marriage—are viewed as a marriage "crisis," a cause for alarm and moral panic on the part of politicians, religious leaders, and societies' moral authorities.

Yet, however morally questionable and varied their local forms, these transformations have involved a profoundly important shift in gender norms and expectations. That shift involves the recognition of the value of educating not only sons but also daughters, of allowing them to wait for marriage as they pursue their educational goals, and of encouraging them to work outside of the home, even after marriage (Adely 2012; Smith-Hefner 2019). Where educational opportunities are open to both young men and young women, women have often moved exceptionally quickly to take advantage of these opportunities. And where there are available employment opportunities for educated women—and where parents recognize the benefits of their daughters' employment—women have put their educations to work.

The complicated constellation of factors that lead young women to delay marriage—and, typically, childbearing—emerges in interesting and sometimes surprising ways. Not uncommonly, the change toward waiting entails a far-reaching shift in gender norms, social identity, and intimate relations. The shift in identity and sociality involves a movement away from a primary focus on social and familial responsibility to a concern with personal fulfillment and some degree and variety of self-actualization.

Having said this, in the many areas of the Global South where educational achievement does not easily translate into employment opportunities—and, equally important, where reigning cultural and religious sensibilities assign primary responsibility for family support to men—men may well experience the status, honor, and economic disappointments of waithood disproportionately and with particularly stigmatizing effects (Wyrod 2016). Non-employment or underemployment is a major hurdle for young men hoping to achieve social maturity through marriage. Waithood's effects are compounded and are particularly debilitating in those contexts where marriage costs are exceptionally high, pushing its achievement out of reach for ever-growing numbers of men.

A partial solution to the challenge may include temporary labor migration, where such opportunities exist. Alternately or in addition, the situation may be momentarily neutralized through the pursuit of even more higher education, or simply by biding one's time networking with peers, killing time playing sports and drinking, and otherwise dealing with the liminal hardship of "wait frustration" (cf. Schielke 2015). As a pervasive and pressing social phenomenon, then, waithood not only reshapes the always multidimensional and socially momentous transition from youth to adulthood, it is also linked to urgent existential issues of gendered status and social recognition, concerns that extend beyond securing a job to social life and civic participation more broadly (Honwana 2014).

The chapters in this volume employ the waithood concept as a guiding frame for rich ethnographic studies of young men's and young women's lives in various states of waithood across the Middle East, sub-Saharan Africa, Latin America, Asia, Europe, and the United States. In this volume, we adopt an expansive view of "waithood," with a focus on both agency and constraint. In some areas of the world, waiting before marriage and childbearing is deliberate, and signals a significant reshaping of the perceived social and cultural desirability of marriage and the acceptability of permanent singlehood. This is certainly true today in many parts of Europe and North America, but also in countries such as Iran (Chapter 10, this volume) or Rwanda (Chapter 6, this volume). However, as shown in the majority of the chapters in this volume, even in areas of the world where marriage delays are occurring and overall marriage rates are declining, the institution of marriage is still viewed favorably by most women (and men), and is culturally and sometimes religiously linked to childbearing. In such cases, men and women may not be opting out of marriage, but rather are forced out by social, economic, and political conditions that constrain young people's options and agency.

As these chapters clearly show, this important distinction between agency and constraint is evident between those areas of the world where waithood is largely involuntary and young people have little choice but to wait (for a job, an opportunity, a partner) and those areas of the world where marriage delay and waithood involve a significant measure of social and individual choice. While many young people may prioritize education, self-development, and employment across varied social contexts to strategize and maximize their available options, other young people find themselves "stuck" (Sommers 2012) and must find creative ways to bide their time while waiting for opportunities that may never materialize.

The studies in this volume reveal that whether voluntary or involuntary, the phenomenon of youth waithood necessitates a recognition of its consequences: a profound reconfiguration of gender and family roles; newly emergent forms of courtship, marriage, and intimate relationships; and the real possibilities of permanent singlehood and childlessness. The chapters in this volume thus speak to four major themes: 1) the frustrations of waithood and the struggles for dignity in nation-states where political-economic circumstances hinder the achievement of adulthood, especially for men; 2) the ways in which educational opportunities, especially for young women, have led to new aspirations, including desires to defer marriage and motherhood until later (or more radically to forego them completely); 3) the ways in which marriage deferrals are leading to fundamental shifts in women's (and men's) social lives, including permanent states of singlehood, especially among educated women; and 4) the impact of delayed marriage on delays in childbearing, especially among educated women, who may eventually experience frustration in their inability to find partners and to become mothers at later ages.

In each of the fifteen chapters in this volume, the authors, most of whom are anthropologists, offer original concepts to help describe and nuance our understandings of waithood in the diverse societies represented in this volume. In Table 0.1, entitled, "Waithood: A New Conceptual Vocabulary," we provide a summarizing overview of these chapters, the ethnographic locations of the authors' studies, and the attending conceptual frameworks they offer. Table 0.1 is thus designed to introduce readers to the new conceptual vocabulary offered throughout this volume, including the locations of these key concepts.

Table 0.1. Waithood: A New Conceptual Vocabulary.

Term	Author(s)	Countries	Definition
Active waithood	McLean	Sierra Leone	Young men's (*youthmen's*) particular investments in planning and striving for educated futures in preparation for a better life; because education is a highly valued life goal, seeking education while waiting to become a full adult is seen as a way to escape poverty and obtain a better future
Conjugal conundrums	Thornton	Dominican Republic	Marriage in the Caribbean is religiously valorized but difficult to enact, especially among impoverished male Christian converts who, by virtue of competing obligations, are precariously situated between the authoritative prescriptions of the church and powerful sociocultural and economic imperatives that discourage the adoption of marriage and the nuclear family model

(continued)

Table 0.1. *continued*

Term	Author(s)	Countries	Definition
Delayed adulthood	Masquelier	Niger	Young men's inability to reach maturity despite being of age, while also practicing time management to embrace delays, fill time, and prepare for the future; this occurs through receiving emotional and material support from peers, exchanging information about jobs, training opportunities, and other resources to orient themselves toward possible futures; thus, young men aim to shatter the temporality of aimless deferral and recreate a sense of purposeful waiting
Emergent waithood	Berry	Guatemala	The places and moments where marriage practices are changing for women, and the ways in which institutions (including the state and NGOs) are shaping marriage practices and reproduction differently; institutions may create conflicting or harmonizing incentives and pressures on women's marital and reproductive lives; however, through these institutional influences, some young women are modeling new possibilities for life trajectories beyond the household and into public and professional spheres
Extended singlehood	Smith-Hefner	Indonesia	Young people in a context of universal marriage nonetheless pursuing higher education, employment, and "self-development," while delaying marriage and extending the period of singlehood, the effects of which are more significant for women who may age out of the "market" and face difficulties identifying a suitable, equally well-educated match
Female reproductive temporality	Vialle	France	Women wait to become mothers because they envisage a reproductive temporality that is based not only on biological, but also social, relational, and temporal factors; women thus seek to satisfy a number of conditions that they deem necessary in order to welcome and raise children, within a temporality that they consider both socially and biologically appropriate

(continued)

Table 0.1. *continued*

Term	Author(s)	Countries	Definition
Giving oneself time	Sadruddin	Rwanda	How young and aspiring women negotiate their womanhood in the wake of sweeping transformations in norms around marriage, education, and gender; "giving oneself time" can be understood as a liminal and aspirational period in which young women belonging to a privileged professional segment of Rwandan society "find themselves" as they contemplate marriage and, to some extent, motherhood
Intentional waithood	Conclusion	Global	In societies where economic and political constraints are not so pronounced and stressful, young people take advantage of opportunities to postpone marriage and childbearing by choice; this phenomenon is significantly gendered, as educational and employment opportunities become more widely available for women around the world
Never-marriedness	Lamb	India	The condition of never having married, putting never-married single women into a unique and anomalous social category, different from separated, divorced, and widowed women; positioned outside the norm, never-married single women see features of their society not easily recognized by others—systems of gender and sexuality, kinship and marriage, and social class—which they must both work within and strive to redefine as they endeavor to achieve forms of everyday well-being and belonging without being married
Politics of waithood	Singerman	Middle East (specifically Egypt, Jordan, and Tunisia)	Young people are engaging in a politics of waithood as they demand dignity and an end to economic and political marginalization; the financial and social challenges of waithood and its liminal status have fueled these political demands, taking a most obvious turn during the Arab Spring
Postponed adulthood	Schulz	Uganda	A deeply paradoxical set of challenges whereby young men frame their aspirations and struggles to attain

(continued)

Table 0.1. *continued*

Term	Author(s)	Countries	Definition
			seniority status as a matter of blocked occupational opportunities on one hand, and, on the other, of the double bind of obligatory marriage and the deeply risky nature of marital intimacy
Refusing to settle	Adely	Jordan	The experiences of single women who have migrated for professional opportunities, who have lived on their own for as much as a decade and are beginning to reckon with the long-term possibilities of staying single; as time passes, many become concerned about finding a suitable partner and marrying, but on their own terms; they insist on living a life of dignity
Reproductive waithood	Inhorn	United States	The condition of women waiting to become mothers, both intentionally (on their paths to professional fulfilment) and unintentionally (because of the difficulties they face in finding a committed reproductive partner); compelling evidence suggests that educated women's growing use of egg freezing reflects unintended reproductive waithood, which, in turn, is tied to gender-based disparities in men's and women's educational achievements, with women surpassing men around the globe
Tactics of marriage delay	Howlett	China	A wide array of interpersonal strategies that people in many cultural contexts pursue to negotiate between the personal and the social in the domain of marriage decisions; the tactics of marriage delay include efforts to avoid bad marriages as well as efforts to achieve emotional and personal fulfillment while waiting for good ones; in some cases, people reject marriage, but more frequently they feel excluded from it, due to hypergamic norms, increasing social inequality, and the rising costs of marriage and childrearing; in addition, queer-identified individuals often face legal exclusion even as they come under pressure to enter "marriages of convenience"

(continued)

Table 0.1. *continued*

Term	Author(s)	Countries	Definition
Unintentional waithood	Conclusion	Global	The plight of young people in resource-poor settings, where increasing numbers of young men and women are being forced to delay marriage and family formation, with profound consequences for their gender identity and social welfare
Voluntary waithood	Babadi	Iran	When the motive behind young peoples' extended singlehood is psychological and not economic; with the continued economic and emotional support of their parents, middle-class young people are enjoying their period of singlehood, engaging in self-exploration and identity formation by pursuing higher education, travelling, part-time exploratory careers, and dating; they also tend to be cynical about marriage (given parents' problematic marital relationships), as well as their own idealist requirements for the perfect partner
Waithood	Introduction	Global	The term originally introduced by Diane Singerman to describe an extended period of young adulthood in which marriage and childbearing are delayed, sometimes indefinitely, thereby preventing the transition to full adulthood; waithood, in its original meaning, refers to unintended delays, which are often due to political and economic realities that force young people into a state of deferred adulthood; but, increasingly, waithood is planned and aspirational, as when young women around the globe delay marriage and childbearing to pursue their educations and careers
Waithood choice	San Román	Spain	Many women using ART waited to become mothers not because of material constraints but by personal choice; choosing to wait does not prevent them from feeling completely adult, nor affect the belief that they can procreate later, after doing other things that they also want to do (such as travelling or "enjoying life"); however, when "the right time" for motherhood comes, women may find that their opportunities to reproduce "naturally" have diminished

Part I. Waithood, Statehood,
and the Struggle for Dignity

In Chapter 1, "Youth, Economics, and the Politics of Waithood: The Struggle for Dignity in the Middle East and North Africa," Diane Singerman updates her original path-breaking waithood argument and sets out a framework for the three chapters that follow in this section—all of which take up young people's responses to state policies that have presented serious roadblocks to their achieving full adulthood. Singerman's chapter offers important new data from Egypt, Jordan, and Tunisia, which indicate that economic policies and poor-quality education continue to pose challenges for young people and have resulted in considerable social precarity, not least of which is widespread and extended marriage delays. Across MENA countries, there is still evidence of a "marital imperative" which closely links marriage to the achievement of adult status. Adding to its urgency, marriage in this region of the world is considered to be the only context for legitimate sex. As Singerman notes, this does not necessarily prevent young people from engaging in intimate relationships, but it places them at risk of social and familial disapproval—and in some countries possible legal punishment—if they do. Yet marriage continues to be a high-risk endeavor for young people—one in which large sums of money are expended, particularly by the groom and his family. Singerman cites 2012 statistics from Egypt to argue that, although there has been some reduction in the costs associated with marriage, expenses can still easily require five to eight years of a young man's wages.

Very high rates of youth unemployment across the MENA region—in some countries approaching 40 percent—have only exacerbated this pattern of marriage delay. Young people have pursued higher education as a strategy for addressing the labor market, but because of the poor quality of schooling and dearth of available positions, even a college degree cannot guarantee a secure job. Singerman points out that an unemployed man is not only considered an unacceptable marriage partner; his situation will likely result in his being unable to accumulate the considerable funds required to pay for marriage and, with it, complete the transition to social adulthood.

Singerman's larger interest goes beyond the demographics and economics of delayed marriage, however, to the broader *politics of waithood* and in particular the state's response to young people's plight. Across the MENA region, the "demand for dignity" (*karama*) is a rallying cry for youth movements seeking social and economic justice. States have not been consistently sensitive to youth demands, but young people's continuing calls for recognition and social justice have had some success, particularly with regard to women's rights. Singerman is careful to point out that these achievements are not solely the product of the aspirations and efforts of disaffected youth; rather, they build on and reinforce larger grassroots movements. Her insight is nonetheless deeply important, emphasizing the need to recognize the desires of young people for dignity, as well as their potential for social change as they endeavor to not only improve their own lives but participate in their nation's development.

In Chapter 2, "'Trusting Is a Dicey Affair': Muslim Youth, Gender Relations, and Future-Making in Southwestern Uganda," Dorothea E. Schulz takes up the role of the state as well in her examination of postponed adulthood, or the predicament of unemployed young men in Mbarara, Uganda, as they struggle to achieve seniority status amid blocked occupational opportunities, while at the same time, they face the "risky" double bind of obligatory Muslim marriage. In Uganda, neoliberal reforms and economic restructuring have led to growing disparities between the rich and "ordinary folks" and between younger and older generations. Young men are blamed by their elders for sitting around doing little or nothing to improve their lives. However, Mbarara youth describe their situation as one of "stuckness"—the result of having limited opportunities and few basic assets on which to draw. As members of a religious minority, Muslim men face multiple hurdles to the achievement of masculine adulthood. Although they pursue higher education and obtain university degrees, Schulz emphasizes that the poor quality of Muslim-founded schools makes their graduates non-competitive for the few jobs that are available.

While Ugandan men accept or even desire a wife who is willing to work and contribute income to the household, a Muslim man is nonetheless expected to be the main support for his family and dependents. As in Egypt, young men in Uganda view marriage as risky—a "dicey affair"—because of the considerable costs involved, but also because of the perceived "untrustworthiness" of women, linked by many young men to women's recent educational and economic gains. As a result of these and other influences, Ugandan women are depicted as "demanding" and "difficult to satisfy," a perception that only exacerbates men's fears of being unable to adequately provide. But Schulz finds that, in contrast to arguments that would frame the problem as one of young people embracing a neoliberal self that emphasizes individual above community and kin, young men are drawing on their social relations as possible sources of sponsorship and advancement. Young Muslim men also look to their religion as a frame of normative reference that fosters some measure of accountability and trust—not just in financial dealings but in spousal relations as well.

Themes of failed economic policies and their effects on frustrated youth are also critical to an understanding of the situation of young, educated Nigeriens. In Chapter 3, "Waiting at the *Fada*: Young Men, 'Tea Circles,' and Delayed Adulthood in Niger," Adeline Masquelier explores the lives of recent male graduates who had hoped to secure white-collar jobs only to discover that their higher education has decreased their employment opportunities. As in the Ugandan example, structural adjustment programs and economic reforms have widened social inequalities and have severely restricted the options for young job-seekers; "greedy elders" are also viewed as an obstacle to employment, wealth, and social maturity.

In urban Niger, then, young men are forced into *delayed adulthood*—unable to find jobs despite their educations, unable to marry as they wait for financial security, and unable to achieve adult status in the community of senior men. And although it is considered below their status as educated "intellectuals," they struggle to cobble together piecemeal or part-time work when they can. Much of their waiting time, however, is spent in *fadas*, or neighborhood tea circles, where they gather to strategize imagined futures. Masquelier describes this time spent in the *fadas* as "purposeful waiting," a time when young men carefully brew tea and talk, and in the process regain some control over how time unfolds. In the *fadas*, young men offer each other a measure of support lacking in their broader social lives, support that takes the form of gestures of respect and recognition, advice on sex and romance, and even, on occasion, financial assistance.

In the final chapter in this section, Chapter 4 on "Emergent Waithood: Institutions and Marriage Delays among Mayan Women in Guatemala," Nicole S. Berry explores the effects of various institutions at state and local levels on the experience of waithood and marriage delays for Indigenous Mayan women. Berry considers state policies, as well as those of local community groups and foreign nongovernmental organizations, as they attempt to frame Indigenous women's roles and futures, especially with regard to marriage and reproduction. She identifies the moment as one of *emergent waithood*, that is, a period of dramatic social and cultural change when at least some women are pursuing education and work and, in the process, delaying marriage and conception. Although limited in number, these women model new possibilities for life trajectories beyond the household and into public and professional spheres. Berry's study highlights the importance of recognizing multiple and shifting institutional pressures and their effects over time on the emergence and experience of waithood for Guatemalan women.

Part II. Gender, Education, and the Aspiration for Autonomy

Building on themes introduced in Part I—particularly the contributions of the state and of state policies that directly or indirectly play a role in supporting marriage delays among youth—the chapters in Part II focus more specifically on the educational piece of the waithood puzzle. Young people pursue education both as a strategy of self-development and social advancement and as a way of biding time while waiting for the political and economic situation to improve. Even in situations where a diploma does not translate directly into desired employment, it may translate into enhanced status and recognition and an increased sense of self-worth. Like their male counterparts, young women seek higher education for all of these reasons, often with the additional hope of contributing to the support of their families and achieving an important measure of autonomy. Young women may use marital delays in pursuit of education as a strategy as well as a tactic to improve their economic situation and life possibilities by waiting to identify the best possible marital match.

In Chapter 5, "Active Waithood: *Youthmen*, Fatherhood, and Men's Educational Aspirations in Sierra Leone," Kristen E. McLean presents the picture of a country emerging from a protracted civil war and repeated economic and health crises, where young men struggle to move forward in their lives with limited means. The term *"youthmen"* is used in Sierra Leone to describe young men living in a liminal state, not yet able to obtain the necessary capital to marry and achieve the formal status of adults. In this context, McLean argues, education is increasingly valued not only for the future possibilities it offers but for providing a sense of agency in an otherwise precarious context. Pursuing further education as a form of *active waithood* is seen as the means by which a young man may transition from a *youthman* to a proper man. Indeed, education is linked not only to future employment possibilities, but also to modernity and a sense of "becoming somebody."

And yet, despite education's promise, a young man's educational trajectory is not uncommonly derailed by unexpected fatherhood. Unlike the context of waithood described by Singerman for young people in MENA countries, where non-marriage (at least in the ideal) precludes sexual activity and pregnancy, young men in rural Sierra Leone not infrequently produce children outside of wedlock while still in high school or university. Although the young man in question may be unable to afford the cost of a wedding, fathers of illegitimate children are nonetheless expected to be responsible and to provide support for both the child and the child's mother. Often, the financial burden proves too heavy to bear and the young man may be forced to leave school to seek employment. In such cases, fathers may shift their focus from their own education to that of their children as a means of carving out a dignified future as proud fathers of educated offspring.

Education is also a highly valued asset in post-genocide Rwanda, but factors into young women's experience of waithood in rather different ways from those described for the *youthmen* of Sierra Leone. Aalyia Feroz Ali Sadruddin's Chapter 6 on "'Giving Oneself Time': Marriage and Motherhood in Urban Rwanda," focuses on the situation of young professional women in Kigali, Rwanda, who have deliberately postponed marriage to pursue higher education and careers. Rwanda is unique among post-conflict areas in that women's social and political roles and participation have increased dramatically in the aftermath of the 1994 genocide that left the nation with a population estimated to be 70 percent female. The women in Sadruddin's study are all in their thirties, unmarried, and work in a wide range of fields, including medicine, law, architecture, and data analysis. All of them, moreover, are the primary breadwinners for their natal families.

Rather than emphasizing marriage and childbearing, these women focus on work and the capacity to support their families as critical markers of adulthood and of self-worth. They uniformly described their liminal, unmarried state as *giving oneself time*. That is, they do not view waithood as something imposed upon them but embrace it as an important phase in their life course. Not only does their singlehood allow them the time to pursue an education and career, but it also affords them the space to come to know themselves better and to prepare themselves to make the best possible choices when they do decide to marry. Sadruddin argues that the decision to postpone marriage and motherhood on the part of these young women should not be seen as a form of resistance to traditional ex-

pectations. Rather, in "taking time" for themselves, they embrace
waithood as a transitional period of preparation for these momentous next steps in life, including future marriages and motherhood.

The final two chapters in this section by Zachary M. Howlett and
Nancy J. Smith-Hefner address the issue of "over-educated," "older"
women and the difficulties they face in identifying an appropriate
marriage partner. In both cases—and similar to the youth described
by McLean and Sadruddin—women may see waithood as a space
for self-cultivation and advancement, but most have not altogether
given up on the idea of marriage.

Zachary M. Howlett's Chapter 7 on "Tactics of Marriage Delay in
China: Education, Rural-to-Urban Migration, and 'Leftover Women,'"
focuses on the experiences of educated rural-to-urban migrant
women. Howlett places rural women's pursuit of education within a
broader context of *tactics of marriage delay* among women striving to
reconcile traditional gender demands of filial responsibility to parents with their own desires for autonomy, self-determination, and
a companionate marriage. These young women—still unmarried in
their late twenties—are often labeled by others with the derogatory epithet "leftover." In many cases, however, they use education
as a strategy to escape the oppressive gender norms of their rural
communities. Education is among the "delay tactics" identified by
Howlett as the means by which young women avoid parental pressure to marry, while they improve their situation and search for a
suitable partner—one who will ideally not impose patriarchal gender expectations with regard to childcare and housework and will
hopefully not be physically abusive.

Other common tactics for marriage delay include renting a temporary, "counterfeit" boyfriend to introduce to parents on the holidays and developing a "virtual relationship" via computer games
and online media. However, the most common tactic for women's
marriage delay is "hitting an edge ball," which Howlett describes as
a strategy of "conformity in resistance." In this case, conformity references the high value placed on education among Chinese. Women
draw on ideals that link filial piety to academic excellence and use
their continuing educational success both to underscore their filial
obedience to parents and to further delay marriage, while carving
out a space for personal autonomy.

The final chapter in this section on gender and education is Chapter 8, "Too Educated to Marry? Muslim Women and Extended Singlehood in Indonesia." In it, Nancy J. Smith-Hefner offers a similar
example of women delaying marriage in Indonesia to pursue educa-

tion and employment, while balancing concerns of responsibility to family and, in this case, religious piety. She considers the situation of Muslim Javanese university students and the growing influence of varieties of Islam on the shape and experience of youth waithood. Over the past several decades, average age at first marriage has risen considerably among Javanese, particularly among Muslim women, many of whom have entered a state of *extended singlehood*. Mothers who were forced to quit school and marry at a young age now encourage their daughters to delay marriage in order to finish school and go to work, so that they will not depend on their husbands and can help support their natal families and siblings. Statistics confirm that Indonesian women are in fact going to work, and at much higher rates than women in other Muslim-majority countries such as Jordan or Egypt.

As elsewhere in the Global South, youth in Indonesia—even pious Muslim youth—have also embraced the ideal of romantic love as the proper foundation for a modern, companionate marriage. However, a growing body of conservative Muslim clerics and religion teachers and a flourishing Muslim youth literature insist that unchaperoned premarital familiarization is sinful and can easily lead to fornication. Smith-Hefner finds that a surprising number of contemporary Javanese youth say they reject modern dating as immoral. Many postpone engaging in relationships with the opposite sex until they have achieved their academic and career goals. When they finally turn to marriage, women find themselves in a particularly difficult situation. Many have moved away from their natal communities, a traditional source of marriage candidates. Sometimes referred to as a "marriage crisis," "older" educated women also face a narrowing pool of equally well-educated marriageable men willing to negotiate work and family roles within a companionate marriage. Smith-Hefner considers the appeal for educated Javanese women of Muslim marriage bureaus, brokers, and matchmakers, who have stepped in to quickly match educated Muslim women with partners for marriage "without dating"—and sometimes with less-educated Muslim men.

Part III. Delayed Marriage and the Meanings of Singlehood

The four chapters that make up Part III of the volume offer a somewhat different angle on marriage delay from that presented in earlier chapters. They address contexts in which waithood is accompanied

by marriage delays that were not necessarily a goal or intended outcome. In these examples, marriage may exist as an ideal, but may
not be considered a feasible solution to other competing social, personal, or economic concerns. In such contexts, young people express
a marked ambivalence toward marriage and may feel that singlehood is on balance more fulfilling than what marriage seems to offer. In other cases, singlehood is simply extended for so long that
marriage simply never happens.

In Chapter 9, "Conjugal Conundrums: Conversion and Marriage
Delay in the Contemporary Caribbean," Brendan Jamal Thornton
looks at marriage delay in the Dominican Republic, where formal
marriage is "not always perceived as sensible or even worthwhile"
and is often avoided completely in favor of more informal arrangements. Legal marriage exists in the Dominican Republic as an ideal
and is encouraged by the Church (particularly the growing Pentecostal Christian community) as the only morally acceptable option.
Nonetheless, childbirth often happens outside of marriage and is
considered natural and without social disgrace. Formal marriage offers a woman stability and respectability, but it is only practical if her
husband is able to provide.

Legal marriage also offers respectability and security for Dominican men. But for many it comes at too high a cost. Thornton describes the divided and multiple masculine obligations a man often
shoulders: obligations to his wife and children, to his family of origin, to his male friends, and to children that he may have fathered
with other women. For both men and women, then, more flexible,
informal unions are preferable to the legal ties of formal marriage,
and despite the efforts of the church, informal unions remain the
norm. However, Thornton addresses the *conjugal conundrums* faced
by young impoverished male Christian converts, who, by virtue of
competing obligations, are precariously situated between the prescription to marry by the Church, and powerful sociocultural and
economic imperatives that simultaneously discourage the institution of marriage and the nuclear family model.

Mehrdad Babadi's Chapter 10, "Between Cynicism and Idealism: Voluntary Waithood in Iran," picks up on this theme of widespread ambivalence toward marriage among urban middle-class
Iranian youth. In Iran as elsewhere, age at first marriage is rising
and is correlated with higher levels of education. The young people
in Babadi's study are the sons and daughters of parents who saw
their own hopes for personal and economic advancement dashed
by the realities of life in post-revolutionary Iran. Iranian parents

have shifted their hopes and aspirations onto their children and are willing to support them both emotionally and financially for as long as they are able. Not uncommonly, they urge their children *not* to marry too early and to take the time instead to explore life in its different dimensions—including relationships with the opposite sex.

Despite the efforts of the Islamic state to address what it views as the moral turpitude of the current generation, most of the young people in Babadi's study describe having had several intimate relationships of varying degrees of seriousness. In discussing their relationships, young people express both extremely high expectations and cynicism regarding the possibility of their achieving long-lasting happiness and stability. They point to the high levels of divorce and marital dissatisfaction in their parents' generation and worry about the difficulties of finding the perfect mate. Babadi thus argues that the phenomenon of marriage delay in this case is best described as *voluntary waithood*, with many young middle-class Iranians making a deliberate decision to put off marriage until sometime in the indefinite future. While they may eventually marry, young Iranians have prioritized individualistic goals of educational advancement, professional development, and self-actualization, taking advantage of their parents' support to do so.

In the two final chapters in this section, Fida Adely and Sarah Lamb consider the predicament of women in Jordan and in India who, for a variety of different reasons, find themselves single—and then must strategize to come to terms with their unmarried status. In both Jordan and India, single women must struggle against a situation in which marriage is a given, women living on their own are an anomaly, and the reputations of single women are a focus of gossip and public concern.

Adely's Chapter 11, "Refusing to Settle: Migration among Single Professional Women in Jordan," highlights the experiences of single Jordanian women who have migrated from their provincial homes to the capital city of Amman for work. These women are educated professionals, many with degrees in technical fields. They come to the city for the purpose of employment and frequently encounter opportunities for further education and even greater mobility. One expected side-effect of this experience is the postponement of marriage. While migration to the city hypothetically offers the women a larger pool of marriage partners and increases the likelihood of their meeting someone interested in developing a companionate relationship, the women report encountering prejudices related to class differences and biases against their provincial backgrounds.

As they approach their late twenties and early thirties, however, many of the women in Adely's study report facing increasing pressure from their families to marry. But in interviews they insist that they would not marry just to marry—"they would not settle." The women explained that their experiences living on their own had significantly changed what they wanted from marriage and made it harder for them to "tie the knot." And because they were working and had their own income, they had the security of knowing that they could take care of themselves financially whatever the case. Adely describes their situation aptly as *refusing to settle*: that is, these Jordanian women might marry if an appropriate candidate appeared, but they were not willing to give up their hard-earned gains just for the sake of marriage.

Sarah Lamb's Chapter 12, "Never-Married Women in India: Gendered Life Courses, Desires, and Identities in Flux," also focuses on single women who have never married, in this case, in the context of West Bengal, India. Lamb explores in ethnographic detail single women's life histories and aspirations, their reasons for not marrying, and their navigations through their singlehood status. She does so through the stories of four older Bengali women who have reached a permanent state of *never-marriedness*. The women come from varied backgrounds. Medha is from a very poor, rural family but had managed to become a college professor. Indrani received her PhD in electrical engineering in the United States; after holding a high-salaried job for some years in New York City, she returned to Kolkata to care for her ailing grandmother. Sukhi-di, now seventy-six, was the third of twelve children. She pursued her education up to the BA level and had held several important professional positions that involved her travelling around rural Bengal. Subhagi came from a very poor family as well as a disadvantaged class; she worked all her life as a day-laborer and never married despite repeated offers.

In their narratives and in those of the other women in her study, Lamb finds that women rarely articulate their aspirations in terms of a drive for individual independence or desire to live alone. Their stories thus complicate understandings of the autonomous individual at the heart of much public discourse on the rise of singlehood in modern societies. In their narratives, women place particular emphasis on their desires to work to support their (extended) families—and their taking considerable satisfaction in being able to do so. Lamb argues that what these women seek is new forms of recognition, belonging, and intimate sociality beyond the conventions of marriage. The women's stories illustrate how they attempt to do so through a variety of means: cultivating longstanding ties to natal kin, finding ways to adopt a child of their own, living with non-kin, and cultivating recognition and collegiality through meaningful work.

Part IV. Delayed Childbearing and the Quest for Motherhood

In the final section of this volume, the attention turns to how delays in marriage have also led to delays in childbearing—and what these delays mean for women's paths to motherhood. In many societies around the globe, a woman's age at first childbirth is increasing, often due to her pursuit of education and career, and concomitant delays in marriage, as described in earlier chapters. But when the cost of delayed marriage is the loss of a woman's reproductive potential, the results can be devastating and technological solutions difficult.

The three chapters in this section of the volume assess these issues in both Europe and North America, where educated women have been delaying first pregnancies, often beyond the point where they can easily conceive. As shown in these chapters, the reasons for delayed childbearing—along with increasing age-related infertility—are not straightforward. For instance, childbearing delay cannot be "blamed" on women's educational achievement alone. Nor can assisted reproductive technologies (ARTs) necessarily solve the infertility problems brought on when women reach an age where ovarian reserve (i.e., the number of high-quality eggs) begins to decline.

The issue of blame is taken up directly in Chapter 13, "Blamed for Delay: French Norms and Practices of ART in the Context of Increasing Age-Related Female Infertility." In it, Manon Vialle examines the increasing demand for ARTs in France, largely due to the infertility problems experienced by women in their late thirties and early forties. Yet, in France, state-subsidized ARTs are restricted to "therapeutic" applications, usually in cases where young married couples are struggling to conceive due to "pathological" problems such as blocked fallopian tubes or premature menopause. The varied reasons why older women may have "put off" conception are rarely considered in this restrictive French reproductive regime, which Manon describes as both conservative and reactionary.

Yet, as Manon shows in her study of French women, all of them in their forties, women's personal hurdles to childbearing can be quite substantial, making women feel "unready to mother." Manon explores these multiple factors affecting what she calls *female reproductive temporality*—the fact that reproductive timing is not only biological, but also social, relational, and material in nature. For example, many French women wait to become mothers because they cannot find a partner, or one who is also "ready" to become a father. Serious material considerations, including the high cost of raising a child in major French cities, also comes into play, as do women's perceptions that their own bodies still "feel young," even when serious ovarian aging is already underway. By exploring the many factors that lead older French women into ART clinics, Manon argues persuasively that the French model of ART is seriously out of touch with the present-day realities of French women's reproductive lives.

Chapter 14, "Waiting Too Long to Mother: Involuntary Childlessness and Assisted Reproduction in Contemporary Spain," offers a somewhat different perspective on why women in Spain are also waiting—sometimes too long—to become mothers. Beatriz San Román explores Spain's changing fertility regime, one in which motherhood has shifted from an "inescapable fate" of women's lives to something that women can now choose to do—or not. Spanish fertility rates have been in sharp decline since the 1970s, with the mean age of Spanish women at first birth now one of the highest in the European Union. This delay in childbearing has mainly been attributed to structural factors, such as unfavorable working conditions, low wages, and job instability. However, this structural analysis of delayed childbearing may be missing the point when it comes to social and affective dimensions of Spanish women's contemporary existences.

Through an analysis of Spanish national fertility survey data, as well as in-depth interviews with Spanish women who have resorted to ARTs after struggling with age-related fertility issues, San Román argues that postponing motherhood may, in fact, be a *waithood choice*. For many Spanish women, the decision to put off childbearing has been made not on the basis of material constraints, but rather as a means of achieving other life goals and forms of personal fulfillment, most of them linked to the consumption of goods and services. However, like many of the French women in Vialle's study, Spanish women may have inaccurate knowledge of the female reproductive lifespan; thus, women's waithood "choice" may result in the "shock" of unexpected infertility. In such cases, the mother's "choices" are restricted, especially as child adoption has become increasingly difficult in Spain. Thus, "waiting too long to mother" may lead to great uncertainty, with motherhood only achieved through the use of donor eggs.

The final chapter of this volume, Chapter 15, "The Egg Freezing Revolution? Gender, Education, and Reproductive Waithood in the United States," by Marcia C. Inhorn returns to issues of gender and education, asking how they might be linked to women's fertility postponement. Over the past decade, single American professional women in their late thirties and early forties have increasingly turned to a new ART called oocyte cryopreservation (aka, egg freezing) as a way to preserve their fertility. Media reports often suggest that these women's "selfish" educational and career ambitions are the main reason why they are using egg freezing to intentionally "delay," "defer," or "postpone" their childbearing. However, an in-depth ethnographic study of more than one hundred American women who turned to egg freezing shows that women themselves offer a quite different interpretation. In fact, the main reason why women were freezing their eggs was due to the lack of a stable partner with whom to pursue marriage and childbearing. Although most women said that they felt empowered and relieved to have frozen their eggs in order to preserve their remaining reproductive potential, they also lamented the fact that men were so hard to find.

As Inhorn argues, this "man deficit" (Birger 2015), and thus the growing momentum toward egg freezing, bespeaks an underlying but little discussed global reality: namely, women are now outstripping men in higher education by the millions, resulting in the lack of equally educated partners with whom to pursue marriage and childbearing. As shown in this chapter, these gender-based educational disparities are occurring in more than one-third of the world's nations, not only in the United States. Thus, as women rise in their educational pursuits, they will increasingly face a dearth of comparably educated men, which—if they want educational parity in their marital partnerships—will affect their future reproductive trajectories. In short, although egg freezing has been touted for its "revolutionary" potential—namely, as an empowering technology that creates new career options and family formations—egg freezing may in fact be a costly technological concession, whereby educated women are literally "buying time" while experiencing *reproductive waithood* beyond their individual control.

In conclusion, these chapters point to the inextricable entanglements between gender, education, employment, marriage, parenthood, and their "delays," which have major impacts on the lives and well-being of young people in virtually all societies around the globe. To our knowledge, this is the first systematic ethnographic exploration and comparison of waithood, as it plays out in its many forms on almost every continent. The lives of young people are very much at stake in this discussion of waithood. Thus, it is incumbent upon scholars to explore the "waithood" state of being, among young people whose path to adulthood has—for one reason or another—been put on hold.

Nancy J. Smith-Hefner is Professor of Anthropology and Chair of the Department of Anthropology at Boston University. A specialist of Southeast Asia, gender, and Islam, she is author of *Khmer American: Identity and Moral Education in a Diasporic Community* (University of California Press, 1999) as well as numerous book chapters and journal articles. Her recent book, *Islamizing Intimacies: Youth, Sexuality, and Gender in Contemporary Indonesia* (University of Hawaii Press, 2019), is a study of the changing personal lives and sexual attitudes of educated, Muslim Javanese youth against the backdrop of a resurgent interest in more normative forms of Islam. Smith-Hefner received her BA, MA, and PhD from the University of Michigan.

Marcia C. Inhorn is the William K. Lanman, Jr. Professor of Anthropology and International Affairs in the Department of Anthropology and MacMillan Center for International and Area Studies at Yale University, where she serves as Chair of the Council on Middle East Studies. A specialist on Middle Eastern gender, religion, and health, Inhorn is the author of six award-winning books, including *America's Arab Refugees: Vulnerability and Health on the Margins* (Stanford University Press, 2018). She is (co)editor of ten books, founding editor of the *Journal of Middle East Women's Studies* (*JMEWS*), and coeditor of Berghahn's "Fertility, Reproduction, and Sexuality" book series. Inhorn holds a PhD in anthropology and an MPH in epidemiology from the University of California, Berkeley.

References

Adely, Fida. 2012. *Gendered Paradoxes: Educating Jordanian Women in Nation, Faith, and Progress*. Chicago: University of Chicago Press.
Ahearn, Laura M. 2001. *Invitations to Love: Literacy, Love Letters, and Social Change in Nepal*. Ann Arbor: University of Michigan Press.

Autor, David, and Melanie Wasserman. 2013. *Wayward Sons: The Emerging Gender Gap in Labor Markets and Education.* Cambridge: Massachusetts Institute of Technology Press.

Birger, Jon. 2015. *Date-onomics: How Dating Became a Lopsided Numbers Game.* New York: Workman Publishing.

Chan, Angelique, Gavin W. Jones, and Paulin Tay Straughan, eds. 2008. *Ultra-Low Fertility in Pacific Asia: Trends, Causes and Policy Issues.* London: Routledge.

Cohen, Philip N. 2013. "Marriage Is Declining Globally: Can You Say That?" 12 June. Family Inequality blog. Retrieved 8 May 2019 from https://familyinequality.wordpress.com/2013/06/12/marriage-is-declining.

Dhillon, Navtej, and Tarik Yousef, eds. 2011. *Generation in Waiting: The Unfulfilled Promise of Young People in the Middle East.* Washington, DC: Brookings Institution Press.

Eberstadt, Nicholas, and Apoorva Shah. 2012. "Fertility Decline in the Muslim World: A Demographic Sea Change Goes Largely Unnoticed." *Policy Review* 173: 29–44.

Fry, Richard. 2017. "The Share of Americans Living without a Partner Has Increased, Especially among Young Adults." Pew Research Center, 11 October. Retrieved 8 May 2019 from https://www.pewresearch.org/fact-tank/2017/10/11/the-share-of-americans-living-without-a-partner-has-increased-especially-among-young-adults/.

Goldstein, Joshua R., and Catherine T. Kenney. 2001. "Marriage Delayed or Marriage Foregone? New Cohort Forecasts of First Marriage for US Women." *American Sociological Review* 66(4): 506–19.

Hirsch, Jennifer, and Holly Wardlow, eds. 2006. *Modern Loves: The Anthropology of Romantic Courtship & Companionate Marriage.* Ann Arbor: University of Michigan Press.

Honwana, Alcinda. 2014. "'Waithood': Youth Transitions and Social Change." In *Development and Equity: An Interdisciplinary Exploration by Ten Scholars from Africa, Asia, and Latin America,* ed. Dick Foeken, Ton Dietz, Leo de Haan, and Linda Johnson, 19–27. New York: Brill.

Inhorn, Marcia C. 2012. *The New Arab Man: Emergent Masculinities, Technologies, and Islam in the Middle East.* Princeton: Princeton University Press.

———. 2018. "The Arab World's 'Quiet' Reproductive Revolution." *Brown Journal of World Affairs* 24: 147–57.

Inhorn, Marcia C., Daphna Birenbaum-Carmeli, Jon Birger, Lynn Marie Westphal, Joseph O. Doyle, Norbert N. Gleicher, Dror Meirow, Martha Dirnfeld, Daniel S. Seidman, Arik Kahane, and Pasquale Patrizio. 2018. "Elective Egg Freezing and its Underlying Socio-Demography: A Binational Analysis with Global Implications." *Reproductive Biology and Endocrinology* 16: 70.

Jones, Gavin W. 2005. "The 'Flight from Marriage' in South-east and East Asia." *Journal of Comparative Family Studies* 36(1): 93–110.

Khosravi, Shahram. 2017. *Precarious Lives: Waiting and Hope in Iran.* Philadelphia: University of Pennsylvania Press.

Lake, Roseann. 2018. *Leftover in China: The Women Shaping the World's Next Superpower*. New York: W. W. Norton & Company.

Livingston, Gretchen, and Juliana Menasce Horowitz. 2018. "Most Parents—and Many Non-Parents—Don't Expect to Have Kids in the Future." Pew Research Center, 12 December. Retrieved 15 March 2019 from https://www.pewresearch.org/fact-tank/2018/12/12/most-parents-and-many-non-parents-dont-expect-to-have-kids-in-the-future/.

Ortega, Josue, and Philipp Hergovich. 2017. "The Strength of Absent Ties: Social Integration via Online Dating." Retrieved 8 May 2019 from https://arxiv.org/pdf/1709.10478.pdf.

Roser, Max. 2016. "Global Population Falling as Human Fertility Rates Decline." Principa Scientific International, 11 July. Retrieved 8 May 2019 from https://principia-scientific.org/global-population-falling-as-human-fertility-declines/.

Schielke, Samuli. 2008. "Boredom and Despair in Rural Egypt." *Contemporary Islam* 2(3): 251–70.

———. 2015. *Egypt in the Future Tense: Hope, Frustration, and Ambivalence before and after 2011*. Bloomington: Indiana University Press.

Singerman, Diane 2007. "The Economic Imperatives of Marriage: Emerging Practices and Identities Among Youth in the Middle East." *Middle East Youth Initiative*, Working Paper No. 6, September, The Brookings Institution, Wolfensohn Center for Development, Washington, DC.

———. 2013. "Youth, Gender, and Dignity in the Egyptian Uprising." *Journal of Middle East Women's Studies* 9(3): 1–27.

Singerman, Diane, and Barbara Ibrahim. 2003. "The Cost of Marriage in Egypt: A Hidden Dimension in the New Arab Demography." *Cairo Papers in Social Science* 24 (1/2): 80–166.

Smith-Hefner, Nancy J. 2019. *Islamizing Intimacies: Youth, Sexuality, and Gender in Contemporary Indonesia*. Honolulu: University of Hawai'i Press.

Sommers, Mark. 2012. *Stuck: Rwandan Youth and the Struggle for Adulthood*. Athens: University of Georgia Press.

Wyrod, Robert. 2016. *AIDS and Masculinity in the African City: Privilege, Inequality, and Modern Manhood*. Berkeley: University of California Press.

Part I

Waithood, Statehood, and the Struggle for Dignity

Chapter 1

YOUTH, ECONOMICS, AND THE POLITICS OF WAITHOOD

THE STRUGGLE FOR DIGNITY IN THE MIDDLE EAST AND NORTH AFRICA

Diane Singerman

"It's not a new Egypt until I have enough money to get married," said Ahmed Gamal in 2013, laughing with friends who have started placing bets on who will be the first among them to tie the knot. "It's a country of boys waiting to be men."
—Ahmed Gamal, quoted in Laura Bohn, "Egypt's Marriage Crisis," 2013

Introduction

Research observations typically pile up on top of each other, often raising more questions than they answer. Studying one issue may make another appear more intriguing or puzzling. I distinctly remember one of those moments while living in Cairo in 1985. While discussing the upcoming marriage of one of her daughters, the matriarch of the family with whom I was living began to pull bags of drinking glasses, pots, fabric, pajamas, plates, and other household goods from a small storage space above their bathroom. Widowed at an early age, the mother of seven children had been saving every gift and exploiting every sale for the *gihāz*, or trousseau, of her five daughters, despite limited resources. Although previously unaware of their stored treasures, I knew they were careful about each piaster. Soon, I learned that the struggle to marry off one's children and provide the requisite economic resources was a challenge in household after household, in every city and village in Egypt, across economic and social strata. It remains a challenge today.

Why did this virtual storehouse of household goods saved over decades leave such an impression on me as I studied how women and men negotiate authoritarianism in Egypt (Singerman 1995)? The extent of the financial resources needed to marry was—and is—almost unbelievable, considering the low wages and economic challenges of this community. Within policy and academic circles however, few paid attention to the costs of marriage even though its institutional structure influenced a range of other decisions and goals such as education, employment, migration, savings and investment, social networks, sensitive and highly surveilled norms around intimacy and sexuality, and family cohesion. In addition to the formidable costs of marriage, other key phenomena were adding to obstacles facing the younger generation, such as finding partners and intimacy, marrying, securing jobs, and thus attaining adult status within larger society. A project on youth exclusion in the Middle East and North Africa (MENA) by the Wolfensohn Center for Development at the Brookings Institution led to several publications and rich comparative discussions (Dhillon and Yousef 2009; Singerman 2007), at which point I introduced the term "waithood" in my contribution to the project.

While little data about the cost of marriage existed at the time, more voices were concerned about the growing youth bulge in the region, with large numbers of young people flooding the job market. Due to the nuptiality transition and improvements in health care and female education, the region had one of the largest youth bulges in the world. A youth bulge, demographers argue, can be positive as dynamic young people contribute to their economy and society, with fewer dependent older cohorts "dragging" on the economy. Yet, if young people are unemployed and unfulfilled with few institutions to channel their demands and participation, countries may waste their demographic dividend and experience political volatility.

This complex set of circumstances led to my argument that young people were not following the typical path between a long childhood and shorter adolescence to reach adulthood, but that they were stuck in "waithood" or the long, liminal, period between adolescence and adulthood. Adolescence is associated largely with the teenage years of ten to nineteen, with adulthood typically following, but in MENA adulthood is associated with marriage, rather than one's age or living independently from one's family. Furthermore, due to prevailing (although always changing) social norms influenced by religious values and law, sexuality is housed in marriage and dating among unmarried young people often provoked social anxiety and scandals typically reflected in the press and public realm. While the idea of waithood emerged to describe the predicaments of young people in Egypt due to ethnographic and quantitative research centered there, many of these same trends characterize other MENA countries.

The first part of this chapter explores contemporary dimensions of waithood largely centered on three countries—Tunisia, Jordan, and Egypt—since important new data have been collected and analyzed about these countries. The second half of the chapter presents an argument that links the social and economic predicaments of waithood to political contestation and protest in MENA countries ranging from Morocco in the west to Saudi Arabia in the east. More specifically, young people are engaging in a *politics of waithood* as they demand dignity and an end to economic and political marginalization. The financial and social challenges of waithood and its liminal status have fueled these political demands. Waithood's connection to political contestation took a more obvious turn during the Arab Spring. I have argued elsewhere that young people's particular grievances and circumstances fueled their protests for regime change, dignity, and social justice (Singerman 2013). Waithood was no longer waiting as young people occupied the squares and lit up social media to condemn authoritarian and monarchical rule, torture, political violence, corruption, and arbitrary power. Some scholars disagree with the notion that the Arab Spring was a youth revolution, since people of all ages and from many constituencies joined the protests, including members of trade unions, Islamist movements, civil society organizations, and human rights groups. Nevertheless, there is strong evidence that youth, among them students, were an overrepresented cohort among the protesters across the region, and many women were central to the protests as well.

The call for dignity—or *karāma*—implied that indignity had prevailed for many decades under the old regimes and that young people refused to be the victims of harassment, state abuse, and violence any longer. Social movement "master frames" diagnose a problem in need of redress, offer solutions to the problem, and motivate support for collective action (Snow and Benford 1988). Young women, fighting for dignity and autonomy of the body, demanded new laws, new policies, and further freedom. Many have noted what they see as the failure of the Arab Spring: Egypt returned to a more oppressive, patriarchal, and exclusionary military rule; Syria, Yemen, and Libya disintegrated into civil war; and monarchies such as Morocco, Jordan, Saudi Arabia, the Emirates, and Bahrain weathered the storm. Yet, I argue that we can see a more positive legacy of the Arab Spring in the sustained and at times successful demands for dignity, particularly as they relate to gender equality. Young women and men who demanded dignity continue to engage in public contestation and to support controversial initiatives and movements that have produced policies to enhance women's rights and gender justice, deepen constitutional commitments to equality, and foster greater diversity and new patterns of intimacy and sexual identity (Tadros 2016). Viewing a set of issues in conversation with each other, rather than as discrete, separate variables may minimize the complexity of these issues or possibly exaggerate positive developments since the Arab Spring, but it is important to understand why many young people are still reimagining their future, rejecting the status quo, contesting powerful interests, and renegotiating norms as they continue to struggle with the consequences of waithood.

Methodology

This chapter is based on ethnographic research launched in older areas of Cairo in the mid-1980s and 1990s that was complemented by additional interviews and research in the 2000s about youth, marriage costs, social norms, public policy, and related issues. As mentioned earlier, the influence of savings strategies around marriage is well-known in Egypt, but not integrated into reigning economic analyses of Egyptian political economy—or into research about gender. Aggregating data from a wider and deeper cross section of Egyptian families, and building on ethnographic insights, Barbara Ibrahim and I collaborated with generous colleagues and added a small marriage module to an Egyptian national household expenditure survey about food subsidies that the International Food Policy and Research Institute (IFPRI) conducted with the Egyptian Ministry of Agriculture and Ministry of Trade and Supply in 1999 (Singerman and Ibrahim 2003). Although it included only four hundred households, gathering and analyzing the first quantitative data on national marriage costs led to a broader interdisciplinary conversation about these issues. The survey's data on poverty and consumption allowed for a comparative sense of the financial challenges associated with marriage and the size of what we called the "marriage imperative." There is now far richer scholarship and data on marriage costs after the inclusion of a revised "marriage module" from the 1999 study in gender-sensitive national labor force surveys in Egypt, Tunisia, and Jordan over the last two decades. Professors Ragui Assaad and Caroline Krafft are pioneers in analyzing connections between the labor market, the marriage market, and male and female employment. This chapter draws from this research published by a range of economists and sociologists, coordinated by national statistical agencies and the Economic Research Forum.[1] In addition, further primary and secondary sources were consulted since the Arab Spring erupted in MENA to support arguments about the "politics of waithood" and the demand for dignity articulated by so many young people in and since 2011.

The Components of Waithood

The Costs of Marriage

Understanding the experience of waithood necessitates linking the cost of marriage to other phenomena confronting young people in Egypt. As mentioned at the outset of this chapter, scholars and policymakers rarely studied the cost of marriage; yet ignoring this protracted financial savings campaign distorts young people's priorities, the goal posts of their decision-making, the trajectory of their employment paths, as well as the economic strategies of their parents. If a young man and woman and their families cannot accumulate the expected sums, a marriage may be postponed for many years, an engagement broken, or financial and social expectations scaled back. As Krafft and Assaad (2017: 2) argue, "marriage is the sole socially acceptable route to a number of adult roles, including independent living, socially sanctioned sexual relations, and childbearing," and all parties involved hope to enact the best possible outcome.

I knew from my own ethnographic work in Egypt and through other scholarship that religious, social, legal, and customary norms dictated specific costs that the bride, the groom, the bride's family, and the groom's family are to provide (Hoodfar 1997; Singerman 1995). The six main marital expenses include: housing (typically an apartment, or rooms in the groom's family's apartment if living with relatives provided by the groom and his family); furniture and appliances (split between the bride and groom's family, designated for particular items and related to the value of the *mahr* or prompt dower); wedding celebrations (often multiple celebrations for different stages of the engagement and marriage often paid for by both families); jewelry for the bride (*shabka* largely paid for by the groom and his family); a dower (*mahr* or sum given by the groom to the bride registered in the marriage contract); and the *gihāz*, or preparations for marriage in colloquial Egyptian, which includes smaller items such as kitchen supplies, carpets, linens, and clothes for the bride (largely paid for by the bride's family and the bride).[2]

Scholars continue to suggest that marriage costs are extremely challenging across economic and regional groups within countries, and across MENA. Assaad and Krafft (2014: 8) argue they are "the most substantial investment young North Africans make." I argue elsewhere that it is the most important intergenerational exchange of assets, particularly for women, since Muslim inheritance laws offer female heirs only half of what male heirs of a similar relationship to the deceased will receive (Singerman 2007). Often, women do not even obtain their rightful legal inheritance due to family pressures to keep wealth concentrated in fewer, male hands (Hoodfar 1997).

Krafft and Assaad (2017: 2) confirm earlier arguments that young women can be demanding, since they realize their financial negotiations will impact their future power within the marriage, as well as the economic well-being and social status of their future family. Marriage is therefore a high-risk endeavor, and the bride's side tries to secure at the outset as much certainty about the spouse as possible and the most advantageous living conditions.

Recent data from labor force surveys increase our understanding and knowledge of marriage costs, and quantitative analysis and economic theorizing about marriage markets and hazard models help us understand the interplay between individual and family characteristics (education, employment, income, assets, housing type, consanguinity, region, etc.) and marriage costs. Recent analysis suggests that marriage costs remain formidable and challenging, across the board, even if they have declined in real terms in some countries, such as Jordan (Assaad and Krafft 2014: 9; Salem 2012; Sieverding, Berri, and Abdulrahim 2018).

To understand these costs more specifically, the first 1999 small household expenditure survey, which included detailed questions about the cost of marriage (COM) in Egypt, found that the COM were EGP 20,194 (approximately US $6,000 in 1999). Comparing these costs to household expenditures in the sample, the cost of marriage equaled eleven times annual household expenditures per capita (or the market value of all goods and services, including durable products purchased by a household [excluding one's home]) or four and a half times per capita Gross National Product. The marriage burden was particularly challenging for those rural households living below the poverty line: their marriage costs were fifteen times per capita household expenditures (Singerman 2007; Singerman and Ibrahim 2003).

In the much larger Egypt Labor Market Panel Survey (ELMPS) in 2006, which included more than 8,000 households, marriage costs had risen to approximately EGP 36,789 or US $6,400 (Singerman 2007). Even though marriage costs have declined over time when adjusted for inflation, people's perceptions of marriage costs may be related to the prices of other goods and services and their memories of less expensive, and less consumptive, wedding preparations.

In a more recent analysis of marriage costs from the 2012 ELMPS, Assaad and Krafft (2014: 9) found that total costs for marriages (based on the preceding three years) were around EGP 62,000, or approximately US $10,164. We will have to wait for the next round of the ELMPS to see how marriage costs have evolved, as Egypt experienced economic difficulties and inflation after the Arab Spring. One indicator that the financial burdens of marriage remain challenging is that Atta Selim, a member of the Egyptian Parliament's Legislative Committee, proposed a new "Fund to Finance Marriages of Young Men" that will provide an interest-free, tax-free loan of EGP 60,000 to Egyptian men. The new legislation was approved by the Parliament's Committee of Youth and Sport and endorsed by seventy other Members of Parliament. An article describing the new loan uses the pejorative *'ānis*, or "spinsters," and argues that this law will help older, unmarried women because men who marry older Egyptian women will receive priority for these new loans, as will men with lower incomes (Abdel Khalil 2018; Amin 2018; "MP Submits Draft Law" 2018).

Relying on the 2006 ELMPS, Figure 1.1 portrays how long it would take the groom and the groom's father to save for marriage costs, since the survey also includes detailed earnings data. It offers three sets of calculations: if the groom and the groom's father saved 100 percent of their income, 50 percent of their income, and finally 17.1 percent of their income, which was the official Egyptian gross domestic savings rate at the time (World Bank 2019a). Because it

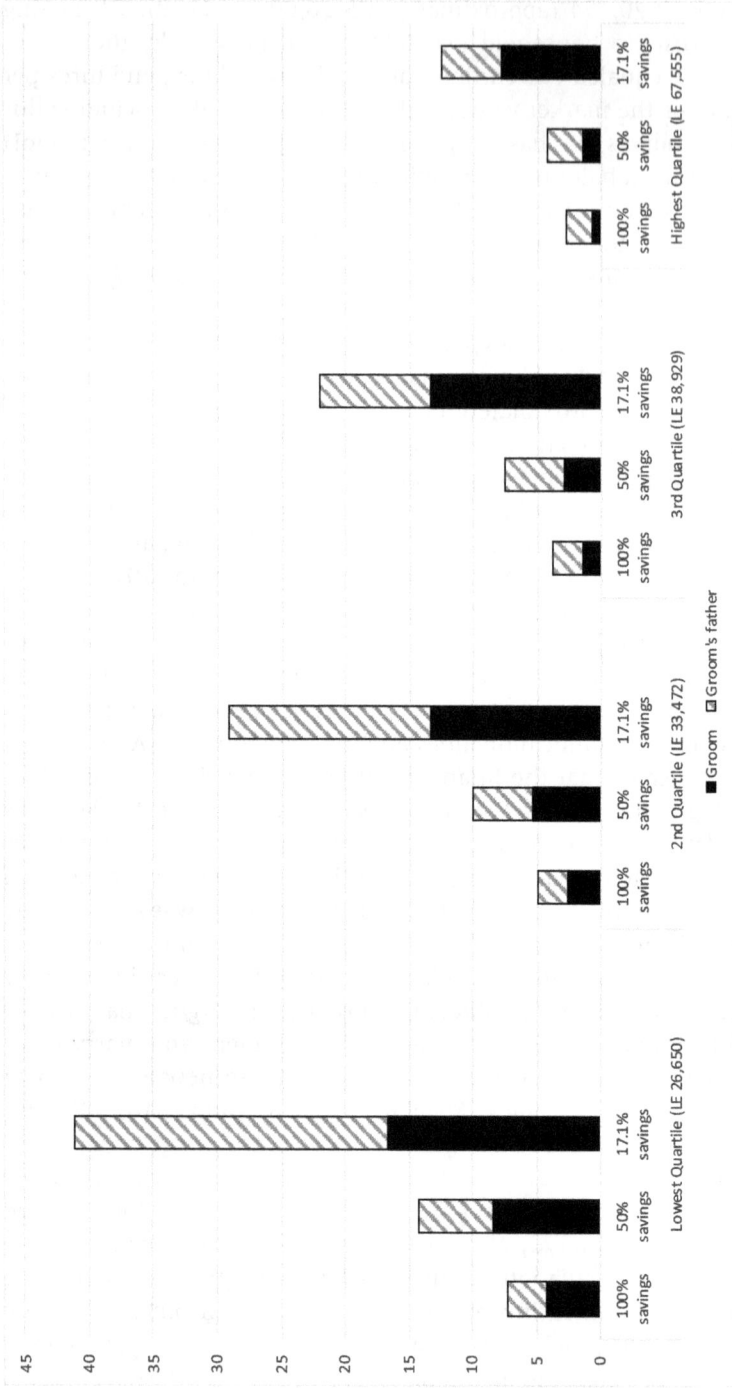

FIGURE 1.1. Years Needed to Save for Groom's and Groom's Father's Share of Marriage Costs, Assuming 100 percent, 50 percent, and 17.1 percent of Earnings Are Saved. Based on data available in the 2006 Egypt Labor Market Panel Survey (ELMPS).

seems impossible to save 100 percent, or even 50 percent, of one's income, this exercise demonstrates the formidable and lengthy savings strategies of Egyptian families around marriage. At the Egyptian domestic savings rate of 17 percent, the lowest income quartile would have to save for marriage costs for approximately forty-two years and even the richest quartile would have to save for fifteen years.

According to the 2012 ELMPS, the "up-front cost of marriage exceeds, on average, eight years of a groom's wages" (Assaad and Krafft 2014: 1). However, this formulation omits the other parties to the marriage who share in the formidable cost: the groom's family and the bride's family. Another way to look at marriage costs is that the main players—the groom, the groom's family, and the bride's family—largely pay one-third of the marriage costs each, although in more rural parts of the country, the groom's family may pay a greater share. According to the 2006 ELMPS, the bride pays very little of the costs of marriage, the groom pays 40 percent of the costs, his family pays slightly less than one-third, and the bride's side contributes about one-third as well. More generally, the groom's side contributes two-thirds of the cost of marriage and the bride's side, one-third (Singerman 2007: 14–15).

Marriage costs vary over time and across countries and subnational regions. In Jordan, the bride and her family contribute very little of the marriage costs, while the groom and his family contribute between 93 and 99 percent of the total cost (Sieverding et al. 2018: 12). In both Jordan and Egypt there are indications that the *mahr*, which is given to the bride from the groom's side, has decreased in popularity or its value has declined, and now both sides share more of the costs of *gihāz*, or preparations for marriage and outfitting the marital home and the bride. Changes in Egyptian divorce law in 2001, and the option of *khul'* or no-fault divorce, has led to much higher sums for the deferred dower, or *mu'akhar*, which is stipulated in the marriage contract as a payment to the bride if the groom divorces her.[3] In a sense, brides or their families have increased the value of the *mu'akhar* as a disincentive to divorce, somewhat like a prenuptial agreement, which has become more popular among wealthier couples in the United States.

In Jordan, the total cost of marriage was also significant. The median total cost of marriage in the 2016 Jordanian Labor Market Panel Survey (JLMPS) (which includes jewelry, housing, furniture, celebration costs, and *mahr*) decreased substantially *in real terms* from 12,600 Jordanian Dinars (JD) (approximately US $17,791) to 11,250 JD (approximately US $16,099) across the two periods (2005–09 marriages and 2012–16 marriages) (Sieverding et al. 2018: 11). It may be the decline in celebration costs that accounts for the lower cost of marriage in real terms (Sieverding et al. 2018). It is interesting to note that in Jordan housing costs for marriage were low in the 2016 JLMPS. Sieverding et al. (2018: 11) note that a "large percentage of respondents in both periods reported having no housing costs upon marriage (74 percent of 2012–16 marriages, and 65 percent of 2005–09 marriages) and this reporting was typical for both renters and owners of housing. The median expenditure on housing was thus zero in both periods." Yet, in the 2010 JLMPS, Rania Salem (2012: 7) calculated that both housing and *mahr* were each 14 percent of total COM. One factor that may account for the differences between the Egyptian and Jordanian surveys is that both women and men were asked about their marriage costs in Egypt and not in Jordan, and perhaps women in Jordan were not as familiar with the costs of housing since the groom and his family typically provide them. Additionally, in Jordan a groom's family may sell off a piece of land to finance the housing costs, but this may go unreported since the groom may not perceive this practice as the same as securing a marital apartment. Rather, it is a more subtle financial transaction (Fida Adely, pers. comm., September 2018).

Unfortunately, the survey instrument for the Tunisian Labor Market Panel Survey (2014) had some problems generating data on marriage costs; thus, we cannot compare marriage costs across the three LMPS's. Nevertheless, important analysis about consanguinity, the relationship between marriage and employment, region, age at marriage, marriage timing, and other factors, has emerged from the Tunisian survey.

Age at Marriage

Surrounding these obvious but largely underappreciated financial struggles to marry, public anxiety and debate arose about intimacy, morality, and sexuality, particularly concerning young, unmarried women and men. For a variety of reasons briefly addressed here, age at marriage for both women and men has risen across the region. Many would argue that improvements in female primary, secondary, and tertiary education were partially responsible for delaying the age at marriage for women as well as changing norms and legislative interventions to raise the legal age at marriage for women (Salem 2012: 5). For example, in Egypt, based on the 2012 ELMPS, 52 percent of those women married between 1980–85 were illiterate compared to 21 percent of the 2000–06 cohort. "Across the same cohorts, the percentage with a secondary degree approximately doubled to 41 percent, and the percentage with a university degree increased almost fourfold, from 5.1 percent to 19.4 percent" (Sieverding 2011: 10). As Egyptian women became more educated, "their average age at marriage increased correspondingly, from 19.8 years among the earliest cohort to 22.0 for the most recent cohort" (Sieverding 2011: 10).

Eliminating "child" marriage had been a goal of many women's organizations in the Middle East, as well as global institutions concerned about high fertility and asymmetric power relations associated with early marriage. Many couples in the region had traditionally been in "age-discrepant" marriages with older men and younger women, reinforcing later male age at marriage rates. But, in the 1990s and 2000s, male age at marriage rose even higher, making the MENA region with the latest age at marriage, outside of China (Mensch, Singh, and Casterline 2005).

Factors delaying marriage are complicated, but men are still marrying at later ages than women while many women are marrying later than those of previous generations. Particularly in Jordan, Morocco, and Tunisia, some women are not marrying at all. In earlier research on Egypt, I suggested that the high costs of marriage and the need to save a great percentage of a groom and his family's wages for marriage may have been a factor in delaying marriage among men, but recent scholarship argues, at least in Jordan, that real marriage costs are in fact declining and therefore may not be a factor in this delay (Salem 2012).

There is general agreement that the number of age discrepant marriages are stable, although the recent labor market panel surveys in Tunisia, Jordan, and Egypt explain that the "median age for marriage for both sexes increased and then fell (in Egypt) or flattened (in Jordan and Tunisia)" (Krafft and Assaad 2017: 10). The median age for Egyptian women to marry is twenty-one and twenty-seven for Egyptian men; for Jordanian women it is twenty-two and twenty-seven for Jordanian men; for Tunisian women it is twenty-seven and thirty-three for Tunisian men (Krafft and Assaad 2017: 10). In Morocco, the spousal age gap widened from seven to eight years, in Egypt, it increased from a six- to a seven-year difference, and in Tunisia it has fluctuated around six years (Assaad and Krafft 2014: 6). Salem notes that for Jordan (and the argument holds for many other nations) "education is the most consistent factor associated with higher ages at marriage" (2012; as cited by Sieverding et al.

2018: 27). In Jordan, although marriage ages have increased slowly in the last few decades and child marriage is uncommon, researchers argue that Jordan's more active rental housing market and other factors reduced the financial pressures surrounding marriage, perhaps only accounting for recent very modest increases at age at marriage (Assaad, Krafft, and Rolando 2017). Nazier and Ramadan (2017) and others examine the ways in which age at marriage, consanguinity, nuclear or extended family living, education, and other factors influence power asymmetries and decision-making among married couples. This is an important avenue to further understand gender dynamics and cultural and material issues (see also Assaad and Krafft 2014).

The universality of marriage is declining in some MENA nations, but not in Egypt, where 95 percent of both women and men marry by age forty (Krafft and Assaad 2017: 9). In Jordan, 15 percent of women are unmarried past the age of forty (Krafft and Assaad 2017: 10), but marriage is nearly universal for men.[4] Late age at marriage is more pronounced in Tunisia, where almost half of all men marry after thirty, as do one-quarter of women (Assaad and Krafft 2014: 5), and 20 percent of men and 22 percent of women are still unmarried at forty (Assaad and Krafft 2014: 9). Not everyone is marrying much later in life, but sizeable numbers of young people are. In Morocco, marriage is no longer considered universal, since 25 percent of women are unmarried by forty years of age, half are married by twenty-five, and 25 percent marry between the ages of twenty-five and forty (Assaad and Krafft 2014: 5).

Sexuality Is Housed in Marriage

As the phenomenon of waithood has grown and young men and women are marrying later, public anxiety and debate about intimacy, morality, and sexuality among unmarried women and men has also increased. Prevailing laws and familial, religious, and social norms discourage unmarried young men and women from intimate relations in MENA but as they stay single longer, it is not surprising that young people are resisting or reshaping those norms, although perhaps not publicly in order to avoid social disapproval (El Feki 2013). Islamist movements and other constituencies have mobilized public support and attracted followers, in part, by referencing the controversies surrounding unmarried young people, intimacy, and sexuality. More research is needed to understand how waithood affects the legal, economic, social, and cultural circumstances of unmarried men and women. For example, sex outside of marriage in

Morocco is punishable by imprisonment of up to one year according to article 490 of the Penal Code, although this law is not always enforced (El Feki 2013: 174) and feminist groups are trying to repeal it (Elouazi 2018). Yet, the National Institution for Solidarity with Women in Distress and UN Women argue that 4 percent of all births in 2009 in Morocco (or 25,000 births) were to single women. New Moroccan non-governmental organizations (NGOs) help single mothers face a bureaucracy that assumed all mothers were married, and now the state allows single mothers to register their child's birth (Newman 2018). One single mother's humiliating experience with civil servants when trying to register her newborn "drove her to self-immolation in the wake of the Arab uprisings" (El Feki 2013: 175). El Feki also reports a study that estimates almost 40 percent of Moroccan young men younger than twenty-five have sexual relations for the first time with sex workers and close to two-thirds frequent this method (2013: 209). While scholars are better today at measuring single aspects of waithood and understanding the links between a youth bulge, educational attainment, and wages on marriage outcomes, for example, there is far less research and analysis of marriage "substitutes," which young people imagine as their sexual practices and norms of intimacy change (see Wynn 2016). Changing the legal environment for single women and men, as well as for single parenthood, is a difficult and controversial challenge that MENA activists are only beginning to address.

The Youth Bulge

The demographic component of waithood, as mentioned earlier, is propelled by a youth bulge, which means that the debates and problems of young people assert themselves more forcefully. While the youth bulge is flattening out a bit globally, almost half the population in MENA is under the age of twenty-four and more than 60 percent are under thirty (UNDP 2016; as cited by McKee et al. 2017). In Jordan, more than 70 percent of the population is younger than thirty (ASDA'A Burson-Marsteller 2018: 58), and in Saudi Arabia, "half the population—roughly 14 million—is under 25" ("Saudi Arabia's Demographic Challenge" 2013). As young people age, the youth bulge may raise other concerns about a greying population, but in many countries in the region it is the problems of youth that fill the headlines. If a youthful population is satisfied and gainfully employed, a country often benefits; however, as the next section demonstrates, the youth bulge in the Middle East is confronting a problematic employment environment.

Youth Unemployment

Very high youth unemployment has intensified waithood in the region and dampened the demographic dividend of a youth bulge,
as Figure 1.2 demonstrates. According to the International Labour
Office (ILO), while youth unemployment has fallen slightly in the
Arab States, followed by Northern Africa, the Arab region still has
the highest youth unemployment rates, at 30 percent in 2017 (ILO
2017: 95).[5] In many countries, political leaders are proposing policies targeted at young people, whether that means focusing on job
creation and entrepreneurial training (typically in the private sector,
including tech start-ups), or relaxing gender segregation as in Saudi
Arabia and Iran, to a lesser extent.

Saudi Arabia has a youth unemployment rate of 28 percent, with
a huge cohort of young people ("Saudi Arabia's Demographic Challenge" 2013). Crown Prince Salman is now trying to mobilize his
youthful population to support his economic diversification plan for
the country, Vision 2030. As he explained in 2017, "seventy percent
of [the Saudi] population is under 30 and we won't allow the 30
percent to hold them back" (McKernan 2017). Figure 1.3 demonstrates that, while youth unemployment rates for Jordan have fluctuated slightly, they are still extremely high and have been growing
steadily since 2010. Since young men and their families provide

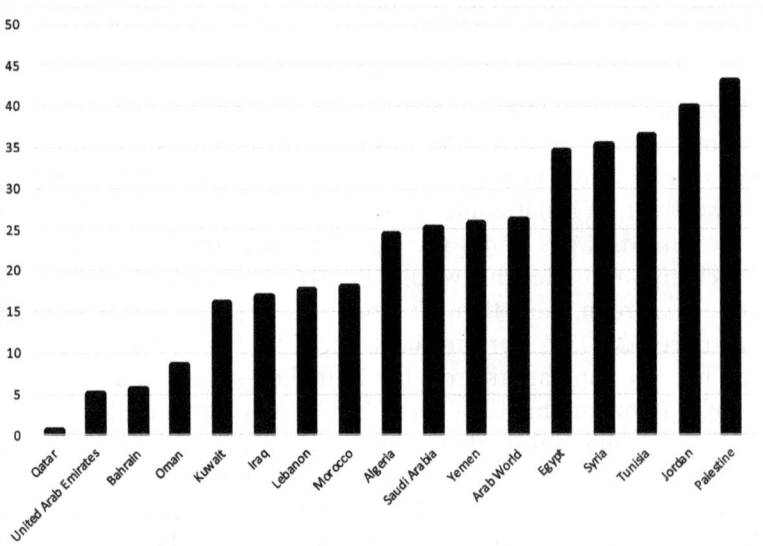

FIGURE 1.2. Youth Unemployment Ages 15–24 in 2017. Based on data available at the World Bank (2019b).

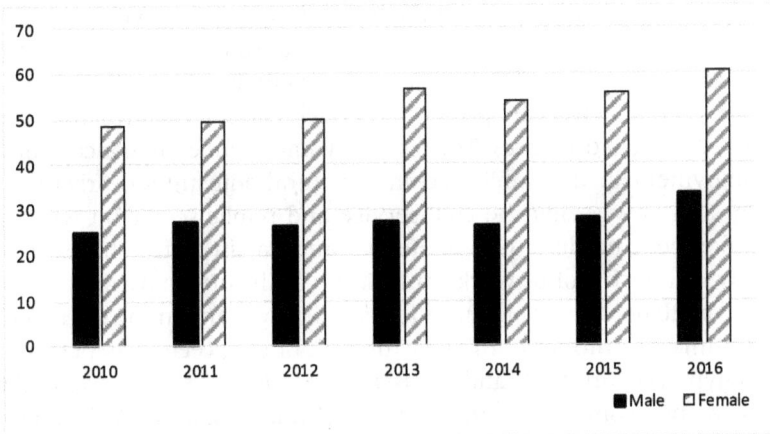

FIGURE 1.3. Male/Female Youth Unemployment Ages 15–24 in Jordan. Based on data available at World Bank (2018).

far more of the marriage costs and since men "must transition into work before they can transition into marriage," male unemployment prolongs waithood, whether because an unemployed man is not a suitable marriage partner or because unemployed men have more difficulty accumulating the expected marriage costs (Krafft and Assaad 2017: 8).

In Tunisia, eight years after the revolution, 36 percent of all youth (15–24) were still unemployed (ILO 2020). Many of the unemployed youth are well educated, and half of university graduates younger than thirty-five are unemployed. It takes university graduates an average of six years to find a stable job. Furthermore, according to the Tunisian government's own statistics, one million youth are not pursuing employment, education, or training (NEET). This is a staggeringly high number in a country of 11.2 million people (Karasapan 2015 as cited by Yerkes 2017: 18).

Some argue that Tunisian young people are voting with their feet; they have migrated abroad in great numbers, including to Syria and Iraq to join the Islamic State. Apparently, Tunisians represent the largest contingent of ISIS's foreign fighters, reaching six to seven thousand recruits by November 2015 (The Soufan Group 2015; as cited by Yerkes 2017: 18). Youth unemployment and waithood are certainly regional drivers of temporary and permanent migration and we have seen skyrocketing rates of out migration from MENA due to political and economic volatility, civil war, and violence following the Arab Spring.

The story of female unemployment differs. The developmental state model in the postcolonial era encouraged educated women to join the public sector because it offered benefits such as maternity leave, equitable pay and promotion policies after childbirth, and secure and safe workplaces. Thus, since women tended to concentrate employment in the public sector, structural adjustment, privatization, and downsizing the civil service and public sector hit female employment harder (Assaad, Hendy, and Yassin 2012). In an ILO study of the school to work transition, youth unemployment rates stood at 20 percent or higher in Jordan and Egypt and in the Occupied Palestinian Territories (OPT) and Tunisian rates exceeded 30 percent. In Egypt, Jordan, OPT, and Tunisia, 40 percent of young economically active women were unemployed (Dimova, Elder, and Stephan 2016: 2). The average female youth unemployment rate for the four countries mentioned above is more than double the male rate at 41.6 and 18.9 percent, respectively (Dimova et al. 2016: 3).

Even though female unemployment figures dwarf male figures, this phenomenon masks the extremely low female participation rates in the region because so many women are not seeking employment and are therefore not included in unemployment figures. Female labor force participation rates in MENA are the lowest of any world region, and in some countries, they have recently declined even further (Assaad, Hendy, Lassassi, and Yassin 2018: 1; Krafft and Sieverding 2018: 5). In Jordan, for example, female labor force participation rates were only 17 percent in 2016 (Assaad, Krafft, and Keo 2018; as cited by Krafft and Sieverding 2018: 6). The ILO (2017: 14) estimates that the regional "gender gap" between young male and female labor force participation rates is the second largest globally, behind South Asia.

A different measurement that captures those not engaged in employment, education, or training (NEET) describes many women who never entered the labor force regardless of their educational status, or who left the labor force after working for a few years before marriage. Shortly after the Arab Spring, Tunisia still had one of the highest NEET rates in the MENA region, estimated at approximately 33 percent of the total number of young people between fifteen and nineteen years old, even though Tunisia had one of the highest female labor force participation rates in the region (ETF 2014; as cited by World Bank 2014: 6). Yet, 60 percent of Tunisian urban female youth (ages fifteen to twenty-nine) were not engaged in employment, education, or training versus 35 percent of male urban youth. In both urban and rural areas, women were almost twice as likely to fall within the NEET category. It is not surprising that many of these young women took part in the Jasmine Revolution in 2010 and more recent protests. Unfortunately, this trend is not limited to the young; 89 percent of the female working age population over thirty in rural areas, and 69 percent in urban areas, is inactive/NEET (World Bank 2014: 6–7).

These component parts of waithood have created great challenges for young people in transitioning to adulthood. To recap briefly: there are large numbers of young people in MENA who are often unemployed; they are single for far longer than those of earlier generations, yet they are not supposed to be dating others, while keeping in the good graces of their families as they find partners and accumulate the formidable costs of marriage. Their experience of waithood is difficult as they struggle to achieve their material and social goals, yet waithood also influences their political perspective as they strive to become adults and citizens.

Dignity, the Politics of Waithood, and Political Contestation

The continued relevance of waithood in MENA, as indicated in the previous sections, means that young people are still in quite a predicament. New literature on youth, youthscapes, precarity, economic insecurity, and structural disadvantages that neoliberalism creates are useful for understanding some of these issues (see Gertel and Hexel 2018; Herrera and Bayat 2010). While this chapter has described some of the economics of waithood, the "politics of waithood" has played out over the last decade as well, with different consequences. Identifying certain initiatives and contestation as the "politics of waithood" does not mean that waithood is causally responsible for the Arab Spring, broader demands for dignity, new laws or executive decrees, or new outbreaks of youth-led or youth-inspired protest. Rather, the idea of the politics of waithood means that we can expect young people to continue mobilizing and agitating for solutions to their problems.[6] This does not mean that they will be successful in realizing their diverse interests, considering the powerful institutions, practices, and elites that dominate civil and political society; instead, it points to some common, shared experiences that propel them to seek change.

The demand for *karāma*, or dignity, articulated in the Arab Spring, was, and continues to be, an expression of the politics of waithood.

In Tahrir Square, Egyptian protesters yelled, "Our dignity is humiliated," "We will die with dignity," and "We demand the end of humiliation and injustice." In Tunis, the demand was for bread, freedom, and dignity. Dignity lays claim to the integrity, safety, agency, and autonomy of the body and protection from arbitrary coercive authority (torture, violence, sexual violence, or arrest without due process) through the rule of law and the justice system (Singerman 2013). One of the most elusive goals for both young men and women is reform of the security forces (whether intelligence, police, or military) so that the state will support and protect—rather than abuse—citizens and their bodies. It is the preponderance of state violence and youthful experiences of that violence that, counterintuitively, has the potential to bind together the struggles of young men and women.

For example, in December 2011, when the Egyptian Supreme Council of Armed Forces (SCAF) charged a sit-in and attacked protesters, soldiers were filmed viciously beating a man and woman. The woman's *hijāb* and black *'abāya* came undone during this brutal attack by many soldiers, revealing her blue bra. Since then, this woman has been known anonymously as "the blue bra woman." Toward the end of Al-Jazeera's film clip, amid a beating from all sides, one soldier jumps on her chest. Next to her, a young man is also getting viciously and repeatedly attacked, but it was the attack on the anonymous "blue bra" woman that received outraged public attention both because of the brutality of the attack and because her body was exposed. There were still forces in Egypt, particularly among the SCAF and its supporters, who blamed her and shamed her for her supposedly "provocative" bra. When the soldiers retreated somewhat, a few people from the sit-in came to her aid, but soon the soldiers charged again and attacked another somewhat older man and woman so brutally that one wonders if they survived. Hafez (2014: 22) wrote that this episode "starkly illuminates the grim ways that women's bodies become sites of social control and moral engineering"; yet it is also instructive that, while the abuse of a young woman's partially naked body led to public scandal, few mentioned the brutal violence against the nearby man. This indiscriminate, asymmetric, and normalized state violence makes the master frame of dignity relevant for the predicaments of both young women and men.

The demand for dignity was a key component of Tunisian protests in 2010 and it remains a master frame of contention throughout the contested period of building a new government and constitution. Aleya-Sghaier (2012:19) suggests the Tunisian revolution "was neither red, nor orange, nor jasmine; it was a 'revolution of dignity.'" Before the revolution, Tunisia's police force dominated and repressed political life. Its corps of 120,000 and 150,000 officers, according to one source, was larger than France's despite Tunisia having only one-fifth of France's population (Aleya-Sghaier 2012: 19). As Aleya-Sghaier argues:

> Violence has been an integral part of the expression of political power in Tunisia since the nation gained independence in 1956. The new state of Tunisia was established through violence. Bourguiba's regime was preserved by the repression and exclusion of its opponents . . . The use of violence to counter popular demands was systemic. (2012: 28)

As protests broke out in Tunisia in 2010 after the self-immolation of Mohamed Bouazizi in Sidi Bouzid, Tunisia's hinterland, the police killings and political violence reinforced the broad demand, articulated by youthful protesters, for dignity, safety, respect, and autonomy of the body. The demand for dignity addresses both state violence and legally mediated ways to exclude citizens from political participation. Yet, it also raises a second structural issue in Tunisia: the economic and political marginalization of its large rural, southern, inland, and provincial population.

The concept *al-hogra*, or contempt, is an intersectional term that men working in the informal sector in Algeria and Morocco have popularized. The informal sector produces 15 percent of Morocco's gross domestic product and employs more than 50 percent of the active urban population (Ilahiane 2021). Economic precarity in Morocco is not only due to the high male and female unemployment figures mentioned above or the low labor force participation rates of women, but also due to the growth of informal sector jobs that come without benefits and job security. In addition, aspects of these activities are often illegal if jobs or economic activities are unregistered, untaxed, or unlicensed. This compromised ethical and moral context of *al-hogra* "refers to various daily micro-practices of injustice and indignation" and the:

> feeling of being deprived or robbed of a basic human right, or for the lack of equal opportunity to shape one's life . . . and is used as a vehicle for social mobilization around overlapping human rights issues such as the right to work, to education, to health, to housing, to justice, to equality, to ethnic and linguistic diversity, to religious freedom, to potable water and electricity, to dignity and respect and so on. (Ilahiane 2021)

Experiences of humiliation and marginalization, whether due to youth unemployment, austerity measures and economic marginalization, poverty, state-sanctioned violence, or sexual harassment, serve to link dignity to another core demand of the Arab Spring—social justice—which means to many people, economic justice. The link here to a "dignity frame" is that economic injustice humiliates and marginalizes young people, in particular. One young plumber and store manager assailed the Moroccan elite as:

> thieves, looters; they are *mufsideen* on Allah's earth [corrupt people]. All they care about is their pockets, their families, and their friends . . . Us, we have Allah. And for us is the street and no education, no health, no housing, no human rights, no Islamic banks. For us shantytowns and living the life of flies on a dead animal skin . . . They made our parents poor and us poor, we will not forgive them. Can you imagine that we have been living in shantytowns for forty years? We will never get out of poverty and *al-hogra*. *Hna mahgureen* [we are humiliated and oppressed]. (Ilahiane 2021)

Tunisians continued to invoke the demand for "work, freedom and national dignity" during the anti-austerity protests in January 2018 ("Tunisia Austerity Protests" 2018). Meanwhile Jordanian protesters condemned the government for its "policy of impoverishment" in June 2018 protests and forced the resignation of Jordanian Prime Minister Hani al-Mulki (Ababneh 2018). The 2018, broad-based, cross-class protests throughout Jordan targeted neoliberalism and more specifically the International Monetary Fund for its mandated price increases for bread, fuel, electricity, and other basic products (Ababneh 2018). Protesters yelled, "Oh, you government of shame. Shame on you. [You] have sold the land and sold the house," and, "We are not poor but were made poor, this is your policy, oh dollar" (Ababneh 2018). In the Jordanian protests, students, women's rights activists, civil society, and trade unions were key actors in the successful protests, which quickly led to a repeal of these new taxes and a new Prime Minister, Omar al-Razzaz.

There are many other examples of similar struggles of the politics of waithood, and some of them concern the dignity and autonomy of women's bodies, specifically. In Algerian and Sudanese protests in 2019, which toppled their rulers, young people and women were critical components of the mobilization as they objected to authoritarianism, military, and police repression, as well as crushing youth unemployment. The politics of waithood and the predicaments of young women are not the only factors in many of these struggles.

Women's movements have been proposing legal changes to secure equal rights for some time, and other movements of nationalism, Islamism, human rights, and the developmental state are active. In Tunisia, for example, the "dignity revolution" led to contestation about equality in the new Tunisian constitution, adopted in 2014 after a two-year deliberative process. A "politics from below" fueled by large-scale protests and women's groups forced a change in the constitution from language about the "complementarity" of women in Article 28 to the equality of women, who as a group, should be afforded equal rights (Charrad and Zarrugh 2014: 230). Article 21, entitled "Equality before the Law," now states: "All citizens, male and female, have equal rights and duties, and are equal before the law without any discrimination. The state guarantees freedoms and individual and collective rights to all citizens and provides all citizens the conditions for a dignified life" (United Nations Development Programme and International IDEA 2014).

This new explicit constitutional guarantee for women has forced the rationalization of many of Tunisia's other laws. In June 2017, the Tunisian President at the time, Beji Caid Essebsi, launched the Individual Freedoms and Equality Committee (COLIBE); one year later COLIBE issued a report that suggested altering Tunisia's Personal Status Code to equalize inheritance between men and women. While on the one hand this new proposal, which is still under debate by parliament, seeks to rationalize constitutional guarantees to gender equality, on the other hand the Tunisian president "insisted that families wishing to continue observing the existing laws surrounding inheritance may continue doing so" (Allahoum 2018). Clearly, some contradictions and tough political battles for dignity and autonomy remain in Tunisia. Yet, the COLIBE report recommends legal reforms that give a child its mother's last name and enable Tunisian women to pass on citizenship to their foreign husbands. The report also suggests ending the death penalty and decriminalizing homosexuality (Dockery and Hassan 2018).

We can see the politics of waithood clearly in Saudi Arabia, where a longstanding demand for dignity and a large youthful population has influenced change in contradictory ways. As the Saudi monarchy realigned internally and Prince Salman emerged as the new powerful royal, press attention focused on King Salman's royal decree that finally allowed women to drive in June 2018 ("Saudi Arabia: Royal Decree" 2017). Yet, we know that, as the monarchy and the international media celebrated Saudi women's newfound mobility, women's rights activists who had demanded the end of male guardianship laws and had previously fought for driving rights were arrested, accused of fostering terrorism and condemned as foreign agents and traitors.[7] The Saudi state opened up movie theaters and allowed women segregated access to sporting events, reinstated physical education for girls in schools, and allowed women to join the armed forces and vote in municipal elections, but it does not permit any organized political movements or activism. In August 2019, a royal decree announced several important changes to guardianship laws, allowing a woman to obtain a passport and travel on her own without a male guardian's permission, register a birth and death, be recognized as the head of a household, and be included in the new gender-neutral definition of a worker (Human Rights Watch 2019), even as women's rights activists continued to be imprisoned in Saudi jails.

Conclusion

This chapter lays out the components of waithood in several countries in MENA, arguing that young people continue to face economic and social problems. At the same time, these issues have encouraged a broader, fundamental political demand for dignity. We can see some positive developments as young women and men fight against sexual harassment through civil society campaigns, establish NGOs, or demand new laws criminalizing harassment in a country like Egypt. While political surveillance, repression, and restrictions on Egyptian civil society frustrate those efforts, youthful disaffection and political demands have been at the center of important, impressive recent protests and uprisings in Algeria, Sudan, Lebanon, and Iraq, some of which have led to national political changes.

Although some MENA governments have tried to decrease youth unemployment and encouraged more job creation and opportunities for young people, some of these issues are beyond national policy initiatives since they reflect larger global trends. Few policymakers recognize, however, the interrelated problems young people face as they struggle to become adults, finish their educations, find employment, accumulate the sums for marriage, and negotiate the years of waithood in meaningful and socially legitimate ways. The complexity of these issues and their impact on each other elude simple solutions, particularly because young people are a diverse constituency with different needs and demands. Recognizing these issues is only part of the problem, and innovative policy interventions are needed on multiple fronts. Most importantly, even if it seems unlikely considering the current political environment in the region, young people must be valued as citizens and agents of change as they try to improve their lives and contribute to their countries.

Acknowledgments

I would like to thank C. Kendall Dorland at American University for her critical help in editing and researching this contribution. I would also like to thank the following for their research assistance on waithood in the past: Kyle Gray, Mohammed 'Alaa Hassan, Anna Olsson, Fatma El-Hamidi, Amina Hegazy, David Spielman, Rania Salem, Maria Buzdugan, David Richards, Mary Breeding, Ali Ozdogun, and Mee Young Han. Special thanks are due to Akhter A. Ahmed and Lawrence Haddad, the International Food Policy Research Institute (IFPRI) for sharing their data and adding a battery of questions on the cost of marriage in Egypt to their survey. The Population Council in Cairo, the American University Senate Research Award (Washington, DC), the New Arab Demography Project of the Social Research Center at the American University in Cairo, and the Mellon Foundation supported components of this research and previous related publications.

Diane Singerman is Associate Professor in the Department of Government, School of Public Affairs at American University. Her research interests lie within comparative politics, gender and politics in Egypt and the Middle East, informal politics, political participation, urbanism, youth, globalization, local governance, and social movements. Recent edited publications include *Cairo Contested: Governance, Urban Space, and Global Modernity* (American University in Cairo Press, 2009) and *Cairo Cosmopolitan: Politics, Culture, and Urban Space in the New Globalized Middle East* (American University in Cairo Press, 2006). Singerman received BA, MA, and PhD degrees from Princeton University and did graduate work at the American University in Cairo.

Notes

1. Much of the statistical data for this chapter is drawn from the Labor
   Market Panel Surveys (LMPS) conducted in Egypt (ELMPS), Jordan
   (JLMPS), and Tunisia (TLMPS). The ELMPS was fielded in 1998, 2006,
   and 2012, the JLMPS in 2010 and 2016, and the TLMPS in 2014. Some
   other sources draw from the 2009–10 Morocco Household and Youth
   Survey (MHYS), the National Survey on Household and Youth (NSHY)
   in Municipal Centers in Tunisia 2012. I am indebted to Professor Ragui
   Assaad for his continued generosity and previous support for including
   a marriage module in the 2006 ELMPS and to Professor Maia Sieverding
   for clarifying some dimensions of the 2014 JLMPS.
2. Economic obligations for one or both parties to the marriage, with the
   possible exception of *fātiha*, are expected around each of these pivotal
   points. Publicly observed stages of the engagement and marriage are typical in Egypt and include: *fātiha* (sealing the engagement between two
   families by reading the opening verse or *sūra* of the Quran), *shabka* ("tying" the couple with a gift of rings or gold), *katb el-kitāb* (formal signing
   of the marriage contract), and *dukhla* or *zifāf* (celebration of the first
   night of joint residence).
3. Men have a unilateral option for divorce at will by pronouncing "I divorce you" three times and simply registering the divorce at the court.
   Women, before 2001, had to prove "harm" under very limited conditions and lengthy court cases.
4. For further discussion of single women in Jordan's cities, see Adely
   (Chapter 11, this volume).
5. The Arab States, following the ILO definition, include Bahrain, Iraq,
   Jordan, Kuwait, Lebanon, Occupied Palestinian Territory (OPT), Oman,
   Qatar, Saudi Arabia, Syrian Arab Republic, United Arab Emirates, and
   Yemen. Northern African states include Algeria, Egypt, Libya, Morocco,
   Sudan, Tunisia, and the Western Sahara.
6. See Honwana (2013) on Tunisian youth.
7. In May 2017, King Salman eased one aspect of male guardianship laws
   by allowing women to access government and health services without
   requiring consent from their male guardians "unless existing regulations
   require it" (Human Rights Watch 2017).

References

Ababneh, Sara. 2018. "'Do You Know Who Governs us? The Damned Monetary Fund': Jordan's June 2018 Rising." Middle East Research and Information Project, 30 June. Retrieved 25 April 2019 from https://merip.org/
2018/06/do-you-know-who-governs-us-the-damned-monetary-fund/.
Abdel Khalil, Hisham. 2018. "Nine Facts about the Draft Law 'Fund to Finance Marriages of Young Men.'" *Al-Yawm al-Sabi'*, 27 August.

Aleya-Sghaier, Amira. 2012. "The Tunisian Revolution: The Revolution of Dignity." *The Journal of the Middle East and Africa* 3(1): 18–45.

Allahoum, Ramy. 2018. "Tunisia's President Vows to Give Women Equal Inheritance Rights." *Al-Jazeera*, 13 August.

Amin, Hiba. 2018. "The Text of the Draft Law is 'Fund for the Marriage of Young People.'" *Elwatan News*, 11 February. Retrieved 20 April 2019 from https://www.elwatannews.com/news/details/3055987?t=push.

ASDA'A Burson-Marsteller. 2018. "A Decade of Hopes and Fears: A White Paper on the Findings of the ASDA'A Burson-Marsteller Arab Youth Survey." Dubai: ASDA'A Burson-Marsteller.

Assaad, Ragui, Samir Ghazouani, Caroline Krafft, and Dominique J. Rolando. 2016. "Introducing the Tunisia Labor Market Panel Survey 2014." *IZA Journal of Labor & Development* 5(15): 1–21. Retrieved 15 August 2019 from https://izajold.springeropen.com/articles/10.1186/s40175-016-0061-y.

Assaad, Ragui, Rana Hendy, and Shaimaa Yassin. 2012. "Gender and the Jordanian Labor Market." Economic Research Forum, ERF Working Paper Series 701, Cairo, Egypt.

Assaad, Ragui, Rana Hendy, Moundir Lassassi, and Shaimaa Yassin. 2018. "Explaining the MENA Paradox: Rising Educational Attainment, yet Stagnant Female Labor Force Participation." March. IZA Discussion Paper Series No. 11385, IZA Institute of Economics. Bonn, German. Retrieved 7 August 2019 from https://www.iza.org/en/publications/dp/11385/explaining-the-mena-paradox-rising-educational-attainment-yet-stagnant-female-labor-force-participation.

Assaad, Ragui, and Caroline Krafft. 2014. "The Economics of Marriage in North Africa." The United Nations University World Institute for Development Economics Research (WIDER) Working Paper No. 2014/067, Helsinki.

Assaad, Ragui, Caroline Krafft, and Caitlyn Keo. 2018. "The Composition of Labor Supply and its Evolution from 2010 to 2016 in Jordan." Economic Research Forum, Working Paper 1183 (April), Cairo, Egypt.

Assaad, Ragui, Caroline Krafft, and Dominique J. Rolando. 2017. "The Role of Housing Markets in the Timing of Marriage in Egypt, Jordan, and Tunisia." Economic Research Forum, Working Paper 1081, Cairo, Egypt.

Bohn, Laura. 2013. "Egypt's Marriage Crisis: Sons and Daughters Too Broke to be Married, Waiting for Adulthood." *NBC News*, 2 November. Retrieved 27 April 2019 from https://www.nbcnews.com/news/world/egypts-marriage-crisis-sons-daughters-too-broke-be-married-waiting-fl na2D11711756.

Charrad, Mounira M., and Amina Zarrugh. 2014. "Equal or Complementary? Women in the New Tunisian Constitution after the Arab Spring." *The Journal of North African Studies* 19(2): 230–43.

Dhillon, Navtej, and Tarik M. Yousef, eds. 2009. *Generation in Waiting: The Unfulfilled Promise of Young People in the Middle East*. Washington, DC: The Brookings Institution Press.

Dimova, Ralitza, Sara Elder, and Karim Stephan. 2016. "Labor Market Transitions of Young Women and Men in the Middle East and North Africa." Work4Youth Publication Series No. 44, International Labour Office, Geneva.

Dockery, Wesley, and Emad Hassan. 2018. "Tunisia: Gay Rights, Inheritance Reforms put Country on Edge." *DW*, 15 August. Retrieved 25 April 2019 from https://www.dw.com/en/tunisia-gay-rights-inheritance-reforms-put-country-on-edge/a-45082954.

El Feki, Shereen. 2013. *Sex and the Citadel: Intimate Life in a Changing Arab World*. New York: Anchor Books.

Elouazi, Sana. 2018. "Sexual Relationships Between Two Consenting Adults Do Not Concern Society." *Morocco World News*, 13 February. Retrieved 25 April 2019 from https://www.moroccoworldnews.com/2018/02/240560/sexual-relationships-adults-morocco-society-mohammed-aujjar/.

ETF (European Training Foundation). 2014. "Young People not in Employment, Education, or Training in the EU Neighborhood Countries." March. Torino, Italy.

Gertel, Jörg, and Ralf Hexel, eds. 2018. *Coping with Uncertainty: Youth in the Middle East and North Africa*. Beirut: Saqi Books.

Hafez, Sherine. 2014. "Bodies That Protest: The Girl in the Blue Bra, Sexuality, and State Violence in Revolutionary Egypt." *Signs* 40(1): 20–28.

Herrera, Linda, and Asef Bayat. 2010. *New Cultural Politics in the Global South and North*. Oxford: Oxford University Press.

Honwana, Alcinda. 2013. *Youth and Revolution in Tunisia*. London: Zed Press.

Hoodfar, Homa. 1997. *Between Marriage and the Market: Intimate Politics and Survival in Cairo*. Berkeley: University of California Press.

Human Rights Watch. 2017. "Saudi Arabia: 'Unofficial' Guardianship Rules Banned. Authorities Should Abolish Entire System." 9 May. Retrieved 20 April 2019 from https://www.hrw.org/news/2017/05/09/saudi-arabia-unofficial-guardianship-rules-banned.

———. 2019. "Saudi Arabia: Important Advances for Saudi Women Freedom to Obtain Passports, But Women Activists Remained Jailed." 2 August. Retrieved 15 September 2019 from https://www.hrw.org/news/2019/08/02/saudi-arabia-important-advances-saudi-women.

Ilahiane, Hsain. 2021. "*Al-Hogra*—A State of Injustice: Portraits of Moroccan Men in Search of Dignity and Piety in the Informal Economy." In *Arab Masculinities: Anthropological Reconceptions in Precarious Times*, ed. Konstantina Isidoros and Marcia C. Inhorn. Bloomington: Indiana University Press.

ILO (International Labour Organization). 2017. "Global Employment Trends for Youth 2017: Paths to a Better Working Future." Geneva: ILO.

ILO (International Labour Organization). 2020. "Unemployment, Youth Total (Percent of Total Labor Force, Ages 15–24) (Modeled ILO estimate)—Tunisia." ILOSTAT database. Retrieved 7 August 2020 from https://data.worldbank.org/indicator/SL.UEM.1524.ZS?locations=TN.

Karasapan, Omer. 2015. "Toward a New Social Contract in Tunisia." Future Development (blog), 27 October. The Brookings Institution, Washington, DC. Retrieved 10 September 2019 from https://www.brookings.edu/blog/future-development/2015/10/27/toward-a-new-social-contract-in-tunisia/.

Krafft, Caroline, and Ragui Assaad. 2017. "Employment's Role in Enabling and Constraining Marriage in the Middle East and North Africa." Economic Research Forum, Working Paper Series 1080, Cairo, Egypt.

Krafft, Caroline, and Maia Sieverding. 2018. "Jordan's Fertility Stall and Resumed Decline: An Investigation of Demographic Factors." Economic Research Forum, Working Paper 1193 (April), Cairo, Egypt.

McKee, Musa, Martin Keulertz, Negar Habibi, Mark Mulligan, and Eckart Woertz. 2017. "Demographic and Economic Material Factors in the MENA Region." *Middle East and North Africa Regional Architecture: Mapping Geopolitical Shifts, Regional Order and Domestic Transformations* 3: 1–43.

McKernan, Bethan. 2017. "Saudi Arabia's Youth Embrace Crown Prince's Desire for Liberalization." *The Independent*, 25 October. Retrieved 25 April 2019 from https://www.independent.co.uk/news/world/middle-east/saudi-arabia-change-youth-crown-prince-modernise-wahhabism-mohammed-bin-salman-a8019876.html.

Mensch, Barbara, Susheela Singh, and John B. Casterline. 2005. "Trends in the Timing of First Marriage Among Men and Women in the Developing World." In *The Changing Transitions to Adulthood in Developing Countries: Selected Studies*, ed. Cynthia B. Lloyd, Jere R. Behrman, Nelly P. Stromquist, and Barney Cohen, 118–71. Washington, DC: The National Academies Press.

"MP Submits Draft Law for State-loans Supporting Marriage for Young People." 2018. *Egypt Independent*, 15 February. Retrieved 25 April 2019 from https://www.egyptindependent.com/mp-submits-draft-law-for-state-loans-supporting-marriage-for-young-people/.

Nazier, Hanan, and Racha Ramadan. 2017. "Marriage Outcomes and Women Empowerment After Marriage: A Three Countries Story." Economic Research Forum, Working Paper No. 1077, Cairo, Egypt.

Newman, Jessica Marie. 2018. "Aspirational Maternalism and the 'Reconstitution' of Single Mothers in Morocco." *Journal of Middle East Women's Studies* 14(1): 45–67.

Salem, Rania. 2012. "Trends and Differentials in Jordanian Marriage Behavior: Marriage Timing, Spousal Characteristics, Household Structure, and Matrimonial Expenses." Economic Research Forum, Working Paper No. 668 (April), Cairo, Egypt.

"Saudi Arabia's Demographic Challenge." 2013. *Stratfor, World View*. Retrieved 25 April 2019 from https://worldview.stratfor.com/article/saudi-arabias-demographic-challenge.

"Saudi Arabia: Royal Decree Allows Women to be Issued Driving Licenses." 2017. *Library of Congress*. Retrieved 25 April 2019 from http://

www.loc.gov/law/foreign-news/article/saudi-arabia-royal-decree-all ows-women-to-be-issued-driving-licenses/.

Sieverding, Maia. 2011. "Women's Contributions to the Cost of Marriage in Egypt: The Role of Education and Employment." Population Association of America 2011 Annual Meeting, Washington, DC, 31 March. Retrieved 25 April from https://paa2011.princeton.edu/papers/111655.

Sieverding, Maia, Nasma Berri, and Sawsan Abdulrahim. 2018. "Marriage and Fertility Patterns among Jordanians and Syrian Refugees in Jordan." Economic Research Forum, Working Paper No. 1187 (April), Cairo, Egypt.

Singerman, Diane. 1995. *Avenues of Participation: Family, Politics, and Networks in Urban Quarters of Cairo*. Princeton: Princeton University Press.

———. 2007. "The Economic Imperatives of Marriage: Emerging Practices and Identities Among Youth in the Middle East." *Middle East Youth Initiative*, Working Paper No. 6, September, The Brookings Institution, Wolfensohn Center for Development, Washington, DC.

———. 2013. "Youth, Gender, and Dignity in the Egyptian Uprising." *Journal of Middle East Women's Studies* 9(3): 1–27.

Singerman, Diane, and Barbara Ibrahim. 2003. "The Costs of Marriage in Egypt: A Hidden Dimension in the New Arab Demography." *Cairo Papers in Social Science* 24 (Spring).

Snow, David, and Robert D. Benford. 1988. "Ideology, Frame Resonance, and Movement Participation." In *From Structure to Action: Comparing Social Movement Research Across Cultures*, ed. Burt Klandermans, Hanspeter Kriesi, and Sidney G. Tarrow, 197–218. Greenwich: JAI Press.

The Soufan Group. 2015. "Foreign Fighters: An Updated Assessment of the Flow of Foreign Fighters into Syria and Iraq." December. Retrieved 25 April 2019 from http://soufangroup.com/wp-content/uploads/2015/12/TSG_ForeignFightersUpdate3.pdf.

Tadros, Mariz. 2016. *Resistance, Revolt, and Gender Justice in Egypt*. Syracuse: Syracuse University Press.

"Tunisia Austerity Protests go on Amid Wave of Arrests." 2018. *Al Jazeera*, 26 January. Retrieved 25 April 2019 from https://www.aljazeera.com/news/2018/01/tunisia-austerity-protests-wave-arrests-180126140735239.html.

UNDP (United Nations Development Programme). 2016. *Arab Human Development Report 2016: Youth and the Prospects for Human Development in a Changing Reality*. UNDP, Regional Bureau for Arab States: New York.

United Nations Development Programme and International IDEA. 2014. "The Constitution of the Tunisian Republic." Translation. Retrieved from 25 April 2019 from http://www.constitutionnet.org/sites/default/files/2014.01.26_-_final_constitution_english_idea_final.pdf.

World Bank. 2014. *Tunisia: Breaking the Barriers to Youth Inclusion*. Retrieved 25 April 2019 from http://documents.worldbank.org/curated/en/753151468312307987/Tunisia-Breaking-the-barriers-to-youth-inclusion.

————. 2018. Modeled International Labor Organization estimate, ILOSTAT database, September.

————. 2019a. "Egypt's Gross Domestic Savings (percent of GDP) in 2006." World Bank National Accounts Data and OECD National Accounts Data Files. Retrieved 25 April 2019 from https://data.worldbank.org/indica tor/NY.GDS.TOTL.ZS?locations=EG.

————. 2019b. "International Labor Organization ILOSTAT Database." Retrieved 27 April 2019 from https://data.worldbank.org/indicator/sl .uem.1524.zs?end=2017&start=1991.

Wynn, Lisa. 2016. "'Like a Virgin': Hymenoplasty and Secret Marriage in Egypt." *Medical Anthropology* 35(6): 547–59.

Yerkes, Sara. 2017. "Where Have all the Revolutionaries Gone?" March. Center for Middle East Policy at Brookings, Brookings Institution, Washington, DC. Retrieved 25 April 2019 from https://www.brookings.edu/ research/where-have-all-the-revolutionaries-gone/.

Chapter 2

"Trusting Is a Dicey Affair"
Muslim Youth, Gender Relations, and Future-Making in Southwestern Uganda

Dorothea E. Schulz

Introduction

I met Amir in Mbarara, southwestern Uganda, soon after I had
started my research on Muslim education in 2012.[1] At that time,
Amir was looking for a job in the non-governmental organization
(NGO) sector, having just received his BA degree in community development studies from Bishop Stuart University in Mbarara. Re-
sponding to my question about his future plans, he said:

> My parents keep telling me that I should get married. But first I need
> to find a job . . . I always felt that working on behalf of your home
> community is important, you know. That is why I asked my parents
> to scrape their money together and help me get a university degree
> in Community Development. And even though prospects to secure
> a job at an NGO are bleak nowadays, I will continue to strive. I feel
> ashamed that my parents have to support me; I detest being stuck. I
> do not just want to sit around and wait for an [employment] oppor-
> tunity to come. As for marriage, yes, it has to come, but frankly, now-
> adays, trusting is a dicey affair. A man cannot be too careful about
> choosing a wife. Finding a good, trustworthy wife who will support
> you is difficult. You risk spending lots of money already during court-

ship only to find out that she and her parents cheated on you. Today's women are only after money; they are selfish.

Prompted by my skeptical response to this sweeping judgment, Amir added:

> They *are* greedy! If you cannot provide for them, they will move over to a man who can offer them more. There are even women who teamed up with their new boyfriend to kill their husband and take whatever he possessed. But we Muslim men are in a slightly better position. If we pick a wife raised properly in a good, respectable Muslim family, chances are much higher that she will not leave you in times of distress and destitution.

Amir's comment on the pitfalls of courtship and marriage might have been unusual in its candor, but it was by no means exceptional. Most young Muslim men whom I came to know over the years of my research in Mbarara similarly highlighted the deeply paradoxical challenges of what might be described as *"postponed adulthood."* They framed their aspirations and struggles to attain seniority status as a matter of blocked occupational opportunities on one hand, and, on the other, of the double bind of obligatory marriage and the deeply risky nature of marital intimacy. Although they recurrently expressed frustration at their own situations of enforced waiting and stressed that marriage was the only way to escape the impasse of protracted youth, they felt highly ambivalent about the prospect of getting married, a step that would expose them to risky intimacy.

When young Muslim men highlight the burdensome, risky, and worrisome nature of their struggles to attain adult status, the complexity of their accounts far exceeds the analytical framework proposed in the literature on gender relations in Uganda. Apart from a recent interest in LGBTQ activism, this literature centers on the persistent subordination of women by highlighting forced child marriage, domestic violence (against women), and women's rights. This literature accurately picks up on important power inequalities and family dynamics in rural and lower-class urban households (e.g., Wyrod 2016). At the same time, the paradigms of "women's subordination" and of "male privilege" gloss over complex shifts in gender dynamics that are evident in many urban households in Uganda. As a result of the expansion of educational opportunities for girls and the media-related spread of middle-class ideals of marital partnership, expectations toward romantic alliance and joint decision-making are rising. As intimated in Amir's remark about the risks of marrying "selfish women," this development, along with the difficulties of unemployment and continued financial dependency, challenges men's abilities to attract and keep wives.

The woes of economic marginality and encumbered prospects of marriage that Amir describes are not limited to young men in urban Uganda. They reflect what a growing number of authors identify as typical structural constraints constitutive of young men's postponed adulthood or involuntary "waithood" around the globe (Dhillon and Youssef 2009; Durham 2017; Singerman 2007). Throughout sub-Saharan Africa, the efforts of male youth to attain adult masculinity and seniority status have been hampered by stark economic inequalities exacerbated through neoliberal reforms (e.g., Comaroff and Comaroff 2006; Honwana 2014; Meiu 2017; Weiss 2004; see also Makhulu, Buggenhagen, and Jackson 2010). By prompting serious delays in marriage and in realizing adult masculinity, these developments call into question what once constituted young men's age-specific "capacities to aspire" (Appadurai 2004; see also Masquelier 2013; Schulz and Diallo 2016).

This chapter recognizes young men's insistence on the involuntary nature of waithood and on their willful pursuit of a way out. The chapter explores the interpersonal and affective dimensions of involuntary waithood in urban Uganda by examining how young Muslim men tackle marriage as the stepping stone for achieving seniority status. Starting with an account of how male Muslim youth in Mbarara, southwestern Uganda, describe what specific dilemmas of involuntary waithood they face, the chapter then zones in on strategies these young men employ to overcome impediments to courtship and matrimonial security and to build futures for themselves.

An analysis of the struggles of male youths to achieve seniority status in urban Uganda requires a life-course perspective that considers how masculinity, as a set of relationally constructed norms and embodied practices, is tied to the particular age-status positionalities of specific categories of "young" men and women. For this reason, this chapter examines how the gender-specific and subjective dimensions of future-making play out for a particular category of male youth in this region. The discussion centers on young Muslim men, whose age-status positionality and future-making capacities, I argue, are defined by their belonging to a religious minority.

Amir's musings on the pitfalls of matrimonial choice and courtship point to a dimension of marital intimacy in times of waithood that has received less attention in comparative literature on youth and waithood. His cautionary remark about treacherous spouses who gang up with lovers to betray or even kill "underperforming" husbands suggests that marital relationships in urban Uganda are infused with considerable distrust about a partner's intentions and reliability. By identifying distrust as a major challenge to young men's situations of waithood, Amir posits an intricate connection between waithood, future-making, and trust. If Amir asserts that "getting married today" requires men to adopt an attitude of healthy distrust toward potential marriage partners and future in-laws, this also sheds light on ongoing reformulations of the terms of courtship and marriage and of the meanings of social relatedness and personhood.

By considering the specific role that dis/trust, as a particular construct of social and affective relatedness, plays in young Muslim men's future-making projects, this chapter contributes to ongoing debates on the significance of "trust," "entrustment," and distrust in social relatedness, in African societies and elsewhere. In his recent book, *Witchcraft, Intimacy, and Trust,* Geschiere (2013) enters a powerful plea for viewing distrust and "envy" as dynamics inherent to family and other intimate relations, in "Africa and beyond." Meinert (2015: 126), in contrast, proposes a historically more specific argument, by interpreting the pervasiveness of distrust in present-day Northern Uganda as the result of civil war–related experiences of violence and betrayal. These arguments invite us to explore, rather than take for granted, how trust and distrust structure relations of social intimacy. Lenk's (2010) conception of dis/trust as a "construction of emotional and discursive relationality" allows me to address dilemmas of waithood that relate to young Muslim men's matrimonial aspirations in particular. The key question is: how do young Muslim men in Mbarara, in their interactions with potential spouses and future in-laws, negotiate relations of intimacy through references to dis/trust as a discursive construction of reliability? By centering attention on the affective and social dimensions of involuntary waithood in Uganda, the chapter ties in with a growing scholarly interest in future-making and notions of futurity. Informed by Appadurai's (2004) understanding of aspiration as a cultural capacity embedded in and constrained by structures of political-economic inequality, the chapter considers how male youth in urban Uganda craft futures within the restricted horizon of expectations available to them. I argue that under current conditions of waithood, young men's efforts to pave a way toward a "future of probabilities" (Appadurai 2004) revolve essentially on a social project of anticipation (e.g., Bell and Mau 1971).

Empirical Research in Mbarara

Uganda is a multiethnic nation in East Africa, with approximately 44 million inhabitants who speak more than forty different national languages. Uganda's postcolonial history has been shaped by successive civil wars along various regional, religious, and ethnic divides. Most Ugandans identify as Christians (among them mainly Catholics, Anglicans, and independent Protestant churches). Muslims form a numerical and political minority in Uganda (Schulz 2013a). The 2014 National Census estimates that 13.7 percent of Uganda's population are Muslim. Most Muslims adhere to Sunni Islam, along with a significant number of Ahmadis and Shi'is.

The young Muslim men who are the main protagonists of this chapter live in Mbarara, a town of about 195,000 inhabitants that forms the administrative center of the Ankole district in southwestern Uganda. I initially met and interacted with these young men while doing research on Muslim education, as part of a broader research project on Muslim-Christian community making and interreligious boundary drawing that I have undertaken since 2012, funded by the German Research Foundation. Because I identified Muslim and Christian youth as important actors involved in religious activism, I was especially interested in gaining insight into the complexities of their social situation and future expectations.

In addition to performing research in the town of Mbarara, I spent extended periods of time in several rural communities located about twenty to thirty miles from Mbarara. As part of my research project on Muslim community making in Mbarara, the investigation also involved regular attendance of "Muslim women's groups" affiliated with two local mosques in Mbarara, as well as interviews with local appointees of the national Muslim organization, a governmental structure established to administer and regulate Muslim affairs.

Empirical research involved living with host families in the different locations, engaging in participant observation, socializing with and conducting more than thirty-five semi-structured interviews with young men and women (Muslims and non-Muslims), and having numerous informal conversations with them, their relatives, and their peers. The interviews were conducted in English or in Ruyankore. I also participated in numerous family and community celebrations, which granted me unique insights into the intricacies of intragenerational struggles.

"Being Stuck": Male Youth and
Involuntary Waithood in Mbarara

What is the particular economic and social context that forms the backdrop to young men's involuntary waithood in urban Uganda, and how do these men understand these challenges? Since the espousal of neoliberal reforms of the 1980s, Uganda's national economy has undergone a radical transformation.[2] Structural reforms have yielded, among other consequences, considerable capital accumulation and concomitant impoverishment of broad strata of the urban population.[3] Rural livelihoods, too, have undergone significant and swift transformation under the neoliberal economic paradigm (Wiegratz 2016: 79–112). The restructuring of the agricultural sector has occurred simultaneously with the concentration of profit in the hands of international companies and domestic players who allegedly belong to a core of people who are either members of, or closely affiliated with, the National Resistance Movement (NRM) government.

As the administrative center of the Ankole region in Uganda's southwest, Mbarara has been a dynamic core of governmental reform policy that aimed at the restructuring of urban and rural markets. When compared to the country's eastern (Wiegratz 2016) and northern regions (e.g., Dolan 2003), the adverse effects of these reforms are less pronounced in Mbarara and its rural hinterlands.[4] This is so because, as the home base to many members of the government and national army, the Ankole region benefitted from considerable financial and technological investment. Mbarara, with its sprawling infrastructure of privatized health provision and higher education and with mushrooming "residential" areas on its outskirts, where highly securitized mansions exist alongside shacks and other makeshift forms of habitation, epitomizes the promises and perils of a national economy revamped as neoliberal. As a consequence of shrinking opportunities for formal employment, in Mbarara, too, finding a regular job in a private company or in the state sector is now more than ever before predicated on personal and family connections to individuals whose influence stretches into the state administration or into business networks that pivot around the political apparatus of the Ugandan state.

Close to the Friday Mosque in downtown Mbarara, squeezed between several main commercial roads, an unruly marketplace area stretches across several streets and building blocks with a sprawling infrastructure of shops, market stands, and street vendors who present their colorful merchandise on little tables next to the street, and grills are set up to serve quick snacks to commuters and passers-by. At numerous corners and spots all around the market area, young *bodaboda* men, the motorcycle taxi drivers, claim their ubiquitous presence, chatting and casually exchanging greetings with passing acquaintances, while keeping a watchful eye on what happens around them, ready at any moment to rush to a potential customer. Right across the street from one of these *bodaboda* taxi areas, a shopping mall that opened a few years ago, along with a branch of the Nakumat supermarket chain, offers merchandise to the rich and the beautiful, thus testifying to the growing wealth, success, and political connectedness of Mbarara's business elite.

Ever since I first noted the dramatic socioeconomic contrast between the two sides of this road, the co-spatiality of these opposites has struck me as a startling illustration of the clashing universes that, if not introduced, have certainly been exacerbated since Uganda's espousal of neoliberalism. The scene encapsulates the exclusions and challenges faced by numerous young men in Mbarara and in contemporary urban Uganda more generally. The two flanking sides of the road offer a vivid *mise-en-scène* of the growing disparity between the rich and "ordinary folk" and of the often-heard dictum that "in Uganda, money makes politics." The shopping mall signals that lavish spending, and the mere ability to partake in consumption, have become important markers of personal achievement as well as of one's family's wealth, success, and connections to the center of power and accumulation in Kampala. The *bodaboda* drivers on the other side of the road stand for the exclusion of a major segment of male youth from the realm of conspicuous consumption. Their waiting for a customer who might emerge from the shopping mall across the street is emblematic of their situation of enforced waithood. The *bodaboda* drivers represent the aborted struggles of numerous young men who either lack education altogether or whose educational degree did not help them secure steady employment, in Mbarara or elsewhere in Uganda. Many of these men reach their thirties without being able to settle down, get married, and build independent homesteads.

Male elders frequently blame young men for their impasse, scolding them for their idleness and tendency to "sit around and wait for a benefactor." For their part, young men vehemently deny these charges by insisting that inactivity is not an option for them. They describe their situation as "being stuck," an expression that highlights the involuntary nature of waithood and the constraints that circumscribe their possibilities for action (see Sommers 2012). Similar to the predicament that youth face in Africa more widely (e.g., Honwana 2014; Momoh 2000), young men in Mbarara lack the basic assets and opportunities to move into an economically stable situation, get married, "provide," and hence achieve seniority status. The abruptness with which the *bodaboda* drivers switch, often within one-tenth of a second, from a posture of seemingly "idle" waiting into a fiery rush for clients epitomizes their ambition. Rather than living in fatalistic acquiescence, their "waiting" involves alertness and readiness to move, act, and search for a livelihood.

Bodaboda drivers' alertness is emblematic of how a broader constituency of urban male youth respond to a situation of "being stuck." In spite of considerable heterogeneity with respect to their educational background and their families' socioeconomic standing, they all struggle to eke out a living by engaging in petty trade and other low-return activities in the informal economy. They rationalize their situation by presenting it as a period of waiting, as one characterized by unattained social status, prompted by economic marginality, but also by daily efforts to forge paths toward adult status.

Young men often express their fear of "remaining stuck" in their current makeshift livelihood strategy, a fear that reflects their acute sense that, as much as they struggle to make ends meet, their occupations constitute deprecated and hence socially insufficient forms of economic activity. The concept of "unemployment" is thus wholly inadequate to describe young men's situation. For one, young men employ themselves in various income-generating activities while waiting for better opportunities to arise. Also, whereas "unemployment" refers exclusively to a marginal position within the labor market, many young men's situation of "being stuck" is as much a social impasse as it is an economic one. Finally, in contrast to the static notion of "unemployment," the term "being stuck," with its stress on involuntary waithood, bears a future-making orientation insofar as it hints at an attitude of "active waiting" (see Masquelier, Chapter 3, this volume) and of exploration, and at the effort to find a way out of their impasse.

Facing Educational Disadvantage: Muslim Youth in Mbarara

Young men's chances to overcome the obstacles they face and move out of their current economic marginality depend to an important extent on the kind of education they receive, as well as on the support they might expect from family members or other sponsors to either start profitable businesses or earn educational degrees. This situation of waithood applies to young men in urban Uganda more broadly and across the socioeconomic divide. Yet there are also obstacles to future-making that apply to young Muslim men more specifically, obstacles that spring significantly from their narrower chances to achieve high-quality education.

As the home area of President Yoweri Museveni and other leading members of the NRM government and military, southwestern Uganda has enjoyed a relatively successful educational infrastructure, benefitting from its elites' preferential integration into the national political economy since the early days of NRM rule.[5] The Ankole region, with its district capital Mbarara, forms part of this economically and politically privileged area, indicated in part by the recent mushrooming of secondary educational institutions and of universities. Yet this educational infrastructure does not benefit Muslim youth to the same degree because many of them attend the schools referred to as the "Muslim-founded schools," which for various reasons, have lower educational standards. As a result of these qualitative discrepancies, Muslim students generally have fewer chances than their Christian peers to find regular employment. Religious affiliation thus constitutes a factor of social differentiation in Uganda, even if this is rarely mentioned officially.

The origins of this structural inequality go back to British colonial administration which, through a number of regionally, ethnically, and religiously founded divisions, created a volatile, sometimes explosive frame for the regulation of rights, entitlements, and political party affiliations (Twaddle 1995). For decades after independence, the lopsided educational system severely impinged Muslim children's employment opportunities (Kiyimba 1986). Following the introduction of universal primary education in the mid-1990s, the national educational sector was reshaped by a flurry of (often privately run) secondary and tertiary educational institutions. The diversification of the educational sector, and the attendant creation of competitive Muslim schools, has benefitted an emergent stratum of well-to-do Muslim urbanites (Schulz 2013a). In contrast, Muslim children of less privileged economic backgrounds still face significant educational disadvantages, largely because the educational degrees offered by Muslim-founded schools do not adequately prepare students for enrollment in Uganda's most prestigious secondary schools (Schulz 2013b).[6] Even in locations where good institutions of secondary and tertiary learning are available, such as in present-day Mbarara, a Muslim youth has fewer opportunities to earn an educational degree as a stepping stone for enrollment at a university or for regular employment, let alone for obtaining one of the coveted positions in the state administration or the private sector. In this situation, many young Muslim men are forced to explore occupational opportunities outside and beyond the career paths enabled by education.[7]

How do young Muslim men view their—sometimes aborted, sometimes successful—efforts to become "proper" Muslim men? How do their dim prospects of regular employment, circumscribed by a narrow labor market and a disadvantageous educational institutional setting, play out in their relationships with young Muslim women?

"Trusting Is a Dicey Affair": Muslim Youth and Gender Relations in Mbarara

Recent scholarship documents how the neoliberal restructuring of society converges with a more comprehensive reshaping of everyday life throughout the Global South. These changes show in the reconfiguration of patterns of social interaction and, notably, in changing frameworks of moral evaluation and religious discourse (e.g., Jones, Hull, and Mohamed 2011; Schielke 2009; Schulz 2012; Smith-Hefner 2005; Wiegratz 2016). Conventional gender norms, values, and judgments are reconsidered and contested, and gendered subjectivities are partly reconfigured (e.g., Cornwall 2016; Mac an Ghaill and Haywood 2016; see also Inhorn 2017). As part of a broader process of moral recalibration, conventional understandings and practices of masculinity are "dislocated" (Cornwall and Lindisfarne 1994). To get a sense of how the recalibration process plays out in the relations between young Muslim men and women in Mbarara, the following discussion centers on how they assess and disagree over the responsibilities associated with normative Muslim masculinity. Their diverging accounts not only reflect ongoing shifts in gender relations but reveal how a discursive register of moral disapproval becomes itself a means to assert, mold, and rework masculine subjectivities in present-day Mbarara.

When young Muslim men in Mbarara chat with each other about their plans for the future, they usually frame their aspirations as a matter of "becoming a proper man who can take care of his fam-

ily." In their view, "proper manhood" refers to a man's capacity to
"provide"—that is, to pay for daily foodstuff, rent, medical expenses,
and school fees for children and to be the gatekeeper to women's
consumption. Their repetitive references to "providing" as a pillar of
adult masculinity shows just how strongly the aspirations of these
young men are geared toward fulfilling the conventional patriarchal
norms that scholars identify as key elements of hegemonic masculinity in Uganda (Dolan 2003; Wyrod 2016: 80–122). Young Muslim
men often stress the desirability of a "financially sound match," an
expression that points to the advantages of being married to a wife
whose education would grant her regular employment and a steady
income. Therefore, to these men, the ideal of the male provider does
not preclude a woman's contribution to family subsistence, as long
as her contribution does not challenge the prerogatives and authority her husband draws from being the main provider.[8]

The marginality of these young men in the labor market fundamentally constricts their "capacity to aspire" to adult masculinity.
Still, holding a steady job does not in itself bear the same symbolic
weight as in Western industrial societies, where employment is considered the cornerstone of hegemonic masculinity (Connell 1995).
In Mbarara, in contrast, men aim to achieve not merely employment alone but financial security in any form. But for young Muslim men, the range of resources and economic options is limited.

My conversations with young Muslim men frequently touched
on the ideas of material uncertainty and work insecurity. Expressed
by the phrase "being broke," this notion formed a leitmotif in young
men's assessment of the crux of their dilemma. Yet while the expression appears to center attention on the economic dimension of
young men's waithood, it provided an astute commentary on their
social impasse as well. "Being broke" captures that young men's inability to achieve financial self-reliance prevents them from marrying and obtaining full seniority status, and hence impedes their
ability to climb up the ranks of intrafamily hierarchy and authority.
Money, in their eyes, works as a currency of social relatedness. Consider, for instance, how Saidi, who in 2013 worked as a (temporary)
driver for a local NGO, described his predicament:

> Nowadays, here in Uganda, becoming a proper Muslim man is a bur-
> den that many youth cannot shoulder. Look at me. I am running
> around without finding a job that would give me security and peace
> of mind. I have tried so many things to move on, but, you see, I am
> still broke. I spend my days worrying about myself and about what

the future might hold for me. If there is no money, how can a man maintain his dignity?

Saidi frames his frustration about his inability to live up to the norms of adult masculinity as a matter of "money shortage," thus presenting money as both the source of his misfortune and its prime solution. This framing points to a "new economics of the person" (Mbembe 2006) in which money becomes an increasingly universal currency of expression and social mediation. Also, in a more immediate sense, my interlocutors' preoccupation with "money" sheds light on a tendency among young Muslim men to define proper Muslim masculinity as a matter of men's capacity to earn and dispense money (see Wyrod 2016: 86) and to invest it in, among other things, matrimonial alliances and conjugal affection.

The importance of male spending power as a requisite for the building of stable matrimonial relationships and the basis for family authority was reinforced by Amir, who, in 2012, was desperately looking for a steady income to honor his late father's request that he marry and start a family on his own. Amir said:

> My problem, you see, is not simply that I cannot find work that would prove to my future in-laws that I will have money coming in steadily and be a good husband and father. Taking care of your family is a big issue nowadays, but it is not everything. How am I to convince a woman that I might be a desirable choice, if I have nothing to give to her? And even if I managed to scramble together some money here and there and give it to her during courtship, where would this leave me? Once we got married, how am I to maintain the impression I made on her, if there is no money coming in steadily? Women nowadays are difficult to satisfy. How will I make sure that she does not talk back to me, blaming me for not giving her some little money on the side? What will I do when she infects our children with her irreverent talk? I risk losing the respect and deference they owe me and with it, my in-laws' esteem and support.

Amir pointedly summarizes a crucial dilemma: in a situation shaped by a heightened social significance of consumption, young men's inabilities to accumulate the resources necessary for consumption makes the cultivation of transactional relationships expedient to the achievement of hegemonic masculinity, yet simultaneously renders them increasingly difficult to obtain in real life (see Enria 2016: 144).

Amir's coupling of a man's authority and spending capacity is not gender-neutral but rests on a specific normative construction of gender hierarchy. His remark that women are "difficult to satisfy" conveys his fear of failure, of being unable to fulfill the heavy burden of financial responsibilities put on an adult man. Amir expresses his anxieties about his inability to achieve and maintain family authority through a moralizing frame that blames women's potential character faults. He makes the ubiquitous risk of his own social failure dependent on his future wife's moral disposition, citing women's propensity for irreverent and greedy behavior as the major factor that could jeopardize his social position within and outside the family. Expressing one's fears about losing control over "independent women" is neither a new phenomenon nor specific to Ugandan society. Similar apprehensions in urban Uganda were noted by Obbo (1980) already in the 1970s. As a set of stereotypical complaints about women's alleged immorality, these allegations illustrate how men disadvantaged by this structural, political-economic impasse couch the dilemma as a moral issue. This moral reframing mirrors the ways discursive schemes in other African societies reflect on shifting gender relations and the dislocation of normative masculinity. Comprised of crude stereotypes about women's "immorality" and "selfishness," this discursive frame signals just how hotly contested dominant gender norms have become under conditions of neoliberal economic reform (Masquelier 2005; Schulz 2001, 2012: 73–95).

Other young Muslim men similarly complained about women's "condescending" demeanor toward men "even if a man made a great (financial) effort during courtship" and about women's desire to "take the upper hand" in romantic relationships and marriage, complaints that, once again, attest to young men's preoccupation with patriarchal decision-making power and family authority. Another grievance was women's alleged propensity to "pick and drop men at their earliest convenience" and to "roam freely"—an expression that alludes to sexual promiscuity. Here, underneath apparent discursive continuities, the object of young men's complaints seems to be changing.[9] Whereas the discursive figure of the "demanding" woman was once aimed primarily at women's greater economic power and potential independence, I found that young Muslim men in Mbarara make this charge mostly in connection with references to a woman's education. The trope of the woman who selects and dismisses men at pleasure speaks volumes about what young men consider the promises and risks of female education. Young men's allegations reflect, first, their sense of losing control over the social mobility of women whose educational background gives them greater leverage in their choice of marriage partners and, second, and more generally, their fear of failure to honor the normative standards of adult masculinity. Young Muslim men's worries materialize in rumors and numerous stories about women who "traded" marriage partners for more promising matches or who, like the female protagonist of Amir's story, even teamed up with their new boyfriends to threaten or disown their initial suitors. As Ali, another man with whom I frequently discussed the challenges of marriage (as shown later in the chapter), put it laconically,

> Today's women cannot be trusted, unless you find someone whose parents have brought her up in a proper way. Most of the time, a girl's parents are the worst. They are so greedy. They will say, "We have not put our girl through school for nothing; now is the moment when her schooling should pay off." They tell their daughters to watch out for a more lucrative match, and when they realize that your job is not steady, they will support her and her new boyfriend to betray you, to rob you of whatever you offered to the girl in good faith.

Other young Muslim men drew similar connections between women's education and their alleged deceitfulness. One interlocutor asserted, "Today's women cannot be trusted, especially if they have been to school. They know their education makes them desirable marriage partners because they can contribute to the family income, and they use this to their advantage." Portraying a girl's schooling as both an advantage and a curse, the remark echoes Amir's concerns about women's dishonesty. The "untrustworthy" woman becomes a master trope that allows men to deflect blame for their socioeconomic difficulties.[10] Young Muslim men use what they see as women's and their parents' deceitfulness to justify extreme caution in the search for a marriage partner and during courtship. In this fashion, young Muslim men employ an attitude of distrust as a chief "strategy" (Carey 2017) for protection from the risky endeavor of courtship and marriage. Becoming an adult man requires them to live with, and pragmatically resolve, the tension between on one side, the marriage-related risks of closeness and entrustment, and, on the other side, the need to maintain a healthy distance as a measure of self-protection.

"Dependable Men Are Rare Nowadays"

Young Muslim men, in their reflections on how to overcome the challenges of waithood, conceive of a man's capacity to "provide" as an essential component of adult masculinity. In contrast, references to a specifically Muslim male identity are largely missing from their definition of proper manhood. Starting from the argument that "masculinity" and "femininity" refer to schemas for being, doing, and feeling that are relationally constructed (Connell 1995; Vera-Sanso 2016: 81), the following discussion centers on how young Muslim women in Mbarara engage in the ongoing construction of ideal masculinity and what role they attribute to Islam in these constructions.

Whereas Muslim men tend to single out "untrustworthy women" as a major object of concern, young Muslim women also approach potential partners with caution. My female interlocutors often deplored that men's inability to act as main "providers" put the growing burden of financial responsibility on women's shoulders. They also insisted that they had little motivation to find employment if their salaries would be spent mostly on their future family's daily survival (see Vera-Sanso 2016: 90–92). When discussing specific cases of courtship and the suitability of individual men, some young Muslim women depicted men's inability to "provide" as a form of moral destitution, implying that their inability was the result of a lack of initiative or outright refusal to change their situations.[11] Muslim women's complaints suggest that they do not contest conventional gender norms and masculinity ideals and rather identify young men's alleged unwillingness to work and "dishonesty" as the main source of their troubles.

Thus, like young men, young Muslim women, rather than explain their suitors' inability to act as "proper men" by economic constraints, describe the current malaise of marital relations as a moral challenge. Many young Muslim women with whom I spoke in the period between 2014 and 2016 maintained that the "main problem of courtship and marriage today" was not the shortage of work opportunities for young men but the unwillingness of these men to become responsible husbands and fathers. As proof, they cited men's alleged reticence to invest their earnings in the building of stable and exclusive relationships with single women, and their propensity to "keep on the side" one or multiple girlfriends, whom they "kept happy and attached" with repeated monetary gifts.

Young Muslim women also framed what they saw as a recurrent problem during courtship and within marriage as a "money problem," thus echoing young men's tendencies to portray money as both the source of and the solution to their impasse. By alleging young men to be unwilling, rather than unable, to provide, young Muslim women deny them the affective disposition of "emergent" adults (Arnett 2000) and portray them instead as irresponsible teenagers who refuse to assume the responsibilities of adulthood.

For some, the safest way to escape the fate of a "duped woman" is to fall back on a religiously founded solution, by searching for a dependable marriage partner "who will respect you because of your education and because of her God-ordained role as a mother and wife." As Aisha, a 22-year-old student whom I first met at a "mosque women's group" meeting in Mbarara in 2013, said:

> When women get married today, their main concern is to avoid the troubles they see in other marriages in which duped women have to endure their husbands' infidelity. Men do not want to content themselves only with one woman; they go astray and keep other girlfriends on the side who will eat up the money needed by his wife to raise his children. The only possibility to make a man see reason is to remind him of God's will. That is why we Muslim girls are in a better position, especially those who have been to school. We only accept the courtship of a suitor who obeys God's commands and who respects us for our education and proper conduct. With God's help, this will protect us from the fate of a duped woman.

Hafiza, another unmarried woman in her early twenties, added:

> For an educated girl, you know, it is not easy to find the right man, but she needs to look carefully and agree with her parents on her choice. A clever man will see the advantages of marrying an educated Muslim girl. A proper Muslim man knows his responsibilities vis-à-vis his wife and children, and that he has duties toward his wife's parents as well. In return, he will have the advantage of an obedient wife who knows how to behave and who does not leave him as soon as things become difficult.

Muslim women in Mbarara, regardless of whether they are already married or still searching for a suitable match, tend to frame their grievances regarding marriage as a moral criticism, not as a comment on the structural constraints that keep men from attaining financial self-sufficiency. As a result, they, too, offer a moral solution: a marriage grounded in what they describe as "Islamic" moral principles. These women believe that their Muslim education and propriety should inspire prospective partners to behave respectfully and support them financially. Submission to "Islamic precepts" is envisioned as a common moral ground and serves young Muslim women as a discursive register to minimize the risks of betrayal and disappointment by future husbands. At the same time, Muslim women and men invoke Islam in specifically gendered ways.

In summary, as much as young Muslim men and women in Mbarara differ in what they identify as the sources of marital trouble, they agree on the three main challenges young men need to tackle to reach seniority status. Young men's marginality within the job market makes it hard for them to establish financial self-reliance as the first step toward marriage. Their uncertain economic situation weakens their chances and leverage vis-à-vis young educated women, which prompts them to distrust potential partners. At the same time, their aspirations to marry and build independent homesteads obliges them to balance the conflicting demands of distrust of and entrustment to women. Finally, young Muslim men need to convince their future spouses and in-laws of the seriousness of their intentions and of the feasibility of their marriage projects.

Finding Ways Out of Involuntary Waithood

While economic marginality constricts the future options of young men regardless of religious background, the state educational system further disadvantages young Muslim men regarding their professional aspirations. How do these young men compensate for these disadvantages? What strategies do they devise to counter the apprehensions of young women and their parents and to convince them of the seriousness of their aspirations?

This section explores how three young Muslim men respond to the constraints and risks of future making in this area of southwestern Uganda. Their examples illustrate how many young Muslim men, in their efforts to overcome their situations of involuntary waithood, fall back on two main resources at their disposal. They build up social capital by investing in support networks that, in the absence of other forms of capital, they hope to convert into employment opportunities and relationships of trust with future in-laws and spouses. In addition, many young Muslim men refer to Islamic precepts and gender norms to justify their own actions vis-à-vis in-laws and their expectations toward women. These Muslim men's responses are specific insofar as they rest on rationalizations that claim a specifically Islamic morality. Invoking proper Muslim manhood minimizes the vagaries of getting married and building a family. In so doing, young men mirror the moralizing solutions proposed by young Muslim women to resolve marriage-related risks and difficulties.

Building Social Capital and Common Moral Ground

Ali illustrates how young Muslim men without starting capital carve out paths toward a predictable future by struggling to attain financial solvency. When I met Ali in early 2016, he had just opened a photo studio on the second floor of a building in one of Mbarara's main commercial streets. At the relatively young age of twenty-nine, Ali had already founded his own business with the help of an uncle, a paternal second cousin "with good connections to the transport sector." Ali also proudly told me that he was soon to be married to a "local girl, very proper, from a very good and reliable Muslim family." Rather than simply striking luck by relying on his rich uncle, Ali had carefully, over time, built a relationship with this uncle as a basis for this sponsorship.

After finishing secondary education at a Muslim-founded school in Mbarara, Ali earned a degree in engineering from the Islamic University in Uganda. Unable to secure employment with the degree, Ali soon grew tired of, as he put it, "hanging around, feeling stuck, and waiting for an opportunity (job) that would never come." He started doing odd jobs on behalf of his paternal uncle who, born into an influential family from the area, had used his closeness to the president's son-in-law to start up business in Southern Sudan. After working for several years for his uncle, first by playing the role of "jack of all trades," then as his driver, and finally as his advisor in business dealings in Juba, Southern Sudan, Ali decided to become his own boss. Having endeared himself to his uncle through his reliability in business affairs, Ali convinced his uncle (who had just shrewdly concluded his affairs in Southern Sudan before business opportunities there started to crumble) to give him some seed money to open a photo studio in Mbarara. Ali also managed to secure from him the means to court a potential bride. About five months before I was introduced to him, Ali had begun to court Nadira, a remote niece of a former Member of Parliament in Mbarara. This marriage into a reputable local family would strengthen his ties to the local political establishment. Over the following year, this courtship involved making numerous material gifts to his prospective bride, visiting his future father-in-law regularly, and "paying his respect" to his future mother-in-law through little services and gifts. Ali also strengthened his friendship to his bride's eldest brother, who, as he explained to me, was a respected member of the local Muslim community and had an important say in deciding on the wedding date and mode of its execution. When explaining his choice of bride to me, Ali stressed her "good upbringing" in a respectable Muslim family and her attendance at a Muslim-founded secondary school, all of which would guarantee "peace and stability in the marriage."

I had a chance to discuss Nadira's marital union with several of her friends whom I knew through a local mosque women's group and who considered Nadira extremely lucky in her choice of marriage partner.[12] These friends maintained that Ali's financial situation was "modest" yet stressed that his Muslim family background, educational credentials, past achievements, and social connections made him a desirable match. All in all, they concluded, Ali was reliable, likely to put his wife "at ease," and therefore "a safe bet," "at least for what a Muslim girl can expect here in Mbarara."

Ali is representative of young Muslim men who, because their educational degrees did not secure them steady employment, need to find other ways to convince prospective wives and in-laws of their financial security and genuine intentions. Ali tackled these challenges by centering his efforts on first cultivating a relationship with his uncle as a potential sponsor of his professional and social career. Compared to many other young Muslim men, Ali was in a relatively privileged position. Family support allowed him to bypass involuntary waithood; his uncle's money and political connections facilitated his access to the marriage market and allowed him to make a desirable matrimonial match. By marrying into a well-respected local Muslim family, Ali felt he increased his chances for future marriage stability and security. As someone whom young Muslim women consider a suitable and safe match, Ali exemplifies how young men and women draw on a shared religious-moral frame of reference to minimize unpredictability and uncertainty.

Making Social Investments

Unlike Ali, Musah could not fall back on family or other sources of financial support to escape involuntary waithood. His efforts demonstrate that young Muslim men who lack both financial capital and favorable social and political connections attribute a central importance to the fostering of social support networks.

Musah was twenty-four years old when I met him in August of 2012. He had initially attended a Muslim school located on the outskirts of Mbarara and later completed secondary education at a regular governmental school. Because his single-parenting mother could not afford to pay his school fees after his father's death, Musah had to drop out of school repeatedly to help his mother make a living, all the while, as he put it, "learning . . . the meaning of hunger and hardship." Ultimately, his efforts to earn a school diploma paid off. A maternal uncle, impressed by Musah's mother's perseverance in supporting her five children single-handedly, covered the remaining years of Musah's education. Musah even earned a degree in social work and social administration from Bishop Stuart University in Mbarara, this time funded by a paternal aunt. When I met Musah in 2012, he eked out a living as a *bodaboda* driver, an occupation he considered only a temporary solution. Whenever I returned to Mbarara in the following years, Musah was still, as he put it, "stuck" in underemployment, a situation that impeded his plans to get married and "move on in life" and was difficult to overcome for his want of "connections" that would allow him "to find some business." Finally, in 2016, Musah started doing odd jobs for the photo studio that Ali, his former classmate, had recently opened in downtown Mbarara. Since then, Musah has been steadily transitioning from his work as a *bodaboda* driver to that of a freelance photographer. In early 2018, Musah became a shop attendant in the photo studio. From the early days of his work at the studio, Musah's initiative had exceeded by far common expectations toward someone only loosely connected to Ali's business. To realize his ambition of steady employment, Musah carefully strengthened his ties to Ali's relatives and in-laws. He signaled his willingness to help through innumerable gestures of disinterested generosity, such as driving around Ali's relatives and mobilizing additional financial support for Ali's and Nadira's wedding from a local businessman. Through these acts of unilateral service, Musah built up a network of support, morally obliging Ali's parents and in-laws to enter into a relationship of reciprocity and recompense. His example illustrates how, in the absence of other forms of capital, social investments are crucial to helping young men realize their aspirations.

Building Trust against All Odds

As we have seen, many young Muslim men and women in Mbarara recognize the risks of marital intimacy, while simultaneously acknowledging the necessity of mutual reliance. Men's and women's cautionary remarks about untrustworthy spouses and their calls for an attitude of healthy distrust vis-à-vis potential spouses and future in-laws suggest that in present-day Mbarara, trust is not a fixed condition of marital unions and social intimacy. Rather, trust as a condition for and feature of marriage needs to be cultivated carefully and over time, by simultaneously maintaining a cautious distance and openness toward the possibility of disappointment. To build

trust under these circumstances is, as Meinert (2015: 119) puts it for
present-day Northern Uganda, a "tricky social achievement" and a
"willed action."

How, then, do young Muslim men in Mbarara generate trustful
relations that will allow them to get married and attain the status of
adult masculinity? What particular form do their social investments
take, and what dynamics of reciprocal obligation and anticipation
do they entail? The example of interlocutor Abdul Rahman helps
answer these questions. Abdul Rahman's acts of "entrustment"
(Shipton 2007) further illustrate his emphasis on the role of Islam
in providing a common moral ground for building ties of trust and
mutual reliance.

I first met Abdul Rahman in 2015, when he was twenty-six years
old. After a rocky schooling experience that forced him to overcome multiple financial hurdles, Abdul Rahman graduated from
secondary school in Fort Portal, Western Uganda. Unable to find
employment in Fort Portal, he moved to his mother's native village
approximately twenty miles away from Mbarara, hoping to make
a living from tea cash crop cultivation. When his maternal uncles
denied him a plot of land because they preferred instead to sell it to
a business man from Kampala, Abdul Rahman moved to Mbarara,
where he started doing odd jobs for the local branch of a Muslim
relief organization, all the while hoping to find permanent employment or scratch together funding to earn a university degree.

Until January 2018, when I talked to him last, Abdul Rahman
had not started, as he put it, "serious courtship preparations," knowing well that unless he was financially sound, "there was no chance
to find a good and honest Muslim wife." Abdul Rahman described
his future aspirations in terms of being self-reliant and of leading
"the life of an honorable Muslim man," which indicates that, to him,
finding a spouse formed only one element in the jigsaw puzzle of
achieving adult masculinity and seniority status. Abdul Rahman felt
very ambivalent about marriage, asserting repeatedly that "one cannot trust women," yet also insisting that a man could not gain full
acceptance into the adult world without entering the unpredictable
grounds of matrimony. Moreover, although Abdul Rahman stressed
his preference for a spouse "who has some educational background
and can contribute to our family income," his comments reveal his
apprehensions about an educated woman's "exaggerated expectations" of her husband. His solution to the dilemma was to search for
a "good Muslim wife" whose upbringing in a "respectable Muslim
family" would ensure her modest behavior and submission to her

husband. Thus, like Ali, Abdul Rahman invoked Islam as a frame of reference that could render conjugal matters and dynamics more manageable and predictable.

To resolve the equally pressing matter of appearing trustworthy to his family and peers, Abdul Rahman, like Musah, engaged in acts of what I call "anticipatory generosity." Before I had even met Abdul Rahman in person, I had heard about his reliability and "readiness to help friends in need." I witnessed numerous scenes in which Abdul Rahman freely offered his assistance, for instance in tricky negotiations between peers and to mobilize loans on behalf of friends or relatives. Although Abdul Rahman confided in me that these commissions put "a heavy strain" on his "sense of dignity," he was eager to intervene and demonstrate his availability. Whenever I asked him whether his favors did not entitle him to compensation, Abdul Rahman vehemently refuted any such thought, maintaining that such services were "part of being social" and should be done "without expecting compensation."[13] Abdul Rahman's popularity and recognition as a generous and reliable person suggest that his cultivation of networks of trust through a performance of disinterested availability was successful.

As Shipton (2007) forcefully argues in his analysis of "fiduciary culture" in Tanzania, trust emerges from various kinds of transfers that, conceived as acts of "entrustment," make others incur debts and oblige them to reciprocate. Graeber (2011) similarly stresses the socially productive nature of "debt" as the motor of diverse, social, moral, and economic relations and transactions. Offering a service and receiving a "gift" are ways of "entrusting oneself" that are predicated on reciprocity. I interpret Abdul Rahman's and Musah's readiness to help and their concomitant refusal of any immediate recompense as acts of "anticipatory generosity." These acts aim to generate trust and become a matter of "entrusting" oneself to someone else, while counting on the recipient's future reciprocation of one's own favor. The acts of "entrustment" thus form part of an elaborate "debt scheme" (Graeber 2011) that at once builds trust and requires trust in order to function.

Abdul Rahman's social engagements illustrate how many young Muslim men seek to channel the outcome of certain social interactions through determined anticipatory generosity. Their actions involve a purposeful reworking of social relations and a reconfiguration of relatedness in the form of trust. Abdul Rahman and others are successful not only because they engage in the "willed" building of trust (Meinert 2015)—that is, in its intentional nature—but

because their acts oblige others to reciprocate. Their behavior constricts the range of possible responses to their actions and renders
the outcome of particular social exchanges more predictable.

Conclusion

This chapter analyzed the social possibilities and affective perils of
young Muslim men's involuntary waithood in Uganda by stressing the
importance of anticipation and aspiration to their future-making efforts. Young Muslim men in Mbarara have a limited range of options
to escape the predicaments of involuntary waithood, yet rather than
content themselves with "simply waiting," they directly and strate-
gically tackle structurally engrained obstacles to adulthood by initiating alternative pathways toward manhood. Their dogged building
of networks of mutual reliability belie elders' frequent complaints
about these young men's lack of initiative and propensity to "merely
complain."

Ali, Musah, and Abdul Rahman, the three young Muslim men
whose aspirations are detailed in this chapter, opted for different
paths toward adult masculinity, while confronting similar dilemmas
and constraints. They all faced the education-related limited prospects for regular employment that are typical of Muslim youth. Musah and Abdul Rahman represent segments of male urban youth in
Uganda that lack family connections to the political and economic
elite and hence to business opportunities. All three recognized the
necessity to resort to, and purposefully foster, social connectedness.
To young Muslims who have no starting capital in their hands other
than the ability to prove their trustworthiness through their "readiness to help," the only option is to build social capital by obliging
those who are hierarchically superior to reciprocate. Lacking the
necessary economic capital to realize financial self-reliance and reliability, all three men initiated schemes of mutual moral indebted-
ness that connected them to older and more financially successful
individuals. By cultivating trust in this way, they foster important
socioeconomic connections.

The plans that young Muslim men devise to move out of involuntary waithood substantiates a more general point. As Singerman
(2007) and Meiu (2017) observe, under neoliberal economic conditions, youth face a radically changing context of generating social security. Deprived of basic opportunities to achieve seniority

status, young men need to fall back on social relations as a source of advancement. To them and, more generally, to all those disenfranchised within a narrowing labor market, relations of reciprocity to peers and kin as well as new structures of mutual support gain in importance (Schulz 2012: 98–135). The growing dependency of young Muslim men on these structures belies a neoliberal ideology that celebrates the unshackling of the individual from family and social obligations. Rather, building social connectedness, encoded as a form of mutual entrustment, becomes what Morris (2008) refers to as generalized patterns of risk insurance in times of hardship (see also Meiu 2017: 177).

Yet, seemingly paradoxically, young men's increased reliance on social relations goes hand-in-hand with mounting concerns about their inability to trust those whose support they need most. An undercurrent of generalized distrust pervades intimate relationships, the effect of radical alterations of conventional domestic economies reinforced by neoliberal economic reform (Ashforth 1999; Hunter 2010). The development also sheds light on an affective dimension of waithood that young Muslim men perceive as a threat to their sense of self and existential security. While they advocate an attitude of "healthy distrust" to navigate the treacherous grounds of courtship and marital intimacy, these men simultaneously recognize the unsettling effects of distrust, and thus frame "trust" discursively and normatively as a key element of marital relations. They seek to temper the destructive effects of distrust by appealing to Islam as a frame of normative reference, one that should foster accountability and predictability in their interactions with spouses and in-laws. Distrust, as an affective component of involuntary waithood, has become a Pandora's box for young Muslim men.

Dorothea E. Schulz is Professor in the Department of Social and Cultural Anthropology at the University of Münster, Germany. Her research, publications, and teaching focus on the anthropology of religion, political anthropology, Islam in Africa, gender studies, and media studies. Schulz is the author or editor of several books and monographs. She has been a visiting fellow at the University of Chicago and at Harvard University. Schulz has received grants and fellowships from the German Research Foundation, the National Science Foundation, the International Institute for the Study of Islam, and the Cornell University Society for the Humanities.

Notes

1. Throughout this chapter, pseudonyms will be used in reference to interview partners.
2. The restructuring of regional and local economies under the pressure of the International Monetary Fund and World Bank started soon after the National Resistance Movement assumed power (in 1986) and gained in momentum in the 2000s.
3. The Ugandan national economy of 2018 cannot be adequately described as fully neoliberal, yet it has undergone neoliberal transformations in significant ways, supported by unprecedented international financial and technical investment. State involvement in economic and market activity has not been reduced as state and government officials have become even more involved in high-profit business ventures (Wiegratz 2016).
4. As an example of the negative effects of the reforms on rural populations, Wiegratz (2016: 84) diagnoses a "reform-induced economic crisis" for the Bugisu region in eastern Uganda during the late 2000s. This crisis followed a coffee boom of the 1990s during which state actors and organizations became main beneficiaries of the rising world market prices.
5. In Uganda, the availability and quality of educational institutions vary significantly from region to region. Most high-quality schools are located in or near the capital of Kampala, whereas the north and east of the country have benefitted comparatively little from economic and infrastructural investment.
6. Although Muslim-founded schools are officially recognized as elements of the public educational system, most of them cannot compete with regular schools with regard to educational quality, technical equipment, and qualified teachers (Schulz 2013b).
7. Career opportunities offered by transnational Muslim organizations are minimal in Mbarara, in contrast to the US and Nigerian Evangelical and Pentecostal churches that have inundated Mbarara town in recent years and promise young Christians ways to overcome their economic and social impasse.
8. Many young men even went so far as to blame their inability to act as the "provider" for past failed marriage alliances and aborted courtships. Their swift and seemingly unproblematic acceptance of blame for what can be seen as a structurally induced incapacity suggests that they internalize the ability to provide as a nature-given element of normative masculinity (see Enria 2016: 144).
9. See Wyrod (2016: 8–11), who maintains that apparent continuities in the discursive construction of gender relations in Kampala conceal an incipient weakening of "male sexual privilege" (see also Parikh 2012).
10. Wyrod (2016: 89–91) notes that men in Kampala generally portray "the promiscuous woman" as a principal driving force behind the AIDS epidemic.

11. Women's parents similarly deplored young men's inability to generate a steady income and their unwillingness to show them due "respect" (that is, to support them materially) in their role as future in-laws.
12. Nadira was reluctant to talk to me, which I attribute to the fact that Ali had frequently talked to me about his courtship struggles.
13. I noticed, however, that Abdul Rahman was visibly hurt when an older cousin whom he had frequently "helped out" refused to lend him money.

References

Appadurai, Arjun. 2004. "The Capacity to Aspire: Culture and the Terms of Recognition." In *Culture and Public Action*, ed. Vijayendra Rao and Michael Walton, 59–84. Stanford: Stanford University Press.

Arnett, Jeffrey Jensen. 2000. "Emerging Adulthood: A Theory of Development from the Late Teens Through the Twenties." *American Psychologist* 55(5): 469–80.

Ashforth, Adam. 1999. "Weighing Manhood in Soweto." *CODESRIA Bulletin* 2: 51–58.

Bell, Wendel, and James Mau. 1971. "Images of the Future: Theory and Research Strategies." In *Sociology of the Future*, ed. Wendel Bell and James Mau, 6–44. New York: Russell Sage Foundation.

Carey, Mathew. 2017. *Mistrust*. Chicago: University of Chicago Press.

Comaroff, Jean, and John L. Comaroff, eds. 2006. *Law and Disorder in the Postcolony*. Chicago: University of Chicago Press.

Connell, R. W. 1995. *Masculinities*. Berkeley: University of California Press.

Cornwall, Andrea. 2016. "Introduction: Masculinities under Neoliberalism." In *Masculinities under Neoliberalism*, ed. Andrea Cornwall, Frank G. Karioris, and Nancy Lindisfarne, 1–18. London: Zed Books.

Cornwall, Andrea, and Nancy Lindisfarne, eds. 1994. *Dislocating Masculinity: Comparative Ethnographies*. London: Routledge.

Dhillon, Navtej, and Tarik Youssef, eds. 2009. *Generation in Waiting: The Unfulfilled Promise of Young People in the Middle East*. Washington, DC: Brookings Institution Press.

Dolan, Chris. 2003. "Collapsing Masculinities and Weak States: A Case Study of Northern Uganda." In *Masculinities Matter! Men, Gender and Development*, ed. Frances Cleaver, 57–83. London: Zed Publishers.

Durham, Deborah. 2017. "Elusive Adulthoods: Introduction." In *Elusive Adulthoods: The Anthropology of New Maturities*, ed. Deborah Durham and Jacqueline Solway, 1–38. Bloomington: Indiana University Press.

Enria, Luisa. 2016. "'I Must Stand Like a Man': Masculinity in Crisis in Postwar Sierra Leone." In *Masculinities under Neoliberalism*, ed. Andrea Cornwall, Frank G. Karioris, and Nancy Lindisfarne, 136–50. London: Zed Books.

Geschiere, Peter. 2013. *Witchcraft, Intimacy, and Trust: Africa in Comparison*. Chicago: University of Chicago Press.

Graeber, David. 2011. *Debt: The First 5000 Years*. Brooklyn: Melville Publishers.

Honwana, Alcinda. 2014. "Waithood: Youth Transitions and Social Change in Africa." In *Development and Equity: An Interdisciplinary Exploration by Ten Scholars from Africa, Asia and Latin America*, ed. Dick Foeken, Ton Dietz, Leo Haan, and Linda Johnson, 28–40. Leiden: Brill.

Hunter, Mark. 2010. *Love in the Time of AIDS: Inequality, Gender, and Rights in South Africa*. Bloomington: Indiana University Press.

Inhorn, Marcia C. 2017. "The Egg Freezing Revolution? Gender, Technology, and Fertility Preservation in the Twenty-First Century." In *Emerging Trends in the Social and Behavioral Sciences*, ed. Robert Scott and Marlis Buchmann, 1–13. New York: Wiley.

Jones, Gavin, Terence Hull, and Maznah Mohamed, eds. 2011. *Changing Marriage Patterns in Southeast Asia: Economic and Socio-Cultural Dimensions*. New York: Routledge.

Kiyimba, Abasi. 1986. "The Problem of Muslim Education in Uganda: Some Reflections." *Journal of the Institute of Muslim Minority Affairs* 7(1): 247–58.

Lenk, Hans. 2010. "Vertrauen als relationales Interpretations—und Emotionskonstrukt." [Trust as a construction of emotional and discursive relationality]. In *Vertrauen-zwischen sozialem Kitt und der Senkung von Transaktionskosten*, ed. Matthias Maring, 27–44. Karlsruhe: KIT Scientific Publications.

Mac an Ghaill, Mairtin, and Chris Haywood. 2016. "(Dis)locating Masculinities: Ethnographic Reflections on British Muslim Young Men." In *Masculinities under Neoliberalism*, ed. Andrea Cornwall, Frank G. Karioris, and Nancy Lindisfarne, 198–212. London: Zed Books.

Makhulu, Anne-Maria, Beth Buggenhagen, and Stephen Jackson. 2010. "Introduction." In *Hard Work, Hard Times: Global Volatility and African Subjectivity*, ed. Anne-Maria Makhulu, Beth Buggenhagen, and Stephen Jackson, 1–27. Berkeley: University of California Press.

Masquelier, Adeline. 2005. "The Scorpion's Sting: Youth, Marriage, and the Struggle for Social Maturity in Niger." *Journal of the Royal Anthropological Institute* 11(1): 59–83.

———. 2013. "Teatime: Boredom and the Temporalities of Young Men in Niger." *Africa* 83(3): 470–91.

Mbembe, Achille. 2006. "Politics as a Form of Expenditure." In *Law and Disorder in the Postcolony*, ed. Jean Comaroff and John L. Comaroff, 273–98. Chicago: University of Chicago Press.

Meinert, Lotte. 2015. "Tricky Trust: Distrust as a Point of Departure and Trust as a Social Achievement in Uganda." In *Anthropology and Philosophy*, ed. Sune Liisberg, Esther Oluffa Pedersen, and Anne Line Dalsgard, 118–36. New York: Berghahn Books.

Meiu, George Paul. 2017. *Ethno-erotic Economies: Sexuality, Money, and Belonging in Kenya*. Chicago: University of Chicago Press.

Momoh, Abubakar. 2000. "Youth Culture and Area Boys in Lagos." In *Identity Transformation and Identity Politics under Structural Adjustment in Nigeria*, ed. Attahiru Yega, 181–203. Stockholm: Nordic Africa Institute.

Morris, Rosalind. 2008. "Speculations on the Value of Life and Death in South Africa's Age of Epidemic." *Public Culture* 20(2): 199–231.

Obbo, Christine. 1980. "African Women: Their Struggle for Economic Independence." *Women's Studies International Forum* 6(4): 457–58.

Parikh, Shanti. 2012. "Modern Wives, Men's Infidelity, and Marriage in East-Central Uganda." *Culture, Health & Sexuality* 14(3): 361–63.

Schielke, Samuli. 2009. "Ambivalent Commitments: Troubles of Morality, Religiosity, and Aspiration among Young Egyptians." *Journal of Religion in Africa* 39(2): 158–85.

Schulz, Dorothea. 2001. "Music Videos and the Effeminate Vices of Urban Culture in Mali." *Africa* 71(3): 325–71.

———. 2012. *Muslims and New Media in West Africa: Pathways to God.* Bloomington: Indiana University Press.

———. 2013a. "Engendering Muslim Self-Assertiveness: Muslim Schooling and Female Elite Formation in Uganda." *Journal of Religion in Africa* 43: 396–425.

———. 2013b. "What Makes a Good Minority Muslim? Educational Policy and the Paradoxes of Muslim Schooling in Uganda." *Contemporary Islam* 7(1): 53–70.

Schulz, Dorothea, and Souleymane Diallo. 2016. "Competing Assertions of Muslim Masculinity in Mali." *Journal of Religion in Africa* 46: 219–50.

Shipton, Parker. 2007. *The Nature of Entrustment: Intimacy, Exchange and the Sacred in Africa.* New Haven: Yale University Press.

Singerman, Diane. 2007. *The Economic Imperatives of Marriage: Emerging Practices and Identities among Youth in the Middle East.* Washington, DC: Wolfensohn Center for Development.

Smith-Hefner, Nancy J. 2005. "The New Muslim Romance: Changing Patterns of Courtship and Marriage among Educated Javanese Youth." *Journal of Southeast Asian Studies* 36(3): 441–59.

Sommers, Marc. 2012. *Stuck: Rwandan Youth and the Struggle for Adulthood.* Athens: University of Georgia Press.

Twaddle, Michael. 1995. "The Character of Politico-Religious Conflict in Eastern Africa." In *Religion and Politics in East Africa: The Period Since Independence,* ed. Holger Bernt Hansen and Michael Twaddle, 1–15. Athens: Ohio University Press.

Vera-Sanso, Perry. 2016. "Taking the Long View: Attaining and Sustaining Masculinity across the Life Course in South India." In *Masculinities under Neoliberalism,* ed. Andrea Cornwall, Frank G. Karioris, and Nancy Lindisfarne, 80–98. London: Zed Books.

Weiss, Brad, ed. 2004. *Producing African Futures: Ritual and Reproduction in a Neoliberal Age.* Leiden: Brill.

Wiegratz, Jörg. 2016. *Neoliberal Moral Economy: Capitalism, Socio-Cultural Change and Fraud in Uganda.* New York: Rowman & Littlefield International.

Wyrod, Robert. 2016. *AIDS and Masculinity in the African City: Privilege, Inequality, and Modern Manhood.* Berkeley: University of California Press.

Chapter 3

WAITING AT THE *FADA*

YOUNG MEN, "TEA CIRCLES," AND DELAYED ADULTHOOD IN NIGER

Adeline Masquelier

Introduction

"Our parents would like us to get up and go to work. But right now, there is no work. There are only worthless jobs [*aikin banza ke nan*].[1] Me, for instance, I'm waiting, I must be patient," Ibrahim,[2] a 25-year-old university graduate, said as he sat drinking tea with friends in a narrow alleyway in one of the oldest and poorest neighborhoods of Niamey, Niger's capital city. What Ibrahim meant was that he had not yet found a job that matched his conception of what he should be doing since earning a university degree in biology. Rather than accept some lowly form of employment out of step with his professional aspirations, he preferred to wait for the career-track job that would enable him to marry, set up a household, and raise children. He knew this might take a while. When he was not submitting new job applications or checking the status of former applications, he spent most of his waking hours at the *fada*, or "tea circle," playing Scrabble, drinking tea, and commiserating about life's hardships with other unemployed *samari* (unmarried young men).

After Niger's independence in 1960, young Nigeriens who sought social mobility through education were promised automatic admission to the civil service. At the time, a formal education was widely touted as the ticket to a better life. However, since the implementation of neoliberal policies that resulted in the reduction of state bureaucracy and the privatization of certain state services, a high school or university degree no longer guarantees steady employment and professional success. Every year the number of available government posts is dwarfed by the number of job applicants. Employment opportunities are similarly restricted in the formal private sector, which currently employs roughly 4 percent of the population. In the end, *jeunes diplômés* (recent graduates) who attended school to secure well-paid white-collar jobs in the service sector routinely find that education has diminished rather than increased their employability, especially if they cannot draw on their "connections." Many of them worry that the stable middle-class futures—complete with rewarding careers, marriages, and households—to which their education theoretically entitles them are simply out of reach.

In Niger, the world's least literate country, those who receive a tertiary education are a distinct minority: in 2011 there were only 135 university students per 100,000 Nigeriens (Annuaire Statistique de l'Enseignement Supérieur 2012). Although the government has built new schools to accommodate the ever-growing number of registered students, the educational system at all levels is inadequately resourced to fulfill its responsibilities. Among other things, it does not sufficiently prepare young people for the labor market. Unable to find jobs, least of all jobs matching their aspirations, many educated youths—who are designated as *intellectuels*, members of the country's intellectual elite—prefer to remain unemployed rather than take temporary jobs (or labor in the informal economy as do their less educated peers). To engage in low-paid, unskilled labor would be not only demeaning but also potentially damaging. "We cannot debase ourselves by taking menial work when we're educated. *Il faut rester à ne rien faire* [We must continue to do nothing]," is how Sani, a recent university graduate who hoped to work in a government ministry put it. "Public service is my destiny. If I set up *un petit commerce* [petty trade] in front of my parents' house, people will think I've gone nuts." Believing he was destined to a great future, the young man felt he had no choice but to refuse the low-status jobs that would threaten that future—a future that, he and his friends agreed, was worth the wait.

Like many other youths elsewhere in Africa who grapple with deficient education and a dearth of jobs, Sani and Ibrahim have been denied a sustainable pathway to adulthood. Unwilling to reproduce their parents' lives—or merely survive in abject conditions—yet unable to secure the stable livelihoods that, by supporting marriage, a new household, and children, would mark the end of youth, they linger in a state of "waithood" (Singerman 2007; see also Dhillon and Yousef 2009; Honwana 2012). Political scientist Diane Singerman (2007) originally penned the concept of waithood to capture the predicament of young Egyptians who could not find jobs, marry, and "get on" with their lives. In English the suffix "-hood" refers to a variety of things, from a social rank or office, such as priesthood or knighthood, to temporary conditions, such as boyhood or maidenhood. As a portmanteau term describing the stagnation endured by jobless or underemployed young people unable to transition to adulthood, waithood (that is, the *wait* for adult-*hood*) points to the liminal character of this life period and the blurring of threshold experiences that previously marked critical life transitions. To experience waithood is to be caught in a temporal limbo between childhood and adulthood or, as Marc Sommers (2012) put it in his ethnography of jobless Rwandan youth, to be "stuck." Whether it is understood as temporal suspension, social immobility or both, waithood in neoliberal times has translated as second-class citizenship for large segments of the world's youth population.

In urban Niger a visible instantiation of waithood is found at the *fadas*, the tea circles fashioned by *samari* to confront unemployment, boredom, and alienation.[3] "*Samari*, many [of them] do not work, they sit in the street, drinking tea and playing *belote* [card game]. Their *fadas* fill the streets, they are everywhere," is how a civil servant described the shared youth culture "based around hanging out" (Jeffrey 2010: 35) that has developed in urban neighborhoods throughout the country. In the past three decades *fadas* with names such as Biker Junior, Paradis des Jeunes (Youth Paradise), Style Mob, or Jeunes Amis Sérieux (Serious Young Friends) have taken over the streets of Nigerien towns, profoundly modifying the texture of the urban environment. By creating conversation groups that meet at specific spots in full view of their neighbors, young men who are denied social recognition and stable livelihoods turn the streets into vital arenas of masculine sociality. They sit together and, in some cases, delimit the space they occupy with symbolic markers (bricks, old tires, a bench or a slab of cement), carving out spaces of belonging that escape the logics of administrative control while renegotiating the boundaries of community. Even when no one is there, *fadas* frequently function as visual landmarks on the urban scape. *Fadantchés* (*fada* members) make themselves visible in

a landscape saturated with youthful expressions of artistry and ingenuity by adorning the wall against which they sit with the name
of their *fada* (Masquelier 2019a).

The clusters of young men sipping tea in the street suggest that
the implementation of structural reforms aimed at adjusting Niger's
economic structures to global realities has invalidated the most basic
of social contracts—that children will one day mature, become productive citizens, and found households of their own. They conjure
visions of an inverted world in which elders labor while *samari* sit
idly. Though some parents are supportive of *fada* forms of sociality,
others complain tea circles are a waste of time. As a *fada* detractor
puts it: "Every hour young men spend at the *fada* is an hour they
don't spend studying." The man blames *fadas* for allowing *samari*
to avoid responsibility, thereby further delaying adulthood. In his
view, *fadas* are a symptom of indolence rather than a by-product of
unemployment and deprivation: *samari* who join *fadas* are not only
wasting their time but also compromising their futures.

Delayed Adulthood

In this chapter I use the notion of *delayed adulthood* to explore how
samari in urban Niger cope with joblessness, uncertainty, and social
immobility. As a transitive verb, "to delay" means to defer an action,
to make someone (or something) late, to hinder or set back. One
speaks of delaying marriage or a child's development. As an intran-
sitive verb, to delay is to be late (or slow), to loiter, to waste time.
In the passive voice, the verb suggests the happening of an event is
out of one's hand. Writing about delayed adulthood thus hints at
samari's inability to reach maturity despite being of age while also
gesturing to the alleged loitering taking place at the *fada* (specifically
the idea that *samari* "waste" time instead of following plotted life
trajectories). Above all, delayed adulthood refers to the practices of
time management *samari* engage in at the *fada* (embracing delays,
"filling time" and preparing the future). At the *fada*, *samari* receive
emotional and material support from peers; they exchange information about jobs, training opportunities, and other resources so they
can orient themselves toward possible futures. The waiting they do
is not fruitless even if it remains tinged with doubt and anxiety.
Drawing on the polysemic quality of the verb "delay," I argue in
this chapter that *fadas* are both places for hanging out and training
grounds for the cultivation of responsible adulthood.

The *fada* is a masculine space created by young men to fulfill their needs for sociality and self-affirmation. Due to the gendered division of labor and pastimes operating in Nigerien society, few *fadas* have female members. *'Yammata* (young unmarried women) do not openly socialize with boys. Mindful of appearing modest and virtuous, they do not linger in public spaces, much less sit in the street for hours at a time. Their place is at home or in school. Courtship is nevertheless very much on their minds.

Though they ostensibly exclude young women, *fadas* often serve as meeting places for young couples seeking to evade parental control after nightfall. It is also there that *samari* exchange information about romance, sex, marriage, and everything else to do with responsible adulthood, including the management of finances. In sum, the *fada* is where *samari* learn to be men through their interactions, real and imagined, with *'yammata*. In this chapter I explore the tensions between, on the one hand, the culture of waiting that shapes the logic of male sociality (and the attendant discourse on idleness, failure, and victimization) and, on the other, the work of imagination (and planning) through which young men prepare themselves for marriage and social adulthood. Through a focus on some of the distinctive modalities of waiting structuring life at the *fada*, I argue that rather than delaying young men on the path to social maturity, most *fadas* smooth out their transition to adulthood even as they appear to promote idleness by making the waiting more tolerable, even occasionally pleasant.

Methodology

This chapter is based on ethnographic, archival, and photographic research I have been conducting in Niger since 2004. The settings for my study are Dogondoutchi, a small provincial town of heterogeneous Hausa speakers, and Niamey, a multiethnic and multilingual metropolis. I had originally planned to research young men's engagement with Islam as it was a logical extension of an earlier project focused on women's participation in reformist Islamic movements. Since so many *samari* whiled away the days by sitting together at the *fada*, *fadas* became a convenient spot for me to meet young men I knew and make new acquaintances. Eventually I realized that placing the *fada* at the center of my analysis would yield important insights into the lived experience of the young men with whom I spoke. The *fada* became both an ethnographic seat and the conceptual frame for exploring how *samari* fill their time with meaningful occupations in the face of precarity.

Over the course of six trips, I visited more than one hundred *fadas*, conversing with young men, watching them prepare tea, play *belote*, and worry about the future, and learning what mattered to them. I used a combination of in-depth interviews, participant observation, and structured surveys to gather data on young men, their demographic profile, their educational and employment history, their ways of being Muslim, their engagement with popular culture, and their dreams and aspirations. All the interviews were conducted in French or Hausa. Some interviews were followed by additional conversations. I conducted participant observation at the *fada* and in some young men's family compounds during all phases of the research project. The observational data complicated and, at times, contradicted what *samari* told me during our conversations. Thirty older men and women of diverse backgrounds discussed with me the problems of youth and the place of *fadas* in Nigerien society. These conversations were essential for making sense of the wider picture. The photos of *fada* inscriptions I took constituted a pictorial repertoire for my discussion of street life, space, and sociality. Newspaper articles and editorials on *fadas* helped me appreciate the place of irony, condemnation, and censure in the public discourse on *fadas*.

Being Young and Un(der)employed in Neoliberal Niger

As the world's poorest country—routinely ranking at the bottom of the UN's Human Development Index—Niger faces serious hurdles on the road to sustainability and self-sufficiency. A number of factors, including food insecurity, political instability, an anemic industrial sector, and few job prospects outside subsistence agriculture and herding, hinder economic development. Operating under the assumption that lack of development is caused by overbearing state intervention in the workings of market forces, the IMF and the World Bank endeavored to dismantle the statist model that held sway in Niger and restructure the production system in favor of the private sector (Gervais 1995). Starting in the late 1980s the imposition of structural adjustment programs aimed at creating a suitable climate for economic growth led to massive cuts in public services, the elimination of subsidies, and the flexibilization of the labor market. Far from promoting development, however, these economic reforms widened social inequalities. Recruitment in both public and private sectors was severely impacted, with young people bearing the brunt of unemployment. It is a pattern that has played out around the world as international lenders demanded that governments in Latin America, Africa, and elsewhere balance their budgets and restructure their economies. Instead of spurring economic growth and encouraging foreign investments, reforms undertaken in the name of fiscal responsibility and free market ideology have had a devastating impact on ordinary livelihoods, trapping many people into situations of considerable precarity and severely restricting the hoped-for futures of emerging cohorts of job seekers.

In Niger the state remains the largest employer, but since the 1990s it has stopped automatically recruiting young graduates and giving them permanent positions. More recently efforts to boost public expenditures to meet security concerns in the face of extremism have put added pressure on the national budget while reducing the financing of other projects. Niger has some of the world's largest uranium deposits as well as sizable oil reserves, but the prolonged drop in commodity prices on the world market has reduced profitability. Agriculture and herding remain the most important sector of the economy, accounting for 40 percent of GDP and constituting the principal source of income for over 80 percent of the population. Yet, due to drought and other environmental risks, it is also a volatile sector where seasonal underemployment is high. Staving off poverty in rural areas often means migrating seasonally to urban centers and earning precarious livelihoods in the informal sector. (Ironically, though most poor migrants from West Africa en route to Europe travel through Niger, comparatively few Nigeriens themselves migrate to Europe.)

Demography further contributes to the country's economic woes. With an average of 7.3 children born to every woman in 2015, Niger has the highest birth rate in the world. It is also the world's youngest country, with a population growing at 3.9 percent per year. Today roughly 75 percent of Nigeriens are under twenty-five years of age. Consequently, the state is burdened with much higher demands for investments in education and health services than is the case in countries with lower population growths (World Bank 2017).[4] Despite sustained efforts to address the needs of growing cohorts of students, the quality of the learning experience in school has substantially worsened in past decades. Not only are teachers inadequately trained (and at times functionally illiterate) but they are frequently absent from the classroom. Growing numbers of young people attend school, but many of them receive a poor education, leaving them ill-equipped for the job market. Moreover, there are simply not enough schools. Existing schools are starved of funding and qualified teachers. As graduates (and school dropouts) enter the labor market in ever greater numbers, they face an acute shortage of stable, salaried jobs. The private sector has not grown as expected to replace lost governmental jobs. Public sector employment, though harder to find, still provides greater financial security as well as a host of nepotistic benefits. Rather than settling for alternative (and less remunerative) occupations, many prefer to sit and wait until offered a position matching their professional aspirations.

While educated young men often boast they will not work for a pittance, this is nevertheless what many of them actually do. They cannot afford *not* to work. Though they see themselves as better positioned than their uneducated peers engaging in *travail de Vietnamien*—a disparaging term for unskilled, physically taxing labor—the income that educated *samari* cobble together by taking temporary, low-wage jobs is rarely adequate. In this regard, the official unemployment rate (18 percent in 2010) is highly deceptive for it does not account for the significant numbers of precariously employed.[5] The prevalence of informal, poor-quality or temporary jobs in Niger suggests that employment is not a buffer against poverty: a large percentage of the employed population lives on less than US $1.90 per day, hence below the poverty line (World Bank 2017). By focusing strictly on unemployment, one ignores the predicament of those who work but lack job security or work intermittently (or part-time) and are overqualified for their jobs.

Bassirou, who was close to defending his MA thesis in sociology, dreamed of securing a permanent position at an NGO dedicated to reproductive health, his field of specialization. He repeatedly filled out job applications though he rarely heard back about the positions. In the meantime and to support himself, he had joined the existing cohort of *enseignants contractuels* (teachers in contract jobs) and taught French to primary students in a small village. Other young men working temporary jobs told me of educational fellowships abroad, well-paid temporary jobs on development projects, and lucrative positions in the private sector; however, these "select" opportunities were usually granted to wealthy youths with connections. Though I met some successful young men from prosperous and well-connected families (some of whom were members of the select YALI "club"[6]) who faced the future with confidence, most of my interlocutors came from families struggling for financial survival. Among the latter, some could rely on parents to provide shelter and sustenance, regardless of whether the household income came from farming, trade, or the civil service. Others struggled on their own, knowing how tight things were "at home," especially if they had numerous siblings. In the end, whether they have a job or depend on their parents for subsistence (or both), young men often lead lives of considerable precarity. They are always on the lookout for the next employment opportunity. In what follows I write about "un(der)employment" to call attention to the pervasiveness of precarious employment among Nigerien youth without losing track of those who are jobless.

Of Youth and Generation

Nigerien society is divided into youth and elders, but because seniority and juniority are situational concepts, the division may be understood differently depending on the context, allowing people to claim certain age statuses regardless of their actual chronological age. By age seven, boys are supposedly old enough to be sent away from home (to study with a Qur'anic teacher, for instance). However, it is not until they become *samari*, that is, after puberty, that the gender norms that regulate social life take on their full implications. They are given separate sleeping quarters and their access to other men's houses becomes restricted. Since social adulthood is a matter of providing for a dependent, *samari* become fully adult upon marrying for the first time.

A girl, on the other hand, reaches adulthood when she gives birth to her first child. Female sexuality must imperatively be contained within marriage, and most girls marry early. Half of Niger's female population is married by age fifteen.[7] Women's experience of youth is therefore relatively shorter than men's, and their transition to adulthood is not hampered to the same extent by austerity and joblessness. It is not uncommon for fifteen- or sixteen-year-old girls to marry men significantly older than them, especially in polygynous households. That said, young women's path to adulthood is not without hurdles. For one thing, the unemployment rate among young women is higher than that of young men. Moreover, if pursuing an education delays the moment at which young women marry, it does not reduce the pressure to conform to normative ideals centered on marriage, motherhood, and domesticity. Amid concerns about rising immorality stoked by conservative Muslim religious leaders, such ideals weigh heavily on *'yammata*'s shoulders, pushing many of them to prioritize marriage over education. Though the case of young Nigerien women is beyond the purview of this chapter, a consideration of the precarious circumstances facing Nigerien youth must proceed from a recognition of the gendered dimension of their experiences.

Young men unable to find suitable jobs describe their waiting as *zaman kashin wando*, which literally translates to "the sitting that kills the pants." It is, they imply, the immobility they endure while waiting for stable employment—not the manual labor of yesteryear—that frays their clothes. Though it is a mere figure of speech, the "sitting" that burns metaphorical holes in their pants captures vividly the sense of disempowerment un(der)employed young men experience in the absence of decent livelihoods. Trapped in the imposed presentism of mere survival, they feel robbed of the futurity previous generations took for granted. "It's hellish! We don't know what the future has in store for us," lamented Ilyassou, a 24-year-old economics student who drew a meager income by occasionally running errands for a butcher. Seemingly idle and with no place to go, the young man spent much of his waking hours at Étoile, the *fada* he had joined when he was in high school. When I met him, the university had been on strike for months and no classes were held. The young man next to him, who wore stylish sunglasses, slim jeans, and a T-shirt adorned with the face of Barack Obama, remarked: "In Niger youth don't have jobs. So they just sit. Throughout the country, it's the same problem." At Étoile, Ilyassou and the young men he had grown up with found a supportive forum for sharing their disillusions and their dreams away from elders' judgmental stares.

Samari frequently complain that they will not be able to take their rightful place in society until elders give up the positions they currently occupy and stop appointing people based on kinship or political affiliation rather than competence. Having been exposed to discourses on liberal democracy, they refer to themselves as a generation sacrificed by selfish (or incompetent) elders unwilling to concede them their due resources and rights. They occasionally warn that, unless something is done to accommodate their needs, they will erupt. "We are tired of being manipulated by political elites. We are a force to contend with, they should not underestimate us," a young man once told me, alluding to the fact that campaigning politicians visit *fadas*, where they ply young men with gifts of money, tea, and sugar and ask that young men vote for them, knowing full well political leaders rarely keep their promises of helping the younger generation.

Aware that Niger's population growth has attracted mounting concern among international lenders, *samari* occasionally describe themselves as a "ticking time bomb" that the government should defuse by providing substantial educational and employment opportunities. "Rebelling against the old" is a classic modality through which members of an emerging generation strive to secure their place in the world. In this respect, *samari* act like typical youth "thwarted in their search for opportunities and advancement by greedy elders holding on to wealth, jobs, and appropriate support" (Durham 2008: 173; see also Comaroff and Comaroff 1999; Gable 2000). By threatening to upstage elders, young people aim to provoke changes that will ideally translate into an improved economic outlook for their generational cohort (Diouf 2003). Their aspirations are generally ordinary: to secure a decent livelihood, marry, and have children. These aspirations take shape in a social context where, barring severe disability, everyone is expected to contract a marriage and produce children. In this overwhelmingly Muslim society (over 95 percent of Nigeriens are Muslim), unmarried cohabitation is not an option and children born out of wedlock are a source of shame for families.

By marrying and fathering offspring, *samari* not only contribute to social reproduction but they also fulfill a religious duty. Moreover, marriage ensures their fates in the afterlife since married men's acts of worship generate more of the *lada*, or divine reward, necessary for entry into paradise, than single men's. As a manifestation of financial stability and emotional maturity, marriage is a critical step toward social recognition (Masquelier 2005). By demonstrating they can provide for dependents, men build themselves up, accruing respectability as well as seniority. It is worth noting that, while in many countries, young men's inability to afford lodgings for their prospective wives is a major impediment to marriage, this is generally not the case in Niger, where new brides often move in with their in-laws. A young man explained: "It is nice to have your own house once you marry. But you need to stay close to your family. If I live with my family, we can pool our resources. It is better. Moreover, once you are married, your wife is expected to cook for her mother-in-law."

Waiting at the *Fada*

Waiting, when sparked by factors beyond individual control, such as unemployment, diminishes people's capacity to plan their futures.

By signaling the extent to which young male Nigeriens have been
affected by job scarcity, the conquest of the urban landscape by tea
circles makes plain the connection between waithood and social immobility. Yet waithood refers to the global holding pattern in which
young people find themselves; as such, it cannot convey the diverse
forms that waiting takes at the *fada*. At the *fada* young men not only
"wait out" the period of joblessness, but they also cultivate the art of
waiting in a lighthearted atmosphere that dispels gloom and encourages striving. Rather than dwell on the "stuckness" of unemployed
young men, I rely on the concept of waiting to highlight specific
temporalities and tactics of anticipation that have emerged in urban
Niger in contexts of economic uncertainty. Peter Dwyer (2009: 18)
distinguishes between what he calls "existential" and "situational"
waiting. The former is a mode of anticipation with no specific object while the latter is "social, relational and engaged" (Hage 2009:
4). Drawing on Dwyer's typology, I argue that at the *fada*, *samari*
transform some of the existential waiting associated with economic
uncertainty into situational forms of waiting, purposeful (often
small-scale) temporalities in which one waits for explicit outcomes,
such as a few sips of perfectly brewed tea, in the company of other
"waiters." Put differently, *fadas* are places where young men forced
to put their lives on hold regain some sense of control over how
time unfolds.

   In Hausa, Niger's most widely spoken language, *fada* connotes
the elders' council and the chief's court. It is an intrinsically masculine space, specifically suited to the work of conflict resolution
and public deliberation. When university students went on strike
in 1990 to push the state to transition to a multi-party democracy,
they adopted the term to designate their own informal gatherings as
they sat in the street to discuss the country's future. Until then Niger
functioned as a one-party state and, following the 1974 coup and the
establishment of military rule, freedom of expression was severely
curtailed. Upon succeeding Colonel Seyni Kountché in 1987, Colonel Ali Saibou liberalized the country's laws. In the face of union
and student demands to institute a multi-party system, he initiated
the democratization process. With the curfew lifted and freedom of
speech restored, it was no longer unlawful to stay up past nightfall,
and talking about politics no longer landed people in jail.

   In the absence of a structured schedule, the young activists held
tea sessions during which they brewed heavily sugared green tea in
tiny kettles nestled on portable braziers. Like the Yemeni *qāt* chews
that serve as public forums for deliberative selfhoods in the absence

of electoral institutions (Wedeen 2008), their newly created *fadas* facilitated the performance of citizenship in times of political turmoil. As the *samarya* (youth associations created decades earlier by the state to channel youth labor toward agriculture and public works) became increasingly obsolete, they were supplanted by the *fadas*, whose organically evolving, informal structure was better suited to nurture un(der)employed *samari's* professional aspirations and dreams of a better life.

Today the *fada* is an indispensable component of daily life for many *samari* yearning for the stability and security of adulthood—in fact, most cannot imagine life without their *fadas*. It is at the *fada* that *samari* solidify friendships, experiment with politics, develop ambitions, mend broken hearts, and secure support in times of hardship. Aside from serving as spaces of leisure—where members play card games, listen to music, or play with their phones while waiting for the tea to brew—*fadas* fulfill a number of other roles. Some function as rotating credit associations: financial contributions are distributed as a lump sum to members on a rotating basis (so they can purchase a plane ticket or a motorcycle) or used for an emergency. In fact, *samari* typically turn to their *fadas* in times of exigency. As one young man said, "The *fada* is a *tontine* [rotating credit association] in everything but name." Others operate like gangs, relying on the sale of drugs and stolen goods to finance their activities. Because jobless *samari* stay up late drinking tea, they can monitor the street for suspicious activity. *Fadas* thus constitute an informal system of surveillance. *Fadas* are often where *samari* learn to use laptop computers or borrow motorbikes to take their girlfriends on dates. It is also where they compete for prestige by drawing on the power of attire. *Samari* know that dress matters. Many are experts at managing impressions, converting the illusion of prosperity into social capital. They frequently spend resources they do not have on clothes to impress girls, for instance (Masquelier 2019b). As places of competitive sociality, *fada* are criticized for imposing burdensome sartorial requirements on participants yearning to "be somebody." Some of them enforce dress codes—dirty or inappropriate clothing results in fines—and encourage *farotage* (showing off) even if that means overspending.

Although membership tends to cut across ethnic affiliations, educational levels, and religious identities, *fadas* occasionally assemble *samari* from the same ethnic groups. Many *fadas* unite male youths with a common passion for soccer or music or a shared religious commitment. Some of them are but informal conversation groups while others are more structured organizations headed by a governing body (a president, a treasurer, and so on) that controls the group's resources, plans activities, and keeps order among the rank and file. Having slipped into Zarma, the language spoken by a quasi-majority of Niamey residents, the term *fada* now refers to all tea circles or discussion groups that assemble daily in the street around a pot of tea, regardless of age, generational status, and professional activity. Some *fadas* are thus comprised of middle-aged or retired civil servants. The great majority bring together young men who have yet to transition into adulthood. In the popular imagination *fadas* are associated with youth, unemployment, and waithood, and this is why they conjure visions of faineance and moral bankruptcy for many elders.

At the *fada* un(der)employed young men receive support in the form of respect, encouragement, financial assistance, or tips about possible jobs, as well as assurance that their problems are taken seriously. To be sure, jealousy and rivalry sometimes infect relationships between *fadantchés*. Most *samari* nevertheless experience the *fada* as a refuge from the outside world—a place where they can commiserate about their predicament, elaborate ambitious plans for the future, or simply fiddle with their smart phones while waiting for the tea to brew without being accused of laziness or told their dreams are out of step with reality.

Tea, Boredom, and the Temporality of Waiting

Across the Global South the current joblessness afflicting young people in contexts of declining educational resources and dwindling economic opportunities has radically altered their experience of temporality and their sense of agency. In much of the Middle East, many youths while away their days smoking water pipes at cafés or staring at their cell phones with little hope of being able to move out of their parents' homes (Daragahi 2018). In Gaza, where the youth unemployment rate is among the highest in the world, jobless young people are said to be "driving the mattress" because they spend their daylight hours sprawled in bed (Booth and Balousha 2017). In Ethiopia bored young men with no jobs lament that the only change they experience in their daily lives is watching the shadows creep from one side of the road to another with the passing of the sun (Mains 2013). Meanwhile in India young men with worthless degrees ward off boredom by hanging out at tea shops, an activity they describe as "timepass" (Jeffrey 2010). They see themselves as "surrounded by an expanse of featureless time" (Jeffrey 2010: 76) that must somehow be managed, "killed," or filled with activities of various kinds.

For young Nigerien men unable to find stable employment, this waiting is often filled with restlessness, frustration, and ennui. Optimism coexists with anxiety. *Samari* speak of how difficult it is to get rid of their sense of unease about the present—a present that is not becoming a future—and of their boredom. Boredom, Ben Anderson (2004: 750) writes, emerges when "something is 'not-yet,'" that is, when something expected does not occur. Martin Heidegger (1995: 67) fittingly describes boredom as that which turns everything around us, including other human beings, into "a colorless indifference."[8] In short, boredom is about depletion. It signals a diminished ability to experience the world sensually. The restless frustration that accompanies the onset of boredom produces a series of disjunctive moods—with despair quickly following hope—in such a way that one is prevented from ever being "in" the moment and absorbed by it. Walter Benjamin (2003: 1) notes that boredom dissolves "threshold experiences" (events punctuating time) to the extent that "falling asleep, and importantly waking up are perhaps the only such experiences that remain to us." By naming their *fada* MDR, the acronym for Manger Dormir Recommencer (Eating Sleeping Starting Over), a group of *samari* stressed how in boredom, eventhood dissolves and time feels like one long continuum broken up by too few temporal markers (Hassane 2003).

Fadas are more than simple places for passing time, however. They aim to fracture the temporality of aimless deferral in which un(der)employed young men are trapped and recreate a sense of purposeful waiting. They constitute an infrastructure of anticipation that helps *samari* cope with excess time by partaking in sensual pleasures. Time, rather than being endured, is enjoyed. At the *fada*, heavily sweetened green tea is brewed in three rounds from a common (but tiny) pot that sits on a small funnel filled with hot coals. From the clump of tea leaves is extracted with each round a dark, concentrated liquid that *fadantchés* share among themselves whether they are two or twelve. It is neither the quantity of tea ingested nor its actual taste that matters (though some argue the first round is bitter—too bitter, in fact, to be drunk) but rather the satiety and strength it procures as well as the experience of sitting around the teapot, waiting until the assigned *shai-man* (*shai* means "tea" in

Hausa) determines the brew is ready. Making tea takes time: sitting for the three rounds of tea may fill the better part of an afternoon.

During what I call "teatime" (Masquelier 2013), that is, the daily practice of preparing and consuming tea, *fadantchés* spent much time waiting for the tea to brew. Teatime, I argue, ruptures the erratic temporality of boredom while endowing waiting with a pragmatic, purposeful dimension: one knows when and how the waiting ends. Half routine, half ritual, it reinserts young men in the tempo of daily life. In the way it produces eventhood (with a "before" and an "after" the event) and conveys a sense of time well-spent, teatime reinserts bored *samari* in a world of meaningful temporality. The wait for the tea is filled by playing card and other games, engaging in conversations on a range of topics, or watching soccer matches on television (or on one's telephone).

But waiting has its rules, and those who wait, whether they wait for jobs or for tea, must abide by the rules. There are rules for governing the order and the manner in which tea should be served and drunk, for instance. There are also rules for visiting and greeting people at the *fada*. At the *fada* time is structured and socialized through a whole array of practices and routines that make the chaotic uncertainty of the future more manageable. Each day brings activities to anticipate. For *samari* living with an unclear time horizon, time at the *fada* is no longer out of joint; the waiting they experience there is predictable, controllable, and even pleasurable. In the way it structures young men's anticipatory temporalities while enhancing their sense of togetherness, tea-drinking has become an essential dimension of *fada* life. *Fadantchés* sometimes joke that without tea, you cannot have a *fada*; the daily sharing of the sweet brew strengthens the webs of friendship that make up the *fada* while also establishing a routinized activity and a valued sense of homeliness. In the end, teatime is a form of "time work" (Masquelier 2020), that is, a means of customizing temporal experience that enables *samari* hoping for middle-class jobs but largely excluded from salaried employment to reclaim a sense of control over how time should be passed.

Headquarters of Love

Though many elders denounce the *fada* "system" for promoting idleness and ultimately delaying young men's transition to adulthood, most *fadas* actively contribute to social reproduction by nurturing young men's romantic aspirations and helping them navigate the landscape of love and intimacy. Due to its location, the *fada* constitutes a useful observatory for appraising *'yammata* passing by. Once a girl has caught the eye of a *samari*, he must find a way to communicate with her. If he manages to obtain her cell phone number, he can greet her via text message and hope to start a conversation, or he can dispatch one of the *fada's dragueurs* (flirts) and *tchatcheurs* (smooth talkers) who will act as a broker. If the broker's *tchatche* (verbosity) is successful and the young woman agrees to be courted, the whole *fada* stands to benefit. Young men are never just individuals: they are also members of a *fada*. Prominent *fadas* are more likely to attract girls. The *fada's* "fame" (Munn 1986) will likely rub off on the girl's own reputation among her peers and, since *'yammata* tend to operate in cliques, her close friends will likely strike up amorous relations with members of the same *fada*. Through the connections it establishes and the conversations it enables, the *fada* is an important nexus in the geography of romance.

As is the case elsewhere on the continent (Parikh 2015; Stambach 2000), the significant expansion of secondary education in Niger has affected local dynamics of romance and intimacy. The coeducational character of French-type schools means boys and girls sit in the same classrooms. If schools are often where educated *samari* become aware of girls, the *fada* is where they solidify their masculinity and become conversant in the language of love. Today young people increasingly speak of making love-based marriages. They often credit the soap operas they watch for making them aware of the importance of affective bonds in cementing marital ties (Masquelier 2009). By distancing themselves from their parents and grandparents, whose marriages were often arranged, they assert their modern individuality. Yet courtship is also a source of anxiety for young men. As a period marked by emotional intimacy, it is seen as a key prelude to a lasting marriage. Paradoxically, the affective dimensions of the relationship often weaken after the wedding, to be replaced by a more "traditional" focus on the fulfilment of kinship obligations (see Smith 2010).

Winning a woman's heart is not easy, especially when one is struggling to keep up with the material requirements of courtship (young women largely expect to be showered with clothes, beauty products, and other items). Yet even as they denounce the commoditization of love, *samari* see marriage as a way of moving up in the world—and enjoying the lifestyle that comes with financial security. Within prevailing contexts of social immobility, romantic love and the emotional involvement it presupposes are complexly bound up with aspirations of an affluent lifestyle.

"The *fada* is the headquarters of love," Ilyassou, the economics student who sat nightly with friends at Étoile, once told me. Such a bold pronouncement may seem counterintuitive in a gender-segregated society such as Niger's. After all, many parents closely monitor the mobility of their unmarried daughters. There is an unspoken code that prevents many *'yammata* from visiting *fadas*—at least, during the day when neighbors can watch their comings and goings. The *fada*'s comparison to a love headquarters is nevertheless fitting for several reasons. First, the *fada* often functions as a training ground where inexperienced and naive young men are exposed to the language of love, the tactics of seduction, and the basics of sexuality. Sex education at school is rather clinical, and parents avoid the taboo subject of sexuality with their children. Since the minimum of savoir faire necessary to be successful in love is not available from traditional sources, the *fada* is where *samari* learn to negotiate romance and courtship. More than one young man told me he was taught to talk to girls (and use the language of poetry) by fellow *fadantchés* well versed in matters of the heart. *Fadantchés* advise one another on how to cope with the material and emotional dimensions of romance. To be sure, they sometimes tease each other about their amorous conquests and, at times, compete for the same girls—leading to conflict.[9] Occasional disputes notwithstanding, the *fada* provides critical support to young men trying to negotiate the complex terrain of romantic attachments.

Second, in the absence of alternative rendezvous spots, the *fada* is where young lovers meet at night to nurture their romance. Restaurants are too expensive for most Nigeriens, and bars are associated with alcohol consumption and dissolute standards. Except for select establishments patronized by expatriates, there are few cafés where young people can hang out and socialize. Moreover *'yammata* raised in strict households enjoy limited mobility: they are barred from attending public events that are not gender-segregated, including the *soirées dansantes* (dancing parties) *fadantchés* organize. Some of them nevertheless dodge parental control by lying about their whereabouts or waiting until everyone is asleep to sneak out of their homes. Under the cover of darkness, they escape the vigilance of adults to make their way to the *fada*. As "contact zones" (Farrer and Field 2015: 11), spaces in which otherwise morally objectionable encounters are facilitated by nightlife, the *fada* houses the tryst of lovers in need of privacy. Ilyassou met his girlfriend, a high school student, at the *fada* every time the young woman could escape her father's surveillance.

Third, it is at the *fada* that wedding plans become tangibly realized. *Samari* often say they cannot get married without the *fada*, which provides critical emotional, logistical, and financial assistance to the groom. "When a member gets married, his friends from the *fada* contribute toward the cost and organization of the wedding. In fact, it is the most important role of the *fada*," a young man told me. Not only do *fadantchés* contribute substantial funds to cover some of the cost of the ceremony (for instance, tent and chair rentals and music, as well as some of the food served to guests), but they also help the future husband negotiate emotional and procedural hurdles. As a platform for managing events (parties, fundraising events, and so on) through an effective division of labor, the *fada* is well suited to help *samari* plan their weddings and address the problems that inevitably arise, including family disputes and financial shortfalls. By contributing financially and otherwise to fellow *fadantchés'* weddings, *samari* ultimately invest in their own weddings, *delayed* as they may be. Thanks to the webs of reciprocity on which the *fada* is built, they know they will enjoy similar support from fellow members when they marry.

Conclusion

A symptom of the social immobility currently facing numerous young Nigerien men, the *fada* is often dismissed by its critics for promoting idleness, thereby delaying *samari's* transition to adulthood. Elders, in particular, frequently accuse *samari* of not wanting to work and of living parasitically off of their parents' labor. Yet such blanket denunciations obfuscate the variety of pastimes and pursuits that occur at the *fada*. Inasmuch as the *fada* is a place for waiting, that waiting, far from being a passive activity, is generative. In this chapter I accent the agentive dimension of the *samari's* waiting—rather than the state of waithood in which they are trapped—to explore some of the ways in which the *fada* not only constitutes a haven from harsh economic realities but also offers strategies for confronting social immobility.

At the *fada*, life unfolds around certain activities whose rhythms and tempos dictate the forms that sociality takes. *Fadantchés*, excluded from the arenas of power and productivity, convert chronic, fruitless waiting into positive temporalities. By punctuating days (and nights) otherwise characterized by amorphous temporalities, the routinized practice of tea drinking, I argue, restores young men who were "lost in time" to a meaningful schedule structured around teatime. At the *fada*, waiting for tea intersects with other forms of waiting: one waits for the call to prayer signaling it is time for worship; one waits for a girlfriend's phone call or to hear about a job application; at another level, one also waits for adulthood and its attendant responsibilities. If teatime creates a space in which postponement—that is, the time it takes to wait for the tea to be prepared—turns into a pleasurable routine, the experience of delayed adulthood translates into a more open-ended sense of contingency— a space of dashed hopes and painful uncertainty. By describing the multiple, intersecting temporalities of waiting at the *fada* as instances of a wider pattern of delayed adulthood, this chapter highlights the diverse ways in which *samari* "customize" (Flaherty 2003) temporality and create possible futures. By offering the social, technical, and material resources required to court young women and marry them, the *fada* actively contributes to social reproduction. One might even describe it as a motor of social regeneration. Rather than helping delay marriage by disincentivizing young men from finding jobs, as elders frequently claim, the homosociality of the *fada* facilitates romance and promotes matrimony by serving as a forum for the circulation of key cultural and financial capital. In this regard, rather than approaching the *fada* as a male-centered institution that excludes women, we must understand it as a site of romantic fantasies and gendered encounters, in which women orient masculine desires in specific directions. At the *fada*, *samari* turn daily loitering into a gratifying experience of teatime at the same time that they discuss marriage and take steps to position themselves toward adulthood. "It is by belonging to a *fada* that you evolve; you cannot evolve by yourself," a young man who had learned basic computer skills from fellow *fadantchés* told me. In the absence of old predictabilities, *fadas* provide a measure of stability while also serving as critical vectors of self-realization for *samari* longing to endorse the mantle of adulthood.

Acknowledgments

I am indebted to the many young men in Niger who invited me into their lives and generously shared their stories with me over the years that I have been pursuing this project. Research in Niger was supported by Tulane University's Newcomb Foundation, Tulane University's Research Enhancement Fund, and the Glick Fellowship of the School of Liberal Arts. I would also like to thank this volume's editors as well as the reviewers for their valuable editorial suggestions.

Adeline Masquelier is Professor of Anthropology at Tulane University. She has conducted extensive research on religion, gender, health and medicine, and youth in Niger. Masquelier is the author or editor of six books, as well as numerous chapters and articles. Her book *Women and Islamic Revival in a West African Town* (Indiana University Press, 2009) was awarded the 2010 Herskovits Award for best scholarly book on Africa and the 2012 Aidoo-Snyder prize for best scholarly book about African women. She received a PhD in anthropology from the University of Chicago.

Notes

1. The foreign terms used in this chapter are either Hausa or French.
2. All the names of young men cited in this chapter are pseudonyms to preserve the privacy and anonymity of my interlocutors.
3. The plural of *fada* in Hausa is *fadodi*. In the media a frenchified plural often appears. I use this form to accent the cosmopolitan character of young men's conversation groups.
4. According to the Ministry of Education, to maintain current school attendance rates, an additional 3,000 classrooms would have to be constructed and 3,500 teachers recruited each year (World Bank 2017).
5. The informal sector, which provides livelihoods for many youth and children, currently generates 60 percent of Niger's GDP (World Bank 2017).
6. YALI stands for "Young African Leaders Initiative," a program launched by President Obama and aimed at providing professional training and opportunities for networking to young Africans.
7. The average age of first marriage is fifteen for a girl with no education, seventeen for a girl with primary education, and twenty for a girl with secondary education (Institut National de la Statistique 2015).
8. For more on the anthropology of boredom, see Frederiksen (2013) and O'Neill (2017).
9. Fights erupting between two *fadas* frequently stem from disputes over girls.

References

Anderson, Ben. 2004. "Time-Stilled Space-Slowed: How Boredom Matters." *Geoforum* 35(6): 739–54.

Annuaire Statistique de l'Enseignement Supérieur. 2012. Ministère des Enseignements Moyens et Supérieurs et de la Recherche [Ministry of Middle and Higher Education and of Research]. Retrieved 21 November 2018 from http://www.stat-niger.org/statistique/file/Annuaires_Statist iques/MESSRT/Annuaire percent20MESSRT percent202009-2010.pdf.

Benjamin, Walter. 2003. *Selected Writings: 1938–1940*. Cambridge: Harvard University Press.

Booth, William, and Hazem Balousha. 2017. "Trapped between Israel and Hamas, Gaza's Wasted Generation is Going Nowhere." *Washington Post*, 6 August. Retrieved 30 June 2018 from https://www.washingtonpost.com/ world/middle_east/trapped-between-israel-and-hamas-gazas-wasted-ge neration-is-going-nowhere/2017/08/06/47b8bf42-5c18-11e7-aa69-396 4a7d55207_story.html?noredirect=on&utm_term=.0c45bfbb5236.

Comaroff, Jean, and John L. Comaroff. 1999. "Occult Economies and the Violence of Abstraction: Notes from the South African Postcolony." *American Ethnologist* 26(2): 279–303.

Daragahi, Borzou. 2018. "Tunisia's Economic Ills Undermine Democracy." *New York Times*, 4 May, A10.

Dhillon, Navtej, and Tarik Yousef. 2009. *Waiting: The Unfulfilled Promise of Young People in the Middle East*. Washington, DC: Brookings Institution Press.

Diouf, Mamadou. 2003. "Engaging Postcolonial Cultures: African Youth and Public Space." *African Studies Review* 46(2): 1–12.

Durham, Deborah. 2008. "Apathy and Agency: The Romance of Agency and Youth in Botswana." In *Figuring the Future: Globalization and the Temporalities of Children and Youth*, ed. Jennifer Cole and Deborah Durham, 151–78. Santa Fe: School for Advanced Research Press.

Dwyer, Peter D. 2009. "Worlds of Waiting." In *Waiting*, ed. Ghassan Hage, 15–26. Carlton: University of Melbourne Press.

Farrer, James, and Andrew David Field. 2015. *Shanghai Nightscapes: A Nocturnal Biography of a Global City*. Chicago: University of Chicago Press.

Flaherty, Michael. G. 2003. "Time Work: Customizing Temporal Experience." *Social Psychology Quarterly* 66(1): 17–33.

Frederiksen, Martin Demant. 2013. *Young Men, Time, and Boredom in the Republic of Georgia*. Philadelphia: Temple University Press.

Gable, Eric. 2000. "The Culture Development Club: Youth, Neo-Tradition, and the Construction of Society in Guinea-Bissau." *Anthropological Quarterly* 73(4): 195–203.

Gervais, Myriam. 1995. "Structural Adjustment in Niger: Implementations, Effects, and Determining Political Factors." *Review of African Political Economy* 64: 27–42.

Hage, Ghassan. 2009. "Introduction." In *Waiting*, ed. Ghassan Hage, 1–12. Carlton: University of Melbourne Press.

Hassane, H. 2003. "Tuer le Temps dans les Fadas: Chômage, Mode d'Emploi" [Killing time at the fadas: unemployment, instruction manual]. *Tel Quel*, 4 May.

Heidegger, Martin. 1995. *The Fundamental Concepts of Metaphysics: World, Finitude, Solitude*, trans. William McNeill and Nicholas Walker. Bloomington: Indiana University Press.

Honwana, Alcinda. 2012. *The Time of Youth: Work, Social Change, and Politics in Africa*. Sterling, VA: Kumarian Press.

Institut National de la Statistique. 2015. Etude Nationale d'Evaluation d'Indicateurs Socio-Economiques et Démographiques [National Study of Evaluation of Socioeconomic and Demographic Indices]. Retrieved 13 August 2018 from http://www.stat-niger.org/nada/index.php/cata log/94.

Jeffrey, Craig. 2010. *Timepass: Youth, Class and the Politics of Waiting in India*. Stanford: Stanford University Press.

Mains, Daniel. 2013. *Hope is Cut: Youth, Unemployment and the Future in Urban Ethiopia*. Philadelphia: Temple University Press.

Masquelier, Adeline. 2005. "The Scorpion's Sting: Youth, Marriage, and the Struggle for Social Maturity in Niger." *Journal of the Royal Anthropological Institute* 11: 59–83.

———. 2009. "Lessons from *Rubí*: Love, Poverty, and the Educational Value of Televised Dramas in Niger." In *Love in Africa*, ed. Jennifer Cole and Lynn M. Thomas, 204–28. Chicago: University of Chicago Press.

———. 2013. "Teatime: Boredom and the Temporalities of Young Men in Niger." *Africa* 83(3): 470–91.

———. 2019a. *Fada: Boredom and Belonging in Niger*. Chicago: University of Chicago Press.

———. 2019b. "Young Men of Leisure? Youth, Conspicuous Consumption, and the Performativity of Dress in Niger." In *Conspicuous Consumption in Africa*, ed. Deborah Posen and Ilana Van Wyk, 152–71. Johannesburg: Wits University Press.

———. 2020. "The Work of Waiting: Boredom, Teatime, and Future-Making in Niger." In *Time Work: Studies of Temporal Agency*, ed. Michael G. Flaherty, Lotte Meinert, and Anne Line Dalsgård. New York: Berghahn Books.

Munn, Nancy D. 1986. *The Fame of Gawa*. Cambridge: Cambridge University Press.

O'Neill, Bruce. 2017. *The Space of Boredom: Homelessness in the Slowing Global Order*. Durham: Duke University Press.

Parikh, Shanti. 2015. *Regulating Romance: Youth Love Letters, Moral Anxiety, and Intervention in Uganda's Time of AIDS*. Nashville: Vanderbilt University Press.

Singerman, Diane. 2007. "The Economic Imperatives of Marriage: Emerging Practices and Identities Among Youth in the Middle East." *Middle East*

Youth Initiative, Working Paper No. 6, September, The Brookings Institution, Wolfensohn Center for Development, Washington, DC.

Smith, Daniel Jordan. 2010. "Promiscuous Girls, Good Wives, and Cheating Husbands: Gender Inequality, Transitions to Marriage, and Infidelity in Southeastern Nigeria." *Anthropological Quarterly* 83(1): 123–52.

Sommers, Marc. 2012. *Stuck: Rwandan Youth and the Struggle for Adulthood*. Athens: University of Georgia Press.

Stambach, Amy. 2000. *Lessons from Kilimanjaro: Schooling, Community, and Gender in East Africa*. New York: Routledge.

Wedeen, Lisa. 2008. *Peripheral Visions: Publics, Power, and Performance in Yemen*. Chicago: University of Chicago Press.

World Bank. 2017. "Republic of Niger: Priorities for Ending Poverty and Boosting Shared Prosperity." Systematic Country Diagnostic, 28 November. Retrieved 21 November 2018 from http://documents.worldbank .org/curated/en/998751512408491271/pdf/NIGER-SCD-12012017.pdf.

Chapter 4

EMERGENT WAITHOOD
INSTITUTIONS AND MARRIAGE DELAYS AMONG MAYAN WOMEN IN GUATEMALA

Nicole S. Berry

Introduction

Prompted to reflect on patriarchy in Mayan communities in Guatemala, Q'eqchi' leader Emma Carlotta Cucul commented, "Machismo was introduced in the invasion against our grandfathers and grandmothers. Since then, we have been brainwashed for 500 years by people saying that men are more important than women. It's true that we see women working, leading now . . . The changes are impressive, but there is still a lot to be done" (Anonymous 2017, translation by author). Her statement brings together many of the foundational dynamics that young Indigenous women in Guatemala must navigate in decisions to marry: colonialism, patriarchy, and the need to lead their communities.

This chapter considers changing institutional pressures on women associated with these foundational dynamics; more specifically, it examines the Guatemalan state as an accomplice of colonialism, the community as an accomplice of patriarchy, and non-governmental organizations (NGOs) as accomplices of the need to lead. I propose the conceptual trope of *emergent waithood* to draw our attention to places and moments where marriage practices may be changing.

Through the lens of emergent waithood, this chapter examines the influences of institutions in shaping marriage practices among Mayan women in Guatemala. I contemplate how changes in the institutional landscape that have occurred over the last twenty years create conflicting or harmonizing incentives for Mayan women in Guatemala to marry.

My analysis is anchored in my fieldsite, Santa Cruz, a town of about three thousand people, in an area of Guatemala called "the highlands." The highlands are characterized not only by altitude (like Denver, Santa Cruz is also "mile-high"), but also by the relatively marginal lands available for production and by the predominance of Indigenous people who live there. People in Santa Cruz call themselves Kaqchikel Maya, distinguishing themselves from Ladinos, the dominant ethnic identity in Guatemala.[1]

After providing a brief orientation to Guatemala, this chapter begins by considering the premium that has been placed on the stability of reproductive practices, like marriage, in the community, which has arguably created a natural resistance to marriage delays. From the mid-1960s through the mid-1990s, Guatemala was embroiled in a civil war that took a massive toil on Indigenous communities. During this period, the state used violence and genocide in attempts to destroy Indigenous social continuity. In addition to production, reproduction has played a central role in Indigenous community continuity in the face of threats. The chapter then considers the remaking of Guatemala after the 1996 Peace Accords and traces how the government's orientation toward liberalization has led to a postwar boom in NGOs. I offer Santa Cruz as an example of the first generation raised in the NGO-rich landscape that implicitly considers reproduction as an individual resource. These young people have had opportunities not available to previous generations, including access to education, training, jobs, and global travel. As highlighted in other chapters, young women now can engage in a period of self-making that was previously impossible. For some, this has led to a delay in marriage. This is the emergence of waithood that is considered in this chapter. Finally, the chapter turns to the third major institution influencing women's reproductive lives: the state. The postwar Guatemalan state has been anxious to remake itself, primarily through the attempt to extend its resources to all its citizens. Part of this effort to remake itself has meant co-opting regional trends that treat reproduction as a resource for remaking the nation. I look at a state program of trading cash for Indigenous mothers' compliance in behaviors relating to the health and edu-

cation system. Like the emphasis on marriage as a community resource that integrates women more tightly into the fabric of the
community, the orientation toward reproduction as a state resource
is designed to integrate women more tightly into the fabric of the
state, arguably competing with the primacy of the community as
an institutional force. I close by offering an example of everyday
life in Santa Cruz that illustrates the competing incentives shaping
the context in which young women may decide to delay marriage.
While "emergent waithood" highlights new possibilities for self-development, delaying marriage can negatively impact a woman's social standing within her community.

Methodology

The material for this chapter is predicated on my research relationship with Sololá, Guatemala. This relationship began in 1999, when
I was first recruited by the Jefatura de Salud (Office of Health Leadership) to explore high rates of maternal mortality in the province.
That project positioned my local base in Santa Cruz, due to the high
rates of pregnancy-related death that women suffered. At the beginning of 2012, I began a second project looking at NGO attempts
to change reproductive health outcomes. Regardless of my professional interests, I have continued to return to Santa Cruz for personal visits and have kept abreast of major events.

Waithood as a concept signals that reproductive practices are
changing or being remade. My long-term observation of everyday
life in Santa Cruz allowed me to compare the lives—and reproductive practices—of women there from the turn of the century to the
present. Likewise, my personal observation of the development in
Guatemala of the NGO sector in general and the growth of a new
generation of young people has given me sufficient perspective to
identify changing incentives that may influence young women and
their decisions about marriage and procreation.

This chapter also relies on a review of scholarly literature. As my
research agenda is tied firmly to reproduction, I maintain a scholarly interest in the anthropology of reproduction, particularly as it
relates to the Guatemalan state. I review this literature to make a
case for reproduction as a community resource. I also draw on grey
literature and scholarly literature that speaks to state programs that
transfer cash to women to improve health outcomes.

Guatemala: State and Nations

Home to a variety of Indigenous nations, the area now known as Guatemala has been a multiethnic territory since time immemorial. Yet the advent of European colonialism produced a prominent governance challenge for the Guatemalan state: the domination of Indigenous Peoples by a central authority. With varied tactics and effectiveness, state attempts to govern Indigenous nations in Guatemala has produced a bloody history of violence and oppression (Adams 1970). Recently, an estimated two-hundred thousand people were murdered during a thirty-year, state-sponsored genocide against Indigenous Peoples (CEH 1999).

My fieldwork respondents frequently described the Guatemalan state as antagonistic to the well-being and continuity of Indigenous communities. For example, like the participants in both Weismantel's (2001) and Crandon-Malamud's (1991) studies, participants in my research spoke about the state not only as precluding their access to lifesaving resources (Berry 2008), but as actively harvesting bodily products from them (Berry 2010). Respondents described the state as violent, for instance recounting how the government insisted on receiving the bodies of dead villagers and then arguably desecrating them through mandatory autopsies, cutting them up and sewing them back together to be returned for burial (Carpenter, Tait, and Quadrelli 2014).

This antagonistic state also is front and center in anthropological literature. The targeting and killing of anthropologist Myrna Mack during the civil war deterred many scholars from conducting ethnographic fieldwork; thus, the vast majority of anthropological writing during the civil war was theoretically and historically oriented. This research focused largely on the tactics that enabled Indigenous communities to maintain as much autonomy from the state as possible over five hundred years of struggle (Carmack 1988; Handy 1984).

Smith's (1990a) important edited volume exploring state and community struggles emphasized the relationships between modes of production, cultural practices, and relative maintenance of autonomy in Indigenous communities. In reflecting on the lack of shared class identity between Indigenous and non-Indigenous Guatemalans, Smith (1990b: 25–26) pointed to the primacy of shared cultural identity in communities, arguing that "a major element in the maintenance of Indian cultural identity has been Indian resistance to full proletarianization and to capitalist relations of production within the community."[2] As such, there exists a plethora of excellent scholarship on Guatemala detailing novel modes of production that forestalled full community integration into state-supported capitalism. Many of these modes, such as "brokerage" and class divisions within Indigenous communities, were exploitative, but, like subsistence agriculture and regional economies of artisan production, were also predicated on shoring up the relationship between ethnic identity and economy (Grandin 2000; McCreery 1994; Smith 1988). Indeed, Smith (1990b) has argued that state actions in the civil war can be interpreted as an attempt to solve the "Indian problem" by breaking autonomy of production.

Reproduction as a Community Resource: Preserving Marriage

Recently, Dudgeon (2006) has extended the argument that the violence the state wrought against Indigenous communities during the civil war should be read as an attempt to break autonomy through gaining control over *production*, by turning our attention to the impact of the violence on *reproduction*. States in the Americas have a long history of trying to undercut social reproduction of Indigenous communities by remaking reproductive practices. Common examples include the forced sterilization of Indigenous women (Bailey 2006; Lawrence 2000; Vasquez del Aguila 2006) and the forced removal of Indigenous children from their homes (Dawson 2012; MacDonald and Hudson 2012; Miller 1996). Dudgeon argues that the genocide perpetrated by the state against Indigenous Peoples in Guatemala not only disrupted Indigenous economies that allowed community independence but also disrupted the reproductive autonomy on which social continuity depends. From my perspective, Dudgeon's ethnography, which details the impact of violence in Ixil (one of the most hard-hit areas) on men, makes a significant contribution by interrogating what others might consider "cultural identity" and showing how this is predicated on gender relations that undergird both physical and social reproduction of Mayan communities. For example, Dudgeon identifies three important gendered institutions that safeguard autonomy: endogamous marriage, midwifery, and inheritance. He also documents how the civil war disrupted each.

Indeed, other post–civil war ethnographies extend our understanding of the symbolic importance of gender and reproduction to forging the Guatemalan nation. Hale's (2006) examples of popular talk surrounding sex are instructive. In one instance, he related the matter-of-fact narration of a secretary who made sense of young Ladinas dating young Indigenous men in her town with reference to the young men's desires to continue the insurrections of the civil war. She referenced the Indian plan to "kill the men and take the Ladina women" (Hale 2006: 159). As Indians never were able to accomplish this during the civil war, today's young Indian men were "achieving conquest through romance rather than revolution" (Hale 2006: 159). While we need to acknowledge the routine use of the word *conquistar* (what Hale glosses as "achieve conquest") to signify that a man had sex with a woman, the secretary's intertwining of politics and dating brings to the fore important tensions around ethnicity, reproduction, and the state. Her spontaneous commentary highlighted the deep ethnic divisions that still exist; the crux of tension is whether Ladinos or Indigenous Peoples would prevail in Guatemala.

Equally interesting are the gendered dimensions of the commentary that positioned men as the active parties in the effort to forge the Guatemalan nation and women as prizes that men took in this effort. Hale later retells this tale of men as forgers of the nation from the perspective of Ladino men who have relations with Indigenous women. His most evocative and yet commonplace story was of a friend of a friend and his "doting mother [who] mak[es] a special effort to bring young indigenous women home as domestic workers so that [her son] could have sex with them" [sic] (Hale 2006: 160). Hale considered this and numerous similar stories of "sexual predation" predicated on "dominant culture males viewing lower status women as fair game" (Hale 2006: 159). While these stories have shock value, they also help us understand how the reproductive sphere is intertwined with power dynamics that relate ethnicity and gender to nation-building in Guatemala. As Hale pointed out, for Ladino men to impregnate Indigenous women laudably contributed to whitening the nation, whereas for Ladina women to birth the babies of Indigenous men did no such thing.

The symbolic importance of *la mujer Maya* or "the Mayan woman" further builds our understanding of the importance of a particular type of Mayan woman to the Mayan nation. Diane Nelson (1999) reflected on the widespread view of Indigenous women as symbols of Maya and bearers of tradition.[3] Nelson's discussion of Guatemalan jokes about Rigoberta Menchu brings into relief what a Mayan woman is and is not. These jokes highlighted the idea that Men-

chu's position as an activist and international leader, as a childless
woman, and as someone who could afford expensive clothing were
all remarkable in that they conflicted with the popular notion of *la
mujer Maya*. As Nelson argues, Indigenous women have been seen
by both Ladinos and Maya as the emblems of Guatemalan ethnicity
who are realized through their reproductive roles as mothers.

While reproduction is often overlooked in theoretical understandings of the relationship between the Guatemalan state and Indigenous populations in favor of a focus on production, it is of central
importance, both symbolically and instrumentally (Ginsburg and
Rapp 1995). Community autonomy has been predicated on the close
link between production and reproduction. Reproductive autonomy
has been built upon particular gendered practices, including marriage.

In Santa Cruz, marriage lies at the core of identity and subjectivity (Berry 2010). Virtually all able-bodied adults get married. Because the norm is to marry someone from within the community,
marriage creates an ever more complex web of relationships binding
inhabitants of the town. Furthermore, because of patriarchal norms
that emphasize age and gender hierarchy, marriage generates obligations and responsibilities, not only among those marrying but along
entire kin networks. So even if the partnership and co-residence of
a couple were to break down, marriage may endure. As a result,
the community in Santa Cruz arguably maintains a vested interest
in maintaining marriage as an institution that shapes reproductive
practice.

Peace and the NGO Nation:
Delay in Marriage, Investment in Self

Though peace officially came to Guatemala in 1996 through the
Peace Accords, when examined through a lens of state governance,
this agreement sidestepped many of the tensions around production, reproduction, and Indigenous autonomy. Peace was forged on
the notion of a truce between government forces and a small, armed
group of insurgents, without recognizing and encouraging stronger
modes of Indigenous governance or addressing Indigenous autonomy. Nevertheless, the peace process allowed a larger Mayan movement to stake claims on the importance of increasing recognition of
Indigenous identity and rights (Warren 1998). The Peace Accords
made the state immediately responsible for providing basic—and
culturally adequate—services to all citizens of Guatemala.

While the Peace Accords did not necessarily transform central-ized governance, it contributed over the next decades to the trans-formation of much of Guatemala into a nation inundated by NGOs (Rohloff, Díaz, and Dasgupta 2011). Internationally, the Peace Ac-cords coincided with the push toward neoliberal ideologies, which heavily influenced strategies to extend basic services (Chary and Rohloff 2015). Rather than expanding the state, post–civil war re-structuring embraced the role of civil society NGOs, particularly in the health sector. Monies were set aside to contract out to organi-zations that already exhibited a strong track record of working with Indigenous Peoples as a stop-gap strategy. As Maupin (2009) pointed out, however, the availability of funds jumpstarted the formation of new NGOs interested in capturing them. At the same time, the end of fighting made Guatemala a safer, and thus a seemingly more pop-ular destination for foreigners—particularly those who lived close by in North America. Postwar Guatemala was rife for NGO-ization; many tourists remained in the country and started NGOs to fill the notable gaps in health and education. Other international NGOs added Guatemala to their lists of countries served.

Officially, it has been difficult to track the NGO expansion in Gua-temala. While Guatemalan NGOs do have their own legal designa-tion, registering an NGO in Guatemala does not necessarily confer the kinds of financial benefits that attaining official status in North America does. Therefore, NGOs led by foreigners, even those that work only in Guatemala, typically do not complete the legal process to register in Guatemala. Rohloff, Díaz, and Dasgupta (2011: 428) estimated that more than ten thousand health-related NGOs existed by 2011.

The drastic increases in NGO activity that occurred over the last two decades have been impossible to miss in a region like Sololá that boasts a world-class landscape coupled with an overwhelmingly photogenic Mayan population (Sullivan and Berry 2017). Pickup trucks sporting various logos of their parent organizations line the streets. Signs advertising NGOs can be found on buildings, on ban-ners, on telephone poles, and on small cards adorning artisanal products made for the tourist market. For those who live in Sololá, NGO activity is on the front burner in social interactions; residents are frequently involved by contributing to operations, being clients, or providing services—or sometimes by simultaneously occupying more than one of these roles.

Indeed, the picturesque landscape has made Sololá a permanent home to a large expatriate population; access to generous funding and volunteering of North American or European patrons has translated into deep support for NGO activity. This class of NGOs can exhibit much diversity, particularly in relation to its integration with local governance. Yet the aims of these organizations are decisively concentrated in the areas of health and education. The ambit of NGO activities is astounding; diverse forms of sponsorship for families and individuals, poor, sick, young, widowed, disabled, etc. exist. Independent clinics, hospitals, and schools have been built. Unlike larger, international organizations that tend to have a three- to five-year project cycle, the expat-fueled NGO sector has tended toward longevity as well as geographic specificity, with many entering twenty years of working within particular communities.

Santa Cruz is one of the municipalities that has seen enormous changes due to NGO activity. When I first arrived in 1999 to Santa Cruz, the only salaried jobs available were working in the municipality (temporary jobs typically tied to political favors), working as a teacher or judge, working for a "foreigner" (and by this I mean any non-Maya person) as the caretaker of a property, or cleaning and cooking at one of the three hotels or vacation homes. Others who earned money generally did so by working the land or through informal day labor. The number of people from the village who had ever graduated from high school could be counted on one hand.

Yet over the last twenty years, Santa Cruz has been the focus of an expat-fueled NGO sector that concentrates on supporting the educational and leadership development of children and youth, as well as training for post-secondary students. Most notably, children growing up in this municipality have access to extended financial and remedial support of their education. This support begins in elementary school and continues throughout a child's or youth's educational trajectory. The first generation who grew up with this support is coming into early adulthood. I would now need more than my fingers and toes to total up the number of high school graduates in the community. Santa Cruz also boasts many students with various post-secondary degrees. Furthermore, many youth are at least trilingual (having added English into their fluency), have traveled internationally, and have completed skills-based certifications allowing them to work in a trade. Thus, many youth (age twenty-five and under) in Santa Cruz have new opportunities for salaried jobs, including cooking, hotel management, and NGO program management, as well as for skilled contract work as wood workers, metal workers, electricians, and seamstresses.

The expansion of education and work opportunities in Santa Cruz has not led to females surpassing their male peers; yet, this new landscape has heavily impacted what is possible for this generation of females vis-à-vis past generations. In the past, high school graduates tended to be male. Female work outside of the house tended to be restricted to the domestic sphere, such as cooking and cleaning. Now females have access to professional and administrative work (as much as their male peers). Young women reimagining what is possible for themselves has also created different and new possibilities of life trajectories; notably, among this new cohort, we are beginning to see a small number of high-achieving females purposefully delaying marriage, while their male peers marry and have children.

As other chapters in this book, particularly those by Adely (Chapter 11, this volume) and Sadruddin (Chapter 6, this volume), highlight, a delay in marriage for women can have a distinct positive valence. The typical gendered dynamics that surround the matrimonial household in Santa Cruz can be demanding for women. A newly married woman often moves into her in-laws' compound. Gendered divisions of labor accord women responsibility for the domestic sphere, including cooking and cleaning. As in Jordan or Rwanda, marriage delays as a result of extended education mean that a generation of young women now have time for self-development. In Santa Cruz, for example, self-development provides young women with the possibility of professional work.

Compared with the ways in which the institution of the community shapes reproductive practices, the influx of NGO resources produces new possibilities and thus incentivizes new reproductive practices. Whereas community norms emphasize the role of reproduction as a community resource necessary to keep the state at bay, NGO norms emphasize the role of reproduction as an individual choice. Delaying marriage and pregnancy can create a benefit—that is, investment in education and work. Nevertheless, young women in Santa Cruz are under the influence of a third institution that tries to shape their reproductive practices: the Guatemalan state.

The Guatemalan State: Marriage, Motherhood, and the Future of the Nation

While the Peace Accords did not transform representation within governance, they did encourage the state to shift toward the deliberate inclusion of its citizens in state programming. As intimated above, the strategies through which the state attempted to extend its reach and unify the nation under one, theoretically benevolent, government were heavily influenced by neoliberal agendas, tying the Guatemalan state more closely to bilateral and international policy interventions and objectives. In this section, I consider iconic and politically progressive state policies that have dominated Latin American approaches to poverty reduction over the last twenty years. Following the lead of a number of Latin American nations, in 2008, the left-leaning government of President Álvaro Colom Caballeros instituted a conditional cash transfer program called "Mi Familia Progressa" (My Family Progresses or MiFaPro),[4] ostensibly with the goal of helping the poorest families. The government used census data to identify families with children under the age of fifteen or where the mother of the family was pregnant and then selected a subset of eligible families to participate. The government promised to provide each mother with US $36 a month, which was about one-third of a minimum wage salary at the time. In exchange, she promised to meet certain conditions regarding health and education behaviors.

In this section I consider MiFaPro as an attempt to incentivize Indigenous women's reproductive practices in ways that made women and their families more compliant and intertwined with state objectives. Not surprisingly, in a country where ethnicity can be used to cleave a line between the haves and have-nots, 78 percent of the recipients of MiFaPro were Indigenous (Ramírez 2009). The conditions that the state set out for mothers to meet included behaviors that would guarantee mothers' participation in state institutions, such as health clinics and schools, through activities such as keeping up to date on children's vaccination schedules and making sure that children were present in elementary school. Those who failed to meet these conditions would be deregistered from the program. Arguably, MiFaPro was a powerful attempt to demonstrate the unity and legitimacy of the postwar state—one that was inclusive of its poorest citizens and to whom its poorest citizens were responsive.

The advent of MiFaPro was a spectacle in Santa Cruz, and though I was not there to witness it firsthand, it was momentous enough for many friends and acquaintances to discuss it with me. Apparently, the First Lady arrived in a helicopter and announced the program to a crowd of Cruzeños gathered in the town square. Santa Cruz was selected as one of six municipalities to participate in MiFaPro. A World Bank (2009) study estimated that 42.34 percent of the population in Santa Cruz lived in extreme poverty—that is the lowest poverty quintile—at that time. Registration day was similarly spectacular. Like many cash transfer programs in Latin America, money was given to women only. On the appointed day, women lined up with their identification documents in the public square, waiting to be checked against registries. After this bureaucratic step, they were shuffled into the next line, where they received their first cash disbursement from a bank representative. Six hundred and eight-eight women are documented as having been given an identification number, helping create a picture of just how congested the town square must have been (World Bank 2009).

In literature about MiFaPro, the Colom government emphasized that the design of transferring income to female heads of household was a strategic (Moser 1993) approach to support female empowerment.[5] Fajardo (2011) emphasized how MiFaPro was a transformational intervention because it purported to change gendered access to resources, which in turn would change gendered roles and responsibilities.[6] These transformations were thought to ultimately open the door for women to occupy new roles in society.

While the transformational potential of the program remains somewhat opaque, the incentivization of particular gender roles and reproductive practices is clear. In line with Molyneux's (2006) critique of Oportunidades, a Mexican cash transfer program, MiFaPro was predicated on redoubling the naturalness of a dominant femininity—women as mothers and women as carers. Only women who occupied these roles were eligible for state benefits. Furthermore, the program was clear about what types of reproductive practices it encouraged: adherence to the demands of state-run health and education systems. In sum, the program could transform reproduction into a resource that could demonstrate the efficacy of the new Guatemalan state.

Competing Incentives Shaping Reproductive Practices: What Does It Mean to Wait?

Now that we have established how different institutions can approach reproduction as a resource, I consider a recent example of everyday life to illustrate how these different approaches can incentivize different reproductive practices. Maria (a pseudonym) was a smart and talented woman who had pursued educational opportunities and now worked in the administration of an NGO. She delayed marriage and remained single, without children, living with her unpartnered mother. Over the last two decades, Santa Cruz has begun to experience water shortages in the dry season, and when Maria started to work, she decided to use her salary to have a well drilled on her land near where she lived, in the outskirts of town. During the dry season, as water started to disappear, Maria and her family were no longer affected. Yet one day, her water started to run dry too. In trying to get to the bottom of the problem, Maria realized that municipal workers had sunk a line and began to pump water out of her well to supply the rest of the town—without consultation.

This case highlights how competing conceptualizations of reproduction as a resource have inspired competing incentives (see Table 4.1). Reproduction is a central resource used to protect the community against an aggressive state. Maria's example illustrates how, as an institution, the community contributes to conditions that incentivize marriage (and motherhood). Although the town leadership may have discussed many factors when attempting to solve the problem of a lack of water, it is likely that Maria's role as a young, single daughter of an unpartnered mother figured, at least tacitly, into the decision to sink a line into her well. Were Maria or her mother married and co-residing with another family, taking her water would have offended a larger sector of the population. For Maria, her decision to delay marriage put her in a vulnerable position with respect to decision-making by the senior leadership of the town.

The fact that Maria drilled a well at all speaks to some of the incentives connected to the NGO position of emphasizing reproduction as an individual resource. Supporting education and training for employment, this NGO has enabled young Mayan women to create different reproductive trajectories—one currently characterized by emergent waithood. Notably by investing in her own self-develop-

TABLE 4.1. Institutional Incentives Stemming from Alternative Views of Reproduction.

Reproduction as . . .	Emphasis on . . .
community resource	sustaining community autonomy from state; preservation of endogamous marriage
individual resource	education and professionalization; emergent waithood to invest in self
state resource	mothers who are integrated into and responsive to state run programs; incentivizing motherhood

ment, Maria was able to garner the capital necessary to drill the well. She also proffered an individualized conceptualization of the water challenge. While the town conversation had been firmly tied to the responsibility of the leadership to solve a communal problem, Maria responded with an individual solution. That others found it intolerable that she and her family enjoy water while her community suffered from drought was clear in the actions of the leadership and silent complicity of her neighbors.

This chapter, along with many others in the volume, indicate that, although education is generally considered to provide a path for women's advancement, the reality is far more complicated. Education can make it difficult for women to marry in countries like Jordan (Adely, Chapter 11, this volume), China (Howlett, Chapter 7, this volume), and Iran (Babadi, Chapter 10, this volume). Even a successful education does not necessarily lead to anticipated changes in status, like for frustrated Nigerien youth who no longer tolerate the prospect of manual labor (Masquelier, Chapter 3, this volume). Maria's example shows us that education can create transformations—Maria had money, she had diplomas, she had skills, she had the autonomy to travel in Guatemala and internationally. While education could create new possibilities for self-development, at the same time, embracing reproduction as an individual resource and delaying marriage detracted from Maria becoming more deeply enfranchised within her community.

Maria's example also poignantly speaks to how the state incentivizes reproduction as a state resource. As a childless woman, Maria was excluded from the state program intended to transform society. Indeed, the state incentivized not just motherhood, but a certain type of motherhood, leveraging MiFaPro to bind mothers more closely to state systems and to use their subscription to demonstrate state success. The example of Maria's water being pilfered highlights how a focus on transforming individuals' access to resources—particularly those on the bottom of the age and gendered hierarchy— falls short of addressing these negatively constraining structures.

In many ways, emergent waithood in Santa Cruz sheds light on the retrograde nature of state perspectives of Indigenous women. The state not only remains fixated on charitable approaches to alleviating Indigenous poverty, but on motherhood as an Indigenous woman's important contribution to society. From this perspective, we can begin to see how the state's approach to promoting well-being draws on stereotypical, generic, and perhaps antiquated ideas of Indigenous women. Accordingly, waithood exposes the limits of state imagination regarding how to encourage true well-being in Indigenous communities. The advent of a delay in marriage and motherhood in an environment where motherhood is a monetarily rewarded role for women demonstrates that young Indigenous women conceive of, value, and operationalize alternative roles.

Ultimately, this chapter frames how young Indigenous women in Santa Cruz are caught between different institutional pressures, echoing themes from several other chapters in this volume (Babadi, Chapter 10; Howlett, Chapter 7; Thorton, Chapter 9). While young people in Santa Cruz embrace the option of pursuing education and employment, for young women, the potential for self-development can be allied with emergent waithood. At the same time, state and community pressures heavily discourage delaying marriage, which challenges the abilities of young women to participate in both their community and state in the most publicly recognized and celebrated ways.

Many of the chapters in this volume highlight how particular institutions are shaping reproductive contexts, including states (Singerman, Chapter 1; Babadi, Chapter 10; Sadruddin, Chapter 6; Vialle, Chapter 13), families (Howlett, Chapter 7; Adely, Chapter 11), and NGOs (Maclean, Chapter 5). My analysis supports the findings of others in this volume who demonstrate that different institutions can create different pressures to incentivize or deter reproductive practices, like marriage. This chapter deepens our understanding of the origins of institutional desires by drawing on anthropological traditions of examining reproduction as a state resource (Greenhalgh 2008; Krause and Marchesi 2007; Paxson 2004) or as community resources (Boddy 1989; Delaney 1991).

Placing my inquiry within a long-term examination of institutions highlights the importance of shifting institutional pressures in the emergence of waithood. In this example, we can see the rise of new and localized institutions, such as NGOs, that have relatively quickly come to impact incentives to marry. At the same time, we see a shift in how the state has attempted to shape reproductive practice in Mayan communities. During the civil war, it sought to dismantle community control of reproduction through violent means. After the Peace Accords, it attempted to trade cash to married and reproducing Mayan women in exchange for allegiance to state programming and goals. These shifts are grafted onto an ongoing struggle of Mayan communities to seek and maintain their autonomy and dignity. Comparing the underlying views of institutions further illustrates the gains and losses young Mayan women face in deciding to delay marriage.

Nicole S. Berry is Associate Professor in the Faculty of Health Sciences at Simon Fraser University in Vancouver, Canada. Her research addresses international attempts to change reproductive health outcomes among Mayans in Guatemala. Berry is the author of *Unsafe Motherhood: Mayan Maternal Mortality and Subjectivity in Post-war Guatemala* (Berghahn Books, 2010). She holds MA and PhD degrees in anthropology from the University of Michigan-Ann Arbor.

Notes

1. The latest available official population report from the Instituto Nacional de Estadística (National Statistics Institute) in Guatemala estimates a population of 15,073,375 people, 39.8 percent of whom are classified as Indigenous (INE 2012). The population of Sololá is estimated at 464,005 people, 96.5 percent of whom are classified as Indigenous (INE 2013). Estimates of the percentage of the population that is Indigenous are contentious across the Americas, as the rationales of who should be counted not only vary but are politically charged, in many cases creating a sub-estimation of Indigenous Peoples (Lloréns 2002).

2. I acknowledge that supportive terminology for referring to Indigenous Peoples varies across time and space. In this chapter, I have followed Younging's (2018) recommendation to use the term "Indigenous" with a capital "I." Nevertheless, the term "Indian" appears several times in this chapter. This was a popular term in the anthropology of Guatemala, largely because it was the dominant Spanish term used to refer to Indigenous Peoples. As Younging points out, it stems from the perspective of the European invaders, and thus, in the right circumstances, bears a negative connotation. I have retained the use of "Indian" both where authors originally used that term, and to indicate the perspective of those who view Indigenous People negatively.

3. Grandin's (2000) analysis of photographs of K'iche' families from the early 1900s also underscores the importance of the Indian woman for Indigenous communities. De la Cadena (1991) offers a comparative perspective of how gender is implicated in ethnicity by examining why "women are more Indian" in contemporary Peru.

4. For this chapter, I have drawn on the World Bank's project appraisal of the Colom government's application for support of MiFaPro (World Bank 2009), the external evaluation of the program (Gutiérrez 2011), and PowerPoint presentations from directors in the program delivered to various United Nations sponsored seminars on conditional cash transfers, which took place in Chile (Fajardo 2011; Ramírez 2009). I have also consulted Dotson (2014), as well as Sandberg and Tally's (2015) and Gaia's (2010) critiques the program.

5. While I restrict my analysis here to considering MiFaPro as a transformational intervention in the lives of women, Sabates-Wheeler and
   Deveraux, however, have been prolific in furthering our practical and theoretical understandings of what transformational social protection programming looks like (Devereux, McGregor, and Sabates-Wheeler 2011;
   Sabates-Wheeler and Devereux 2007, 2008, 2011; Sabates-Wheeler and
   Roelen 2011).
6. Two main domains were specified from which these transformations
   could take place. First, in order for MiFaPro to begin to distribute income in a particular area, representatives would engage municipal governance to help set up the program. Doing so, designers argued, would
   eventually lead to municipal governance conceptualizing a new role for
   women, as municipal programming did not normally attend to women
   as a category of clients, and certainly not for matters of money. Second,
   designers argued that providing women with a bi-monthly salary would
   contribute to amplifying women's control over resources, most specifically income and decision-making, within the family, ultimately creating
   new gendered roles and division of labor at the household level.

References

Adams, Richard Newbold. 1970. *Crucifixion by Power: Essays on Guatemalan
National Social Structure, 1944–1966.* Austin: University of Texas Press.

Anonymous. 2017. "La mujer indígena es quien lidera la lucha en Guatemala" [Indigenous women are who lead the fight in Guatemala]. *Ima-
genes del Sur*, 18 December. Retrieved 15 September 2018 from http://
www.imagenesdelsur.tv/?q=node/933.

Bailey, Claudia Paz. 2006. "Guatemala: Gender and Reparations for Human
Rights Violations." In *What Happened to the Women? Gender and Reparations
for Human Rights Violations*, ed. Ruth Rubio-Marín, Pablo De Greiff, and
Alexander Mayer-Rieckh, 92–135. New York: Social Science Research
Council.

Berry, Nicole S. 2008. "Who's Judging the Quality of Care? Indigenous
Maya and the Problem of 'Not being Attended.'" *Medical Anthropology*
27(2): 164–89.

———. 2010. *Unsafe Motherhood: Mayan Maternal Mortality and Subjectivity in
Post-war Guatemala.* New York: Berghahn Books.

Boddy, Janice Patricia. 1989. *Wombs and Alien Spirits: Women, Men, and the
Zar Cult in Northern Sudan.* Madison: University of Wisconsin Press.

Carmack, Robert S. 1988. *Harvest of Violence: The Maya Indians and the Guatemalan Crisis.* Norman: University of Oklahoma Press.

Carpenter, Belinda, Gordon Tait, and Carol Quadrelli. 2014. "The Body in
Grief: Death Investigations, Objections to Autopsy, and the Religious and
Cultural 'Other.'" *Religions* 5(1): 165–78.

CEH (Comisión para el Esclarecimiento Histórico). 1999. "Guatemala: Memory of Silence, Report of the Commission for Historical Clarification: Conclusions and Recommendations." Guatemalan Historical Clarification Commission.

Chary, Anita, and Peter Rohloff. 2015. *Privatization and the New Medical Pluralism: Shifting Healthcare Landscapes in Maya Guatemala*. Lanham: Lexington Books.

Crandon-Malamud, Libbet. 1991. *From the Fat of our Souls: Social Change, Political Process, and Medical Pluralism in Bolivia*. Berkeley: University of California Press.

Dawson, Alexander S. 2012. "Histories and Memories of the Indian Boarding Schools in Mexico, Canada, and the United States." *Latin American Perspectives* 39(5): 80–99.

De la Cadena, Marisol. 1991. "'Las Mujeres son más Indias': Etnicidad y Género en una Comunidad del Cuzco" ['Women are more Indian': Ethnicity and gender in a community in Cuzco]. *Revista Andino* Ediciones de las Mujeres 9: 7–47.

Delaney, Carol Lowery. 1991. *The Seed and the Soil: Gender and Cosmology in Turkish Village Society*. Berkeley: University of California Press.

Devereux, Stephen, J. Allister McGregor, and Rachel Sabates-Wheeler. 2011. "Introduction: Social Protection for Social Justice." *IDS Bulletin* 42(6): 1–9.

Dotson, R. 2014. "Citizen-Auditors and Visible Subjects: Mi Familia Progresa and Transparency Politics in Guatemala." *Polar-Political and Legal Anthropology Review* 37(2): 350–70.

Dudgeon, Matt R. 2006. "Reproduction and Gender in Guatemala's Genocide." Unpublished manuscript.

Fajardo, Neftalí Hernández. 2011. "Guatemala Programa 'Mi Familia Progresa'" [The Guatemalan program 'My Family Progresses']. Sixth Seminar on Conditional Cash Transfers. Santiago, Chile.

Gaia, Elena. 2010. "*Mi Familia Progresa*: Change and Continuity in Guatemala's Social Policy." *Social Policy Review* 22: 199–223.

Ginsburg, Faye D., and Rayna Rapp. 1995. "Introduction: Conceiving the New World Order." In *Conceiving the New World Order: The Global Politics of Reproduction*, ed. Faye D. Ginsburg and Rayna Rapp, 1–17. Berkeley: University of California Press.

Grandin, Greg. 2000. *The Blood of Guatemala: A History of Race and Nation*. Durham: Duke University Press.

Greenhalgh, Susan. 2008. *Just One Child: Science and Policy in Deng's China*. Berkeley: University of California Press.

Gutiérrez, Juan Pablo. 2011. *Evaluación de Impacto de Mi Familia Progresa* [Evaluation of the impact of My Family Progresses]. Mexico: Instituto Nacional de Salud Pública.

Hale, Charles R. 2006. Más que un Indio [More than an Indian]: *Racial Ambivalence and Neoliberal Multiculturalism in Guatemala*. 1st ed. Santa Fe: School of American Research Press.

Handy, Jim. 1984. *Gift of the Devil: A History of Guatemala*. Toronto: Between The Lines.

INE (Instituto Nacional de Estadística). 2012. *Caracterización Estadística República de Guatemala 2012* [Statistical Characterization of the Republic of Guatemala 2012]. Guatemala: Guatemala.

———. 2013. *Caracterización Departamental Sololá 2013* [Characterization of the Department of Sololá 2013]. Guatemala, Guatemala.

Krause, Elizabeth L., and Milena Marchesi. 2007. "Fertility Politics as 'Social Viagra': Reproducing Boundaries, Social Cohesion, and Modernity in Italy." *American Anthropologist* 109(2): 350–62.

Lawrence, Jane. 2000. "The Indian Health Service and the Sterilization of Native American Women." *American Indian Quarterly* 24(3): 400–19.

Lloréns, Jose A. 2002. "Etnicidad y Censos: Los Conceptos Básicos y Sus Aplicaciones" [Ethnicity and censuses: Basic concepts and their applications]. *Bulletin de l'Institut Français d'Études Endines* 31(3): 655–80.

MacDonald, David B., and Graham Hudson. 2012. "The Genocide Question and Indian Residential Schools in Canada." *Canadian Journal of Political Science/Revue Canadienne de Science Politique* 45(2): 427–49.

Maupin, Jonathan Nathaniel. 2009. "'Fruit of the Accords': Healthcare Reform and Civil Participation in Highland Guatemala." *Social Science & Medicine* 68(8): 1456–63.

McCreery, David. 1994. *Rural Guatemala, 1760–1940*. Stanford: Stanford University Press.

Miller, James Rodger. 1996. *Shingwauk's Vision: A History of Native Residential Schools*. Toronto: University of Toronto Press.

Molyneux, Maxine. 2006. "Mothers at the Service of the New Poverty Agenda: Progresa/Oportunidades, Mexico's Conditional Transfer Programme." *Social Policy & Administration* 40(4): 425–49.

Moser, Caroline O. N. 1993. *Gender Planning and Development: Theory, Practice and Training*. London: Routledge.

Nelson, Diane M. 1999. *A Finger in the Wound: Body Politics in Quincentennial Guatemala*. Berkeley: University of California Press.

Paxson, Heather. 2004. *Making Modern Mothers: Ethics and Family Planning in Urban Greece*. Berkeley: University of California Press.

Ramírez, Andrés. 2009. "Los Programas de Tranferencias Condicionales en la Crises: Mi Familia Progresa Guatemala" [Conditional transfer programs in the crisis: My family progresses Guatemala]. First Seminar on Conditional Cash Transfers, Santiago, Chile.

Rohloff, Peter, Anne Kraemer Díaz, and Shom Dasgupta. 2011. "'Beyond Development': A Critical Appraisal of the Emergence of Small Health Care Non-Governmental Organizations in Rural Guatemala." *Human Organization* 70(4): 427–37.

Sabates-Wheeler, Rachel, and Stephen Devereux. 2007. "Social Protection for Transformation." *IDS Bulletin* 38(3): 23–28.

———. 2008. "Transformative Social Protection: The Currency of Social Justice." In *Social Protection for the Poor and Poorest: Concepts, Policies, and*

Politics, ed. Armando Barrientos and David Hulme, 64–84. London: Palgrave MacMillan.

———. 2011. "Transforming Livelihoods for Resilient Futures: How to Facilitate Graduation in Social Protection." Future Agricultures Consortium Working Paper 23. Brighton: IDS.

Sabates-Wheeler, Rachel, and Keetie Roelen. 2011. "Transformative Social Protection Programming for Children and their Carers: A Gender Perspective." *Gender & Development* 19(2): 179–94.

Sandberg, Johan, and Engel Tally. 2015. "Politicisation of Conditional Cash Transfers: The Case of Guatemala." *Development Policy Review* 33(4): 503–22.

Smith, Carol A. 1988. "Destruction of the Material Basis of Indian Culture: Economic Change in Totonicapán." In *Harvest of Violence: The Maya Indians and the Guatemalan Crisis*, ed. Robert S. Carmack, 206–31. Norman: University of Oklahoma Press.

———, ed. 1990a. *Guatemalan Indians and the State: 1540 to 1988*. Austin: University of Texas Press.

———. 1990b. "Introduction: Social Relations in Guatemala over Time and Space." In *Guatemalan Indians and the State, 1540 to 1988*, ed. Carol A. Smith, 1–30. Austin: University of Texas Press.

Sullivan, Noelle, and Nicole S. Berry. 2017. "Good Intentions and Murky Ethics." *Anthropology News* 58(6): e61–e67.

Vasquez del Aguila, Ernesto. 2006. "Invisible Women: Forced Sterilization, Reproductive Rights, and Structural Inequalities in Peru of Fujimori and Toledo." *Estudos e Pesquisas em Psicologia* 6(1): 109–24.

Warren, Kay B. 1998. *Indigenous Movements and their Critics: Pan-Maya Activism in Guatemala*. Princeton: Princeton University Press.

Weismantel, Mary J. 2001. *Cholas and Pishtacos: Stories of Race and Sex in the Andes*. Chicago: University of Chicago Press.

World Bank. 2009. "Project Appraisal Document on a Proposed Loan in the Amount of US $114.5 Million to the Republic of Guatemala for the Expanding Opportunities for Vulnerable Groups Project." Washington DC: World Bank.

Younging, Gregory. 2018. *Elements of Indigenous Style: A Guide for Writing by and about Indigenous Peoples*. Edmonton: Brush Education, Inc.

Part II

GENDER, EDUCATION, AND THE ASPIRATION FOR AUTONOMY

Chapter 5

ACTIVE WAITHOOD

YOUTHMEN, FATHERHOOD, AND MEN'S EDUCATIONAL ASPIRATIONS IN SIERRA LEONE

Kristen E. McLean

Introduction

African conceptualizations of "waithood" refer to youth living in a period of suspension between childhood and adulthood, essentially "stuck" (Sommers 2012) or "waiting for adulthood" (Honwana 2014: 29). This phenomenon refers to the challenges associated with transitions to adulthood, as African youth struggle to find a stable living in order to marry, build homes, and support their families. Theorists like Honwana (2012, 2014) and Sommers (2012) argue that these challenges stem from a context of social and economic crisis driven by failed neoliberal economic policies, poor governance, and political instability that have left young Africans largely jobless.

In West Africa, the term *youthmen* has emerged to describe men living in this liminal position—those who have failed to attain adulthood despite their biological age (Momoh 1999; Utas 2005). Of note, like the term "youth," which is overwhelmingly used in African settings in reference to men (Shepler 2010), the same holds for the concept of *youthmen* (Mabala 2011). The term refers to men who have "outgrown youth" chronologically but not socially, men who look like adults but are not yet accepted by society as such (Utas

2005: 150). In Sierra Leone, an economic crisis, propelled by the country's decade-long civil war (1991–2002) and recent Ebola epidemic (2014–15), has made it exceedingly difficult for young men to afford to marry and establish households, key markers of social adulthood. For many, remaining single or engaging in informal relationships while awaiting employment is preferable to enduring the humiliation of not being able to provide for a family (Enria 2016).

Unlike notions of waithood in the Middle East and North Africa (Dhillon and Yousef 2009; Singerman 2007), which convey a sense of passively "waiting," African conceptualizations of waithood have been described as more dynamic. As Honwana argues, African youth in waithood "are not inactively lingering and waiting" but are "dynamic and use their agency and creativity to invent new forms of being and interacting with society" (2014: 30). Rather than remaining idle, African youth are improvising forms of livelihood in the informal economy, building social networks, and actively planning for their futures (Finn and Oldfield 2015; Gilbert 2018; Masquelier 2013; Vigh 2009). As this chapter demonstrates, young men are particularly invested in planning and striving for educated futures in preparation for a better life, a productive endeavor that I refer to as "*active waithood.*"

For many young Sierra Leoneans, education is a highly valued life goal, for it is seen as a way to escape poverty and obtain a better future (Betancourt et al. 2008). Though it does not guarantee employment, if often allows one to earn enough income to enable a happy, fulfilling life (Collier 2012). For many, education has also been associated with a return to normalcy following the social upheaval caused by the war (Zuilkowski and Betancourt 2014). Despite its appeal, however, pursuing an education in the postwar context is an experience fraught with challenges. First, men are becoming fathers at young ages. Unlike other contexts where men experience waithood, in West Africa it does not necessarily apply to childbearing (Utas 2005). Indeed, it is common for men in Sierra Leone to engage in sexual relations and have children outside of wedlock, though it is socially frowned upon. Men's ability to continue their education after becoming a father is often prohibited by their economic circumstances, made more precarious by the demands of fatherhood. Another challenge has been the interruptions to schooling men have faced due to the war and, more recently, the Ebola epidemic, which have threatened a meaningful sense of life progress.

Despite these challenges, this chapter demonstrates that many young men still hold out hope of continuing their education, either by planning their own return to school or transferring their educational aspirations onto their children. In what follows I show that, despite their categorization as *youthmen*, young Sierra Leonean men are not inactively resigned to waiting. Nor are they resigned to focusing on the "here and now," in contrast to what others have observed about African youth in waithood (Honwana 2012: 30). Rather, planning for and pursuing an education for many provides a sense of forward life momentum, demonstrating a type of "active waithood." For them, education embodies hope for a more secure future and supplies a means for garnering dignity and respect that propels them closer to adulthood.

Sierra Leone: A Brief History

Between 1991 and 2002 Sierra Leone was engaged in a brutal civil war that resulted in fifty thousand deaths, the displacement of two million citizens, and the destruction of the majority of the country's infrastructure (Human Rights Watch 2003). A rebel movement emerged under the banner of the Revolutionary United Front (RUF), which captured approximately 80 percent of the countryside and later occupied the capital of Freetown. The various factions, including the Sierra Leone Army and Civil Defense Forces, in addition to the RUF, recruited and abducted children and youth, forcing them to participate in the conflict, in which thousands of civilians were systematically raped and tortured (Amowitz et al. 2002).

The social and economic consequences of the war have been devastating. Sierra Leone has important mineral resources, most notably diamonds, but during the war mines were either shut down or seized by rebel forces. Many remain unopen to this day in various states of disrepair. Commercial agriculture, which includes mainly cocoa, coffee, and palm oil exportation, was similarly destroyed. Though the country has come a long way in terms of recovery, poverty levels remain high and indicators of economic and human development are consistently some of the lowest in the world (Wang 2007).

In addition to the devastation wrought by the civil war, Sierra Leone was also severely impacted by the 2014–15 West African Ebola crisis, which resulted in more than fourteen thousand cases and nearly four thousand deaths by the end of the epidemic (WHO 2016). During this time, the country's already weak economy came to a virtual standstill, with GDP plunging from 20.7 percent in 2013 to just 4.2 percent in 2017 (World Bank 2018). Sierra Leone currently ranks 179th out of 188 countries on the Human Development Index, with over half its population of more than seven million living on less than $1.90 per day (UNDP 2018). Unemployment and underemployment characterize 70 percent of the country's population, a large portion of whom are young people between the ages of fifteen and thirty-five (NAYCOM and MYES 2012). In addition to the economy, social sectors including health and education also suffered severely, highlighting underlying fragilities.

Yet, once deemed "The Athens of the West," Sierra Leone has a rich educational tradition and is home to West Africa's first college (Bledsoe 1992). Colonial education was first instituted as a consequence of British Christian missionary bodies in the late nineteenth century. At independence in 1961, Sierra Leone inherited the British-style colonial education system, which was largely aimed at educating civil servants and government administrators and excluded much of the interior of the country (Collier 2012). However, in the 1990s the Education for All movement encouraged the educational system to be more inclusive. The country currently hosts a mixture of government and private schools, the latter generally run by religious organizations.

Sierra Leone's education system was severely impacted by the country's civil war, during which schools were targeted for destruction and many teachers fled the country (MEST 2007). By the late 1990s, an estimated 70 percent of school-aged children had no access to education (MEST 2001), and as a result many students today are several years beyond the typical age for their grades (Betancourt et al. 2008). In the decades following the end of the war, the government has committed to rectifying this situation, as evidenced by the Education Act 2004, which requires all children to complete a basic education (defined as six years of primary school and three years of junior secondary school). Official policies have abolished school fees at the primary level, and more villages now have access to schools. As a result, school enrollments have increased across all levels (MEST 2018), including in tertiary institutions, thanks in part to the establishment of distance education programs (World Bank 2013).

Despite these improvements to the education system, many challenges remain. Though technically primary school is "free," unofficial fees persist, making it difficult for families to afford to send their children to school. The education sector also suffers from poor classroom conditions, overcrowding, unqualified teachers, and a lack of secondary school facilities in some chiefdoms (Wang 2007). As a result, many children do not complete school. At the primary level, the completion rate is around 75 percent, but falls to 40 percent for junior secondary school and just 22 percent for senior secondary school (MEST 2018). Girls, in particular, experience disproportionately high rates of incompletion, especially at the secondary level. This persists despite government efforts to boost female enrollment by providing officially free junior secondary school enrollment to girls in the Northern and Eastern districts (MEST 2007). Factors inhibiting girls' schooling include sexual violence, exploitation from male teachers, and early pregnancy. It is estimated that nearly three out of every ten schoolgirls are excluded from education at some point due to pregnancy (MEST and UNICEF 2016), and rates are thought to have increased during the Ebola epidemic as a result of long-term school closures (MEST 2018).

Research Setting and Methodology

This chapter draws on fifteen months of ethnographic research undertaken between August 2015 and December 2016 in Sierra Leone. The study focused on young fatherhood, masculinity, and family well-being. While education was not the primary focus of this project, the relationship between manhood and *buk lanin* (formal education), as well as the social expectation of fathers to educate their children, emerged organically from conversations with young men. Furthermore, since my research was carried out during the Ebola epidemic (though as it was winding down), when schools, businesses, and other social activities were put on hold, many adults and children were left waiting for their "normal" lives to resume. Thus, in their narratives, men often emphasized the urge to continue schooling.

The research was conducted in the Kono District of Sierra Leone, a diamond mining area in the Eastern part of the country. Kono was heavily impacted by the country's civil war, particularly as rebel groups sought control of its lucrative mines. As a result, Kono struggles with challenges including high rates of poverty and unemployment and limited access to health and social services (SSL and ICF International 2013). Study sites include Koidu Town, Kono's largest urban center, in addition to several nearby towns and villages that were selected based upon either their history of conflict or exposure to Ebola. Located just sixty miles from the epicenter of the outbreak in neighboring Kailahun, individuals living in Kono were severely impacted by the death, destruction, and added stressors associated with the epidemic.

During fieldwork, I lived and worked with a diverse group of fathers and their family members. Participants included 106 fathers, between the ages of eighteen and thirty-nine (based on local definitions of youth), and thirty-nine female partners and other female family members. Men ranged in age, ethnic group, marital status, socioeconomic status, and religious background. While many aspired to jobs in the government, financial, or non-governmental organization sectors, high rates of unemployment often meant that men engaged in whatever work was available, from mining and farming, to petty trading or commercial motorbike riding. Nearly all men were precariously employed and struggled to meet their families' basic needs, regardless of their jobs. Similarly, though many men hoped to complete their secondary degrees or attend one of the country's universities or polytechnic institutes, levels of education ranged considerably (see Table 5.1), and all men struggled financially to obtain what education they did have. Due to the focus of this chapter, the individuals discussed represent a self-identified group of

TABLE 5.1. Sample Characteristics (N=106).

		Number (N)	Percent (%)
Age	18–24 years	26	24.6
	25–31 years	47	44.3
	32–39 years	33	31.1
Religion	Muslim	56	52.8
	Christian	49	46.2
Tribe	Kono	68	64.1
	Other	38	35.9
Relationship Status	Married	36	34.0
	Engaged (*put kola*)	26	24.5
	Girlfriend	30	28.3
	Single	14	13.2
Education	None	6	5.7
	Some primary	10	9.4
	Some junior secondary	21	19.8
	Some senior secondary	56	52.8
	Some college	10	9.4
	Technical school	3	2.8
Employment	Mining	25	23.6
	Trade/vocational work	15	14.2
	Commercial bike riding	15	14.1
	Unemployed	14	13.2
	Farming	13	12.3
	Business/petty trading	12	11.3
	Other	12	11.3

educationally "successful" men—those who prided themselves on their intellect or perseverance and saw education as a means to successful personhood. Study objectives were addressed via semi-structured interviews and life-history narratives, which were carried out in Krio, Sierra Leone's lingua franca. These interviews were audio-recorded, with permission, and translated into English during the transcription phase. Fieldwork also included participant observation and informal interviews with young men and their families in their homes and neighborhoods, worksites, and places of recreation and worship. Fieldwork was accompanied by detailed, handwritten notetaking. In what follows, pseudonyms are used in order to protect participants' confidentiality.

Men's Educational Aspirations

As anthropologists have noted, there is an understanding of education in many African contexts as being "salvational" by leading people toward a better future (Stambach 2010: 372). Despite the reality that formal schooling often does not translate into jobs, many youths continue to approach education as a vital endeavor, full of possibilities (Stambach 2017). In Sierra Leone, youth are migrating to urban areas in vast numbers in order to pursue an education. Their aspirations are humble: to complete secondary school, and for some, to move on to college. Unlike their fathers' generation, young men increasingly see education as important for fostering a successful future, primarily by increasing their chances of securing stable employment in a growing market-driven economy. Education therefore invites the possibility of financially catering for one's family, a crucial marker of manhood and adulthood (Enria 2016). Men also perceived that obtaining an education would provide a more reliable path to security beyond employment. According to one young *okadaman* (commercial motorbike rider), an education is preferable because "bike will finish, money will finish, but education will never finish. You will die with education and live with education; you move with education."

In addition to providing security, the growing value of education mirrors a global shift in gender norms and identities toward a greater concern with personal development and self-actualization. Richards (1996: 138) has written about education in Sierra Leone, for example, as a "passport to modernity" because it inspires hope and access to an imagined "good future" regardless of whether it directly translates to employment. Sierra Leonean men often associate education with a sense of advancement that fosters feelings of pride and self-worth. One man, an unemployed father, explained, "education makes you feel good, like you are someone who has intelligence. Because you have learned, you can be proud in the community. You feel big." Men with an education beyond primary school often boasted that they were "taken seriously" in the community and asked to participate in community leadership roles. Oldenburg (2016) describes a similar phenomenon among men in the Eastern Congo, where education has enabled them to be "intellectual" and "modern," imbuing them with social prestige. Noting that education is a social field that is also inherently political, Stambach (2017: 13) observes that it "discursively empowers people with authoritative responsibility." Importantly, an education can better position people to participate in political decision-making and otherwise contribute to society.

One reason that education may be so highly coveted by youth in Sierra Leone is that it can be incredibly difficult to obtain. The education system in Sierra Leone has been interrupted on numerous occasions over the course of young men's lives, and they expressed frustrations over these multiple setbacks. A further challenge to completing one's education is the often-unwelcome news of pregnancy during one's school-going years, a trend that appears to be on the rise. Though access to contraceptives is slowly improving, until recently it was largely inaccessible outside of major urban centers. In Sierra Leone, pregnant girls are formally banned from attending school (Amnesty International 2015), and young men are also generally expected to drop out in the case of unplanned pregnancy. Further, men are often required to reimburse the girl's family for their lost investment in her education or promise to send her back to school once the child is weaned. The prospects for employment without an education are grim and often require dangerous or socially undesirable work. Thus, many men fear that becoming a father too soon will ruin their futures. However, despite the strains associated with early fatherhood, many men continue to prioritize their educations, often fighting to continue against the odds.

Mark's Story

Mark attended primary school in a small town in Kono known for its lucrative diamond mines. When the war broke out, he and his family fled the town, which became a stronghold for rebel forces in the east. During this time, Mark was fortunate to continue his education by attending various primary schools run by the United Nations, first in Bo, then in Freetown. Eventually he was able to return to Kono to complete secondary school. He explained with pride that in his teenage years he was an avid member of the Literary and Debating Society. He was also proud of his command over the English language; during this time he even earned the nickname Theo, for the thesaurus he always carried in his back pocket.

According to Mark, as he got older, he became influenced by his peers, who took him to nightclubs and introduced him to women. Before he knew it, in his third year of junior secondary school, he had impregnated his new girlfriend. Mark was overcome with worry as to the shame this news would bring his family and how it would impact his education. While many young men in Mark's position are faced with dropping out of school in order to support the mother and child, Mark was fortunate that his family was financially stable and could support him. Still, the stress of having to care for a young child impacted his ability to concentrate on his studies, and though he completed his secondary coursework, he was unable to pass the country's university entrance exams.

Now, at twenty-six years old, Mark is living alone in Koidu and working as a file clerk for a local clinic. His son, currently nine, lives in the village with his mother and her family. Though Mark and the child's mother are no longer a couple, he still visits her often to see his son and provide financial assistance for his food and education. By local standards, Mark is considered lucky to have completed secondary school and obtained employment. However, he yearns to continue his education by attending university. His plans are impeded by his financial state; given his current responsibilities and meager salary, Mark cannot afford the fee to retake the entrance exams. This he describes as one of his biggest challenges:

> I have realized the importance of education, so I have made up my mind to go back to school. I had planned to start this year, but with the commitments I have, the money is not enough. The private WASSCE [West African Senior School Certificate Examination] I want to take costs 600,000 Leones [approximately US $85]. That is what I am fighting for right now, so that I can achieve that step.

When I asked Mark about the obstacles he faced in reaching his goal of attending university, he responded by referring to all of his past circumstances. "I still have the belief that the pregnancy has been one of the root causes for my current struggle," he explained. But

Mark is determined to persevere. He stays at his office after work to meditate on the issue, planning when he will retake the exam and how he will pay for it. He is determined, in part, because he believes a higher level of education will enable him to better care for his child—care in this setting being intricately tied to financial provision. Currently he feels embarrassed at times when he is unable to provide for all of his child's basic needs. Mark also imagines that an advanced education will allow him to "be someone" in the future. Thus, he prepares devotedly for his entrance exams by studying e-books on his phone, for example. "I read, and after every section I take a test, and then I am rated," he explains, "so through that I am still learning, because I want to be part of the [educational] system. If I am not within that system, then I am not prepared to be a man."

For many men like Mark, interruptions to their educations are common over the course of their young lives. Despite their ages and the fact that they have become fathers, many continue to hold out hope of reaching their educational goals. Typically, those who have managed a secondary level of education have done so at a high cost to themselves or their families, and the thought of not being able to complete that education—particularly by passing the WASSCE—can be almost unbearable. Not only will education likely improve their financial circumstances, but it also contributes to a sense of success in and of itself.

Masculinity, Fatherhood, and the Importance of Formal Education

When I arrived at the community center, I quickly found Lamin waiting for me in the courtyard. Lamin had invited me to attend his son Alhaji's graduation from nursery school, and he wanted us to arrive early so he could introduce me to the school's principal, Mr. Sandi. After introducing me to Mr. Sandi and Alhaji's teachers, Lamin led me to our seats near the front of the room, where we waited for the program to start. Eventually, parents began to arrive, with little children trailing behind them, dressed in miniature graduation gowns and caps. The adults (mostly mothers) fussed over their children's outfits and fixed the girls' hair. They set up tables, complete with tablecloths and plastic flowers, and brought out food and drinks—sweet beverages made of rice and milk. Alhaji arrived with his mother (Lamin's ex-girlfriend) and her entire extended family—aunts, grandmothers, siblings, etc. Clearly this was a major social event. Alhaji, who was normally shy around me when I greeted him at his father's shop, bounded right up to me, with a big smile on his face. At Lamin's request, he recited for me the speech he would be giving as part of the graduation ceremony and then ran off to join his friends. I observed Lamin laugh as his son fluttered about the room, full of excitement.

Finally, the program started. The chairman of the event was introduced, and we were led in opening prayers. The school's principal and teachers were introduced next and invited on stage. Then the children came up, one by one, starting with the students in nursery class one. A child would go on stage, deliver a short, rehearsed speech, and then the audience would clap while the student's family rushed onto the stage to hug and praise their child. When it was Alhaji's turn, Lamin was very concerned with filming the performance, his camera up and on right away. And as Alhaji spoke, I watched Lamin's face light up with pride and delight. Following his recitation, Lamin scurried up on stage alongside the other family members to share in his son's celebration. Upon returning to our seats, he immediately showed the video of Alhaji to a friend in the audience, clearly proud of his son's accomplishment.

In Sierra Leone today being a "good" father is directly tied to one's ability to educate—and thus secure life opportunities—for his children (Morrell 2006). Fathers often described provision of education as part of their role to provide for children's basic needs. Because affording school fees can be a challenging endeavor for many in this context, men tend to experience great pride and accomplishment when able to invest in their children's education. For some young men who are unable to continue their own educations due to financial constraints or conflicting social responsibilities, it is through their children's schooling that their future aspirations regarding education, and thus social advancement, can still be achieved.

Lamin's educational journey was one particularly defined by struggle and sacrifice. His father died when he was a baby, and his mother struggled to pay his school fees. Growing up, he often went to school on an empty stomach or was driven from school for not paying tuition. When he was in secondary school, Lamin worked nights as a security guard to help finance his way. He would get home from school each day around 4:00 pm, sleep for two hours, and then head to work. He made a meager salary and hardly slept, but he continued in this way because of his passion for learning.

According to Lamin, the girls at school were attracted to him because of his intellect. They would elicit his help with their schoolwork, and in return they would bring him food and occasionally pay for his books. In his second year of senior secondary school, Lamin's girlfriend became pregnant with Alhaji. Upon learning of the pregnancy, the girl's parents reported him to the Family Support Unit of the local police, and he had to sign a document agreeing to financially support the woman and child. He was also required to refund the girl's family for their losses, due to her interruption in schooling, and to pay to send her back to school. Seven years later, Lamin is still struggling to pay the woman's school fees, despite the fact that she has now left him. "Because I am not working and I do not have much money to satisfy her needs, she decided to break off the relationship," he explained.

To Lamin, education is incredibly important, and though his educational path was wrought with hurdles and he feels unable to continue, he still aspires to pursue an educated future for his son, Alhaji. He explained:

> I even want him to get a standard education more than me. I am praying for that. That is why I am taking the commitment to build him up, because I did not go to nursery school. I only started my education in class one [primary school], but the war affected my education badly. I was on the verge to be promoted to class three in the year 1992 when the war broke out in Sierra Leone, so for eleven years I did not hold a pen, and I did not enter a classroom.

Indicating his dedication to his son's future success, Lamin first enrolled Alhaji in nursery school at just one year old. He is also quite involved in his school affairs, beyond simply paying tuition (toward which, he says, all of his earnings go). "I even asked his teachers to give me their contact numbers so that I can be contacting them about how the child is doing," he said. Lamin works at his mother's store, which is located next to my office space on the main road that runs through Koidu Town, and I would often see him sitting with Alhaji in the evening hours, helping with his math or writing in a little composition book.

It is not uncommon for young fathers in this context to behave like Lamin in terms of their child's education, where both paying school fees and ensuring that children succeed in school are seen as important components of fatherhood. In fact, men are becoming increasingly involved in their children's education by attending school meetings, enforcing study hours, helping their children with homework, or arranging for private tutoring. These trends contradict the "masculinities in crisis" literature (Lindsay and Miescher

2003), which depicts African men as irresponsible and neglectful of children, but they fall in line with new research pointing to changing notions of fatherhood that value intimacy and emotional engagement with children (Smith 2017). These new norms, I argue, provide other ways in which men can support their children as fathers, particularly as they face struggles to provide financially.

Men tend to be highly invested in their children's education for many reasons. One of the main motivations for having children in Sierra Leone is for the "benefit" (namely financial) children are expected to provide their parents and caregivers in old age (Bledsoe 1992). Explained a young farmer named Mohamed:

> I am no longer going to school, so now I want to groom my children. I have had some little education . . . It is just like a plantation. It is now fine for me to plant, and then later, when I have grown old, I will be able to harvest. So, when you have a child and you raise that child well as a father; then, when you are old, he/she too will be able to take care of you.

Thus, investing in a child's education is often seen as an investment in one's future wealth, important in a country without any form of social security for aging adults. But beyond material security, children are also more generally associated with a brighter future, as in "maybe tomorrow the child will become somebody." Importantly, the idea of an educated child with a sound future appealed to men, as they hoped a child's success would reflect positively on themselves. This is certainly the case for Sahr, a 24-year-old father who left school halfway through his senior secondary studies: "Now I have got my child, and if I have money I will send him to school so that even if I am not able to make it in life, he will come and make it and I will get the name, that he is Sahr's son."

In Sierra Leone, men are often able to see themselves in their children, and their children's successes can thus feel like their own. As Morrell (2006) has noted for South Africa, material conditions can constrain how men understand and express fatherhood, resulting in the kind of fatherhood in which one's children become part of one's identity. In this way, fatherhood becomes intertwined with the process by which men come to understand who they are in society. Especially for those who yearned to continue with their own educations but felt unable to do so, investing in a child's education becomes the next best alternative, for it provides a way of "moving forward" with their educational aspirations. Not only do men not want their children to struggle (as they themselves have struggled), but they want to set them up for the best possible chance of success, which will benefit *both* their children and themselves.

Ebola, Containment, and Active Waithood

Because education is so important to one's sense of self and the impression of forward mobility, young men felt incredibly frustrated when schools were closed during the Ebola epidemic. For many, this was the second time that their education had been interrupted for a substantial period of time, the first being during the civil war. Though schools were formally closed for about one year, within some communities it took up to two years before schools were properly functioning again. As one young man explained, "Everybody was scared. Even when they declared schools open again it took some months before children began to go to school because of the fear." Men enrolled in school at the start of the epidemic were suddenly prevented from taking exams and graduating to the next level. This caused them to worry about their future stability and capacity to obtain employment. They further worried that their children would fall behind in school and forget what they had learned. They were also concerned about the personal and social consequences of these academic closures, one man quoting how "an idle mind is the devil's workshop."

Prohibited from working and continuing in their educational aspirations (either for themselves or their children), many men reported experiencing a heightened sense of stagnation during the Ebola period. They commonly reported feeling "stuck" and unable to "go forward." As one man explained:

> During the Ebola period you cannot just get up and say, "I want to go to that neighbor," or you do not just hear about a funeral and go there. We were just stuck. You just stay in one place; you do not go either this way or that. Nobody moves. It tightened us. To always stay in one place like statues is very bad.

Harman (2014) has noted the devastating consequences of school closures during the Ebola epidemic in Liberia. She explains that parents are highly invested in their children's education in this context and that an extended break is seen as interrupting their progress. They hope to raise children who will "enable them to die feeling proud of the accomplishments they achieved as a person and a member of society." Schooling, Harman (2014) further argues, is in part a way to continue living, a way for people to be able to "put something between themselves and a crisis." She notes that, despite official closure of educational organizations, many people in Liberia continued to provide informal instruction to students in private settings. I also found that people in Sierra Leone improvised in the face of school closures.

Osman is one such person. At twenty-seven years old, he lives with his extended family in an amputee camp just outside of Koidu Town, that was built shortly following the end of the war. Osman is an amputee. Despite the difficulties he faced during the war, however, he managed to complete secondary school. When his family fled to Guinea as refugees, he attended a United Nations–run school there. He then returned to Kono, eventually finishing secondary school in 2012. Despite his injury, his family was adamant that he continue schooling so he would not end up having to beg for a living. Osman's mother had encouraged him, saying, "You need to go school; you still have a future. Just because this has happened to you does not mean that your life has come to an end." Fortunately, Osman excelled in school. "I was very smart when I was in school," he told me, "I was always in the top five of my class."

Like his parents, Osman is similarly adamant that his children advance and excel in their education. Given his recent unemployment, he has decided not to pursue a higher education for now so that his family can invest what they have in educating his two young children, currently six and nine years old, one girl and one boy. "I am still proud even though I am unable to continue with education for now," he explained:

> But really things are difficult, and why actually I have suspended the school affairs is because I do not have enough funds to continue my education. I want to continue, but that support is not there. I have two children, and both of them are schooling presently. So instead of saying that I will be responsible for only myself and abandon their affairs and they end up negatively tomorrow, I will carry the blame. So it is better for me to sponsor the children instead of myself.

When schools were closed during the Ebola epidemic, Osman became distressed regarding the interruption to his children's education. He was particularly worried about his daughter's future.

While men tend to have the same educational aspirations for children of either gender, there is often an increased concern about girls as they age. As Osman elaborated:

> In Sierra Leone as a girl child grows to age thirteen or fourteen, when
> her breasts start to project, she will consider herself matured. Then
> she will engage in sexual activities at that early age, and she will get
> pregnant. I want to stand against that. I want her to be focused on
> her education.

In other words, he did not want his daughter to make the same mistake he had made, by having a child during his school-going years.
"But the Ebola time was so hard," he told me. "It stopped people's
freedom of movement. It spoiled the children's schooling. It spoiled
many things." He worried that schools being closed meant that his
children might go astray.

One way in which Osman contributed to the community (and to
the continuing development of his own children) was by volunteering with Handicap International, which was sponsoring a project to
keep children active in learning throughout the epidemic. Though
bans on social gatherings were frequent during the height of the
crisis, they were slowly beginning to lift as the outbreak waned.
During this time, before schools had officially reopened, Osman facilitated classes from his veranda in the camp as part of the program.
Children would come at allotted times by class, and they would sit
together and study what they had learned before the closure of
schools in order to "keep their minds fresh." Osman was given a ra-
dio and batteries so he could benefit from some of the educational
programming that was being aired during this time. In his free time,
he would listen, studiously take notes, and then pass the information he learned along to the students.

Osman enjoyed this work and found it fulfilling, not only because
it allowed his and others' children to "stay fresh," as he put it, but
because it also gave him something valuable to do with his time,
which was especially welcome after months of remaining idle and
confined to his home. Osman required that all the children living in
his compound attend the classes, as he was concerned that they too
not remain idle. By engaging in such activities, he was able to experience a sense of momentum regarding his educational aspirations
for his children. Importantly, he felt less stuck.

In pursuing private classroom instruction, some fathers, like Osman, made the most of a difficult situation. While their children
may not have been formally progressing in school by advancing to
the next class, they were at least not falling further behind. Interestingly other opportunities presented themselves during the Ebola epidemic for men to plan for their children's futures. For marginalized
male youth like Lamin, mentioned above, the Ebola epidemic in-

troduced opportunities for employment that would otherwise have been unavailable. Many young men seized upon these opportunities in order to save money that could later be spent on education once schools reopened.

Generally, these jobs were not ideal and carried with them a significant risk to men's health. Lamin, for example, was hired as a cleaner at an Ebola Treatment Unit. There his responsibilities included cleaning toilets, mopping up vomit, changing patients' dressings, as well as what was referred to as DBM (Dead Body Management), or washing and preparing the bodies of deceased patients. Due to the nature of the risk involved, this work came with the constant fear of infection in addition to stigmatization by peers and neighbors. Though the risk was great and the social consequences discouraging, Lamin decided it was worth it, because he wanted to be able to pay for Alhaji's school fees in the coming year. Importantly, this was Lamin's first salaried job, his first chance to fully support his son without the help of his mother. As he explained, "It was there that I started earning my first money. I was paid three million Leones [approximately US $428 per month] so I was able to take care of my child." This he considered to be a worthy sacrifice, as it helped him to feel that he was contributing productively to his son's future during a period of time when life felt like it had reached a standstill. For other young men like Lamin, these new jobs fostered by the Ebola economy were welcome for similar reasons, namely, that they helped them to be better fathers.

Conclusion

As illustrated in this chapter, young men in Sierra Leone highly value formal education. As a social resource, they associate it with hope and the possibility of a bright future, and as such the pursuit of education may be just as important as its ends (Stambach 2017). Importantly, educational attainment is intricately wound into men's identities and feelings of self-worth; it is linked not only to future employment prospects, but also modernity and a sense of "becoming somebody" (Langevang 2008). Many men, despite becoming fathers at young ages and experiencing interruptions to their educational trajectories, still hold out hope of an educated future—both for themselves and their children. Indeed, if a man is unable to continue his own education, due to financial constraints or conflicting social responsibilities, it is through his children's education that his future aspirations can often still be met. During the Ebola epidemic, men's educational plans were often put on hold, threatening a sense of life progress. However, many young men sought out ways in which to stay mentally "fresh" or actively plan for their educational futures. This, in the context of death and destruction, was a way to continue living (Harman 2014).

In Kono, where traditional paths to adulthood via marriage or home-building are largely inaccessible, education can serve as a means by which men engage in *active waithood*. For those who are unable to complete their own schooling, they recalibrate their aspirations with an eye toward the next generation. Indeed, a child's educational success can serve as a proxy for a father's own success, allowing these men to carve out dignified futures. These findings resonate with Finn and Oldfield's (2015: 38) depiction of young men in Freetown, for whom time spent waiting is neither "empty time" nor a "tired acceptance of social and economic marginalization," but instead an opportunity to innovate and actively plan for the future. Ultimately this research refutes perceptions of African *youthmen* as immobile and unmotivated and emphasizes the agentive ways in which these men strive to succeed not only for themselves but for future generations.

Acknowledgments

Fieldwork for this research benefited from the generous funding of multiple agencies including The National Science Foundation (Grant No. 1528395), the Wenner-Gren Foundation (Grant No. 9216), the Yale MacMillan Center for International and Area Studies, and the Yale Anthropology Department. The author further benefited from dedicated time to write and reflect on this work from a P.E.O. Scholar Award and a Minerva–United States Institute of Peace Scholar Award.

Kristen E. McLean is Assistant Professor in the International Studies Program at the College of Charleston. She recently completed a Peace and Security Fellowship with the United States Institute of Peace. McLean works on issues related to youth, gender, violence, and health in post-conflict and humanitarian settings. Her current book project is an ethnography of fatherhood, masculinity, and family well-being in eastern Sierra Leone. McLean holds a BA and MPH from Emory University and a PhD in anthropology from Yale University.

References

Amnesty International. 2015. *Shamed and Blamed: Pregnant Girls' Rights at Risk in Sierra Leone*. London: Amnesty International Publications.

Amowitz, Lynn L., Chen Reis, Kristina H. Lyons, Beth Vann, Binta Mansaray, Adeyinka M. Akinsulure-Smith, Louise Taylor, and Vincent Iacopino. 2002. "Prevalence of War-Related Sexual Violence and Other Human Rights Abuses Among Internally Displaced Persons in Sierra Leone." *JAMA* 287(4): 513–21.

Betancourt, Theresa S., Stephanie Simmons, Ivelina Borisova, Stephanie E. Brewer, Uzo Iweala, and Maria de la Soudière. 2008. "High Hopes, Grim Reality: Reintegration and the Education of Former Child Soldiers in Sierra Leone." *Comparative Education Review* 52(4): 565–87.

Bledsoe, Caroline. 1992. "The Cultural Transformation of Western Education in Sierra Leone." *Africa* 62(2): 182–202.

Collier, Ebenezer S. 2012. *Primary and Secondary Education in Sierra Leone: An Evaluation of >50 Years of Practices and Policies*. Freetown: Sierra Leonean Writers Series.

Dhillon, Navtej, and Tarik M. Yousef, eds. 2009. *Generation in Waiting: The Unfulfilled Promise of Young People in the Middle East*. Washington, DC: Brookings Institution Press.

Enria, Luisa. 2016. "'I Must Stand Like a Man': Masculinity in Crisis in Post-war Sierra Leone." In *Masculinities Under Neoliberalism*, ed. Andrea Cornwall, Frank G. Karioris, and Nancy Lindisfarne, 136–50. London: Zed Books.

Finn, Brandon, and Sophie Oldfield. 2015. "Straining: Young Men Working Through Waithood in Freetown, Sierra Leone." *Africa Spectrum* 50(3): 29–48.

Gilbert, Julia. 2018. "'They're my Contacts, Not my Friends': Reconfiguring Affect and Aspirations Through Mobile Communication in Nigeria." *Ethos* 83(2): 237–54.

Harman, Eva. 2014. "Schooling, Urgency, and Hope for Movement Ahead of the Ebola Crisis in Liberia: Perspectives from Recent Fieldwork." *Cultural Anthropology Online*, 7 October. Retrieved 10 January 2019 from https://culanth.org/fieldsights/schooling-urgency-and-hope-for-movement-ahead-of-the-ebola-crisis-in-liberia-perspectives-from-recent-fieldwork.

Honwana, Alcinda. 2012. *The Time of Youth: Work, Social Change and Politics in Africa*. Sterling: Kumarian Press.

———. 2014. "'Waithood': Youth Transitions and Social Change." In *Development and Equity: An Interdisciplinary Exploration by Ten Scholars from Africa, Asia and Latin America*, ed. T. Dietz, L. Haan, and L. Johnson, 28–40. Leiden: Brill.

Human Rights Watch. 2003. *"We'll Kill You If You Cry": Sexual Violence in the Sierra Leone Conflict* 15(1A). Retrieved 15 September 2018 from http://www.hrw.org/reports/2003/sierraleone.

Langevang, Thilde. 2008. "'We are Managing!' Uncertain Paths to Respectable Adulthoods in Accra, Ghana." *Geoforum* 39(6): 2039–47.

Lindsay, Lisa A., and Stephan Miescher, eds. 2003. *Men and Masculinities in Modern Africa*. Portsmouth: Heinemann.

Mabala, Richard. 2011. "Youth and 'The Hood': Livelihoods and Neighbourhoods." *Environment and Urbanization* 23(1): 157–81.

Masquelier, Adeline. 2013. "Teatime: Boredom and the Temporalities of Young Men in Niger." *Africa 83*(3): 470–91.

MEST (Ministry of Education, Science and Technology). 2001. *National Education Master Plan*. Freetown: Government of Sierra Leone.

———. 2007. *Sierra Leone Education Sector Plan: A Road Map to a Better Future, 2007–2015*. Freetown: Government of Sierra Leone.

———. 2018. *Education Sector Plan 2018–2020—Getting is Right: Service Delivery, Integrity and Learning in Sierra Leone*. Freetown: Government of Sierra Leone.

MEST (Ministry of Education, Science and Technology) and UNICEF. 2016. *Sierra Leone—A National Assessment of the Situation of Out-of-School Children in Sierra Leone*. Freetown: Government of Sierra Leone.

Momoh, Abubakar. 1999. "The Youth Crisis in Nigeria: Understanding the Phenomena of the Area Boys and Girls." Conference on Children and Youth as Emerging Categories in Africa, 4–6 November, Leuven, Belgium. 4–6 November.

Morrell, Robert. 2006. "Fathers, Fatherhood and Masculinity in South Africa." In *Baba: Men and Fatherhood in South Africa*, ed. Linda Richter and Robert Morrell, 13–25. Cape Town: HSRC Press.

NAYCOM (National Youth Commission) and MYES (Ministry of Youth Employment and Sports). 2012. *Sierra Leone Youth Report 2012: Youth Development*. Freetown: Government of Sierra Leone.

Oldenburg, Silke. 2016. "'I Am an Intellectual': War, Youth, and Higher Education in Goma (Eastern Congo)." *AnthropoChildren* 6. Retrieved 11 April 2019 from https://popups.uliege.be/2034-8517/index.php?id=2489.

Richards, Paul. 1996. *Fighting for the Rainforest: War, Youth and Resources in Sierra Leone*. Oxford: James Currey.

Shepler, Susan. 2010. "Post-war Trajectories for Girls Associated with the Fighting Forces in Sierra Leone." In *Gender, War, and Militarism: Feminist Perspectives*, ed. Laura Sjoberg and Sandra Via, 91–101. Santa Barbara: Praeger.

Singerman, Diane. 2007. "The Economic Imperatives of Marriage: Emerging Practices and Identities Among Youth in the Middle East." *Middle East Youth Initiative*, Working Paper No. 6, September, The Brookings Institution, Wolfensohn Center for Development, Washington, DC.

Smith, Daniel J. 2017. *To Be a Man Is Not a One-Day Job: Masculinity, Money, and Intimacy in Nigeria*. Chicago: University of Chicago Press.

Sommers, Marc. 2012. *Stuck: Rwandan Youth and the Struggle for Adulthood*. Athens: University of Georgia Press.

Stambach, Amy. 2010. "Education, Religion, and Anthropology in Africa." *Annual Review of Anthropology* 39: 361–79.

———. 2017. "Student Futures and the Politics of Possibility: An Introduction." In *Anthropological Perspectives on Student Futures: Youth and the Politics of Possibility*, ed. Amy Stambach and Kathleen D. Hall, 1–16. New York: Palgrave Macmillan.

SSL (Statistics Sierra Leone) and ICF International. 2013. *Sierra Leone Demographic and Health Survey 2013*. Freetown, Sierra Leone and Rockville, Maryland.

UNDP (United Nations Development Programme). 2018. *UNDP Sierra Leone 2017 Annual Report: The Next Phase of Development*. Freetown: UNDP Sierra Leone.

Utas, Mats. 2005. "Building a Future? The Reintegration and Remarginalization of Youth in Liberia." In *No Peace, No War: An Anthropology of Contemporary Armed Conflicts*, ed. Paul Richards, 137–54. Athens: Ohio University Press.

Vigh, Henrik. 2009. "Youth Mobilization as Social Navigation: Reflections on the Concept of Dubriagem." *Cadernos de Estudos Africanos* 18/19: 140–64.

Wang, Lianquin. 2007. *Education in Sierra Leone: Present Challenges, Future Opportunities*. Washington, DC: World Bank.

World Bank. 2013. *Republic of Sierra Leone: Higher and Tertiary Education Sector Policy Note*. Washington, DC: World Bank.

———. 2018. *GDP Growth (Annual percent)*. Retrieved 15 September 2018 from https://data.worldbank.org/indicator/NY.GDP.MKTP.KD.ZG.

WHO (World Health Organization). 2016. *Ebola Situation Report—30 March 2016*. Geneva: WHO.

Zuilkowski, Stephanie S., and Theresa S. Betancourt. 2014. "School Persistence in the Wake of War: Wartime Experiences, Reintegration Supports, and Dropout in Sierra Leone." *Comparative Education Review* 58(3): 457–81.

Chapter 6

"GIVING ONESELF TIME"
MARRIAGE AND MOTHERHOOD IN URBAN RWANDA

Aalyia Feroz Ali Sadruddin

Introduction

I first met 32-year-old Chrisie Umutoni through our mutual friend
John Rusagara in New Haven, Connecticut, in the spring of 2016.[1]
While Chrisie was in the process of completing a two-month internship in internal medicine at the Yale School of Medicine, I was in
the midst of preparing to move to Rwanda to conduct fieldwork for
my PhD. As a graduate student from Kenya studying in the United
States, I was always eager to connect with fellow Africans abroad.
Chrisie and I clicked immediately, something John had predicted
when he introduced us to each other. "You two ladies have to connect because *muri impanga* (you are twins)! You are both obsessed
with school, take life way too seriously, and are definitely going to
get married late." Even though Chrisie and I did not refrain from
giving John a hard time about his self-proclaimed "brotherly judgments," we knew well what he meant. After all, we were two single
East African women in our late twenties who were pursuing advanced degrees. Although we had certainly thought about marriage,
it was not a priority, at least for the time being. Nor was it something
that looked like an immediate possibility. "So much has to happen
in my professional life before I start looking for a man," said Chrisie

during our conversation. "I do not want to get married in haste. I just have to trust that all of those things will happen. For now, I have to focus on finishing my specialization."

Chrisie had ambitions. She had wanted to become a medical doctor since she was a child. Excellent grades at the end of her high-school career granted her the opportunity to attend the University of Rwanda to pursue a bachelor's degree in medicine. She credited her Kenyan mother and Rwandan father as her primary sources of inspiration. Despite her determination to advance further in her education and professional life, she could not help but wonder whether she was living her life in the "right" or "wrong" way. She explained:

> You know how it is. We can get educated and have careers but there is still some kind of judgment from our families and people in our communities. But I feel like things for some young women [like us] are changing at home. People are seeing that they cannot just put us in one box. We can put ourselves in different boxes. Do I want to find my dream man and give birth to beautiful children? Of course I do. I also want to finish this final year at school and travel to Zanzibar, my dream destination.

As a Rwandan-Kenyan who had twice traveled to the United States to receive additional training as a medical student, Chrisie was aware of her privileged position and the freedom she had to make her own professional and personal decisions. Although her parents, with whom she lived in Mwogo, Bugesera (located in Rwanda's eastern province), were not members of Rwanda's economic elite, they invested whatever resources they had toward educating Chrisie and her younger sister, Yvette. "Different women have to deal with different expectations and pressures. This is why women like us who have the chance to change things up a little should go for it! I want young African girls to look at other African women for inspiration." The almost five-hour tête-à-tête about education, marriage, womanhood, and everything in between that I had with Chrisie in 2016 was the first of many. As contemporary social norms go, we became friends on Facebook and met each other frequently when I was in Kigali, Rwanda's capital, during the course of my fieldwork. Her mother and father, who took much interest in my research on aging and late-life care practices, became my surrogate parents, and through me, cultivated a long-distance friendship with my parents in western Kenya. Today, Chrisie works as an internal medicine specialist at King Faisal Hospital in Kigali, the largest referral hospital in Rwanda. In December 2018, she traveled to Zanzibar.

In this chapter, I examine how young women negotiate their womanhood by "giving themselves time" in the wake of sweeping transformations in norms around marriage, education, and gender roles in contemporary Rwanda. In this context, the Kinyarwandan notion of *kwiha igihe* means "giving oneself time." *Kwiha igihe* can be understood as a liminal period in which young women belonging to a particular professional segment of Rwandan society find themselves as they contemplate marriage and motherhood. As I argue, the period of giving oneself time is a deeply reflective process, something that women in this phase of life deal with individually and collectively. It is a time for women to generate solidarity with other women and to figure out their next steps. Importantly, women view this in-between period as a privilege: they are conscious that their education and economic independence provide them a degree of flexibility to engage in complex debates about what it means to be women in Rwanda today. Despite its current exclusivity, this period of liminality is something that the women, whose stories inform this chapter, hope will become a more common phenomenon in Rwanda (and in Africa more broadly) as more young women get educated.

I divide this chapter into two sections. In the first section, I explore the predicaments of Rwandan women, who are under immense pressure to "rise up" as innovators and as leaders due to increased investment on behalf of the government in their advancement. Coupled with these pressures are varying uncertainties about how to follow in the footsteps of women from earlier generations who rebuilt Rwanda in the aftermath of the 1994 genocide, hold on to their jobs in the city, and economically support their families. In the second section, I discuss women's perspectives on marriage and motherhood.

Women in Post-genocide Rwanda: A Brief Description of the Context

Rwanda is a country in central East Africa that is bordered by Uganda, Tanzania, Burundi, and the Democratic Republic of Congo. Most people who have heard of Rwanda have likely done so because of the 1994 genocide that took place there between two of the country's three ethnic groups: the Hutu and the Tutsi. With an estimated total of one million deaths of Tutsi and politically moderate Hutu in one hundred days, the Rwandan genocide has been widely acknowledged as the most efficient conflict in modern history (Des Forges 1999; Prunier 1995).[2] The genocide left an indelible mark on Rwandan society, rupturing the fabric of social, economic, and family life. Most of the people who were killed during the genocide were Tutsi men. In addition, Hutu men who were perpetrators during the conflict were either imprisoned or fled to neighboring nations. The stark absence of men translated into 54 percent of Rwanda's post-genocide population being comprised of women, who in both rural and urban areas took on a range of challenging tasks in an attempt to rebuild the country (Hunt 2017; Newbury and Baldwin 2000; Zraly, Rubin, and Mukamana 2013).[3] For example, in rural areas, women mobilized and formed support groups as they cleaned streets, buried bodies, and raised orphaned children. It is estimated that one hundred thousand children became orphans as a result of the genocide, with many suffering from a broad range of mental and physical wounds (Kuehr 2015; Veale and Quigley 2000). In urban areas, women joined the government, seeking to establish a sense of stability and normalcy from the top down (Karp and Banducci 2008; Powley 2003).

Twenty-five years after the genocide, the visibility of women across all spheres of Rwandan society is striking. Changes in the 2003 constitution, which instituted a 30 percent quota for women in elected positions, have resulted in Rwanda having the highest percentage—64 percent—of women in parliament in the world (Abbott and Malunda 2016; Atkeson and Carrillo 2007). Outside the political realm, the post-genocide Rwandan constitution also stipulates that, in addition to having inheritance rights in their birth family, women can also inherit land from their husbands (Burnet 2011). One of the key architects of women's equality is incumbent president Paul Kagame. Popularly referred to as "Africa's feminist president," Kagame has been adamant about the involvement and advancement of Rwandan women within and outside of government.

I should note that policies and debates about women in Rwanda have not gone without criticism. Critics of Kagame's government argue that moves to integrate women into public office have more to do with generating international investment than with addressing more pressing issues, such as poverty and political oppression, which are pervasive in Rwanda (Berry 2015; Burnet 2008; Reyntjens 2004; Straus and Waldorf 2011; Thomson 2018). Although aspects of this literature raise key points about the challenges related to the politics of womanhood and gender in contemporary Rwanda, they are not the focus of this chapter. Instead, I turn my attention to the challenges and contradictions of urban-dwelling women, like my friend Chrisie, who have benefited from education and training initiatives instituted by the Rwandan government and international development agencies. As I illustrate, these women are under increased pressure from society to rise up, to innovate, and to become leaders in their respective fields. In addition to being the primary breadwinners for their families, they are burdened with the legacy of the women from previous generations—their grandmothers, mothers, and aunties—who raised them with limited resources and who helped to rebuild Rwanda after the genocide. Older women's achievements are sources of inspiration and anxiety. Simply put, failure to maintain a certain level of excellence and economic autonomy in their professional lives has cascading effects on the lives of young Rwandan women. As a result, many seek to give themselves time before making decisions to get married and to become mothers.

Fieldwork with Young Women

Rwanda has been the primary locus of my research since 2014. Even though my research focuses on aging and late-life care practices in urban and rural Rwanda, I had numerous opportunities to speak with young women from different social, economic, and educational backgrounds during the course of my fieldwork. In fact, I spent a substantially larger amount of time at the beginning of my research with younger women than I did with elderly persons, my primary interlocutors, who worried that I would "get bored" if I was in their presence for too long. Elderly persons frequently introduced me to young women at community meetings and church services who were close to me in age, encouraging us to share our life experiences with one another. Some elderly persons in rural areas who had grandchildren or other family members living and working in Kigali also introduced me to them. These connections became crucial, establishing a strong level of trust between me and my interlocutors.

I would also not have been able to conduct research with young women in the way I did if it were not for my friendship with Chrisie. Given that we had become good friends and that she had made me a member of one of her WhatsApp chat groups, "The KGL XX Squad," I had privileged access into her and her friends' worlds as an anthropologist while simultaneously being able to be an active member of the group. In addition, being a member of this chat group translated into my getting invited to various social events, which ranged from private hangouts at friends' homes to public gatherings at coffee shops, markets, music shows, and nightclubs whenever I was in Kigali. The fact that I was single, from East Africa, and still a student cultivated a sense of shared identity between the young women and me. Even though I was an "outsider," in many senses, the uncertainties I was experiencing—especially with respect to my personal and professional life—mirrored those of the young women with whom I worked. This theme came through poignantly across my interviews. As Chrisie told me during our first meeting: "turi bamwe, abanyamashuli batarashyingirwa" (we are the same, educated but unmarried). Furthermore, I appreciated the ways in which this group of women engaged with me about my research. For example, many challenged me to think more critically about its purpose and "realness." All in all, my conversations with these women felt like shared therapy sessions. In this chapter, I draw on interviews that I conducted with twenty-two women from this group between June 2016 and September 2017 (refer to Table 6.1 for additional demographic information).

Fears of Failing and Pressures of Living in KGL

Kigali, or KGL as young women called it, was becoming an increasingly vibrant city. The multifaceted transformation of Kigali as Rwanda's capital and as an African city afforded them various opportunities to interact with people from across Africa and the world. All of these women, for example, attended a range of youth summits hosted in Kigali, received opportunities to travel (either to countries within or outside of Africa), and underwent additional educational and professional training in the city. As Juliette, a 29-year-old urban planner who was born in Byumba (a town in northern Rwanda) and who had studied at the University of Rwanda, told me, "This place makes me want to keep improving. I like that I can apply my skills and meet people from different countries. I feel like I am helping to build something. Things here are not easy but the vibe and the hustle is exciting."

Despite the relative economic security that this group of women enjoyed, as a result of having an academic diploma or degree, life in the city was far from easy. Both *abakobwa bavukiye mu mujyi* (women born in the city) and *abakobwa bavukiye mu cyaro* (women born out-

TABLE 6.1 Demographic Information of Young Women Interviewed for this Research.

Inter-view	Birthplace	Age	Profession	Living arrangement	Relationship status
1	Musanze, Rwanda	32	Data analyst	Living as a paying guest	In a three-year relationship
2	Nyagatare, Rwanda	28	Research assistant	Renting a house with three women	Recently engaged
3	Bujumbura, Burundi	29	Medical doctor	Living as a paying guest	Single
4	Kigali, Rwanda	31	Research assistant	Living with family of six	Dating for six months
5	Kigali, Rwanda	32	International development	Living with family of eight	Recently engaged
6	Kigali, Rwanda	25	Researcher: Ministry of Health	Living with family of six	Single
7	Kinshasa, DRC	27	Young women's start-up	Living as a paying guest	Recently broken up
8	Muhanga, Rwanda	28	Program manager at a German-headed NGO	Living as a paying guest	In a two-year relationship
9	Gisenyi, Rwanda	29	IT consultant	Renting a house with four women	Recently engaged
10	Johannesburg, South Africa	31	Researcher at UNICEF (United Nations Children's Emergency Fund)	Living with family of five	Dating for eight months

11	Gisenyi, Rwanda	27	Barista and concept designer	Renting a house with three sisters	Single
12	Nairobi, Kenya	32	Medical doctor	Living as a paying guest	Single
13	Huye, Rwanda	34	Medical doctor	Renting a house with one woman	Engaged for one year
14	Byumba, Rwanda	28	Lawyer	Living alone	Recently broken up
15	Kibungo, Rwanda	29	Urban planner	Renting a house with three women	Single
16	Kampala, Uganda	30	Architect	Living with maternal aunt	No time to date (for now)
17	Brussels, Belgium	31	Trainee at Belgian Embassy	Living with mother's extended family	Single
18	Kampala, Uganda	35	Vice-manager at a local bakery, baby-sitter, cook	Living in a house with three siblings	Single
19	Kigali, Rwanda	34	Accountant at a five-star hotel	Living alone	In a five-year relationship
20	Muhanga, Rwanda	31	Completing PhD in Public Health	Living in a house with five women	Single
21	Huye, Rwanda	32	Teacher at a private school in Kigali	Living alone	Dating for three months
22	Kampala, Uganda	33	Artist and designer	Living with family of three	Preparing to get married

side the city) acknowledged that Kigali was not for everyone. Recurring through my interviews were stories of young women from rural areas who had come to the city with the hopes "of doing something" but who left the city feeling disillusioned due to the challenges associated with finding sustainable employment. The fact that this particular group of women had either acquired a bachelor's degree or other academic diploma and were able to find jobs made them increasingly conscious of their situations. They were *abanyamahirwe* (the lucky ones). Success in finding jobs, however, did not mean that women took their situations for granted. "It is not easy to find and then hold on to a good job," said 31-year-old Clarisse, who, at the time of our interview, had been working as a trainee at the Belgian Embassy for four months. As a result, having a good job added more pressure on women to perform and to advance professionally, since society regarded them as the next generation of women who had the potential to "take Rwanda to the next level." Joline, twenty-nine years old, articulated this theme clearly in her interview:

> Have you seen the women in our government? They are doing so much! They are our role models. And I know that some people who visit Rwanda think our woman are just for show, but I do not think that. It is nice to see women work like that. Sometimes my friends and I talk about whether we will be able to bring it like those women, you know? I hope we will not be the generation that just messes everything up.

She continued by saying:

> I want to be good at my job and make sure that I can stand as an example to other young Rwandans. We still have many children who are not getting the schooling they deserve. This is why those of us who have jobs have to work hard because not everyone in our country is in our situation. Even if I wanted to get married, I would have to have money. Life without work is very difficult because everything is so expensive.

The prospect of unemployment triggered a deep sense of fear and uncertainty in the minds of women. For them, failing in the city was not an option. They had to be *abakobwa bashikamye* (tough women).

Another key reason that women feared failing in the city was because of the extent to which their families depended on them. All of them were either primary or partial breadwinners, contributing various amounts of their income to their family members. Additional economic responsibilities included women purchasing school items for their siblings, paying for medication for their family members, and contributing to the rent of their families' homes. Take Beatrice's case, for example: at thirty-five years old, she had worked very hard to become an assistant manager at one of Kigali's most popular bakeries. Her mother, who was sickly, lived in Kampala, Uganda, where Beatrice was born. Her father had died when she was an infant. As the oldest child in her family, she was responsible for taking care of three of her younger siblings with whom she lived in a small one-bedroom house that she rented for 150,000 Rwandan Francs (roughly US $170) per month. In order to earn an extra income, Beatrice worked as a babysitter-cum-cook for three European families. She used a portion of the salaries she received from both of her jobs to pay her rent and to purchase food and other necessary supplies for her siblings. The other portion of her salary went directly to her mother. She explained why she did this:

> I am not here for myself but for my family. Life in Kigali is not easy. This is why I have to work the extra jobs. Because I grew up in Uganda, I was able to learn good English and get a bachelor's degree in business administration. This degree has helped me a lot. I want to do another degree, but for now I have to take care of my family. I cannot afford to be careless.

Kigali was also an increasingly expensive city. "The city knows how to take from us," said Clementine, a 32-year-old, who worked as a substitute teacher at a private school in Kigali and lived in a studio apartment. She went on to say, "Things do not get cheaper. We have to eat, pay rent, and also help our families. Our money is not ours." These sentiments were not specific to Clementine. All of the women—including the four who were born and lived with their families in Kigali—expressed anxieties about the expensive nature of the city. As indicated in Table 6.1, most of the women either rented houses in neighborhoods outside the city center where rent prices were more affordable or lived as paying guests with family friends. In addition to splitting the cost of rent, women who lived with other women also shared food and clothes as a way of saving money. They all either walked or commuted to work via public transport. Only two women's families owned a car, which they shared. Women who lived as paying guests also carried out various household tasks, such as cooking, cleaning, and shopping for food, in the homes in which they lived. Avoiding these tasks was not an option, as doing so would reflect negatively on their parents, especially their mothers, who would be blamed for not instilling them with good values and a sense of respect. Although women did not necessarily mind fulfilling these tasks, they mentioned feeling over-whelmed about juggling their personal and professional obligations. Being educated or having jobs did not exempt them from perform-ing what they described as "home tasks." Even in the cases where women did not carry out these tasks, either because they had house helpers or other (typically younger female) family members who took them on, the basic societal expectation was that they know how to cook, clean, and run their homes. Fears of failing and pres-sures that came with living in Kigali meant that these women, even if they were dating or in long-term relationships, did not feel ready to get married. They needed more time.

Kwiha Igihe: Giving Oneself Time

Kwiha igihe (giving oneself time) was how young women described their current phase of life. As I came to understand it, this period of liminality was a time for women to take stock of their current situations and to prepare for their futures. It was a busy and chal-lenging time in which women were working and supporting their natal families. To be clear, women in this phase of life did not view themselves as girls but as women. Marie, a 28-year-old lawyer who had recently broken up with her boyfriend of two years, described this phase as a "middle period":

> I guess I understand this time as that which comes after university but before the marriage period. Does that make sense? Even though I am no longer with my ex, I have this time to decide what I want to do next. I want to get married and have children but feel like I need to make sure that I am ready. So, for now, I am just working, meeting with my friends, and planning for my future.

The process of giving themselves time, therefore, allowed women to prepare for *inshingano z'ubuzima* (real-life responsibilities), pri-marily marriage and motherhood. As a result, *kwiha igihe* is elemen-tal in that it allows women to effectively plan for their futures on their own terms. None of the women wanted to make rash deci-sions that would have a negative impact on their lives or those of their family members. This "after university but before marriage pe-riod" (to borrow Marie's phrase), despite its emotional difficulties and economic responsibilities, was viewed as a privilege. "Not every

Rwandan woman has this time to just focus on their own hustle," emphasized Marie. In this regard, giving oneself time was an active period. Women were constantly trying to improve, whether by acquiring new skills in their professions or by thinking of alternative ways in which they could assist their families. Work was a dominant characteristic of this phase of life, as Uwase explained:

> This time is all about work. We are not just working alone but also with other women. I feel strong when I look around and see women working hard and trying to support their families and help advance the country. Working and sending money home makes me feel like I have value as a daughter and citizen of Rwanda seriously.

What I describe as *kwiha igihe* in Rwanda resonates with Alcinda Honwana's concept of *liggey* in Senegal. In Wolof, *liggey* means "work" and is a celebrated marker of adulthood. The ability to work and to provide for oneself and others defines a person's self-worth and position in the family and community (Honwana 2013). At its core, work is intertwined with dignity. Without work, there is no dignity. As Honwana explains, the absence of work results in many young people in Senegal and elsewhere in Africa experiencing "waithood." With respect to my research, the work that young Rwandan women carried out and the ways in which they socially and economically supported their families infused them with a deep sense of pride and responsibility. Work made them feel "useful" and "needed."

Giving oneself time also involved women coming together to form support groups with each other. Friendship was a crucial component of this phase of life. All of the women I interviewed belonged to a strong group of friends with whom they met and kept in close contact. Friendships were especially important for women who did not have family members in Kigali who told me that it was difficult to survive in the city without some form of social and emotional support. Even women who lived as paying guests with close or distant relatives, as well as those who lived with family, emphasized the centrality of friendship. Friends were another form of family for women. Physically meeting friends or chatting with them on WhatsApp afforded women opportunities to talk and to exchange information on issues such as work, family, money, relationships, and marriage. Further, being a part of a close group of friends provided women access to spaces in which they could "be real with each other" and not worry about "having to be perfect all the time." In Chrisie's words, "my friends are my other family. There are times when I get tired and wonder whether all of this effort to be excellent is worth it. But then when I see my girls, I feel better. They give me hope."

In her previous research and in her chapter for this edited volume, anthropologist Adeline Masquelier (2013; Chapter 3, this volume) shows that unemployed men in Niger often convene in *fadas* (tea circles) as a way of seeking support and building solidarity. Masquelier argues that this method of coming together is a crucial strategy for men to defy boredom at a time where economic opportunities are hard to come by. There is overlap between my research in Rwanda and Masquelier's research in Niger. Both of our findings show how young people come together to generate kinship, relationality, and solidarity with one another as they strive to make sense of their identities and aspirations in a rapidly changing world. For Rwandan women, coming together at friends' homes, in cafés, or at church was a way for them to motivate and support each other as they strategized about their futures. In contrast to Gilbert's research (2018: 237) in Nigeria, where "women's present realities see them as stuck in the house enduring long periods of time," the Rwandan women I interviewed were not as constrained by physical space. Many, for example, hosted their friends in their small houses where they would share food, exchange clothes, and talk about their problems. The fact that all of the women in my research owned smartphones and had access to the internet (even if only during work hours) also meant that they were able to maintain some level of contact with their circle of friends wherever they were. Many had formed chat groups with names such as "Les Filles," "#XoXo," and "The Crew," in which they updated and exchanged up-to-date information with each other.

While the weight accorded to giving oneself time was pronounced in my interviews, Rwandan women were also conscious of the consequences of giving themselves *too* much time. They did not want to be in this liminal period for the rest of their lives. Even women who were single, or who were not interested in being in relationships during the time of our interviews, revealed their desire to get married and have children one day. However, the social and economic responsibilities that characterized this phase of their lives resulted in them holding off on marriage and motherhood.

Marriage and Motherhood

The women I interviewed explained marriage and motherhood as "real-life responsibilities." As a result, they did not see themselves as *abagore buzuye* (full women). Although none of these women had children outside of wedlock, they knew many educated and non-educated women in this situation. Six out of the twenty-two women, for instance, had siblings who had children prior to marriage. Depending on the circumstance, women who had children but were not married were treated in different ways by society and members of their families and communities. As a medical doctor, Chrisie encountered many cases of this kind:

> I see many women who are pregnant and unmarried. Some of them are very scared because they worry about how they will be able to take care of their children. It is not just uneducated women in the rural areas. The same thing happens with educated and rich women. Rich women are lucky because they do not really need men to pay for things . . . but still . . . their children need fathers too.

She continued:

> In Rwanda, marriage and motherhood are big parts of women's lives and identities. Women in my situation are lucky because we won't take much shit from men, you know? Not all young women are in the same situation. Many of my friends have either left their men or have had their men leave them because of these things. I feel like we forget that marriage and fatherhood are also things that make men *men* [Chrisie's emphasis].

Similar to other countries in sub-Saharan Africa, marriage and parenthood are essential rites of passage for young women and men in Rwanda (Hunter 2010; Lawson 2013; Smith 2014; Zraly et al. 2013). Both are markers of social adulthood. Rwandan women with whom I worked wanted to marry "good men." They were also fearful of divorce. "I do not want a man who comes and goes but a man who stays," said Dominique, who, despite being single at the time of our interview, was not against the idea of marriage. As illustrated in Table 6.1, most of the women in my research were in long-term relationships or had recently started to date. Women in long-term relationships were in the process of preparing to get married, noting that they would do so as soon as they and their partners were able to accrue enough funds.

As I was repeatedly told, getting married was expensive. Marriage was also not an event that took place *just* between a woman and a man. Rather, it was described as a union between families and communities. Therefore, women and their partners had to dedicate a lot of thought and money to the event. For example, some women told me that they and their partners had opened joint bank accounts in which they deposited small amounts of money for their wedding whenever they were able. As Odette, a good friend of Chrisie's told me, "It is not easy, Aal. My people in the village keep telling me that I will be an old mother if me and my man keep waiting to get married, but we cannot do it right now. Everyone will come and drink beer and eat meat, you know?" Odette had been engaged to her fiancé, Olivier, for three years. Although committed to each other, both worried about what would happen to their relationship if they "got late" in getting married and having children. Odette and I became good friends through our common link with Chrisie. On 15 November 2018, she contacted me via WhatsApp to let me know that Olivier proposed to her after getting promoted at work. Her text message to me read: "We have enough money to get married, Aal! We are hoping to get married in March 2019. Will you be here?"

The seriousness that women and their partners attached to marriage led them to attend church services and consult with priests and nuns about how to prepare to be good wives and good husbands. Even though most, if not all, of the women I interviewed were in better economic positions than most Rwandans, none of them wanted to rush into marriage. Waiting to get married was viewed as a privilege. In addition, women acknowledged that they had to find men who were "willing to work with them" or "be patient." The men who were dating or were in long-term relationships with the women with whom I worked were also trying to do something with their lives, as Chrisie explained:

> They also have responsibilities to fulfill. It is not just women who are doing the hard work. Most of my friends who are in relationships are with men who are in the same situation. Sometimes things do not work out, though. Like for me . . . I was in a long relationship, as you know . . . but he wanted to get married and have children very quickly, and I was still in medical school. I did not want to have a baby and then give it to my parents. Even my parents were not too happy with how he behaved, but his mind was set. I do not know if I will find someone like him again, but I hope some fine man will come along soon.

Chrisie's desire to find a "fine man" for future marriage and motherhood was shared by the other single women in the study, even though some were not currently looking for such partners. Women who were single, such as Beatrice for instance, admitted to not wanting to remain "alone for life." Beatrice told me that she was "hopeful that when her time came, she would find her husband." This is despite the fact that she was already considered "old," according to Rwandan standards. Women also noted wanting to be in long marriages, telling me that divorce was tolerable only in the event of physical and emotional abuse. To be clear, the women I interviewed did not view marriage or motherhood as ending their sense of independence, fracturing their friendships, or hindering their professional lives. Rather, they viewed marriage and motherhood as a new phase of their lives.

Waithood in Contemporary Africa: A Shift from Young Men to Young Women

The term "wait adulthood" or "waithood" has emerged as a prominent theme in academic and public discourses about youth and their pathways toward social adulthood globally. Coined by the political scientist Diane Singerman (2007)—whose research in Egypt illustrates that young people remain single for extended periods of time as they are unable to afford the high costs of marriage—academic research on waithood has primarily centered on young men's experiences. This trend is especially pronounced in the social science record from sub-Saharan Africa. Overall, research on waithood from this region paints a rather dismal picture of young people's lives, describing them as being "stuck" in a perpetual state of liminality, which, in most instances, results in "failed" or "incomplete" adulthood (Christiansen, Utas, and Vigh 2006; Hansen 2005; Utas 2005).

The descriptor of "stuckness" is particularly relevant to my research in Rwanda. Introduced by the anthropologist Marc Sommers (2012: 7), the notion of stuckness describes the situation of young Rwandan men who, in the context of mounting social and economic pressures and tight-fisted state economic policies, find it difficult to "become adults in traditionally accepted ways" and to get "recognized as men in Rwandan society." Sommers also argues that men's inability to become adults has a "trickle-down" effect on women, who, as a result of being dependent on men, are themselves unable to assume their place in society as women. While it is true that young men and women across sub-Saharan Africa face a broad range of social, economic, and political challenges in their everyday lives (i.e., unemployment and limited-to-no civil liberties), more research on the gendered nature of these realities is required.

Social science literature on youth living in urban and rural Africa has evolved considerably in recent years. Rather than assess youth realities and futurities from a vantage point of "social death" (Christiansen et al. 2006; Vigh 2006), social scientists, including anthropologists, have increasingly started to examine the dynamic ways in which young African men (and, to some extent, women) are navigating the rapidly evolving social, economic, and political landscapes of the countries in which they live (Honwana 2013; Pike, Mojola, and Kabiru 2018). For example, in his extensive research with young men in Guinea-Bissau, anthropologist Henrik Vigh (2016: 224) emphasizes how, in a country confounded by decades of civil strife, young men make morally complex decisions in order to "gain better lives for themselves and their families." Similarly, Juliet Gilbert (2018) reveals how young women in Nigeria, who are often restricted by failing institutions, family and church pressures, and the fear of others' jealousy, form friendships with others through their mobile phones and BlackBerries. Drawing from literature on youth, time, and productivity (Jeffrey 2010; Masquelier 2013), Gilbert demonstrates how the ownership of cell phones affords women crucial opportunities to form social relations and develop friendships across multiple spaces.

Despite the emergence of this new literature, women's experiences of waithood remain understudied (Cole 2016; Gilbert 2018; Mojola 2014; Smith 2009 are notable exceptions). African feminists, such as Nigerian author Chimamanda Ngozi Adichie and Zimbabwean novelist NoViolet Bulawayo among others, have responded to these gaps in the academic literature, providing rich analyses of the micro- and macro-complexities that characterize African women's everyday lives in the context of dramatic social and economic change across the continent. Through their literature and activism, Adichie (2012) and Bulawayo (2013) have broadened the lens on womanhood in contemporary Africa, moving away from simplistic narratives that have long portrayed African women as subservient, lacking agency, and stymied by structures of patriarchy. By putting African women at the center of their analyses and unapologetically challenging Western stereotypes, their writing has catalyzed a veritable excitement on gender issues, generating fresh perspectives on topics such as work, responsibility, agency, and the place of African women in the world.

I have sought to contribute to these debates in this chapter as a Kenyan woman and anthropologist by showing how young, educated, and urban-dwelling women in Rwanda are trying to strike a balance between their personal and professional lives. On the one hand, they are expected to match the achievements of women from previous generations who by taking on key leadership roles managed to establish normalcy in the country after the genocide. On the other hand, they are expected to fulfill social and cultural obligations by getting married and becoming mothers. Such competing anxieties, as I have shown, cause many young women to reconsider and delay the timing of marriage. By focusing on their careers and supporting their families, they attempt to make something of themselves before getting married and becoming mothers.

Conclusion

In this chapter, I have shown how young, educated women in urban Rwanda are prolonging marriage and motherhood by "giving themselves time." Although being educated and having a job in the city distinguishes them from most young Rwandans, these achievements come with a host of expectations from family and society. Therefore, being a young, educated, and employed woman in contemporary Rwanda requires determination and discipline. As a result, Rwandan women immerse themselves in particular forms of decision-making, self-reflection, and friendships as they strategize about their futures. While the women whose perspectives and experiences inform this chapter do not paint a general picture of womanhood in contemporary Rwanda, they illustrate how women who have acquired some level of education and who, compared to the majority, are economically stable, strive to make the transition to full adulthood. They frequently ask themselves questions such as: Are we doing things the right or wrong way? Have we put "real life" on hold for too long because of education? What will happen to us if we do not get married or birth children? Will people think of us as women who do not care about our ideals and values? The anxieties embedded in these questions are not specific to young women in Rwanda. As indicated in other chapters in this edited volume, women are grappling with these anxieties globally.

Aalyia Feroz Ali Sadruddin is a PhD candidate in the Department of Anthropology at Yale University. Her research focuses on aging, kinship, and social recovery in post-genocide Rwanda.

Notes

1. Aside from Chrisie, all personal names and nicknames are pseudonyms.
2. The Rwandan genocide of 1994 is officially referred to as the "Genocide against Tutsi." While there is no doubt that Hutu militia specifically targeted Tutsi, politically moderate Hutu were also systematically killed during the conflict. Ethnicity is a complex and controversial topic in Rwanda. In an attempt to transcend ethnic divisions and create a "post-ethnic society," the current government calls for a collective Rwandan identity. (For more information, refer to Eramian 2014.)
3. For more information, see https://www.inclusivesecurity.org/how-women-rebuilt-rwanda/, retrieved 2 February 2020.

References

Abbott, Pamela, and Dixon Malunda. 2016. "The Promise and the Reality: Women's Rights in Rwanda." *African Journal of International and Comparative Law* 24(4): 561–81.

Adichie, Chimamanda Ngozi. 2012. *We Should All Be Feminists*. New York: Anchor Books.

Atkeson, Lonna Rae, and Nancy Carrillo. 2007. "More Is Better: The Influence of Collective Female Descriptive Representation on External Efficacy." *Politics and Gender* 3: 79–101.

Berry, Marie E. 2015. "'Bright Futures' Fade: Paradoxes of Women's Empowerment in Rwanda." *Signs* 41(1): 1–27.

Bulawayo, NoViolet. 2013. *We Need New Names: A Novel*. New York: Black Bay Books.

Burnet, Jennie E. 2008. "Gender Balance and the Meanings of Women in Governance in Post-genocide Rwanda." *African Affairs* 107(428): 361–86.

———. 2011. "Women Have Found Respect: Gender Quotas, Symbolic Representation, and Female Empowerment in Rwanda." *Politics and Gender* 7(3): 303–334.

Christiansen, Catrine, Mats Utas, and Henrik E. Vigh. 2006. "Navigating Youth, Generating Adulthood: Social Becoming in an African Context." Uppsala, Sweden: Nordic Africa Institute.

Cole, Jennifer. 2016. "Giving Life: Regulating Affective Circuits among Malagasy Migrants in France." In *Affective Circuits: African Migrations to Europe and the Pursuit of Social Regeneration*, ed. Jennifer Cole and Christian Groes, 197–222. Chicago: University of Chicago Press.

Des Forges, Alison. 1999. *Leave None To Tell the Story: Genocide in Rwanda*. New York: Human Rights Watch.

Eramian, Laura. 2014. "Ethnicity Without Labels? Ambiguity and Excess in 'Postethnic' Rwanda." *Focaal—Journal of Global and Historical Anthropology* 70(2014): 96–109.

Gilbert, Juliet. 2018. "'They're my Contacts, Not my Friends': Reconfiguring Affect and Aspirations Through Mobile Communication in Nigeria." *Ethnos* 82(2): 237–54.

Hansen, Karen Tranberg. 2005. "'Getting Stuck in the Compound': Some Odds against Social Adulthood in Lusaka, Zambia." *Africa Today* 51(4): 3–16.

Honwana, Alcinda. 2013. "Youth, Waithood, and Protest Movements in Africa." *African Arguments*, 12 August.

Hunt, Swanee. 2017. *Rwandan Women Rising*. Durham: Duke University Press.

Hunter, Mark. 2010. *Love in the Time of AIDS: Inequality, Gender, and Rights in South Africa*. Bloomington: Indiana University Press.

Jeffrey, Craig. 2010. *Timepass: Youth, Class, and the Politics of Waiting in India*. Stanford: Stanford University Press.

Karp, Jeffrey A., and Susan A. Banducci. 2008. "When Politics is not Just a Man's Game: Women's Representation and Political Engagement." *Electoral Studies* 27(1): 105–15.

Kuehr, Manuela Elisabeth. 2015. "Rwanda's Orphans: Care and Integration During Uncertain Times." *Stability: Journal of Security and Development* 4(1): 1–15.

Lawson, Shannon L. 2013. "Tales, Tropes, and Transformations: The Performance of Gusaba no Gukwa in Rwanda." PhD dissertation. Athens, OH: Scripps College of Communication, Ohio University.

Masquelier, Adeline. 2013. "Teatime: Boredom and the Temporalities of Young Men in Niger, Africa." *Journal of the International African Institute* 83(3): 470–91.

Mojola, Sanyu A. 2014. *Love, Money, and HIV: Becoming a Modern African Woman in the Age of AIDS*. Berkeley: University of California Press.

Newbury, Catherine, and Hannah Baldwin. 2000. *Aftermath: Women in Postgenocide Rwanda*. Working Paper No. 303. US Agency for International Development.

Pike, Isabel, Sanyu A. Mojola, and Caroline W. Kabiru. 2018. "Making Sense of Marriage: Gender and the Transition to Adulthood in Nairobi, Kenya." *Journal of Marriage and Family* 80(5): 1298–1313.

Powley, Elizabeth. 2003. *Strengthening Governance: The Role of Women in Rwanda's Transition*. Washington, DC: Hunt Alternatives Fund.

Prunier, Gérard. 1995. *The Rwanda Crisis: History of a Genocide*. New York: Columbia University Press.

Reyntjens, Filip. 2004. "Rwanda, Ten Years On: From Genocide to Dictatorship." *African Affairs* 103(411): 177–210.

Singerman, Diane. 2007. "The Economic Imperatives of Marriage: Emerging Practices and Identities Among Youth in the Middle East." *Middle East Youth Initiative*, Working Paper No. 6, September, The Brookings Institution, Wolfensohn Center for Development, Washington, DC.

Smith, Daniel Jordan. 2009. "Managing Men, Marriage, and Modern Love." In *Love in Africa*, ed. Jennifer Cole and Lynne M. Thomas, 157–180. Chicago: University of Chicago Press.

———. 2014. "Fatherhood, Companionate Marriage, and the Contradictions of Masculinity in Nigeria." In *Globalized Fatherhood: Emergent Forms and Possibilities in the New Millenium*, ed. Marcia C. Inhorn, Wendy Chavkin, and José-Alberto Navarro, 315–335. New York: Berghahn Books.

Sommers, Marc. 2012. *Stuck: Rwandan Youth and the Struggle for Adulthood*. Athens: University of Georgia Press.

Straus, Scott, and Lars Waldorf. 2011. *Remaking Rwanda: State Building and Human Rights after Mass Violence*. Madison: University of Wisconsin Press.

Thomson, Susan. 2018. *Rwanda: From Genocide to Precarious Peace*. New Haven: Yale University Press.

Utas, Mats. 2005. "Building a Future? The Reintegration and Remarginalization of Youth in Liberia." In *No Peace, No War: An Anthropology of Contemporary Armed Conflicts*, ed. Paul Richards, 137–54. Athens: Ohio University Press.

Veale, Angela, and Padraig Quigley. 2000. *In-depth Assessment into the Situation of Orphans in Rwanda*. Kigali, Rwanda: MINALOC/UNICEF.

Vigh, Henrik E. 2006. "Social Death and Violent Life Chances." In *Navigating Youth, Generating Adulthood: Social Becoming in an African Context*, ed. Catrine Christiansen, Mats Utas, and Henrik E. Vigh, 31–60. Uppsala, Sweden: Nordic Africa Institute.

———. 2016. "Life's Trampoline: On Nullification and Cocaine Migration in Bissau." In *Affective Circuits: African Migrations to Europe and the Pursuit of Social Regeneration*, ed. Jennifer Cole and Christian Groes, 223–44. Chicago: University of Chicago Press.

Zraly, Maggie, Sarah E. Rubin, and Donatilla Mukamana. 2013. "Motherhood and Resilience among Rwandan Genocide-Rape Survivors." *Ethos* 41(4): 411–439.

Chapter 7

TACTICS OF MARRIAGE DELAY IN CHINA
EDUCATION, RURAL-TO-URBAN MIGRATION, AND "LEFTOVER WOMEN"

Zachary M. Howlett

Introduction

In China, the pejorative label "leftover woman" (*shengnü* 剩女) is often attached to women who are not married by their late twenties. In a society where marriage rates are high, the demeaning implication of this label is that these women are unwanted, possessing some stigma that disqualifies them from the marriage market. Commonly perceived as "childish" and "silly," they are not recognized as having reached full adulthood, for which marriage and childbirth are a prerequisite. Their stigma, however, often merely consists of being well-educated and successful. In a society where the social norm is for women to "marry up" to a man who is older and wealthier, outperforming men in school and work makes it difficult to find a mate. The vast majority of women in China eventually marry: as of the 2010 census, only 2 percent remain single after the age of thirty-five (UNICEF 2014). Nevertheless, the discourse of leftover women has become a focal point for a sense of moral crisis in Chinese society. Derided as "picky" and "careerist," these women get blamed for China's low birthrate (now far under the replacement rate) as well as for a perceived decline in Confucian family values.

This chapter adds to a growing body of research that shines a critical light on this discourse. Far from being responsible for a decline in family values, leftover women in China, like women who marry late elsewhere (see Inhorn, Chapter 15, this volume), generally want to get married but struggle to find suitable partners (Fincher 2016; Gaetano 2015; Ji 2015; To 2015). Confronting a resurgence of gender inequality and patriarchal mores in China, these women are innovative social actors who strive to reconcile the "traditional" demands of filial duties, like childbirth and eldercare, with the "modern" desires for autonomy, self-determination, and a companionate marriage (Ji 2015).

I bring a fresh perspective to the leftover woman phenomenon by considering an under-examined contingent of these women: educated rural-to-urban migrants. Education and migration are closely connected in China. During the reform and opening era (1978 onward), the state has removed many Mao-era strictures on population movement, unleashing the largest migration in human history (Merkel-Hess and Wasserstrom 2009). Hundreds of millions of migrants now seek their livelihoods in China's urban centers. But China maintains a restrictive two-tier system of household residency (*huji* 户籍), and those without urban residency lack equal access to education, health care, and welfare. For most migrants, success on the National College Entrance Exam, known as the Gaokao (高考), provides the only viable pathway to full urban citizenship and the social benefits that this status confers (Howlett 2021). For this reason, people say that study can "change fate" (*gaibian ming* 改变命). But for many women of rural origin, rural-to-urban migration has an added incentive: escaping the gender norms of rural places. In many places in the countryside, a "traditional" culture that "values men over women" (*zhongnan qingnü* 重男轻女) remains particularly strong.

The scholarly literature on migrant women tends to focus on blue-collar migrants (Gaetano 2015; Jacka 2005; Yan 2008; Zheng 2009). Conversely, the literature on leftover women mostly centers on the experience of well-educated urbanites in China's largest metropolises (Fincher 2016; Gaetano 2014; Ji 2015; To 2015). Even when this literature addresses the lives of migrants, its urban focus means that it tends to give short shrift to an important dimension of their existence: the way in which their families and communities "back home" affect their decisions about love, education, and marriage.

Thus, the experience of educated rural-to-urban migrant women remains understudied. But more attention to this group is needed given its considerable social significance. Following China's massive expansion of higher education beginning in the late 1990s, women from peripheral places have been increasingly using education as a springboard to the cities.[1] As in many places, women in China have overtaken men in college enrollment (see also Inhorn, Chapter 15, this volume). Women of rural origin, though they are underrepresented in China's top colleges, have begun participating in higher education in unprecedented numbers. According to a 2008 survey of four national- and provincial-level universities, rural women, though they constituted 27 percent of the broader population, made up only 17 percent of college students (Wang et al. 2013). Although 17 percent is still relatively small, this number is certainly much greater than it was prior to the 1990s, when *all* women made up around 25 percent of the college population (Liu, Li, and Yang 2015: 37; Xu 2018).[2]

Though educated rural women generally want to find husbands, many strive to deflect social pressure to marry early in their search for an emotionally satisfying, physically safe, and tolerably egalitarian relationship. At the same time, they wish to be filial daughters and support their parents and relatives. In this chapter, I examine the tactics that educated rural-to-urban migrant women use to carve out space for their own autonomy, emotional fulfillment, and self-development in the context of delayed marriage.

Daughters aim to be recognized as valuable and filial, avoid "bad marriages," and thrive emotionally and professionally. But achieving these different goals, which in theory should overlap, often requires reconciling a contradiction between personal ideals and social norms. Although I focus on the experiences of educated rural-to-urban migrant women, the tactics of this group are similar in many respects to those of others who postpone marriage, including educated women of urban origin as well as leftover men. Each of these groups has a unique experience, but their commonalities should not be overlooked. By the same token, the tactics of marriage delay in China are likely to have close analogs cross-culturally.

Thus, the *tactics of marriage delay* form an analytical trope with broad cross-cultural relevance. This term encapsulates a wide array of interpersonal strategies that people in many cultural contexts pursue to negotiate between the personal and the social in the domain of marriage decisions. Delay has different connotations in different places and times: sometimes it is voluntary and sometimes involuntary; often it is a mixture of both. Consequently, the tactics of marriage delay include efforts to avoid bad marriages as well as efforts to achieve emotional and personal fulfillment while waiting for a good one. In some cases, people reject marriage, but more frequently they feel excluded from it. This exclusion has complex causes, including hypergamic norms, increasing social inequality, and the rising costs of marriage and childrearing. In addition, queer-identified individuals often face legal exclusion even as they come under pressure to enter "marriages of convenience." Since these factors are not unique to China but are shared across many societies, the tactics of marriage delay are widespread.

Focusing on migrant leftover women in China, I consider three main types of marriage-delay tactics: keeping up appearances, creating virtual worlds, and hitting "edge balls" (*cabianqiu* 擦边球). The former two tactics both involve an altered relationship with conventional reality, through either fabrication or fantasy. Keeping up appearances refers to the practice of leading a double life: fabricating an image of conformity to placate nervous parents and relatives. Creating virtual worlds involves pursuing various emotional escapes, such as romantic computer games or online relationships. Both keeping up appearances and creating virtual worlds entail a disconnect between ideal and reality. In the former tactic, women maintain a persona that conforms to the social norm of a trajectory toward early marriage, but this appearance ultimately proves unsatisfying: it defers rather than resolves the conflict between personal and social ideals. In creating virtual worlds, women pursue a personal fantasy that fulfills their own deeply felt ideals, but it is often impossible to transform this virtual reality into a tangible and satisfying social arrangement.

By contrast, the tactic of hitting an edge ball seeks to bring personal and social ideals into better alignment through negotiation. In ping pong, an edge ball is one that strikes the edge of the table: it is technically in bounds but impossible to return. In social terms, an edge ball is a strategy that forces a compromise: hitting an edge ball makes an effective demand for recognition by packaging personal aspirations in a form that pays strategic and often sincere obeisance to conventional social norms. In this chapter I focus on the most common edge-ball strategy: pursuing higher education to defer marriage. In so doing, women buy time by playing one Confucian ideal, the pursuit of education, against another one, early marriage and childbirth. The prominence and success of this strategy means that leftover women are almost by definition well-educated.

Leftover Women, Leftover Men

This chapter focuses on women, but men can also be leftover. As educated women increasingly outnumber educated men, two types of people generally find it difficult to find a spouse: high-status women and low-status men (Ji and Yeung 2014). Like leftover women, the latter, pejoratively described as "bare sticks" (*guanggun* 光棍), have become the focus of a moral panic (Greenhalgh 2015). Since early times in China, childless men have been instigators of rebellion and unrest. Painfully aware of this history, the state sees these bare sticks as a source of social instability. To some degree, the difficulty of men in finding wives is a result of China's distorted gender ratio at birth, which peaked at 121:100 (men to women) in 2004 before falling to 113:100 in 2017 (Central Intelligence Agency 2019; Gaetano 2017). This demographic crisis is exacerbated by the tendency of rural women to marry into the cities (spatial hypergamy) and that of high-status men to have multiple "wives" (a legal spouse and one or more secondary wives or "little thirds," *xiaosan* 小三). But as in other places in the world, the fundamental issue is economic (see Singerman, Chapter 1, this volume): the difficulty of ordinary men in attracting mates is a financially enforced waithood. In this patrilineal society, the groom's family bears the brunt of marriage expenses, of which the big-ticket item is a house. With skyrocketing real-estate prices, the cost of marriage has soared out of reach for many men.[3]

Ironically, the waithood of leftover women also derives partly from economic issues, although in a contrasting sense. Usually well-educated, women who postpone marriage tend to possess a relatively high degree of financial security; however, they struggle to find a partner who is willing to give them equal authority in a relationship, which is importantly symbolized by financial contributions to the household. These women often wish to shoulder a large share of these expenses, which would give them equal say over conjugal property, but find themselves rebuffed by many potential suitors (Ji 2015). This treatment produces a problem for leftover women that is the opposite of that of leftover men: rather than being excluded from marriage because they are financially insecure, leftover women are excluded (in part, at least) because they are *too* secure.

But whereas leftover men often never marry, the majority of left-over women eventually do.[4]

Methodology

I have been studying education, mobility, and marriage in China since 2008. After carrying out preliminary research in Shanghai, I conducted two years of continuous fieldwork in China's southeastern Fujian Province from 2011 to 2013. The focus of my research was the College Entrance Exam, including its ramifications in family life. To investigate how experiences vary between rural and urban places, I split my time between three field sites: Xiamen, a coastal metropolis with a population of approximately 4,000,000; Ningzhou, a backwater agricultural city (population approximately 800,000); and Mountain Town, a rural county seat (population approximately 80,000).[5] In all three places, I served as a volunteer teacher at under-resourced high schools. In this participant-observer role, I talked with dozens of students and their parents about their hopes for the future, including plans for matrimony and work. I socialized with teachers, many of whom were struggling with their own dilemmas around marriage. I also conducted focus groups of undergraduate students and interviewed postgraduate students about their educational experiences and plans for the future. My language of communication was Mandarin, and all translations are my own.

In the summer of 2016, I carried out a month of follow-up research, re-interviewing teachers and accompanying them to reunions with former students. Four years after my initial fieldwork, these young people had now become recent college graduates and, in many cases, were facing increased parental pressure to find a mate. In the winter of 2017, I conducted a further month of field research in another region of China, southwestern Yunnan Province. In addition to my on-the-ground field research, I have kept in touch with many respondents via social media, telephone, and email.

Education and "Terror of Marriage"

After worrying for decades about "overpopulation and underdevelopment" (*renkou duo, dizi bao* 人口多, 底子薄), Chinese policymakers now face a demographic paradox: high rates of marriage but very low birthrates (Jones 2007; Raymo et al. 2015). This pattern departs from the norm in many countries, where falling birthrates have been accompanied by declines in marriage.

Although marriage continues to be nearly universal in China, change may be on the horizon. The number of new marriage registrations has plummeted in recent years, falling 30 percent between 2013 and 2018.[6] At the same time, the age at first marriage is rising (Raymo et al. 2015). This trend is particularly marked in urban areas. In Shanghai, China's largest city, the average age of first marriage rose from 26.7 to 30.1 for men and from 24.4 to 28.1 for women between 2005 and 2014.[7] These figures are significantly higher than the national averages, which are 26 for men and 23.9 for women (Raymo et al. 2015). Meanwhile, birthrates in China, despite the abandonment of the one-child policy in favor of a two-child policy in 2015, remain low. The Total Fertility Rate, a measure of the average birthrate, is now 1.62 (as of 2016), which is just a little higher than that of Japan, at 1.44.[8] As a result of these trends, China, like other East Asian societies, faces the specter of an "elderquake" or "grey tsunami" (Keimig 2017). By 2030, one in four people in China will be over the age of sixty (United Nations 2015).

For Chinese state leaders, these trends present an existential challenge: how to maintain economic growth, and thus political legitimacy, in a period of social aging and declining births. For Chinese parents, these developments are similarly worrying. In the context of inadequate social welfare guarantees, the rearing of filial offspring has long been a family's best insurance against old age. Given these concerns, it is little surprise that women's rising age at first marriage has spawned a moral panic.

But the discourse of leftover women unfairly stigmatizes women for larger social problems. As in other countries, declining childbirth is closely correlated with the rising costs of having a child (Jones 2007; Raymo et al. 2015; Shi 2017). And instead of women being careerist and picky, as the leftover discourse maintains, men are frequently the fussy ones. In China as in other patriarchal societies, it has long been the social ideal that women should marry up (female hypergamy). Having internalized this norm, men are often unwilling to pursue an egalitarian relationship with a woman of equal or higher social status. Granted, many women themselves follow the hypergamic ideal, preferring an older and more successful husband (Nakano 2018). But unmarried women in their thirties frequently say that they are willing to marry a younger or less-educated man (Gaetano 2014; Ji 2015). As in other countries, an emergent trend of marrying down, or hypogamy, appears to be taking hold among educated women in China, although they report difficulty in finding men who are "open-minded" enough to pursue such an unconventional arrangement (cf. Inhorn and Smith-Hefner, Introduction, this volume).

As elsewhere in the world, these trends are closely tied to women's increasing educational attainment (Charles 2011). Since China's era of reform and opening began in the late 1970s, women have caught up with and started to surpass men in many measures of education. The proportion of women in college rose from 23.4 percent in 1980 to 33.7 percent in 1990, and from 40.9 percent in 2000 to 50.8 percent in 2010 (Liu et al. 2015: 37). In 2016, it reached 52.5 percent, and in the same year the number of women in postgraduate institutions also surpassed that of men for the first time.[9] Of course, women have achieved these gains despite the persistence of a highly gendered division of labor that largely locks them out of the highest echelons of power. Women continue to be underrepresented in top-tier colleges and in STEM (science, technology, engineering, and mathematics) fields (particularly in the "harder" disciplines and subfields), from which China's state leaders and captains of industry are largely selected (Guo, Tsang, and Ding 2010; Liu and Neuhaus 2013; Wang et al. 2013; Xu 2018). Still, there is no doubt that women's increasing participation in higher education has been a "silent revolution" (Liang et al. 2013).

Notably, women have achieved these accomplishments amid a broader resurgence of gender inequality and patriarchal norms. Although the governing Communist Party pays lip service to gender equality, much ordinary life continues to be governed by cultural logics that regard women as inferior (Engebretsen 2015; Fong 2002; Friedman 2006; Rofel 2007; Sangren 2000; Zheng 2009). In many ways, the Mao era (1949–76) was a period of relatively rapid strides in equality between the genders, which resulted from the state's muscular intervention in people's private affairs. Marriages had to be approved by one's work unit, for example. Women were encouraged to work, and men were prohibited from engaging in polygamous relationships. But in the era of reform and opening, the Party-state has largely withdrawn from its close supervision of marriage. This privatization of marriage gives individuals greater scope for personal choice but has resulted in the partial resurgence of gender norms of the pre-socialist decades of the 1920s and 1930s, when it was common for men to take multiple wives and for a woman's parents-in-law to have say over conjugal property (Davis 2014). Women's overall participation in the labor market has decreased.

Women were the first to get laid off during the restructuring of the state-led economy during the reform era and have been increasingly expected to stay at home (Liu 2007). The rate of employment for women between the ages of twenty and fifty-nine fell from 84 percent in 1990 to 74 percent in 2010; of the 26 percent unemployed women, 40.5 percent are full-time homemakers (Fincher 2016: 36; UNICEF 2014: 38). In broad terms, the reform period has been marked by the partial resuscitation of a "patriarchal bargain" in which women's recognition is inextricably tied to procreation and domestic labor (Kandiyoti 1988).

In urban areas, where the one-child policy was strictly enforced, parents have tended to invest equal time, money, and energy in the education of girls, who as singleton children represent the family's "only hope" (Fong 2002, 2006). But in rural areas, where the one-child policy was never so strictly enforced, large families are common. Patrilineal norms remain strong, meaning that people see sons as necessary to continue the lineage. Many parents continue to cite the old Confucian adage that the worst sin against filiality is not to have a son (*bu xiao you san, wu hou wei da* 不孝有三, 无后为大). Granted, parents in some rural areas have developed a preference for daughters, whom they perceive as more filial than boys (Shi 2017). But the distorted sex ratio at birth testifies to continued son preference, which remains the norm in many places, including my field sites in rural Fujian. In deference to these patrilineal norms, an important exception to the one-child policy allowed rural parents to have two children if the first was a girl. And parents who were "unlucky" enough to have two daughters were often willing to bear the steep fines and penalties so that they could "keep trying" until they produced a male heir. As a result, families of three or four children are common in my field sites. Typically, the elder siblings are daughters, who often work as migrant laborers to support the education of younger siblings, particularly boys (cf. Smith-Hefner, Chapter 8, this volume).

In this context, it is by no means a given that a daughter's education will be supported. Yet girls are widely considered by parents and teachers to be superior to boys in academic diligence, even as they suffer under the sexist bias that they are "naturally" inferior in math and science. In my rural field sites, many of the star students are girls. But despite their academic achievements, their parents and grandparents (including mothers and grandmothers) will frequently sigh, "You are such a good student. It is just such a pity that you were not born a boy!" Of course, many parents have a change of heart upon witnessing a daughter's educational achievements. And a girl who is nurtured to success can increase the status of rural parents, who become the envy of less forward-thinking neighbors. For instance, a woman of rural origin who was pursuing her PhD in sociology at Xiamen University reported that her father's financial support of his daughters' education made him the laughingstock of her village while she was growing up. But when both she and her little sister got into college, he was elected village head. Still, girls largely continue to be seen as "scattered water," unworthy of equal emotional and financial investment because they marry out of their natal household (*jia chuqu de nü'er, po chuqu de shui* 嫁出去的女儿, 泼出去的水).

Even in the cities, teachers tell girls that marriage is their "second big chance to change fate after the Gaokao." Girls are admonished to get a high score on the exam so they can "catch a big fish" (a materially successful husband). As soon as girls finish high school, they come under pressure from parents, teachers, and administrators to find spouses. The shift in parental priorities from academics to marriage can be dizzying. One young woman, the daughter of a Chinese teacher in my rural field site, told me that as soon as she passed the Gaokao, from one day to the next, her mother went from warning her to avoid boys to admonishing her to go on a diet: she was to "make herself attractive" to prospective mates. Even greater pressure falls on women who do not attend academic secondary school or who fail the big test. As a high school principal said in an online community for educators, if a girl does not get into college, she should get married immediately.

Once married, however, many new wives feel alienated in the gender roles that they are expected to perform. From the very beginning, they often face tremendous pressure to give birth to a baby boy. Men of means—the big fish—may not even agree to marrying legally until a woman has born a son. Women are generally expected to do the heavy lifting—albeit often with the help of grandparents—of childcare and domestic work, and many resent this norm. As a newlywed head teacher in Ningzhou told a friend over lunch, "When I ask my husband to help with the housework, he just says, 'Other women can take care of a child, why can't you?' Nothing infuriates me more than that kind of talk!" In many cases, men enforce gender norms with physical abuse. In the countryside in particular, women face epidemic levels of domestic violence (Parish et al. 2004; Zhao and Zhang 2017). The topic is under-researched, making the available statistics patchy; however, some researchers report a prevalence rate of domestic violence against women in rural areas as high as 66 percent (Zhao and Zhang 2017:193). Among my rural respondents, accounts of abuse are common.

Under such circumstances, it is unsurprising that women initiate the majority of divorces and have high rates of suicide, especially in rural areas (Kleinman et al. 2011). Although suicide rates are falling overall, women in rural areas are two to five times more likely to kill themselves than women in cities (Zhang et al. 2014). Observing these trends, many young women fear marriage. As one woman of rural origin, a graduate student and "leftover" at the age of twenty-seven, said, "I live in terror [*kongju* 恐惧] of marriage."

Counterfeit Boyfriends: Keeping Up Appearances

When it comes to delaying marriage, educated migrant women from the countryside have an advantage over their counterparts of urban origin. Women who migrate to the cities are removed from the most direct and constant form of social pressure to marry: the pressure that comes with living in proximity to parents. Many unmarried women of urban origin continue to live with their parents after college. By contrast, women who move to urban areas usually see their family only during holidays, especially Chinese New Year, when family members, many of whom may themselves be migrants, reconvene in the family's hometown to celebrate.

This geographical separation from family members means that educated women of rural origin, like other rural-to-urban migrants, often find themselves leading double lives. Their existence in the city becomes a backstage to their frontstage life back home, for which they construct a persona that conforms to their parents' ideals of feminine chastity and marriage-mindedness. Of course, it is rare for women not to want to get married at all, but they often feel less urgency than their parents do. Moreover, their standards for a good match may differ substantially. Daughters tend to emphasize companionship, emotional fulfillment, and acceptance of their desires for a career and self-development, whereas parents often stress physical characteristics, success, and financial stability (Gutmann 2019).[10]

As daughters pursue their lives and careers in the city, they often feel like they are "performing" (*biaoyan* 表演) or "putting on a show" (*zuoxiu* 作秀) for their parents and relatives. The particularities of these performances can vary widely. In many cases, women make up fictive boyfriends, or embellish the virtues of men with whom they are romantically involved. In others, women may conceal the fact that they are dating from their parents for fear that they may not approve of their efforts to "gain experience" before "settling down." Many describe a "disconnect" (*tuojie* 脱节) between their "real self" (*zhenzheng de wo* 真正的我) and the self that they portray to their family. As a recent college graduate from Ningzhou put it, "In my mother's ideal, I am a traditional virtuous lady [*shunü* 淑女], but she doesn't understand the real me." And as a twenty-something administrative assistant from a rural background commented, "I feel like I am always pacing back and forth between ideal and reality."

Such performances are relatively easy to maintain at a distance, but the annual pilgrimage home for Chinese New Year gives parents and relatives an opportunity to interrogate daughters at close range. The pressure to bring a boyfriend home for the holidays can become enormous. But introducing a boyfriend to one's parents is tantamount to engagement. Few couples will take this step until they are "ready." To respond to the demands of eager parents, daughters have increasingly resorted to an extreme tactic: renting a "counterfeit boyfriend" (*jiazhuang nanyou* 假装男友). Some counterfeit beaus advertise their services online, but women find them more frequently through their social circles or by word-of-mouth. Sometimes a friend or a coworker can assume the role as a favor. One of my respondents, an unmarried professional in Xiamen from rural Hunan Province, asked a man in her gym if he would be her counterfeit boyfriend. In some cases, an unmarried man and an unmarried woman will reciprocally perform this labor of dissimulation on a barter basis; men, too, may face great pressure to bring a girlfriend home for the holiday, though usually not until a later age. In recent years, counterfeit romances have become a favorite topic of the media and soap operas, which regale their audiences with stories about "fake lovers who become real" (*nongjia chengzhen* 弄假成真).[11]

In real life, however, this transformation from counterfeit to genuine is probably rare. Far from closing the gap between the matrimonial ideals of parents and those of daughters, the counterfeit phenomenon painfully dramatizes this disconnect. In this respect, the dilemmas of heterosexual and cisgender leftover women overlap with those of another cohort for whom a chasm looms between "traditional" social ideals and personal aspirations: gay or non-cisgender persons who are living in the closet (Engebretsen 2015; Zheng 2015). The latter likewise avail themselves of counterfeit boyfriends and girlfriends to deflect parental pressure to marry. Such subterfuges frequently extend even into marriage, as gay men and women engage in marriages of convenience, either with a complicit or (as is often the case) an unknowing spouse. In this way, too, their experience parallels that of leftover women. Even though most leftover women eventually marry, this decision frequently involves settling for a less-than-ideal mate: many women eventually give in to the pleas of parents to get married first and fall in love later. Ironically, the reality of such marriages is not too far from that of the counterfeit strategy: couples are told that if they dutifully perform their social duties, real love will follow. But it is common for women to regret this choice. Representing the views of many, a Ningzhou English teacher of rural origin told me she regretted her decision to succumb to social pressure when she "finally" married at thirty:

> Honestly, I don't know if my husband and I ever had real feelings for each other. He has always accepted me, but we lack an emotional foundation (*qinggan jichu* 情感基础) . . . I was too naïve when I married my husband. I thought I was fulfilling my social duty, but I didn't realize how much I would have to sacrifice my personal goals . . . I have a couple of college classmates who are still unmarried. One of them says she will never get married. I really admire her strength. If I had been stronger, I would have resisted longer.

Virtual Worlds: Computer Games, Popular Culture, and Online Relationships

Women's leftover years are frequently lonely. When the reality of dating provides little room for the fulfillment of personal romantic ideals, women often resort to various forms of fantasy to fill the gap. One of the most pervasive types of fantasy is not conventionally categorized as such: the pursuit of online relationships on China's social media platforms, such as QQ or WeChat. These platforms enable strangers to meet each other online, and many women will cultivate flirtatious or romantic friendships with men whom they never see in the flesh. For example, a twenty-something office worker from rural Guangdong Province spoke in rapturous terms about her "fiancée," a man from faraway Liaoning whom she had met on WeChat. Although she assured her parents that she had a boyfriend, she had never actually seen him in "real life" despite having chatted with him for nearly two years. Skeptics might object to my characterization of such relationships as fantasy. They might point out that virtual relationships can be as real as offline ones and sometimes transform into physical relationships, which is certainly true. But in many cases, these virtual relationships never become viable marriage matches. Rather, they perform the function of creating a virtual space for companionship and mutual wish-fulfillment.

For many unmarried women, such online relationships constitute the main source of romantic companionship. Many others may have real-life relationships yet find them deeply unsatisfying. One such woman, another Ningzhou high-school teacher from a rural background, maintained an on-again, off-again long-distance relationship with her high-school boyfriend. She did not want to marry him, but despite having ended the relationship several times, she continued to face considerable pressure from her family and her boyfriend's family. Unable to find another suitable candidate in her immediate social milieu, she cultivated friendships online, which she herself characterized as an escape. These online relationships gave her emotional solace but did not transform into viable partnerships. Frequently, the men whom she met online misrepresented themselves, or otherwise turned out to have some personal or financial defect that made them unacceptable as real partners.

Of course, the pursuit of online relationships represents only one type of virtual activity that women engage in to provide themselves with a modicum of emotional fulfillment during their leftover years. A panoply of popular culture including soap operas, dating shows, and novels caters to the leftover demographic, promising wish-fulfillment and escape from everyday reality. In recent years, a special type of computer game has even emerged to appeal to this market. An example of this genre is the mobile dating simulation role-playing game, *Love and Producer* (*Lian yu zhizuoren* 恋与制作人), released in 2017. In this game, women assume the role of a television producer who must revive the fortune of her father's production company while choosing between four heartthrob suitors. These men vie for the affection of the protagonist by giving her expensive gifts, inviting her to candlelight dinners, and reading her bedtime stories. Players even receive texts and telephone calls from their imaginary lovers. The game, which has over four million active users, provides many women with a diversion from the difficulty of finding a real-life partner (Feng 2018). As an enthusiast reported, "Love is not always just as one wishes, but a virtual romance can be a compensation" (Huang 2018).

But rather than validating women in their decision to combine marriage with the pursuit of personal development, these popular cultural products, which are closely supervised by state censors, often normalize and reinforce the popular wisdom of the leftover discourse that educated unmarried women are "careerist" and "picky." For example, the popular 2015 television show *Let's Get Married* (*Zanmen jiehun ba* 咱们结婚吧) seeks to persuade viewers that the 32-year-old female protagonist must either conform to traditional marriage standards, such as hypergamy, or forever remain single; similarly, the enormously popular dating show, *If You Are the One* (*Fei cheng wu rao* 非诚勿扰), reinforces the common perception that educational success dampens marriage prospects, for example by highlighting how female contestants conceal postgraduate degrees from potential suitors (Feldshuh 2018).

Educated migrant women, who are far removed from the supervision of their immediate family, may easily slip into the solace of wish fulfillment and fantasy, which provides a ready diversion from the difficulty of finding a suitable mate. While these virtual worlds offer emotional respite from the loneliness and despair that may characterize the leftover existence, they often remain ultimately unsatisfying. Granted, fantasy can be a laboratory for working out one's personal ideals and for imagining new forms of aspiration; however, virtual relationships, whether in social media or a computer game, provide only limited comfort for unmarried women. And the state-curated fantasies of popular culture often merely reflect the normalizing strictures of the leftover discourse, which blames women themselves for their marriage-less state.

Hitting an Edge Ball: The Academic Diligence of Rural Women

In contrast to the tactics of keeping up appearances and creating virtual worlds, neither of which bridge the gap between personally held ideals and conventional social norms, the tactic of hitting an edge ball provides a way of negotiating with social norms to bring them into closer alignment with personal ideals. The most prominent edge-ball strategy, women's pursuit of higher education, is demonized for being responsible for women's marriage crisis. Yet women of rural origin generally do not see education as a way of avoiding marriage altogether but rather as a method of squaring the circle between filial obeisance and the pursuit of self-development.

The phrase "to hit an edge ball" generally refers to a strategy of conforming to the letter of the law while disobeying its spirit. It often has a negative connotation, although people also admire the skill, ingenuity, and luck that hitting a good edge ball requires. People mainly use the expression in the realm of policy or regulatory regimes.[12] In personal life, it is generally employed for humorous effect. But I think it is useful to theorize edge balls as a wider social phenomenon in China and beyond. In China as in many places, ordinary people employ many ingenious strategies to push back against power. As the old saying goes, "Above there are policies and below there are countermeasures" (*shang you zhengce, xia you duice* 上有政策, 下有对策). An important such countermeasure, edge balls negotiate with the law—be it formal or customary—by packaging a demand for recognition in a form that cannot be refused. They represent an important strategy of social innovation and creativity: edge balls sneak new forms of social arrangement into existence by paying lip service to conventional social norms. In so doing, they create new "facts on the ground" that can lead to lasting social change.

In China, being a good student is one of the main ways in which children express filial obedience to parents. But the virtue of scholarly assiduousness has conventionally been seen as a masculine trait (Kipnis 2011). By outdoing men in such "masculine" virtues as academic diligence, women are asserting themselves as equals to men in filial devotion. As a girl in my rural field site told me over lunch in the cafeteria, "I think that [girls work harder than boys because of] a disobedient attitude [*bufu xinli* 不服心里]. China is a patriarchy, and girls want to prove their worth."

Of course, in urban areas, it is more generally accepted that daughters, who in many cases are singleton children, should have equal access to education. But over 40 percent of the population is still officially categorized as rural.[13] As I suggest above, many rural women, who are proportionately underrepresented in college, must fight oppressive gender norms to secure access to higher education. This fact is dramatically demonstrated by their descriptions of negotiations with family members over education and marriage. Many women of rural origin are allowed to attend college only after an older sister has "gone out to work" to pay for the college tuition of her younger siblings. They are painfully aware of this sacrifice, which male children are rarely asked to make. An academically talented girl can resist the pressure she faces to start working and get married upon the completion of compulsory schooling, which currently ends at grade nine. But as the pressure to marry intensifies in her twenties, postgraduate education often provides the most viable route toward further delaying marriage and carving out a space for personal autonomy. Some speak of the decision to pursue a master's degree or PhD in terms of increasing their "power of choice" (*xuanzequan* 选择权) in life. Many say that postgraduate education is a way of "maintaining their independence" (*baochi duli* 保持独立) until they can find a man who "accepts" (*jieshou* 接受) them.

In this Confucian society in which education is so deeply valued, postgraduate education is a way of increasing one's status and value. For students of rural origin, graduate school provides a second chance to achieve admission to elite universities in China's largest cities, which is frequently denied them in the Gaokao owing to regional test-score disparities (Howlett 2021; Wang et al. 2013; Yeung 2013). But for college-educated women from peripheral places, attending graduate school may also be a second chance to escape gender norms that they perceive as oppressive. One such woman, a star student from Ningzhou, had narrowly missed the cutoff score to attend Peking University in Beijing, one of China's most elite colleges, when she underperformed on the Gaokao in 2012. Both she and her parents had been devastated by this failure. But the young woman eventually fulfilled her Beijing dream when she secured admission to a prestigious doctoral program at the university right out of college. Her parents initially opposed her graduate school plans, admonishing her to find a husband and settle down in their hometown or in nearby Xiamen. But when they saw the prestigious seal of Beijing University on a graduate school admissions letter, their hearts melted. The letter was her edge ball.

Women also see graduate school as a "platform" (*pingtai* 平台) for meeting suitable mates, reasoning that well-educated men are more likely to share their outlook on life and marriage. Many university administrators, who refer to late marriage as a crisis, consider it their social duty to help women in graduate school find husbands. To this end, universities sponsor social events for singles. Although most women do not intend to defer marriage indefinitely, obtaining an advanced degree—particularly a PhD—can make it exceedingly difficult for them to find a husband. For this reason, people call "female PhD's" (*nü boshi* 女博士) the "third sex" (*disan xingbie* 第三性别), a chauvinist label that testifies to the discrimination that they face in the marriage market.

Conclusion

By surpassing boys in school, girls of rural origin deflect pressure to drop out and marry early. For many, pursuing higher education in the big city is not only about achieving social mobility but also about escaping the patriarchal ethos of rural places. But they often also see it as a way to find a good husband. In addition, professional success enables women to take better care of their families. For these reasons, filiality and liberation are inextricably interlinked in women's quests for recognition.

The strategies of keeping up appearances and creating virtual worlds mainly reinforce, or at least leave unchallenged, the disconnect between personal ideals and social norms. To be sure, keeping up appearances gives people a hidden backstage for the pursuit of alternative forms of flourishing. And virtual worlds can be places in which people imagine new forms of social arrangement. But by themselves neither of these tactics presents an overt challenge to conventional patriarchal bargains. By contrast, the edge ball of academic diligence packages personal aspirations in a form that is difficult for supporters of conventional mores not to recognize.

This chapter argues that women who delay marriage in China are innovative social actors who are shifting norms around women's participation in higher education, even as Chinese society more broadly witnesses a resurgence of patriarchal patterns. The choice to delay marriage is often a way of avoiding the possibility of a bad marriage, which many women fear. This possibility is particularly real for women in the countryside, where rates of domestic violence and suicide are relatively high. The norm of hypergamy means that the very strategy that women use to get out of the countryside—the pursuit of higher education—forces them into waithood. Most women in China eventually marry, frequently "settling" for a partner that they deem substandard. But many, like the teacher from Ningzhou, regret that choice. And while marriage was until recently nearly universal in mainland China, increasing divorce and falling marriage rates signal change on the horizon. Elsewhere in East Asia, such as Hong Kong and Tokyo, rising numbers of women have started to remain single into their thirties and even forties; in these places, many women reject the norm that they should get married and bear children even as they embrace the social duty of eldercare (Nakano 2018).

These trends raise real questions about the future of marriage in China. If women experience conventional marital arrangements as oppressive, will they seek to transform them or avoid them altogether to find new forms of flourishing outside of marriage? Already, an emergent social trend of hypogamy, though still only beginning, may be taking shape. And rather than pursue divorce, which is still stigmatized in China, many women live separately from their husbands to maintain space for their personal aspirations (and in some cases to ensure their physical safety). The experience of non-heterosexual and non-cisgender subjects in China also suggests ways of thriving outside of heteropatriarchal norms, even as it underscores the difficulties faced by queer subjects, among whom we must count "female PhDs," in achieving recognition within those norms. Whatever directions these trends take, they imply two things: First, the tactics that women employ to pursue livable, recognizable lives do not end with marriage but continue in various forms throughout their lives. Second, these tactics point to emergent ways of being and flourishing that pose fundamental challenges to any form of state power that would define women's value largely in terms of their procreative contribution to the body of the nation.

Zachary M. Howlett is Assistant Professor of Anthropology at Yale-NUS College at the National University of Singapore. After completing his BA in German studies at Brown University, he spent several years in China working as a teacher, translator, and interpreter. He later received MA and PhD degrees in anthropology from Cornell University. Howlett is a sociocultural anthropologist who focuses on education, mobility, and marriage in China. His forthcoming book is *Meritocracy and Its Discontents: Anxiety and the National College Entrance Exam in China* (Cornell University Press, 2021).

Notes

1. According to the China Statistical Yearbook, between 1999 and 2009, the number of university students in China quadrupled from 5 million to 20 million and now hovers over 27 million (http://www.stats.gov.cn/english/statisticaldata/annualdata/, retrieved 3 January 2019). See Yeung's (2013) discussion of higher education expansion.
2. The number of rural women is likely much higher in vocational and technical colleges, where the percentages of women and people of rural origin are relatively high (see Yeung 2013).
3. As a result, an increasing number of couples are deciding to enter into a "naked marriage" (*luohun* 裸婚), which refers to the practice of getting married without the usual material accoutrements of a house, car, etc.
4. Greenhalgh (2015) suggests that over 10 percent of men expected to marry between 2005 and 2025 will fail to find a partner.
5. Ningzhou and Mountain Town are pseudonyms.
6. See "China's Marriage Rate Plummets" (2018).

7. Refer to Chunhua Ma's (2018) report. Ji and Yeung (2014) report similar 2005 numbers for Shanghai.
8. I take these figures from World Bank data. See https://data.worldbank .org/indicator/SP.DYN.TFRT.IN?locations=CI-JP-CN, retrieved 3 January 2019. Since many births in China are unregistered, the precise fertility rate is difficult to estimate.
9. See "Women Dominate Higher Education in China" (2017).
10. For example, many parents forbid their daughters from marrying a man under a certain height since they fear that short offspring will face pervasive discrimination.
11. See, for example, http://news.sina.com.cn/s/qw/2016-02-01/doc-ifxn zanm3908098.shtml, retrieved 29 January 2020.
12. See, for instance, Minghuan Li's (2012) discussion of how transnational migration brokers hit edge balls to help their clients migrate overseas.
13. According to the 2017 China Statistical Yearbook, 42.65 percent of the population was rural in 2016.

References

Central Intelligence Agency. 2019. "The World Factbook China." Retrieved 23 April 2019 from https://www.cia.gov/library/publications/the-world-factbook/geos/ch.html.

Charles, Maria. 2011. "A World of Difference: International Trends in Women's Economic Status." *Annual Review of Sociology* 37(1): 355–71.

"China's Marriage Rate Plummets." 2018. People's Daily Online, 29 June. Retrieved 24 April 2019 from http://en.people.cn/n3/2018/0629/c900 00-9476075.html.

Davis, Deborah S. 2014. "Privatization of Marriage in Post-Socialist China." *Modern China* 40(6): 551–77.

Engebretsen, Elisabeth L. 2015. *Queer Women in Urban China*. Abingdon: Routledge.

Feldshuh, Hannah. 2018. "Gender, Media, and Myth-Making: Constructing China's Leftover Women." *Asian Journal of Communication* 28(1): 38–54.

Feng, Jiayun. 2018. "Love and Producer: The Chinese Mobile Game that has Millions of Women Hooked." SupChina, 16 January. Retrieved 24 April 2019 from https://supchina.com/2018/01/16/love-and-producer-the-chinese-mobile-game-that-has-hooked-millions-of-women/.

Fincher, Leta Hong. 2016. *Leftover Women: The Resurgence of Gender Inequality in China*. London: Zed Books.

Fong, Vanessa L. 2002. "China's One-Child Policy and the Empowerment of Urban Daughters." *American Anthropologist* 104(4): 1098–109.

———. 2006. *Only Hope: Coming of Age Under China's One-Child Policy*. Stanford: Stanford University Press.

Friedman, Sara. 2006. *Intimate Politics: Marriage, the Market, and State Power in Southeastern China*. Cambridge: Harvard University Asia Center.

Gaetano, Arianne M. 2014. "'Leftover Women': Postponing Marriage and Renegotiating Womanhood in Urban China." *Journal of Research in Gender Studies* 4(2): 124–49.

———. 2015. *Out to Work: Migration, Gender, and the Changing Lives of Rural Women in Contemporary China.* Honolulu: University of Hawai'i Press.

———. 2017. "Women, Work, and Marriage: Challenges of Gendered Mobility in Urban China." In *China's Urbanization and Socioeconomic Impact,* ed. Zongli Tang, 109–24. Singapore: Springer Singapore.

Greenhalgh, Susan. 2015. "'Bare Sticks' and Other Dangers to the Social Body: Assembling Fatherhood in China." In *Globalized Fatherhood,* ed. Marcia C. Inhorn, Wendy Chavkin, and José-Alberto Navarro, 359–81. New York: Berghahn Books.

Guo, Congbin, Mun C. Tsang, and Xiaohao Ding. 2010. "Gender Disparities in Science and Engineering in Chinese Universities." *Economics of Education Review,* Special Issue in Honor of Henry M. Levin 29(2): 225–35.

Gutmann, Matthew. 2019. "Favorite Sons and Leftover Daughters: Men, Marriage, and Gender Equality in China." In *Men Are Animals: An Anthropology of Sex, Violence, and Biobabble.* New York: Basic Books.

Howlett, Zachary M. 2021. *Meritocracy and Its Discontents: Anxiety and the National College Entrance Exam in China.* Ithaca, NY: Cornell University Press.

Huang, Lanlan. 2018. "Chinese Women are Addicted to Virtual Boyfriends, So What?" *Global Times,* 11 January. Retrieved 24 April 2019 from http://www.globaltimes.cn/content/1084398.shtml.

Jacka, Tamara. 2005. *Rural Women in Urban China: Gender, Migration, and Social Change.* Armonk: M. E. Sharpe.

Ji, Yingchun. 2015. "Between Tradition and Modernity: 'Leftover' Women in Shanghai." *Journal of Marriage and Family* 77(5): 1057–73.

Ji, Yingchun, and Wei-Jun Jean Yeung. 2014. "Heterogeneity in Contemporary Chinese Marriage." *Journal of Family Issues* 35(12): 1662–82.

Jones, Gavin W. 2007. "Delayed Marriage and Very Low Fertility in Pacific Asia." *Population and Development Review* 33(3): 453–78.

Kandiyoti, Deniz. 1988. "Bargaining with Patriarchy." *Gender and Society* 2(3): 274–90.

Keimig, Rose Kay. 2017. "Growing Old in China's New Nursing Homes." PhD dissertation. New Haven: Yale University.

Kipnis, Andrew B. 2011. *Governing Educational Desire: Culture, Politics, and Schooling in China.* Chicago: University of Chicago Press.

Kleinman, Arthur, Yunxiang Yan, Jing Jun, Sing Lee, Everett Zhang, Tianshu Pan, Fei Wu, and Jinhua Guo. 2011. "Introduction: Remaking the Moral Person in New China." In *Deep China: The Moral Life of the Person: What Anthropology and Psychiatry Tell Us about China Today,* ed. Arthur Kleinman, Yunxiang Yan, Jing Jun, Sing Lee, Everett Zhang, Tianshu Pan, Fei Wu, and Jinhua Guo, 1–35. Berkeley: University of California Press.

Li, Minghuan. 2012. "'Playing Edge Ball': Transnational Migration Brokerage in China." In *Transnational Flows and Permissive Polities,* ed. Barak Kalir and Malini Sur, 207–28. Ethnographies of Human Mobilities in Asia. Amsterdam: Amsterdam University Press.

Liang, Chen, Hao Zhang, Danqing Ruan, Cameron Campbell, and James Z. Lee. 2013. *Wusheng de geming: Beijing Daxue yu Suzhou Daxue shehui laiyuan yanjiu, 1949–2002* [Silent revolution: The origins of Peking University and Soochow University undergraduates, 1949–2002]. Beijing: SDX Joint Publishing Company.

Liu, Bohong, Ling Li, and Chunyu Yang. 2015. "Gender (In)Equality and China's Economic Transition." In *Revisiting Gender Inequality: Perspectives from the People's Republic of China*, ed. Qi Wang, Min Dongchao, and Bo Ærenlund Sørensen, 21–57. Comparative Feminist Studies. New York: Palgrave Macmillan.

Liu, Jieyu. 2007. *Gender and Work in Urban China: Women Workers of the Unlucky Generation*. Abingdon: Routledge.

Liu, Ning, and Birgit Neuhaus. 2013. "Gender Inequality in Biology Classes in China and Its Effects on Students' Short-Term Outcomes." *International Journal of Science Education* 36(10): 1531–550.

Ma, Chunhua. 2018. "The Pressure to Get Married is Tearing China's Families Apart." *Sixth Tone*, 3 January. Retrieved 24 April 2019 from http://www.sixthtone.com/news/1002866/the-pressure-to-get-married-is-tearing-chinas-families-apart.

Merkel-Hess, Kate, and Jeffrey N. Wasserstrom. 2009. "A Country on the Move: China Urbanizes." *Current History* 108(717): 167–72.

Nakano, Lynne. 2018. "In the Shadow of the State: Families and Single Women in Three East Asian Cities." American Anthropological Association Annual Meeting, San Jose, 16 November.

Parish, William L., Tianfu Wang, Edward O. Laumann, Suiming Pan, and Ye Luo. 2004. "Intimate Partner Violence in China: National Prevalence, Risk Factors and Associated Health Problems." *International Family Planning Perspectives* 30(4): 174–81.

Raymo, James M., Hyunjoon Park, Yu Xie, and Wei-Jun Jean Yeung. 2015. "Marriage and Family in East Asia: Continuity and Change." *Annual Review of Sociology* 41(1): 471–92.

Rofel, Lisa. 2007. *Desiring China: Experiments in Neoliberalism, Sexuality, and Public Culture*. Durham: Duke University Press.

Sangren, P. Steven. 2000. *Chinese Sociologics*. London: Athlone.

Shi, Lihong. 2017. *Choosing Daughters: Family Change in Rural China*. Stanford: Stanford University Press.

To, Sandy. 2015. *China's Leftover Women: Late Marriage among Professional Women and Its Consequences*. Abingdon: Routledge.

UNICEF. 2014. "Women and Men in China: Facts and Figures 2012." 1 September. Retrieved 2 January 2019 from http://www.unicef.cn/en/publications/comprehensive/2065.html.

United Nations. 2015. "World Population Ageing 2015." Retrieved 28 August 2020 from http://www.un.org/en/development/desa/population/publications/pdf/ageing/WPA2015_Report.pdf.

Wang, Xiaobing, Chengfang Liu, Linxiu Zhang, Yaojiang Shi, and Scott Ro-
zelle. 2013. "College Is a Rich, Han, Urban, Male Club: Research Notes
from a Census Survey of Four Tier One Colleges in China." *The China
Quarterly* 214 (June): 456–70.

"Women Dominate Higher Education in China." 2017. *People's Daily Online*, 28 October. Retrieved 24 April 2019 from http://en.people.cn/n3/
2017/1028/c90000-9285962.html.

Xu, Duoduo. 2018. "Is Gender Equality at Chinese Colleges a Sham?"
Sixth Tone, 5 April. Retrieved 24 April 2019 from https://www.sixthtone
.com/news/1002051/is-gender-equality-at-chinese-colleges-a-sham
percent3F.

Yan, Hairong. 2008. *New Masters, New Servants: Migration, Development, and
Women Workers in China*. Durham: Duke University Press.

Yeung, Wei-Jun Jean. 2013. "Higher Education Expansion and Social Stratification in China." *Chinese Sociological Review* 45(4): 54–80.

Zhang, Jie, Long Sun, Yuxin Liu, and Jianwei Zhang. 2014. "The Change
in Suicide Rates between 2002 and 2011 in China." *Suicide and Life-
Threatening Behavior* 44(5): 560–68.

Zhao, Ruohui, and Hongwei Zhang. 2017. "Family Violence and the Legal
and Social Responses in China." In *Global Responses to Domestic Violence*,
ed. Eve S. Buzawa and Carl Buzawa, 189–206. Cham: Springer.

Zheng, Tiantian. 2009. *Red Lights: The Lives of Sex Workers in Postsocialist China*.
Minneapolis: University of Minnesota Press.

———. 2015. *Tongzhi Living: Men Attracted to Men in Postsocialist China*. Minneapolis: University of Minnesota Press.

Chapter 8

TOO EDUCATED TO MARRY?
MUSLIM WOMEN AND EXTENDED SINGLEHOOD IN INDONESIA

Nancy J. Smith-Hefner

Introduction

Demographic studies indicate that across East and Southeast Asia women are achieving dramatically higher levels of education than those of previous generations and have even begun to surpass the educational achievements of men. Rising levels of women's education accompany rising levels of female participation in the urban workforce and correlate with marriage delays and even non-marriage among women ("Asian Demography" 2011; Jones 2004). Indonesia has followed this pan-Asian pattern regarding women's educational achievement, employment, and delayed marriage (Jones 2009). Unlike some other Asian countries, however, Indonesia has been slow to shift away from the pattern of universal marriage that once defined the region. In Indonesia, there remains a widespread expectation that—unless mentally or physically impaired—all young people will marry. The "marital imperative" weighs most heavily on young women. Those who delay marriage to pursue tertiary degrees are in an especially precarious position. Because most Indonesian women prefer to marry someone of at least the same age and educational level as themselves, and because most men look to marry "down" with regard to age and education, many educated women find it challenging to identify an appropriate match in a narrowing field of candidates (A. Utomo 2014).

The situation of educated middle-class women in Indonesia is in many ways similar to that reported for middle-class women in Vietnam and China (Earl 2014; Howlett, Chapter 7, this volume). In those countries as in Indonesia, successful family planning programs have resulted in a significantly smaller average family size. Parents now focus greater attention and resources on relatively fewer offspring. At the same time, families have come to recognize the value of educating daughters with an eye to future employment. For many young women, putting off marriage is a strategy of self-development and future economic security; importantly, it also allows them to "repay the moral debt" owed to their families. Postponing marriage leads to difficulties, however, if marriage is put off for too long.

Drawing on a long-term study of university-educated youth in the city of Yogyakarta, in south-central Java, Indonesia (Smith-Hefner 2019), this chapter examines the situation of middle-class Muslim Javanese women who have delayed marriage in order to pursue education and employment, and the hurdles they face when they finally turn to look for a suitable partner. In recent decades, Indonesia has seen a pronounced shift away from the authoritarian developmentalist morality of the New Order state (1966–98) to the growing influence of different varieties of Islam in both public and private realms. Young people and their elders report a marked generational shift away from parentally arranged marriage; today, youth in both urban and rural areas of the country identify romantic love as the proper foundation for a modern, companionate marriage based on shared values and understandings. Rather than embracing this new freedom of marital choice, however, an increasing number of Javanese young people—including educated Muslim women— reject modern dating as a way to identify a possible marriage partner as un-Islamic and immoral and are turning instead to varieties of Muslim matchmaking services in their effort to meet their ideal match (Smith-Hefner 2005, 2019).

This chapter examines the affinities and tensions between modernizing impulses emphasizing romantic love, companionate marriage, and self-development and those focused on the cultivation of Muslim piety. The discussion aims to describe and assess the personal and social benefits and challenges for women who embrace a more conservative Muslim model of marriage (see Schulz, Chapter 2, this volume). My interest is in simultaneously teasing out the role that religion—in this case, Indonesian Islam—plays in the broader social phenomenon of delayed marriage or "waithood." More generally, I consider the degree to which the waithood model as it has been formulated for the Middle East is a useful framework for understanding a widespread pattern of *extended singlehood* among educated youth in Indonesia. By this, I refer to the pattern whereby increasing numbers of young people are delaying marriage in order to pursue education, employment, and "self-development" and, in the process, extending the period of unmarried youth.

Fieldwork in Yogyakarta

Indonesia is a Southeast Asian nation of some 17,000 islands and nearly 270 million inhabitants. Eighty-seven percent of Indonesians identify as Muslim, making Indonesia the most populous Muslim country in the world (Pew Research Center 2010). The city of Yogyakarta, on the Indonesian island of Java, is the administrative capital of what is known as the "Special Region of Yogyakarta." The city proper has a population of 400,000 residents. However, if one includes the surrounding provinces that comprise the Special Region, that figure rises to 3,600,000. Yogyakarta is an important center of Javanese culture and history, as well as the site of Indonesia's only still-functioning sultanate. It is also widely known as a "city of students" (*kota pelajar*) and is home to several hundred private, state, and Muslim secondary and tertiary institutions—among them the prestigious Gadjah Mada University, Indonesia's oldest and second largest university. According to the 2010 census, almost 92 percent of Yogyakarta's population identifies as Muslim.

The focus of my research over the past fifteen years has been on Yogyakarta's Muslim university students—that is, young people who are at a stage in their lives where they are consciously preoccupied with crafting a future while struggling to position themselves vis-à-vis the rapidly evolving social scene around them. Over the course of my project, I conducted in-depth interviews with more than 250 students, most of whom were affiliated with either Gadjah Mada University or the nearby State Islamic University (UIN Sunan Kalijaga). I conducted all interviews in either Indonesian or in Javanese and translated them to English when needed. In addition to interviews, I engaged in focus groups and informal discussions with hundreds more young people. I also carried out ethnographic observations among their teachers, parents, friends, and religious leaders.

While my interviews were broad and covered an array of topics having to do with Islam, education, and social change among Muslim Javanese youth, this chapter focuses mainly on young women.

The Times Have Changed

Indonesian young people, as well as their parents and teachers, recognize and frequently comment that the "times have changed" (*zaman sudah berubah*) and today's youth have many more opportunities than were available to prior generations. During President Suharto's "New Order" regime (1966–98) an aggressive and comparatively successful Family Planning Program was undertaken; the period also saw a vast expansion of educational opportunities, including for girls and young women, in both urban and rural areas of the nation. These developments converged to bring about a widespread recognition of the benefits of "smaller high-quality families," as well as new understandings of family, gender relationships, and the role of children. New Order directives initiating compulsory schooling, first through grade six and, beginning in 1989 through grade nine, have succeeded in achieving near-universal primary education and dramatically increasing participation in secondary and tertiary education (Hull and Jones 1994: 61; Oey-Gardiner 1991). Between 1965 and 1990, the percentage of young adults with basic literacy skills skyrocketed from 40 percent to 90 percent. The percentage of youths completing senior high school grew from 4 percent to more than 30 percent in the same period (Hefner 2000: 17; Hull and Jones 1994). Equally important, New Order economic policies shifted emphasis from agriculture and agrarian development to a program of industrialization and light manufacturing that resulted in widespread urbanization. The percentage of the population living in Indonesian cities rose from 17 percent in 1970 to 31 percent in 1990, and is now approaching 55 percent (US Library of Congress n.d.).

New employment opportunities in factories, the greatly expanded civil service, and the service sector served as an incentive for parents to keep their children in school with an eye to obtaining a well-paying job and a foothold in the emerging middle class. Many of the new service and factory jobs are particularly well-suited to women who, as in other developing economies, are considered more flexible, deferential, and disciplined than men (Wolf 1996: 150; see also Jones 1994). Although progress in attainment of the government's goal of universal education through grade nine for all young people slowed for a period of time in the aftermath of the economic and political crisis of 1997–98 (Jones and Hagul 2001), the breadth and quality of schooling in Indonesia today are vastly greater than those of Indonesia in the 1950s and 1960s.[1] Perhaps most significantly, the expansion of educational and economic opportunities has affected the situation of girls and women even more dramatically than that of men, allowing them to catch up with and, in some areas, even surpass male achievements (Jones 1994: 31; Parker and Nilan 2013: 81–82).[2]

Linked to the possibility of stable employment and economic security, a university degree has quickly become the marker of upward mobility and middle-class status. Javanese parents uniformly express the desire that their children—now, daughters as well as sons—"go further and achieve more" than they were able to achieve (*melebihi orang tuanya*), and many make considerable personal and financial sacrifices to support their children's academic success. This is true not only of urban parents but of rural parents as well, who not uncommonly report selling off ancestral rice fields (*sawah*) and house land (*pekarangan*) to put their children through school. As in a growing number of Muslim-majority countries (see Adely 2012), the academic achievement of one's offspring is viewed as a reflection of one's success at parenting; a diploma carries with it considerable prestige (*gengsi*) for the bearer as well as for his or her family.

Whatever its precise status and economic benefits, the expansion of educational opportunities has had a profound effect on contemporary Javanese family roles and gender conceptions. The most immediate index of this change has been the postponement of marriage and the prolongation of the period of unmarried singlehood. Young people, most markedly young women, are marrying at significantly older ages as they put off marriage until they have finished their schooling. In 1965 the mean age at first marriage for females in Indonesia was 18.6 years; in 1971 it was 19.3 (Jones 1994: 75–81). New marriage legislation enacted in 1974 set the minimum marriage age at nineteen for males and sixteen for females and enshrined the notion that young people may not be forced into marriages against their will. By 1990 the mean age of first marriage for females had climbed to 21.6 years (Jones 1994: 80). These statistics do not distinguish between urban and rural areas, but studies indicate that while urban centers like Yogyakarta—where the mean age at first marriage for females in 1990 was 24.1[3]—have led the way in patterns of delayed marriage, when level of education is controlled for, there is little difference between cities and the countryside (Jones 1994: 89).

Women and Work

Commentaries from young people indicate that they and their parents are keenly aware of these dramatic changes. Sitting on the porch outside her parents' house, Inayah,[4] a student in her fourth and final year studying English literature at Gadjah Mada University, offered the following observation as her mother nodded in agreement,

> It's different from when my mom was young. She had to quit school and get married when she was only seventeen because her parents thought if she got much older she wouldn't be marketable (*tidak laku*) and she'd end up an old maid (*perawan tua*). Nowadays women who marry young are laughed at, "How come she's married, she's so young" (*Kok kawin, masih muda*)! Women want to finish their educations first and if possible to work before marrying. And it's not just city people who think that way. If they can afford to, rural people send their daughters to the city to go to school, and they get married later, too.

As Inayah notes, Javanese women are not only postponing marriage to seek knowledge through higher education; they are also planning to put that knowledge to work (Nilan 2008; Smith-Hefner 2007). Young women who do not work after graduation are derided by their peers as having wasted their time, effort, and money (*rugi sekali*). Most young Javanese women today—including religiously observant Muslims and even politically active Islamists—see women's employment both as a personal necessity and an unambiguous social good. As important for most women, employment outside the home is viewed as a pathway to personal security and autonomy, in particular where marital ties and family supports may be less than certain. Many university women recount how their own mothers—ordinary Muslims as well as those religiously observant—had repeatedly advised them of the wisdom of a woman having her own money so that she is not dependent on the generosity of her husband and can support herself and her children if circumstances require. Mothers who themselves were forced to leave school at a young age in order to marry are particularly insistent that their daughters finish their educations and go to work.

This broader link—between education, work, and autonomy—is often expressed in parents' comments with regard to the fact that their daughters will be allowed to choose their own husbands. Bu Suharti, a high school teacher in urban Yogyakarta and mother of three daughters and one son, matter-of-factly stated what many other mothers of young women told me: "As for my daughters, they will choose their own husbands. We cannot choose their husbands for them; we can only offer advice. But my husband and I have given them lots of education so that they can make good decisions." The link to autonomy is clear. It is education that prepares young women to make good marital choices, and it is education that offers them the possibility of working, not only to help their husbands support their families, but to support themselves and their children if necessary.

What is more, a woman who has her own money has the means to help her parents or siblings if the need arises. Bu Suharti continued,

> And with education, they can help their husbands support their families, not just stay home with the children. No! I feel strongly that the wife has to have her own income. That way if she wants to give some money to her younger sibling or to her parents, and if her husband disagrees, she can just say, "I have my own money." If she has no money of her own, he'll feel it's a drain. But if she has her own money, it's fine. She can say, "I have my own income."

Many young women report being painfully aware of the sacrifices their parents made in supporting their children's education and express their hope to "repay the moral debt" (*mbalas budi*) by assuming the financial burden of schooling their younger siblings or helping their parents financially in other ways (see Parker and Nilan 2013). This ethical concern for the support of parents and siblings is to a significant degree "gendered"—that is, the theme looms far larger in the personal narratives of young women than young men. In my interviews over the years it was not uncommon for young women to comment, "I want to work after I graduate to make my parents happy"; "I know how much my parents have sacrificed to support my education, I want to work so that I can repay their sacrifice"; "I want to be an example for my siblings and when I graduate I plan to support their schooling." The gendered difference in ethical and financial responsibility among Javanese has long been noted in the ethnographic literature. Javanese women in particular are identified, and identify themselves, as being more careful with money; once married, they are typically the ones to manage the household budget (Brenner 1995; Smith-Hefner 1988). By contrast, men—in part as a reflection of their greater autonomy—spend relatively more time hanging out in the public sphere eating, drinking coffee, smoking cigarettes, and pursuing women (*cari cewek*). As they approach their mid-twenties, young men are expected to begin putting aside money with an eye to eventual marriage and setting up households of their own.

World Bank statistics on women's employment confirm these ethnographic observations. Data for 2013 indicate that 47.6 percent of Indonesian women ages fifteen and older were employed.[5] The significance of these figures is clear when they are compared with employment figures from other Muslim-majority countries. The percentage of Indonesian women ages fifteen and older who are part of the workforce is almost *four times* higher than the percentage of working-age females employed in Jordan (at 12.1 percent), almost three times higher than the percentage of Egyptian women (at 16.8 percent), and over twice as high as the percentage of working women in Tunisia and Morocco.[6] According to social demographer Ariane J. Utomo (2014: 1688), who draws on data from Indonesia's Central Bureau of Statistics (BPS), the percentage of Indonesian women in the labor force is even higher—57 percent in 2000—up from 32 percent in 1971.

The Imperative to Marry

As with Bu Suharti quoted above, most Javanese parents now recognize the right of their daughters to choose their own husbands. At the same time and no less importantly, the great majority ask their daughters to put off serious involvement with the opposite sex—certainly while they are still in high school and, for most, during their time in college as well. Their concern is twofold. On the one hand, parents point to the situation of many women in their own generation who stopped their schooling in order to marry and who, as a result, never completed their degrees. On the other hand, parents fear the possibility that romantic involvements will result in pregnancy and bring shame to the family with similar results: the young woman would have to drop out of school to marry.

And yet, although Javanese parents warn their daughters to avoid relationships that could interfere with their studies and potentially prevent them from graduating, the fear of *never* marrying is also a palpable source of tension—not only for parents but for young

women as well. There is a pervasive and strong "marital imperative" among Indonesian Muslims, and young people, like their parents, regard marriage and children as an absolute social and moral
"given." In interviews, young people regularly referred to marriage
as a "religious duty" as well as an important means of repaying the
debt owed to parents for their care and upbringing. For Indonesian Muslims, marriage is also a mark of social maturity, and those
who opt not to marry suffer real and severe social stigmatization
(Parker 2008). There is a widespread assumption that those who do
not marry are in some sense "defective" or incomplete (*tidak sem-
purna*). Even homosexuals report that they experience strong social pressures to enter into heterosexual unions (Blackwood 2010;
Boellstorff 2005).

The Australian sociologist, Gavin Jones, describes Indonesia as
following a pattern of "universal marriage," defined as a country
where less than 5 percent of women are still single in their late
forties. In Indonesia in 2005, Jones and Gubhaju (2008: 11) write,
only 2 percent of Indonesian women in their late forties were never
married. Although this pattern has shifted in many areas of South
and Southeast Asia and may eventually shift in Indonesia as well
(see Jones 2005), marriage is still regarded as a required and valued
rite of passage and social standing for the overwhelming majority of
Indonesian youth. According to this near-universal norm, women
who reach their mid-twenties and are not yet married are considered "old maids" (*prawan tua*), and anxious concern is expressed
over their "marketability" and, in particular, their declining fertility.
In addition to being a religious requirement and a means to repay
one's moral debt to parents, marriage is closely linked to the imperative that one provide a grandchild *keturunan* (lit., descendant)
for eager grandparents. Age twenty-five was frequently cited by my
respondents as the optimal age for a woman to marry because it is
considered to be the peak of a woman's fertility, after which time
her ability to bear children is believed to decline rapidly.

Moral Panics

The widespread delays in youth marriage and the extended period
of unmarried singlehood have led to repeated public moral panics
that focus on the fear of unchecked sexual licentiousness among
unmarried youth. Conservative Muslim voices have been the most
insistent in these public debates on youth morality. Most such

spokespersons offer a simple and consistent message: young people should avoid any unchaperoned interactions with unrelated members of the opposite sex. The fear is that such interactions could easily lead to religiously illicit sexual relations (*zina*). They therefore urge young people already involved with someone to either end the relationship or marry quickly. Such public debates have in turn fueled the ascent of a new variety of Muslim youth preachers and relationship consultants (see Hoesterey 2008; Smith-Hefner 2009) specifically dedicated to offering religious guidance to youth on matters of sexual propriety in Islam; the same phenomenon has given rise to a no less pervasive genre of youth literature focusing on the social anxieties and moral perils of "youth in waiting."

Widely available and inexpensive handbooks and guides for unmarried youth offer practical advice and moral counsel on how to navigate the insecurities and moral temptations of singlehood. Many of the authors of these handbooks also work as professional consultants for schools and businesses and as motivational speakers for Indonesia's huge number of Muslim educational and religious organizations, as well as electronic and print media outlets. Not uncommonly, these consultants are themselves young people, only slightly older than the age of my respondents. They typically draw on their own relationship experiences in offering advice to their "younger siblings," who are wondering how, when, and with whom they will marry. Books with such topically unambiguous titles as *Single until Married: Making the Most of Singlehood* and *Single but Productive* encourage their readers to avoid inappropriate relations with members of the opposite sex, keep their emotions under control, and make the most of the period of unmarried singlehood. Authors remind their readers that although their "soulmate rests in God's hands" (*jodoh di tangan Tuhan*), this does not mean that one should simply wait for one's partner to appear. "Your soulmate may rest in God's hands, but if you are not prepared for him when he appears, he may not even notice you and walk right by!" (Kholid and Agustina 2013: 12; Saputra 2016). Authors therefore encourage their readers to actively work on "improving themselves" in order to become the most attractive—and, more specifically, pious—marriage candidates possible. Activities like keeping oneself busy through religious study and devotion, pursuing education and professional training, and engaging in charitable and social work activities like volunteering at a Muslim orphanage or teaching in a Qur'anic preschool are promoted as positive strategies for addressing sexual frustration and marital uncertainty.

Despite the widespread incidence of public moral panics, official statistics on levels of premarital sex among Indonesian youth are surprisingly low (in the range of 10–12 percent). Higher levels of sexual activity are reported by men than women and by non-Muslims than Muslims, with most instances of intercourse occurring within long-term relationships (Ford, Shaluhiyah, and Suryoputro 2007; I. Utomo 2002).[7] Though the reliability of survey questionnaires that focus on youth sexual behavior is somewhat problematic, the young people in my research reported similarly conservative attitudes with regard to premarital sex. What is more, multiple ethnographic studies, including my own, have found that, among those youth who do engage in sex, the use of contraceptives is not prevalent (Ford et al. 2007; I. Utomo 2003). Women say they worry about the possibility of negative side effects of the pill and even of condom use on long-term fertility. Young people (women as well as men) cite the embarrassment of purchasing contraceptives—especially the fear of encountering someone they know at the shops and kiosks where prophylactics are sold. Many young people, importantly, cite their moral principles ("my most basic principles") as keeping them from engaging in premarital sex, or at least from engaging in behaviors that could result in pregnancy. A young woman who becomes pregnant out of wedlock is quickly married to her impregnator. If he cannot be found, the pregnant woman will be married to a willing substitute in order to "cover up the shame" (*menututupi aib*).

Too Educated for Marriage

All of the young people I interviewed expressed a palpable level of anxiety over finding a marriage partner; however, the anxiety is notably more acute among young women. Although the age of first marriage has risen for both men and women, the increase is most marked among women. And it is women who have been identified as the focus of what has been referred to by scholars as a "marriage crisis" or "marriage squeeze" (Jones and Yeung 2014; A. Utomo 2014). The phenomenon refers to the difficulties many educated young women face in finding partners due to an imbalance in the number of available men or to young women putting off marriage for "too long" and aging out of the marital market.[8] Facing a narrowing pool of marriageable men, educated women scramble to identify a partner who is willing to negotiate work and family roles within the context of a "modern," companionate marriage.

Indonesian men have long been able to marry without social stigma into their thirties and, more rarely, even into their forties; male marriage at later ages is also not thought inappropriate for fathering and raising children. By contrast, women and public commentaries on young women express a consistent and high level of concern for the prospect of waning fertility after the age of twenty-five; as a result, an unmarried woman in her late twenties is almost universally regarded with a mixture of trepidation and concern. Children are eagerly anticipated and are expected to arrive soon after marriage. Young people regularly report, "If I am ready to marry, then I am ready to become a parent." None of the women in my survey contemplated a life alone as an attractive option, not even those who were finishing advanced degrees or already had secure employment or a career. Even among those women who had been supporting themselves for some time and very likely would be able to support themselves in the future, none could imagine the possibility of remaining unmarried.

Seriously Seeking Marriage

Mahmudah is representative of many of the unmarried, highly educated women in my study, and her story illustrates many of the themes introduced above. She is a tiny figure with a round face and a huge smile. She dresses in what is locally identified as "Saudi style," in a long solid-color robe and matching headscarf that reaches all the way down below her hips. It is a style of dress rather uncommon in Indonesia. Mahmudah is now completing an MA degree, but it is taking her longer than expected due to her work responsibilities. She has worked as a nanny and tutor overseas and as a religion teacher in Yogyakarta. She is currently a supervisor in a girls' boarding school. At thirty-four years old, Mahmudah has been actively and anxiously searching for a marriage partner for the past six years. She says,

> People consider me an old maid. If by age twenty-five a girl hasn't yet married, she's considered "unmarketable," an old maid, or not normal. That's how villagers think almost everywhere across Indonesia—and not just villagers . . . I mean, well, I don't feel that way, but it's the parents who feel embarrassed because others look at them and think, "Wow, their daughter isn't married and she's already so old! What's she waiting for?"

Mahmudah explains that at least part of her problem is that most of her cohort is now married. When she returns to her village, there is no one who might be a possible match. "I've lost my community," she says.

Because of her conservative dress, Mahmudah tends to attract men looking for a religiously conservative wife who will assume a subservient position within the marriage. Notwithstanding her conservative bearing, however, Mahmudah is looking for someone who views marriage in companionate terms—as a "partnership" in which both husband and wife will share familial responsibilities. She says she is above all looking for a partner with whom she can "dialogue," one who is willing to work with her as "part of a team," and can grow together with her over time. She admits that while she was initially hoping to find someone who shared her same level of education, she no longer feels that is critical, so long as he is "flexible" and "willing to compromise." She explains,

> I'm really serious [about marrying], and I'm not picky. Maybe I used to be. Like when I got my BA and I felt I really had to have someone with a BA. But now I don't think it's a problem, what's important is that we can connect. We can talk and come to an agreement about things. And we can work together as a team. No problem. We can improve things as we go along in the process of getting to know each other.

She is also looking for a husband who will understand her desire to continue to work. Like many other women in my survey, Mahmudah takes her responsibility to her parents seriously and has furthered her education at least in part so as to be able support them in their old age. Her burden is double as she was adopted by her maternal aunt as a toddler and has both her biological and adoptive parents to support. She says,

> I've been working part time since I was nineteen to help pay for my studies, and when I finally graduate, I will work full-time. Work is really important to me. I could never marry a man who didn't allow me to work. I have to be realistic. I have two sets of parents to think of. If I wasn't allowed to work, what would they do?

Repeated attempts to meet with young men, especially those recommended by her friends and colleagues as possible candidates for marriage, have made Mahmudah realistic about her options and increasingly willing to make compromises. But she has discovered that too many men find her educational status and experience intimidating and quickly withdraw their interest once they learn about her achievements. This masculinist anxiety figured frequently in my interviews: many men stated quite openly that they fear that a woman with more education and experience than themselves will want to "take the lead" in family decision-making and will compromise the husband's social standing. Mahmudah shares,

> Lots of guys just back down when they find out about my education and experience. They wonder if I would be happy as their partner because they haven't done anything like that. They feel inferior (*minder*). They say, "Later, if we marry, I'll be behind, and you'll be in front making the decisions and I won't be able to do anything at all." . . . I tell them, that's not how it should be. We have to complement each other (*kita harus saling melengkapi*). "There will be moments when I'm in front and moments when you are in front. How could it ever be that I would be the one to lead the prayers? Not possible! But maybe in the education of our child, I would know more, and I would lead there." And they would reply, "I'm just not sufficiently self-confident." "Well, okay, if that's the case."

As these comments illustrate, one of the distinguishing features of gender-role normativity in Muslim Indonesia today is that, even while the movement of women into higher education and post-marital employment has been broadly accepted, the idea that the husband remains the "head of the household" (*kepala keluarga*) remains strong. That conviction informs and injects a measure of tension into male perceptions of highly educated women and adds to the difficulties that older educated women face in identifying a possible partner.

An Extended Courtship

Febriyanti offers an example of another common pattern among educated women—that is, marriage delay within the context of an extended courtship. At the age of thirty-one, she has an MA and is a lecturer in history at an Indonesian university. Febriyanti plans to go on to get her PhD but emphasizes that she is anxious to marry first. She realizes that if she were to go abroad unmarried, she would return home in her mid- to late thirties and her chances of ever marrying would be slim. In fact, Febriyanti has had a serious a serious boyfriend for the past six years. He has a BA in business administration and works as a consultant on intermittent projects. Although she is anxious to marry, the couple has encountered multiple challenges that have resulted in repeated postponements.

Febriyanti, like many of the other women in my study, links marriage first and foremost to the desire to have and to raise children, to make her parents happy (*membalas budi*), and to fulfill the requirements of her Islamic faith. Febriyanti said, "Of course it's a given that I will marry. For me it's a way of honoring my parents and God. Because I believe that marrying is a form of devotion, of worship." Like Mahmudah, Febriyanti has been working on her own since she obtained her BA and emphasizes her plans to continue working in order to help support her younger siblings as well as her family, especially her parents. Her father's health is poor, and he is no longer able to pay for the education of Febriyanti's youngest brother. Febriyanti has been paying her brother's tuition for the past several years and has encouraged him to progress toward an MA as well.

Although she sometimes despairs that she will never marry, Febriyanti says that she has invested so much time and energy in her relationship with her current boyfriend that she feels she cannot break it off. She worries that at her age and with her level of education, finding someone else would be difficult. She too reports that what she wants above all is a life partner who values and recognizes the importance of shared commitment and dedication to a mutual conjugal project. But the years of waiting to marry, she says, have made her more realistic. Not one to hedge her bets, while she waits, she continues with her plans to apply to a PhD program abroad.

Marriage without Courtship

Despite the difficulties educated women encounter in securing a marriage partner, very few say they would consider asking their parents to arrange a marriage for them. Whereas just one or two generations ago, the majority of marriages in Indonesia were parentally arranged, today the percentage of arranged marriages has dropped precipitously (Jones 1994). Acknowledging what is in social fact a widespread increase in female autonomy, especially among educated women, parents say they "do not dare" to make arrangements for their daughters, fearing they would be blamed later if the marriage did not work out.

Rather than turning to parents, some Muslim women are turning to a variety of different types of Muslim marriage bureaus and brokers or matchmakers to find a partner. Many of these women subscribe to the admonition heard in conservative Muslim and Islamist circles, that all premarital socialization with unrelated members of the opposite sex is sinful. Over the past fifteen to twenty years this cultural conviction has given rise to the growing, albeit not yet universal, belief that "there is no dating in Islam—only *ta'aruf*" (meeting for the purpose of deciding whether or not to marry). At least some have decided that *ta'aruf* or quickly marrying without extensive premarital familiarization is a reassuring solution to a marriage market under pressure.

Nindy is one of those women who turned to a Muslim matchmaking service to find a husband. Tall, with an oval face, she hardly looks like someone who would have any trouble finding a partner. But Nindy had attended sex-segregated Muslim schools all of her life and was painfully shy. At thirty-three years old, she had never had a boyfriend. She explained that her cousin literally pushed her to attend several mass matchmaking events, filling out the requisite paperwork for her and on one occasion even forcing her into a waiting taxi so she would arrive on time.

Increasingly popular in post-resurgent Indonesia (which is to say, since the late 1990s), these large-scale matchmaking events are typically organized by religious individuals or organizations of a moderately conservative inclination who are motivated by the conviction that it is their moral duty to help Muslim singles meet and marry. Matchmaking meetings attract anywhere from fifty to several hundred singles, almost always more women than men. To enroll in the event, participants submit their "biodata" to a committee that then facilitates the exchange of data and subsequent meetings between participants. Biodata typically include information on religion, age, height, weight, and complexion, and a succinct statement about what one is looking for in a marital partner. The requirements for participating are simple but strict: one must be single, serious in one's matrimonial intentions, and ready to marry quickly. Some organizations also offer to pay for wedding expenses and even include a honeymoon package to Bali or Singapore.

Nindy eventually met her husband at one of these mass matchmaking events. Now thirty-six with a two-year-old daughter, Nindy married just shy of thirty-four years of age and got pregnant immediately. At the time she married, Nindy had already finished her BA and had worked for some time as an assistant teacher at a school for children with special needs. She has since taken the national exam to become a civil servant and now has a full-time teaching position. Her husband is two years younger than she is and has only a grade-school education. He makes a modest income as a salesclerk in an office supply store. Nindy explained, "When we finally met, I don't know why, but I felt sympathy for him (*saya simpati*) right away. He seemed like a good person and easy-going. And we were both mature and ready to marry. So why not? Maybe this was my intended match (*jodoh*)."

Because they were both serious and ready to marry and because Nindy was concerned about her age and anxious to have a child quickly, just one week after they met, the couple decided to marry. The marriage took place as soon as arrangements could be made with their two families—that is, within a few months. According to Nindy, "We married quickly and without dating because we were both ready and because of my age. I wanted a child, so why wait?"

The differences between Nindy and her husband with regard to age, education, and income, are unusual, but the couple's arrangement underscores the innovative role played by Muslim matchmaking services. Their organizers assure their participants that so long as both parties are serious about marriage and willing to live according to the principles of the Qur'an and the Sunnah, their marriage will succeed. Central to these principles is the ideal that wives recognize their husband's role as the moral guide and leader of the family (*imam, pembimbing*) and the reaffirmation that the wife will take primary responsibility for the household and the children.

As the popularity of *ta'aruf* has spread, not all women who choose to marry by religious arrangement are "older" (that is, over twenty-five). Especially among young women active in one of Indonesia's new Islamist movements, one encounters women in their twenties who see Muslim marriage services as a way to avoid what they view as the inevitable sin involved in dating as well as the dreaded possibility of becoming an "old maid" (*perawan tua*) and no longer "marketable" (*tidak laku*). Dina, for example, married by *ta'aruf* when she was just twenty-four and still in medical school. Her parents had asked her to wait on marriage until she had finished her internship and become a doctor, but she was worried about how long those achievements might take. Dina belonged to a *tarbiyah* religious study group, a Muslim Brotherhood–influenced educational movement that has become popular on Indonesian university campuses since the 1990s (Bubalo and Fealy 2005; Machmudi 2008). As with Muslim Brotherhood–inspired groups in the Middle East, *tarbiyah* groups are organized in a small, networked manner, with a nonetheless significant measure of teacher-student hierarchy. The group in which Dina was active had discussed with their teacher (*guru ngaji*) the benefits of marrying quickly without dating, and everyone had agreed it was the right route to take. Rather than an event-specific religious bureau, responsibility for the marital selection and arrangement was the responsibility of Dina's religion teacher. Dina explained,

> My parents wanted me to wait to marry until I finished my medical studies and set up my practice, but I told them that I was interested in marrying by *ta'aruf* so they would be prepared for that. But when it happened, it was unexpected. The process was so fast. I knew him (the guy who would become my husband) but we weren't friends or anything. We were both involved in *tarbiyah* religious study groups, but not the same one and we had different teachers . . . So, one day my teacher suddenly asked me, "Do you have any plans to marry? Are you ready?" And lots of other questions like "What's your idea of marriage?" and "What kind of household do you envision?" It was because the guy who is now my husband had signaled his interest in marrying me. And I told my teacher yes, I was ready to marry.

The couple met several times to discuss their expectations, but always with both of their religion teachers present as chaperones. In those meetings, Dina made certain that her future husband would agree to allow her to work. He assured her that he considered her medical work as a "blessing" to others and that *as long as she could find time to care for their future children,* he would agree to it. It took their families several months to make the wedding arrangements because the groom's parents lived some distance from Yogyakarta. During that time the couple only rarely met and never without a chaperone present; nonetheless, as Dina describes it, the process was quite romantic. She recounts that the fact that she and her future husband met so rarely only heightened the anticipation:[9] "It's really true what people say: that it's so much more romantic to date after you've married (*pacaran setelah menikah*)."

Indonesian Women and Waithood

As in so many other newly developing countries in the world, educational and economic expansion in Indonesia has resulted in significant marital delays for growing numbers of young people, especially in the ranks of the country's new and aspiring middle class. Indonesian waithood's most striking social effect is seen in the difficulties faced by young, educated women in identifying an appropriate marriage partner, difficulties compounded by these women's age and educational attainment relative to that of the pool of available men. As most Indonesian men continue to marry "down," "older" women with too much education find they have educated themselves out of the marriage market and are "unsellable" (*tidak laku*). While some education in a female marriage partner is regarded as a positive, many men continue to fear that women with too much education will challenge their position of authority within the family.

The situation of Indonesian women parallels in many ways that of women in other Asian countries such as China and Vietnam who are also postponing marriage in order to pursue higher education and employment. In those countries too, there is a perceived "marriage crisis," one that is often blamed on women being too self-centered and "picky." These popular assumptions are belied, however, by educated women's stated desires to delay their marriage in order to work so they can lessen the economic burden of parents and help with the support and schooling of younger siblings. Indonesian women aspire to a measure of personal autonomy through these achievements, but that does not preclude their desires for companionship and social and familial belonging. Young, educated women are anxious to marry and have children—not only as the fulfillment of a moral debt owed to parents and their perceived social role but as an important requirement of their faith.

In Indonesia, the "marriage crisis" is widely framed as a crisis of youth morality and it is Indonesian Muslim groups that have stepped in to offer a moral and religious solution. Muslim organizations offer young people an alternative to the moral uncertainties of dating by identifying potential partners who share religious principles and a vision for a shared household while simultaneously holding out the promise of a romantic, companionate relationship. Rather than returning to reliance on parental matches, many young people embrace the promise that, if one comes to the process well prepared and puts one's future in God's hands, it will all work out in the end. But the economic and ethical terms of the problem's resolution are unambiguous and important: they involve *affirming* the new middle-class realities of women's education and professionalism, while also *working to assure* that both spouses abide by Islamic ethical norms—ethical norms that include the recognition of the husband as the family leader and the wife as the household manager and caregiver of children.

The social and cultural concomitants of the phenomenon of marriage delay or "extended singlehood" in Indonesia and in Asia more broadly then offer a contrast with those reported for the Muslim Middle East. Unlike at least some areas of the Middle East, the growing incidence and prolongation of waithood in Indonesia has not primarily been the consequence of male unemployment and the steeply rising costs of marriage (Ghannam 2013; Hasso 2010; Singerman 2007). Nor has the phenomenon been consistently linked to growing male frustration leading to depression, disillusionment, or religious radicalism (Schielke 2008). Waithood in Indonesia is less an unavoidable set of circumstances that constrains youth possibilities, than an aspirational period of extended singlehood in which young people, particularly young women, pursue newly available options—not only for themselves, but for their families. The public concern regarding waithood's spread in Indonesia has, similarly, less to do with social or political unrest than with the concern of a new generation of Muslim preachers to ensure that, even as delayed marriage and women's higher education become part of the new Indonesian reality, these developments are brought squarely into alignment with Islamic ethical norms.

Nancy J. Smith-Hefner is Professor of Anthropology and Chair of the Department of Anthropology at Boston University. A specialist of Southeast Asia, gender, and Islam, she is author of *Khmer American: Identity and Moral Education in a Diasporic Community* (University of California Press, 1999) as well as numerous book chapters and journal articles. Her recent book, *Islamizing Intimacies: Youth, Sexuality, and Gender in Contemporary Indonesia* (University of Hawaii Press, 2019), is a study of the changing personal lives and sexual attitudes of educated, Muslim Javanese youth against the backdrop of a resurgent interest in more normative forms of Islam. Smith-Hefner received her BA, MA, and PhD from the University of Michigan.

Notes

1. By 2008, 84 percent of Indonesian youth between the ages of thirteen and fifteen were enrolled in junior high school, 55 percent of those between the ages of sixteen and eighteen were enrolled in senior high school, and 17 percent of college-aged youth were enrolled in tertiary institutions (Parker and Nilan 2013: 80–81).
2. In 2014, according to UNESCO statistics, women's secondary school enrollment had essentially caught up with men's at 99 percent gender parity (UNESCO Institute for Statistics, "Education, Indonesia," http://data .uis.unesco.org, retrieved 2 March 2017). World Bank statistics for the year following (2015) indicate that at the tertiary level, women's enroll-

ment (at 32.8 percent) had surpassed men's (at 29.4 percent) (World Bank Gender Data Portal, "Indonesia," http://datatopics.worldbank.org, retrieved 12 March 2017).

3. By 2005, that figure had risen to 25.7 years (Jones and Gubhaju 2011: 51).
4. In order to protect the identity of respondents, all names are pseudonyms.
5. http://search.worldbank.org/data?qterm=employment+in+Indonesia, retrieved 21 August 2014.
6. http://search.worldbank.org/data?qterm=employment+in+Egypt; http://search.worldbank.org/data?qterm=employment+in+Jordan; http://search.worldbank.org/data?qterm=employment+in+Morocco; http://search.worldbank.org/data?qterm=employment+in+Tunisia, retrieved 21 August 2014.
7. However, unlike the pattern found in some other Asian contexts, living together outside of wedlock—in Javanese, *kumpul kebo* or "the mingling of water buffalo"—is not at all widespread in Indonesia, and is a target of strong religious and societal disapproval.
8. Young people often cite an imbalance in the overall number of Indonesian men relative to women as creating this crisis. But statistics do not bear this out. It is not the overall number of men relative to women that is the problem, but the number of desirable men with the appropriate level of education.
9. Early reports on the relative satisfaction of couples who have married by *ta'aruf* indicate that these unions are, in fact, quite happy (see Ardhianita and Andayani 2005).

References

Adely, Fida. 2012. *Gendered Paradoxes: Educating Jordanian Women in Nation, Faith, and Progress*. Chicago: University of Chicago Press.

Ardhianita, Iis, and Budi Andayani. 2005. "Kepuasan Pernikahan Ditinjau dari Berpacaran dan Tidak Berpacaran" [Marital satisfaction viewed from dating or not dating]. *Jurnal Psikologi* 32(2): 101–11.

"Asian Demography: The Flight from Marriage." 2011. *The Economist*, 20 August. Retrieved 4 April 2016 from https://www.economist.com/briefing/2011/08/20/the-flight-from-marriage.

Blackwood, Evelyn. 2010. *Falling into the Lesbi World*. Honolulu: University of Hawaii Press.

Boellstorff, Tom. 2005. *The Gay Archipelago: Sexuality and Nation in Indonesia*. Princeton: Princeton University Press.

Brenner, Suzanne A. 1995. "Why Women Rule the Roost: Rethinking Javanese Ideologies of Gender and Self-Control." In *Bewitching Women, Pious Men: Gender and Body Politics in Southeast Asia*, ed. Aiwa Ong and Michael G. Peletz, 19–50. Berkeley: University of California Press.

Bubalo, Anthony, and Greg Fealy. 2005. *Joining the Caravan? The Middle East, Islamism, and Indonesia*. Paper No 5. NSW, Australia: The Lowey Institute.

Earl, Catherine. 2014. *Vietnam's New Middle Classes: Gender, Career, City*. Copenhagen: Nias Press.

Ford, Nicholas J., Zahroh Shaluhiyah, and Antono Suryoputro. 2007. "A Rather Benign Sexual Culture: Socio-sexual Lifestyles of Youth in Urban Central Java, Indonesia." *Population, Space and Place* 13(1): 59–76.

Ghannam, Farha. 2013. *Live and Die Like a Man: Gender Dynamics in Urban Egypt*. Stanford: Stanford University Press.

Hasso, Frances. 2010. *Consuming Desires: Family Crisis and the State in the Middle East*. Stanford: Stanford University Press.

Hefner, Robert W. 2000. *Civil Islam: Muslims and Democratization in Indonesia*. Princeton: Princeton University Press.

Hoesterey, James B. 2008. "Marketing Morality: The Rise, Fall and Rebranding of a Gym." In *Expressing Islam: Religious Life and Politics in Indonesia*, ed. Greg Fealy and Sally White, 95–112. Singapore: Institute of Southeast Asian Studies.

Hull, Terence H., and Gavin W. Jones. 1994. "Demographic Perspectives." In *Indonesia's New Order: The Dynamics of Socio-economic Transformation*, ed. Hal Hill, 164–68. Honolulu: University of Hawaii Press.

Jones, Gavin W. 1994. *Marriage and Divorce in Islamic South-East Asia*. Singapore: Oxford University Press.

———. 2004. "Not 'When to Marry' but 'Whether to Marry': The Changing Context of Marriage Decisions in East and Southeast Asia." In *Untying the Knot: Ideal and Reality in Asian Marriage*, ed. Gavin W. Jones and K. Ramdas, 3–58. Singapore: NUS Press.

———. 2005. "The 'Fight from Marriage' in South-east and East Asia." *Journal of Comparative Family Studies* 36(1): 93–119.

———. 2009. "Women, Marriage, and Family in Southeast Asia." In *Gender Trends in Southeast Asia: Women Now, Women in the Future*, ed. T. W. Devashayam, 12–30. Singapore: Institute of Southeast Asian Studies.

Jones, Gavin W., and Bina Gubhaju. 2008. *Trends in Age at Marriage in the Provinces of Indonesia*. Singapore: Asian Research Institute, National University of Singapore.

———. 2011. "Regional Differences in Marriage Patterns in Indonesia in the Twenty-first Century." In *Changing Marriage Patterns in Southeast Asia: Economic and Socio-cultural Dimensions*, ed. Gavin W. Jones, Terence H. Hull, and Maznah Mohamad, 50–61. New York: Routledge.

Jones, Gavin W., and Peter Hagul. 2001. "Schooling in Indonesia: Crisis-Related and Longer-term Issues." *Bulletin of Indonesian Economic Studies* 37(2): 207–31.

Jones, Gavin W., and Wei-Jun Jean Yeung. 2014. "Marriage in Asia." *Journal of Family Issues* 35(12): 1567–83.

Kholid, Setia Furqon, and Ina Agustina. 2013. *Jangan Jatuh Cinta! Tapi Bangun Cinta!* [Don't fall in love, build love]. Sumedang, West Java: Rumah Karya Publishing.

Machmudi, Yon. 2008. "The Emergence of *New Santri* in Indonesia." *Journal of Indonesian Islam* 2(1): 69–102.

Nilan, Pam. 2008. "Youth Transitions to Urban, Middle-class Marriage in Indonesia: Faith, Family and Finances." *Journal of Youth Studies* 11(1): 65–82.

Oey-Gardiner, Mayling. 1991. "Gender Differences in Schooling in Indonesia." *Bulletin of Indonesian Economic Studies* 27(1): 57–79.

Parker, Lyn. 2008. "To Cover the Aurat: Veiling, Sexual Morality, and Agency among the Muslim Minangkabau, Indonesia." *Intersections: Gender and Sexuality in Asia and the Pacific* 16: 1–76.

Parker, Lyn, and Pam Nilan. 2013. *Adolescents in Contemporary Indonesia.* New York: Routledge.

Pew Research Center. 2010. "Muslim Population of Indonesia." Retrieved 9 January 2019 from http://www.pewforum.org/2010/11/04/muslim-population-of-indonesia/.

Saputra, Effendi. 2016. *Walau Jomblo, Tetap Produktif* [Single but still productive]. Jakarta: Media Komputindo.

Schielke, Samuli. 2008. "Boredom and Despair in Rural Egypt." *Contemporary Islam* 2(3): 251–70.

Singerman, Diane. 2007. "The Economic Imperatives of Marriage: Emerging Practices and Identities Among Youth in the Middle East." *Middle East Youth Initiative*, Working Paper No. 6, September, The Brookings Institution, Wolfensohn Center for Development, Washington, DC.

Smith-Hefner, Nancy J. 1988. "Women and Politeness: The Javanese Example." *Language in Society* 17(4): 535–54.

———. 2005. "The New Muslim Romance: Changing Patterns of Courtship and Marriage among Educated Javanese Youth." *Journal of Southeast Asian Studies* 36(3): 441–59.

———. 2007. "Javanese Women and the Veil in Post-Suharto Indonesia." *The Journal of Asian Studies* 66(2): 389–420.

———. 2009. "'Hypersexed' Youth and the New Muslim Sexology in Contemporary Java." *Review of Indonesian and Malay Affairs* 43(1): 209–44.

———. 2019. *Islamizing Intimacies: Youth, Sexuality, and Gender in Contemporary Indonesia.* Honolulu: University of Hawaii Press.

US Library of Congress. n.d. "Urbanization." Retrieved 10 January 2019 from http://countrystudies.us/indonesia/33.htm.

Utomo, Ariane J. 2014. "Marrying Up? Trends in Age and Education Gaps among Married Couples in Indonesia." *Journal of Family Issues* 35(12): 1683–1706.

Utomo, Iwu Dwisetyani. 2002. "Sexual Values and Early Experiences among Young People in Jakarta." In *Coming of Age in South and Southeast Asia: Youth, Courtship and Sexuality*, ed. Lenore Manderson and Pranee Liamputtong, 207–27. Richmond: Curzon Press.

———. 2003. "Reproductive Health Education in Indonesia: School versus Parents' Roles in Providing Sexuality Information." *RIMA (Review of Indonesian and Malaysian Affairs)* 37(1): 107–34.

Wolf, Diane L. 1996. "Javanese Factory Daughters: Gender, the State, and Industrial Capitalism." In *Fantasizing the Feminine in Indonesia*, ed. Laurie J. Sears, 140–62. Durham: Duke University Press.

Part III

DELAYED MARRIAGE AND
THE MEANINGS OF SINGLEHOOD

Chapter 9

Conjugal Conundrums
Conversion and Marriage Delay in the Contemporary Caribbean

Brendan Jamal Thornton

Introduction

Legal or "traditional" marriage in the Caribbean has for decades posed a unique challenge for social scientists and Caribbean people alike. The problem, as it has been framed in the literature, is based on the disconnect between the ideals of religious doctrine—primarily the pervasive Christian ideal of marriage—and the prevailing reality of common-law unions in Caribbean family ideology and organization (including the regular attribution of "matrifocality" and "male marginality" to Caribbean domestic units). Historically, the Caribbean has consistently low marriage rates relative to the rest of the world. Conjugal ideals of "romantic, monogamous, enduring marriage and co-residence," while familiar and, at least in some ways, desirable, are largely impractical for many Caribbean peoples, often being viewed as inappropriate or deemed "not for us" (Barrow 1995: 57, 65). Instead, formal marriage is commonly avoided, as it does not represent a functional option to many men and women who see the institution as limiting. The conflict here between cultural ideal and practical reality is especially acute for evangelical Christian converts who must balance the demanding expectations of the faith with the actualities of everyday life and conventional negotiations of sociality, intimacy, and relatedness in the region. Perhaps surprisingly, even after conversion, common-law unions perdure despite additional pressure to formalize sexual relations through marriage upon joining the church. Drawing on insights from my ethnographic work in the Dominican Republic as well as the anthropological and sociological literature on marriage and the family in the Caribbean, this chapter considers the notion of "waithood"—or what it means to postpone marriage—in an area of the world where deferred marriage is more often the norm than the exception and where certain conjugal unions, even for the faithful, remain quixotic and present just as many relational conundrums as they do reasonable solutions to the elemental matters of romance, reproduction, and prosperity in today's Caribbean.

Delayed marriage has been the Caribbean norm for years. However, to postpone marriage here does not necessarily imply extended singlehood since any number of conjugal union types might prevail in the place of formal marriage. The Caribbean, understood in general terms, stands in contrast to other regional cases explored in this volume, not only for its long-term and relatively stable commitment to extra-legal unions and flexible approach to conjugality, but also for the relatively permissive degree of sexual license men and women enjoy alongside the widespread Christian propagation of sexual modesty and restraint. With this considered, alongside the data explored below, the emergent conditions of waithood globally may not correspond evenly with the established and enduring patterns of marriage delay, long observed in the Caribbean. If waithood is to be theorized here, it must account for the strategic and routine modes of deferral and avoidance that Caribbean people have employed for decades in their efforts to manage local desires as well as social expectations when it comes to reproductive partnerships and procreative goals.

It can be said that, while marriage in the Caribbean is religiously valorized, it is difficult to enact. In what follows, I draw special attention to the key dilemmas fueling marriage delay by focusing on the *conjugal conundrums* facing impoverished male converts who, by virtue of competing obligations, are precariously situated between the authoritative prescriptions of the church that oblige them to marry and powerful sociocultural imperatives that discourage adoption of the nuclear family model and disincentivize marriage at an early age. Because of their structural position and, presumably, as devout converts, their greater commitment to the church and its ideals, the male faithful experience these dilemmas more forcefully than anyone else: marriage at once urgently compelled by their church membership but no more easily realized. A focus on these and other men helps throw the perennial question of whether or not to marry and when into sharper relief and sheds valuable light on how Caribbean men and women differentially experience the conjugal conundrums underlying deferred marriage throughout the region.

Considering marriage delay and the waithood concept in relation to the Caribbean is instructive because it reminds us that reproductive unions are by definition elastic; legal marriage is but one (albeit popular) possibility among many. The Christian institution of marriage, along with its endorsement of the nuclear family, cannot be viewed as essential to reproduction, even where Christian moral values predominate. Indeed, there is nothing natural or inherently superior about co-residential, monogamous, and/or stable unions, much less those that are "divinely ordained." Caribbean family ideology and organization demonstrate the limited and contextual efficacy of Christian marriage; time and again Caribbean people choose extra-legal partnerships over those sanctioned by law or religious rite in ways that belie the universal appeal of formal matrimony and betray its ostensible suitability and attractiveness across time and space.

Caribbean Family Ideology and Organization

The subject of marriage and family is not new to the sociology and anthropology of the Caribbean. In fact, research on the Caribbean family constituted an important segment of the primordial bedrock of Caribbean studies in social science from the 1950s through the 1970s and produced a great deal of empirical work illuminating the structure and function of kinship organization and ideology across the region.[1] The lion's share of this output highlights the frequency and apparent ordinariness of extra-legal family formation, delayed or late entry into marriage, and the prevalence of women-headed households, especially—though not exclusively—among Afro-Caribbean, poor, and working-class families (Rubenstein 1983: 283).[2]

Noting important deviations from the nuclear family model, this scholarship draws specific attention to three conjugal union types that are popular in Caribbean countries; these are commonly referred to as visiting, common-law, and legal marriage. *Legal mar-*

riage, the only union formally sanctioned by law or by religious rite, refers to a union where partners live together in the same household and are "married" by lawful or religious ceremony. *Common-law* marriage refers to unions where partners share a common household but are not legally married and therefore lack the social status and formal sanctioning afforded to couples in legal marriages. And, lastly, *visiting unions,* the most flexible if least prestigious of the three union types, refer to consensual partnerships between individuals who are neither officially married nor living in a common-law union; in visiting relationships, couples do not share a household and their union is not sanctioned by legal or religious prescription. Raymond T. Smith (1988: 111) summarizes the range of meanings as follows: *legal marriage* is a legally contracted union; *common-law marriage* is a co-residential non-legal union; and a *visiting union* is a union that is neither legal nor co-residential. Regardless of union status, Caribbean peoples might consider themselves or others to be "married" or refer to their partners as "spouses" in any three of these arrangements—that is to say that the legality of one's union status is sometimes obscured by the colloquial use of terms like "husband" and "wife" inasmuch as they are applied indiscriminately to a variety of conjugal scenarios. In the Dominican Republic, for instance, it is customary to refer to domestic partners or longtime romantic companions as *esposo* and *esposa,* whether or not the individuals concerned are legally married or even share a residence.

While the nuclear family model, along with formal, legal marriage, is aspirational throughout the Caribbean—a marker of social status and respectability (Wilson 1969: 78) and a cultural ideal readily acknowledged if not enthusiastically endorsed across economic classes—common-law and visiting unions are commonplace and tend to be institutionalized among the poor and working classes for whom childbirth out of wedlock is perceived as natural and transpires without social disgrace (Barrow 2001: 422). Caribbean people distinguish between legal and non-legal unions, to be sure, but generally acknowledge the range of unions to be legitimate, even inevitable, conjugal arrangements. At the same time, they assign varying degrees of respectability to each status according to pervasive patriarchal Eurocentric and Christian moral values that structure the ethics of family formation from above (Barrow 2001: 422; Reddock 2005: 80; Safa 1998: 206; also see Clarke 1957; Wilson 1969). Formal marriage, however unlikely for some, is nevertheless considered the most prestigious and respectable option, while visiting unions garner the least esteem but are no less prevalent (e.g.,

Roberts and Sinclair 1978: 64–65).[3] In general, the rules governing Caribbean family formation are not rigid, therefore permitting considerable sexual freedom and accommodating a variety of possible domestic configurations (Powell 1986: 83). Extra-legal unions are the prevailing norm, and it is not uncommon for married men to have mistresses or for women to have children with several different men throughout their lifetime. This relatively laissez-faire attitude toward conjugality and childbearing characterizes the flexible approach to marriage, residence, and partnering patterns typical of social and sexual relations in the Caribbean.

The normalcy afforded common-law and visiting unions and the resulting social dynamics are defining characteristics of the Caribbean region according to several demographic indicators. According to Powell (1986: 83) and others, roughly 70 percent of all births in the Caribbean happen in non-legal unions (compare that with only about 15 percent globally), and it is estimated that at least one-third of Caribbean households are headed by women.[4] These numbers have changed little over time. Despite a precipitous fall in fertility rates since the 1970s, for example, the ages of women at first marriage and birth of first child in Caribbean countries have remained fairly constant.[5] This contrasts with Europe, Central Asia, and other regions that have witnessed significant delays in family formation over the same time period (Chioda 2016: 45–46). Even considering significant advancements in economic and educational opportunities, especially where it concerns the progress of women—not to mention demographic changes and important political and cultural transformations across the region—family formation in the Caribbean has not changed appreciably for several generations (Barrow 1996, 2001; Douglas 1992: 15–16; McKenzie 1993; Reddock 2005; Roberts and Sinclair 1978; R. Smith 1988: 166).

Marriage and the Christian Church

Popular ideas about conjugal roles and relationships in the Caribbean differ drastically from those enshrined by Christian churches, which more or less unanimously promote marriage as the ideal union. From the perspective of both Catholicism and Protestantism (and any number of its seemingly infinite denominations), legal Christian marriage is the only legitimate and morally appropriate context for sexual contact and childbearing. Any other sexual arrangement outside of monogamous heterosexual marriage constitutes "living in sin." Most conjugal unions in the Caribbean are, therefore, according to its primary religious institutions, immoral, deviant, and sinful, and, as a consequence, deemed incompatible with serving God.

The marriage ideal itself, seemingly ubiquitous throughout the Caribbean, is a product of the pervasive influence Catholic and Protestant Christianities have exercised over the region since it was first colonized (Thornton 2016). Subsequently, Christian churches (not to mention other religious institutions) have exerted strong pressure on couples to marry, but their efforts have been met with varying degrees of success. Caribbean couples remain firmly committed to common-law and visiting unions despite longstanding opposition from some of the largest and oldest cultural institutions in the region. Nearly two decades ago, Barrow (1996: 439) made the telling observation that even in response to ethical damnation, Caribbean people seem unlikely to change their cultural practices when it comes to reproduction and marriage.

Remarkably, even with the considerable expansion of evangelical and, in particular, Pentecostal-charismatic forms of Christianity over the past forty years, little has changed. Pentecostal Christianity tends to be more demanding than other Christian denominations when it comes to the moral identity and ascetic obligations of its flock, including the firm insistence on marriage by religious rite. The expectation is that conversion to Pentecostal Christianity will be followed by a strict transformation in the moral character of the convert. As part of their "rebirth in Christ," the born-again faithful are expected to reform aspects of their life once characterized as sinful. This often means severing social ties with familiars whom they fear might draw them back into sin. In order to ensure godliness, converts follow prohibitions on drinking, smoking, dancing, fornicating, fighting, and swearing, and abide by a bevy of behavioral prescriptions intended to distinguish them from the "unconverted." Among the prescriptions for living a righteous Christian life is formal marriage to another likeminded churchgoer who shares the same spiritual goals. Upon conversion, converts are instructed to terminate any illicit sexual relationships and to seek suitable partners for marriage who will help them in their quest for salvation.

Termination of common-law and visiting relationships, for many churches, is a prerequisite to full membership in the congregation (though it depends on the current policies of the specific church). In many churches, for example, baptism may be withheld until an unlawful union is severed or made regular through the appropriate marriage rites. Some churches reject common-law unions out of hand, while others are more permissive and willing to recognize stable and committed unions as acceptable, if by no means ideal. Because of this, marriage might be sought for no other reason than to facilitate full participation in the faith community and to legitimize one's place among the devoted.

Little evidence exists to suggest that marriage practices have radically changed for the converted. Over the past several decades, Pentecostalism, and charismatic Christianity more broadly, are among the fastest growing forms of Christianity worldwide, with the vast majority of conversions occurring among the poor and popular classes in the Global South. Since the 1970s, Protestant growth throughout the Caribbean and Latin America can be described as impressive. In the Dominican Republic alone, for example, the number of Protestant Christians rose from 1.6 percent of the population in the 1960s to nearly 23 percent today, and of those Protestants, 81 percent are Pentecostal by denomination or identity. Added to that, 52 percent of all practicing Catholics in the country identify as charismatic, a "pentecostalized" form of Catholicism (Pew Research Center 2014: 64). Surprisingly, over that same period, the marriage rate has not changed appreciably. According to UNPD (2008) *World Marriage Data*, the crude marriage rate in the Dominican Republic in 1970 was 4.2 (annual marriages per thousand) and in 2005 it was recorded again as 4.2, exactly the same rate. For comparative purposes, Jamaica's crude marriage rate went up from 4.9 in 1970 to 8.7 in 2006; Cuba's went down from 13.4 in 1970 to 5.0 in 2006; Puerto Rico's decreased from 10.9 in 1970 to 5.8 in 2006; Martinique's marriage rate fell from 5.4 in 1970 to 3.7 in 2006; and Trinidad and Tobago's stayed relatively stable from 6.8 in 1970 to 6.3 in 2005.

It seems that Pentecostals and other evangelical Christian groups, while successful at converting Catholics and others to the faith, have not been as successful at convincing them to marry, at least in the widespread transformative cultural ways they so often claim. Scarce evidence exists to suggest a marriage revolution has attended the otherwise stark charismatic revival that has swept through the Caribbean in earnest since the 1970s and 1980s. To my knowledge, no systematic or comparative study of marriage rates among Protestant families in the Caribbean has ever been undertaken. Much more research in this area is needed to determine to what degree conversion has affected the marriage practices of believers who, by all other indications, appear to be following the same cultural trends of the region.

For the past fourteen years, my ongoing fieldwork and ethnographic research in the Caribbean has focused on impoverished urban communities and the role religious identity plays in the management of everyday life (Thornton 2013, 2016, 2018a, 2018b). Between 2007 and 2009 (with significant follow-up visits in 2010 and 2012), I conducted comprehensive ethnographic research with a Pentecostal community in a poor urban neighborhood of Villa Altagracia in the Dominican Republic. A primary focus of this research concerned conversion and the intersecting themes of gender, cultural change, and the politics of religious authority locally. Accordingly, I collected ethnographic data on a number of related topics, including information about family dynamics, past and present associations and relationships, demographic information, and personal histories. I frequently probed informants on the nature and quality of their social relationships, their evaluations of self and community identity, as well as their ideas about social roles and statuses. Over the course of this work, I observed that while talk about marriage was frequent, few people I knew or interacted with were married in the legal or religious senses. At times, I even observed churchgoers actively work against establishing marriage alliances (see Thornton 2018a). Despite the churches' pleas to the faithful to formalize their domestic unions, legal marriage was the exception rather than the rule. This observation is consistent with patterns of pluralistic family formation nationally and the prevalence of extra-legal unions evident throughout the country. It seems fair to say that, while the ideal is desirable in word, it is irregularly followed in practice. It is difficult to reconcile why so many people, even after conversion, are in no rush to marry.

The reasons, I think, have far less to do with the failures of the church in substantiating the benefits of marriage than they do with the institution's inability to address the structural contradictions in Caribbean culture that, historically, have constrained early marriage and incentivized more flexible alternatives to formal Christian matrimony. For Pentecostal and evangelical Christians specifically, marriage demands additional commitments that are especially difficult to adhere to when combined with the challenging requirements and moral expectations of the faith. Marriage remains a cultural ideal in the Caribbean, but one subordinate to reproduction and childrearing and subject to the evaluative concerns of prudent young adults for whom marriage matters, but often in ways that provide for its realization only later in life.

Reproduction and Childrearing

It is widely held in the Caribbean that while a woman may forego becoming a wife, she ought to become a mother (Powell 1986: 83, 121). Having or raising children is generally viewed as a compulsory, celebratory duty of adulthood, an index of divine favor. According to Dorian Powell's (1986) work on women's familial experiences in Antigua, St. Vincent, and Barbados, motherhood more than wifehood is understood to be the primary basis of feminine identity. She observes that while women are strongly marriage-oriented in these countries, there is little urgency regarding when exactly a woman gets married. Instead, womanhood is more directly tied to the experience of maternity. For the lower classes in particular, marriage is postponed, if it occurs at all, until after childbearing, while those from the upper classes, for whom "illegitimacy" comes at a higher social cost, marriage to someone of the same status and ethnic group is usually a prerequisite to childbirth (Barrow 2001: 422). Sociologist Christine Barrow (1995: 59) reports that for the country of Barbados, at least up to the 1990s, a gap of five years separated the average age of a woman at birth of her first child (her early twenties) and her age at first marriage (her late twenties). It is common for Caribbean women to remain in their natal homes even after childbirth since it is there where they may receive the most support in the face of potentially unreliable fathers. A corollary is that legal marriage is often entered into when partners are past childbearing (M. Smith 1966: xxxiv; Wilson 1969: 77).

The minor emphasis on marriage, it has been argued, is the result of the relatively weak and unstable conjugal bond observed as a hallmark of Caribbean family organization (Safa 2012). The relative indifference toward marriage expressed by the masses combined with the centering of motherhood reflects the high value assigned to familial networks based on consanguineal ties and on the markedly strong bond nurtured between a mother, her children, and her female kin. Based on her extensive work in the contemporary Hispanic Caribbean, anthropologist Helen Safa (1998: 203–4) contends that the conjugal bond between husbands and wives has been weakened over time through consensual unions, labor migration, liberalization of divorce, and the deterioration of men's ability to fulfill the role of economic provider. "Even in male-headed households," she notes, "the strongest bond is often that between mother and child and female kin, rather than the conjugal tie which is emphasized in the nuclear family." This is particularly the situation among the urban, low-income strata where women under stress must rely on their female kin group for stability and aid in cases where men are unreliable, unavailable, or incapable of supporting a family as the primary breadwinner (Safa 1998: 212–13; also see Safa 1995). These kinship networks play a vital role in the area of childcare, especially for those women who pursue economic activities outside of the home and provide the primary safety net against economic and social instability (Powell 1986). These relationships become the foundation for security in woman- and women-headed households where extended family networks based on the support of female kin are a major survival strategy in the absence of material contributions from men, especially for lower- and working-class single mothers (Safa 2012: 229).

Although men often play a dominant role in the household, it cannot be said that they are always or even most of the time the "heads of the family." This is the case if he is absent, his support is uncertain, or if he makes limited or otherwise inadequate contributions to his wife and children. In places throughout the Caribbean where women are more employable than their husbands, or where, because of emigration, women take over the affairs customarily reserved for men in order to compensate for their absence, the traditional father-husband role is undermined or devalued and may be rendered nonessential by the financial stewardship of women and the greater responsibility for childrearing they normally assume. It is based on these tendencies that the term "matrifocality" is so often applied to Caribbean family organization—namely, the central role women assume in the household and the supposedly peripheral role of the father/husband to the domestic sphere and nuclear family. According to the historical sociology and anthropology of the region, greatly influenced by the observations and writings of social anthropologist Peter Wilson (1969, [1973] 1995), men are "marginal" to the household and its affairs, an area defined as the woman's domain and the space where her interests are realized or prioritized and her authority most respected. The man's domain, alternatively, is defined by the street or public sphere where he finds complementary institutions, activities, and values that center on men and male interests, a space where menfolk are said to pursue "reputation," the primary means to social distinction apart from women (Wilson 1971). It follows that if the woman's main sphere of influence is the household, the man's is the rum shop, the street corner, and the public square. This dualistic character attributed to Caribbean social structure is exemplified in the opposing but complementary values of *reputation* and *respectability* outlined by Wilson in his work on the island of Providencia. According to Wilson's model, the alternative values of *reputation* are developed among marginalized men as an adaptive response to their exclusion from more elevated forms of prestige that are epitomized by the principles of upper-class inflected *respectability*, a complex of cultural values rooted in hegemonic Christo-European ideals embodied by the church and nuclear family, and represented by the institution of marriage. The resulting dynamic is one that sees men spending much of their time and resources outside the home—on friends, mistresses, etc., in pursuit of reputation—at the inevitable expense of their wives and children, who would otherwise benefit from their exclusive investment in the household. The result is a weakened conjugal bond diminished by the constant strain of forces that direct husbands' attention and resources away from hearth and home.[6]

Benefits and Limits of Marriage

While legal marriage is viewed as having its benefits, the flexibility of common-law and visiting relationships in the Caribbean offers strategic advantages in a variety of scenarios. To begin with, traditional, legal marriage, from the perspective of many women, promises to afford them the stability and respectability that is unattainable in extra-legal unions. This is in no small part because it better assures them of their partner's financial commitment. This assurance is rooted in the enforceable legal claim to financial support and property rights attending lawful marriage contracts as well as any tangible rewards that may be derived from respectable status in the community (Dirks and Kerns 1976: 47). In a survey of attitudes about marriage conducted by sociologist Barbara Finlay in Azua, Dominican Republic, female respondents who preferred marriage over common-law unions cited the greater rights women could exercise against men if they were legally married, making such statements as: "There is more respect [in marriage], more responsibility, and the woman has more claims against the man"; "There's more support against the man" (Finlay 1989: 58). A lawfully married woman can more confidently depend on her husband's patronage if he is both legally and morally obligated to provide for her and her children. Accordingly, a woman tends not to marry a man until he can prove his economic viability and demonstrate his financial commitment since without those reassurances, he is relatively free to spend his money wherever he wishes and disinclined to invest it primarily in his wife and her household.

Just as elsewhere, economically irresponsible men are viewed as poor spouses (however sufficient they may be as lovers): good enough, perhaps, for a visiting relationship but not good enough for marriage. Finlay's (1989: 63) survey of rural women in Azua, Dominican Republic, found that when asked to describe a good husband, the most common response given was that he should be a provider for his family, "that he spends what he earns on the family's needs and not just on himself." Safa (1998) finds that Dominican female heads of household often avoid marriage and prefer to support themselves if they cannot find a good provider. She contends that it is a lack of marriage partners willing and able to support a family that encourages women to have children out of wedlock and to resist marriage or remarriage (Safa 1998: 212). Marital alliances, following the conclusions of Dirks and Kerns (1976: 48), are typically founded on a couple's willingness to enter into a long-term economic commitment and the man's demonstration of his capacity to do so. Homeownership, in many cases, is the main indication of this capacity and the primary symbol of his readiness for a wife and children (also see Powell 1986: 88; R. Smith 1956: 139). Marriage is regularly postponed until a potential husband can provide and maintain a dwelling of his own. This autonomy is usually the first step toward legalizing a union and establishing co-residential accommodations independent of a wife-to-be's family and their support for her and her children. These and other economic prerequisites for marriage are common and, for the poor and working classes, likely represent the primary deterrent to marriage at an early age (Blake 1961: 134–48).

According to research conducted by Dirks and Kerns (1976: 49) in the British Virgin Islands, most extra-legal unions are initiated under a mode of reciprocity that favors the maximization of short-term social and economic interests and therefore appeals to individuals facing precarious straits or who, as younger individuals, wish to avoid burdensome claims on their resources or freedom. Legal marriage, on the other hand, is usually contracted with the prospect of an enduring, generalized exchange relationship. Although legal unions require investments that promise minimal immediate returns, their value lies in the maximization of long-term objectives, not the least of which include respectability and power in the local community, supportive offspring, and security in old age (Dirks and Kerns 1976). For men and women alike, marriage offers mutual protection against the inclemencies that are bound to beset life over time (Dirks and Kerns 1976: 47). It is for this reason that, with age and changes in fortune or life circumstances, legal marriage becomes a more probable eventuality. By the time men reach their late twenties and early thirties, their commitment to peer groups is somewhat diminished and their potential for securing stable employment more likely achieved or within reach. At this time, formal marriage becomes not just viable, but more desirable. It is therefore possible to interpret differing conjugal elections as "adaptive strategies" to the changing circumstances in which individuals find themselves at different stages of their life cycle (Barrow 1996: 70; Dirks and Kerns 1976).

While legal marriage is viewed as having its benefits it is not always viewed as sensible or worthwhile, even as incentives for formal unions increase with age and changing circumstances. Barrow (1995: 59) observes that while, in general, Caribbean people believe that marriage is the right and proper context for sexual relations and childbearing, marriage can mean a bundle of prescriptions that are not always viewed as practical or even desirable. Among the reasons they might avoid or postpone marriage, women across the Caribbean cite aversions to housework and childcare, potential restrictions on their freedom and independence, constraints on their access to economic support from kin and other men, and greater exposure to domestic violence (Barrow 1995: 59; Finlay 1989: 57–67; Powell 1986: 88; Roberts and Sinclair 1978: 64–67). Moreover, for many women today, marriage and childrearing at too young an age can spoil plans for an education and career. For these reasons, and still others, legal marriage is not always the most expedient option for Caribbean women.

Lifelong fidelity and submission to a husband's authority means increased susceptibility to domestic violence, personal ambitions deferred, perhaps sexual desires suspended or compromised, and other conditions that suggest marriage does not necessarily provide the security or happiness it is purported to yield. Visiting unions, on the other hand, carry few of these disadvantages and are not as disruptive to female autonomy and the ideals of gender equality desired and often expressed by Caribbean women (Barrow 1995: 59). According to Roberts and Sinclair's (1978: 67) survey of women and patterns of reproduction in Jamaica, common-law unions were assessed to be of the lowest value by their female respondents since such unions restrict the freedoms enjoyed in visiting unions but come with all of the constraints of legal marriage while offering none of the apparent benefits. In the Dominican Republic, Finlay's (1989: 57–58) survey of working rural women in Azua suggests more ambivalence; she finds that women there indicate little preference for legal marriage over living with a man in a "free union." According to her respondents, extra-legal unions are preferable to formal marriage since men are largely perceived as unfaithful by nature and, with such low expectations of them, "it's better if the ties are looser."

It is possible, as Safa (1998: 210) puts forward, that as women's expectations of men have increased over time, women are no longer willing to accept male abuse and domination and therefore eschew formal marriage in favor of more advantageous or attractive arrangements. Moreover, as a result of improved economic autonomy, women increasingly take the initiative to end unsatisfactory relationships and perhaps do so today with greater ease thanks to the widespread liberalization of divorce. In any case, incentives to marry early, or to marry at all, have always seemed to be insufficient when it comes to making reproductive decisions in the Caribbean.

Binding Obligations

For men, just as for women, legal marriage can mean respectability and security, but for many it comes at a price they either cannot afford or find too costly to warrant. Marriage may be a long-term goal for men, promising fulfillment of the nuclear family ideal with regular companionship, a respectable household, exclusive sexual access, patriarchal identity, supportive offspring, and security in old age. At the same time, however, marriage in the Caribbean context carries with it a complicated and sometimes irreconcilable division of loyalties leveraged unevenly against men. Whether or not a married or soon-to-be married man can financially support a family of his own is one issue; the other, perhaps more challenging issue, is whether he can manage divergent obligations to his wife and children, to his family of origin, particularly his mother and her household, to his male friends, to children he has fathered with other women, to his siblings, and possibly also to his father and other kinfolk (e.g., R. Smith 1956: 138–39). As these obligations multiply or divide on an individual basis, men, unlike their female counterparts, retain strong financial and moral commitments to individuals outside the nuclear family—even after marriage—putting considerable stress on their ability to meet their conjugal responsibilities. For the poor and working classes, this strain is increased exponentially since the resources needed to fulfill these obligations satisfactorily are often out of reach. Women, comparatively, are bound by fewer financial commitments: a woman's moral obligations according to custom are limited to the household she lives in—that is, her children and the man she is involved with—and not to the extraneous and multiple people to whom men in this context are frequently beholden.

Legal marriage in this way contrasts with common-law and visiting unions that ultimately necessitate fewer and less binding commitments. The few mutual obligations attending common-law and visiting relationships are viewed by the partners to them, both male and female, as being relatively loose, voluntary, and non-binding (Blake 1961: 122). If a man or a woman wishes to end a common-law relationship, the task is not fettered by paperwork or a complicated division of communal possessions, much less the legal settling of debts or reconciliation of joint affairs. This is seen as an advantage, not just by men, but by women as well (Finlay 1989: 59). The flexibility inherent in more fluid, pluralistic approaches to family formation gives men and women alike a strategic advantage over the nuclear family ideal, since for men it lightens the moral burden of meeting conflicting obligations to a multitude of different people and for women it ensures the freedom to choose what is best and most desirable for them as individuals, or as mothers, and promises autonomy from the exercise and violence of male domestic authority. Informal unions benefit both men and women in a cultural context that esteems Christian marriage but does little in the way of providing for its practical achievement.

The cultural politics of marriage delay in the Caribbean are a social and economic negotiation structured by norms of expectation, the necessities of reproductive success, enduring bonds of reciprocal obligation, and desires for happiness, love, and autonomy that are familiar to most young adults across the globe. To postpone marriage in this context has always made sense, where the benefits of formal legal unions are contextual and might only become clear later in life, with increased economic stability and the more likely assurance of material and emotional satisfaction.

Waithood in the Caribbean has less to do with singlehood or "waiting" to form a domestic union (to bear children, to raise a family, etc.) and has more to do with the deliberate and strategic deferral of legal marriage contracts and their attending burdens and restrictions. Whatever new incentives to "wait" might arise, they are inevitably weighed against long-term evaluations of stability, reproductive success, and overall happiness. Even as growing economic and educational opportunities lead men and women to postpone marriage longer than usual, these and other social changes only act to further reinforce a pattern of deferral and avoidance long evidenced in the region.

The Convert's Dilemma

Conventional Christian marriage affirms traditional gender roles for men and women. Once married, men in the Pentecostal church, for example, are expected to assume the responsibility of dependable patriarch, and their authority over the family is avowed and sanctioned by their congregation. For a woman to accept this "patriarchal bargain," her born-again husband is expected to be a reliable provider and to refrain from domestic violence, infidelity, and excessive spending outside the household (on alcohol, entertainment, or other women). With his conversion, his commitment is to be reoriented toward his immediate family and his role as husband and father. From this perspective, his conversion is more than welcome since it shores up the benefits of formal marriage by lessening the likelihood of domestic instability, therefore curtailing the most common conflict between spouses. In theory, the thinking goes, women should value such unions since Pentecostal Christian marriage reinforces the strongest conjugal ties to the nuclear family, ensuring additional support for the domestic sphere where, limited as they might be, women stand to gain the most from their spousal relationship. Moreover, in addition to the legal claims against their husbands that follow from lawful marriage, with their conversions, women also succeed in obtaining spiritual claims, levied by God and enforced by the greater church community. Through the "reformation of machismo" (Brusco 1995) that accompanies this type of conversion, Christian wives have the added reassurance that their husbands will provide for them, as well as remain faithful and non-violent, alleviating concerns a woman might have of a man's suitability as a long-term partner (Austin-Broos 1997; Thornton 2016). Thus, with conversion, marriage should become more likely, even if it provides no obvious incentive to marry young.

At the same time, however, the adoption of a conservative Christian doctrine of marriage ushers in a difficult conflict for believers—one that pits the moral demands of the church, following the radical transformation of conversion, against the established patterns of domestic and kinship relations in the region. While the pressure to regularize one's union before God increases after joining the church, the incentives or reasons to marry or not to marry remain unchanged outside of church doors. The conflict between the cultural ideal of legal marriage and the practical reality of common-law unions is especially acute for evangelical and Pentecostal Christian converts because they must balance the demanding expectations of the faith with the conventions of everyday Caribbean life. There is an assumption that those who have adopted a conservative Christian identity have resolved this dilemma in accordance with the ascetic discipline of the church; however, scarce evidence exists to confirm this to be the case, at least in any generalizable sense.

For younger male converts, conversion presents a conjugal conundrum. Male converts are expected to find an appropriate Christian spouse and marry her soon after joining the church. Once married, Pentecostal husbands must fulfill the lofty expectations that they be Christian patriarchs, spiritual and material wellsprings for family and familiars, and loyal servants of God; they must also, according to social convention, provide financially for their wives, perform as reliable sons to their mothers, and deliver as benefactors to their children. They are also beholden to siblings and friends with whom they have strong moral ties. The church adds additional pressure to fulfill these obligations since being a good Christian husband also means being charitable, reliable, and a moral exemplar to the community (Thornton 2016). With conversion, it becomes harder for men to neglect their conjugal responsibilities and their obligations outside the home because of the added weight of the faith's formal and informal discipline. If, for example, a male convert who has married cannot fulfill the minimum expectations of a born-again husband, his testimony will be thrown into question and the validity of his conversion scrutinized, not only by his wife but also by his congregation and the community at large. To not live up to the community's expectations for Christian men is tantamount to failure, made all the worse by a convert's profession of holiness and declarations of spiritual reform.

Men, therefore, may not be incentivized to marry with any haste, even after conversion. Elsewhere I have discussed several cases from my fieldwork in the Dominican Republic where men evaded the charge to get married despite the explicit directives of their church (see Thornton 2018a). Crucially, conversion alone does not alleviate the economic burden of marriage or resolve the issue of competing obligations to kinfolk. If many already find the obligatory demands of marriage overwhelming and unmanageable, they are unlikely to be able to cope with the additional demands of their faith.

Instead of resolving the conflict through a secondary injunction against extramarital relations and extraneous spending, Christian converts are likely to avoid or delay marriage for many of the same reasons as everyone else. Ultimately, conversion does little to solve the structural contradictions that create irreconcilable expectations for men outside the home, despite reorienting much of their attention onto marriage and the nuclear family. Informal unions perdure because the dilemma of divergent loyalties persists, and men's enduring obligations remain unresolved even after joining the church. This conjugal conundrum is compounded by poverty and financial instability. For the poor and working classes, marriage and the dilemma of increasing obligations is experienced forcefully as an economic obstacle, one that rich people can afford to navigate since they have the resources to respond to proliferating financial responsibilities but which, inevitably, leaves the impoverished with inadequate means to warrant formal marriage.

Conclusion

The ethnographic record suggests that these deep-rooted cultural practices will be slow to change, especially given that even Christian conversion fails to solve the conditions that lead to deferred marriage in the first place. Waithood, or what it means to postpone marriage, in one form or another, has always been a negotiation of changing circumstances in light of demographic shifts or economic and educational advancements; it has also always been a strategic assessment of value in relation to enduring social conventions, economic motives, conflicting obligations, and customary expectations that draw individuals into difficult conjugal scenarios that, at different times and for different people, may or may not inspire entry into romantic monogamous lawful marriage with "respectable" designs on a nuclear family.

Too often it is assumed that marriage is the desirable and obvious answer to economic insecurity or social uncertainty—especially as it concerns the so-called Third World or Global South—when in many cases it may not be. Indeed, the conventional practices of family formation and the indifferent attitudes toward early marriage exhibited in the Caribbean, particularly for the most precarious citizens, indicate otherwise. Safa (1998: 203) makes the important point that any negative view of female-headed households, for example, is largely based on the Eurocentric emphasis on the nuclear family as the preferential norm—and the embodiment of modernity and progress—and mistakenly holds that female-headed households are pathological because of the rupture of the conjugal bond. The same can be said for the generally negative assessment of extra-legal unions and the regular denunciation of what has derisively been called "concubinage" by political and religious leaders alike. Much of the pioneering work on the Caribbean family carried out by the likes of Raymond T. Smith (1956), based originally on his research in British Guyana, sought to denaturalize the nuclear family relationship as a taken-for-granted human universal. His work, along with that of others cited here, demonstrates the virtues of flexible family formation; together, their scholarship highlights the advantages of conjugal versatility while helping to explain the resiliency of informal unions throughout the region.

Delayed marriage or waithood, along with the diverse modes of conjugality observed throughout the Caribbean, is neither maladaptive nor pathological; it is also not new. Even as educational and employment opportunities for women rise in many areas of the world, including the Caribbean, and even as religious enthusiasm intensifies the call for sanctified unions, marriage trends in the Caribbean will be slow to change so long as the benefits of extra-legal alternatives prevail. By assessing the conjugal conundrums at the heart of early marriage delay and troubling the normativity and inherent desirability of the nuclear family model, we can take an important step toward untangling the complicated life decisions seemingly all people make when planning families and futures—whether inspired by God or broader cultural traditions—all while minding the multiple meanings attributed to reproductive and communal life in the contemporary Caribbean and beyond.

Brendan Jamal Thornton is an anthropologist and Associate Professor of Religious Studies at the University of North Carolina at Chapel Hill. Thornton's ethnographic research in the Caribbean is concerned with the social and cultural politics of belief and the role religious identity plays in impoverished urban communities. His scholarship has been published in *Anthropological Quarterly, Religion, Latin American Research Review,* and elsewhere. He is the award-winning author of *Negotiating Respect: Pentecostalism, Masculinity, and the Politics of Spiritual Authority in the Dominican Republic* (University of Florida Press, 2016). He received a PhD in anthropology from the University of California, San Diego.

Notes

1. Notable examples of this work include Blake (1961), Clarke (1957), Henriques (1953), Horowitz (1967), Otterbein (1966), Roberts (1975), Roberts and Sinclair (1978), Rodman (1971), M. Smith (1962a, 1962b), R. Smith (1956, 1973), and Solien (1960). For readers new to the region, the Caribbean has been treated for some time now in both anthropology and in sociology as a "socio-cultural area" (Mintz 1965; also see M. Smith 1965); that is, a diverse geopolitical space united by many shared social structural features owing, at least in part, to common historical experiences of conquest, colonization, slavery and/or peonage, and the development of multiracial and multicultural societies (M. Smith 1965: 19). Despite the diverse linguistic, political, and cultural realities marking the region as plural and divisible, there remains a convincing number of shared characteristics—social and cultural commonalities—that connect distinct Caribbean societies to one another and distinguish them as a group from other global regions. Throughout this chapter I cite studies from an array of Caribbean countries that arrive independently at similar conclusions about marriage and family formation, affirming that, at least in these areas, individual Caribbean societies are much more alike than they are different.

2. Important differences across ethnic groups have been observed—especially pertaining to East Indians (Innerarity 2000: 62; Roberts and Braithwaite 1962; Schwartz 1965; R. Smith and Jayawardena 1959)—not to mention differences across economic status groups. Significant similarities, however, have also been noted. Some work suggests that the same general structural patterns may hold for the middle and upper classes, though the full range of practices are assigned different values (Douglass 1992; R. Smith 1988; see also Barrow 2001: 421–22). Of course, we find unions of all types among all classes of people, regardless of race or ethnic group, but the relative incidence of their occurrence varies in ways that are difficult to measure (R. Smith 1988: 112), and attitudes toward specific family practices and the meanings assigned to them can differ across class, race, age, gender, and religious affiliation (Barrow 2001: 422).

3. It is necessary to point out that, while men might accrue prestige among their peers through demonstrations of virility and sexual potency and may flaunt the existence of "outside" children to enhance their masculinity, women's sexual freedom is constrained by the imposition of dissimilar rules of decorum and modesty (Barrow 2001: 422; Clarke 1957: 91, 96; R. Smith 1956: 141; Thornton 2016; Wilson 1969: 71–72).

In areas throughout the Caribbean, men, as a general rule, are viewed as incorrigible womanizers whose all but inevitable infidelity is treated as regrettable, if nevertheless expected (Otterbein 1966: 69; Thornton 2013). This oft-cited double standard of sexual morality—"what is fame for the man is shame for the woman" (Rodman 1971: 60)—is a pervasive assessment of what is considered respectable for the different sexes, but one that veils the prevalence of extramarital relationships not uncommonly pursued and maintained by women themselves.

4. The percentage of households headed by women in the Dominican Republic, Haiti, and Jamaica in the early 2000s, for example, was 26.8, 42.7, and 44.7 respectively (ECLAC 2000). For other Caribbean islands, see Massiah (1983). For the total number of births globally that occur out of wedlock see UNPD (2015) report *World Population Prospects*. According to World Bank data from 2014, fertility rates have declined steadily in the Caribbean over the past half-century. For example, the total fertility rate per woman dropped in the Dominican Republic from 5.6 (births per 1,000 women) in the early 1970s to 3.1 in the early 2000s; over that same period rates dropped in Cuba from 3.5 to 1.5, in Jamaica from 5.0 to 2.4, and in St. Lucia from 6.3 down to 2.0 (St. Bernard 2003: Table 12).

5. According to census data collected in the 1990s, the average age at first marriage for women in countries like Jamaica, Barbados, Grenada, Saint Lucia, Dominica, and Saint Vincent and the Grenadines was between 31 and 34 years old; for men, it was greater than 34 years old (UNPD 2017).

6. To be sure, the binary that Wilson (1969, [1973] 1995) outlines is in practice much less orderly or prescriptive (see Besson 1993). The allegedly peripheral—or "marginal"—role Caribbean men are said to assume in relation to the family has been challenged by Barrow (1998) and others as essentialist and much too narrowly focused on male contributions to the nuclear family in co-residential conjugal scenarios and not beyond them (as sons, brothers, or uncles, for example). Such an interpretation, they argue, limits men's domestic role to strictly disciplinary and economic matters while reductively positioning men in opposition to women and to the family itself (also see Barriteau 2003).

References

Austin-Broos, Diane. 1997. *Jamaica Genesis: Religion and the Politics of Moral Orders*. Chicago: University of Chicago Press.

Barriteau, Eudine. 2003. "Requiem for the Male Marginalization Thesis in the Caribbean: Death of a Non-Theory." In *Confronting Power, Theorizing Gender: Interdisciplinary Perspectives in the Caribbean*, ed. Eudine Barriteau, 324–55. Kingston: University of the West Indies Press.

Barrow, Christine. 1995. "'Living in Sin': Church and Common-Law Union in Barbados." *The Journal of Caribbean History* 29(2): 47–70.

———. 1996. *Family in the Caribbean: Themes and Perspectives.* Kingston: Ian Randle Publishers.

———. 1998. "Caribbean Masculinity and Family: Revisiting 'Marginality' and 'Reputation.'" In *Caribbean Portraits: Essays on Gender Ideologies and Identities,* ed. Christine Barrow, 339–58. Kingston: Ian Randle Publishers.

———. 2001. "Men, Women and Family in the Caribbean: A Review." In *Caribbean Sociology: Introductory Readings,* ed. Christine Barrow and Rhoda Reddock, 418–26. Kingston: Ian Randle Publishers.

Besson, Jean. 1993. "Reputation & Respectability Reconsidered: A New Perspective on Afro-Caribbean Peasant Women." In *Women & Change in the Caribbean: A Pan-Caribbean Perspective,* ed. Janet Momsen, 15–37. Bloomington: Indiana University Press.

Blake, Judith. 1961. *Family Structure in Jamaica: The Social Context of Reproduction.* New York: The Free Press of Glencoe.

Brusco, Elizabeth. 1995. *The Reformation of Machismo: Evangelical Conversion and Gender in Colombia.* Austin: University of Texas Press.

Chioda, Laura. 2016. *Work and Family: Latin American and Caribbean Women in Search of a New Balance.* Washington, DC: World Bank Publications.

Clarke, Edith. 1957. *My Mother Who Fathered Me: A Study of the Family in Three Selected Communities in Jamaica.* London: George Allen & Unwin Ltd.

Dirks, Robert, and Virginia Kerns. 1976. "Mating Patterns and Adaptive Change in Rum Bay, 1823–1970." *Social and Economic Studies* 25(1): 34–54.

Douglass, Lisa. 1992. *The Power of Sentiment: Love, Hierarchy and the Jamaican Family Elite.* Boulder: Westview Press.

ECLAC (Economic Commission for Latin America and the Caribbean). 2000. *Latin America and the Caribbean—Selected Gender-Sensitive Indicators.* Demographic Bulletin 70.

Finlay, Barbara. 1989. *The Women of Azua: Work and Family in Rural Dominican Republic.* New York: Praeger.

Henriques, Fernando. 1953. *Family and Colour in Jamaica.* London: Eyre Spottiswoode.

Horowitz, Michael. 1967. *Morne-Paysan: Peasant Village in Martinique.* New York: Holt, Rinehart and Winston.

Innerarity, Faith. 2000. "Marriage and Family in the Caribbean." *World Family Policy Forum 2000.* Retrieved 14 May 2018 from https://pdfs.semantic scholar.org/196b/171e32da94bcaf0057db8ab3e9302a253179.pdf.

Massiah, Joycelin. 1983. *Women as Heads of Households in the Caribbean: Family Structure and Feminine Status.* Paris: UNESCO.

McKenzie, Hermoine. 1993. "The Family, Class and Ethnicity in the Future of the Caribbean." In *Race, Class and Gender in the Future of the Caribbean,* ed. J. Edward Greene, 75–89. Kingston: Institute of Social & Economic Research, University of the West Indies, Mona.

Mintz, Sidney. 1965. "The Caribbean as a Socio-Cultural Area." *Journal of World History* 9(1): 912–37.

Otterbein, Keith. 1966. *The Andros Islanders: A Study of Family Organization in the Bahamas.* Lawrence: University of Kansas Publications.

Pew Research Center. 2014. "Religion in Latin America: Widespread Change in a Historically Catholic Region." 13 November. Retrieved 13 February 2019 from https://www.pewresearch.org/wp-content/uploads/sites/7/2014/11/Religion-in-Latin-America-11-12-PM-full-PDF.pdf.

Powell, Dorian. 1986. "Caribbean Women and their Response to Familial Experiences." *Social and Economic Studies* 35(2): 83–130.

Reddock, Rhoda. 2005. "Rethinking Common-Law Unions: Toward a Critical Re-evaluation of Caribbean Family Sociology." *IDEAZ* 4(1–2): 72–85.

Roberts, George W. 1975. *Fertility and Mating in Four West Indian Populations.* Kingston: Institute of Social and Economic Research, University of the West Indies, Mona.

Roberts, George W., and Lloyd Braithwaite. 1962. "Mating Among East Indian and Non-Indian Women in Trinidad." *Social and Economic Studies* 11(3): 203–40.

Roberts, George W., and Sonja A. Sinclair. 1978. *Women in Jamaica: Patterns of Reproduction and Family.* Millwood: KTO Press.

Rodman, Hyman. 1971. *Lower-Class Families: The Culture of Poverty in Negro Trinidad.* New York: Oxford University Press.

Rubenstein, Hymie. 1983. "Caribbean Family and Household Organization: Some Conceptual Clarifications." *Journal of Comparative Family Studies* 14(3): 283–98.

Safa, Helen. 1995. *The Myth of the Male Breadwinner: Women and Industrialization in the Caribbean.* Boulder: Westview Press.

———. 1998. "Female-Headed Households in the Caribbean: Sign of Pathology or Alternative Form of Family Organization?" *The Brown Journal of World Affairs* 5(2): 203–14.

———. 2012. "Class, Gender, and Race in the Caribbean: Reflections on an Intellectual Journey." *Canadian Journal of Latin American and Caribbean Studies* 37(74): 219–42.

Schwartz, Barton. 1965. "Patterns of East Indian Family Organization in Trinidad." *Caribbean Studies* 5(1): 23–36.

Smith, Michael Garfield. 1962a. *Kinship and Community in Carriacou.* New Haven: Yale University Press.

———. 1962b. *West Indian Family Structure.* Seattle: University of Washington Press.

———. 1965. *The Plural Society in the British West Indies.* Berkeley: University of California Press.

———. 1966. "Introduction." In *My Mother Who Fathered Me: A Study of the Family in Three Selected Communities in Jamaica,* ed. Edith Clarke, i–xliv. London: George Allen & Unwin Ltd.

Smith, Raymond T. 1956. *The Negro Family in British Guiana: Family Structure and Social Status in the Villages.* London: Routledge & Kegan Paul Limited.

———. 1973. "The Matrifocal Family." In *The Character of Kinship,* ed. Jack Goody, 121–44. Cambridge, UK: Cambridge University Press.

———. 1988. *Kinship and Class in the West Indies: A Genealogical Study of Jamaica and Guyana.* Cambridge, UK: Cambridge University Press.

Smith, Raymond T., and C. Jayawardena. 1959. "Marriage and the Family amongst East Indians in British Guiana." *Social and Economic Studies* 8(4): 321–76.

Solien, Nancie. 1960. "Household and Family in the Caribbean." *Social and Economic Studies* 9(1): 101–6.

St. Bernard, Godfrey. 2003. "Major Trends Affecting Families in Central America and the Caribbean." Paper prepared for the United Nations: Division of Social Policy and Development, Department of Economic and Social Affairs Program on the Family.

Thornton, Brendan Jamal. 2013. "Residual Masculinity and the Cultivation of Negative-Charisma in a Caribbean Pentecostal Community." In *The Anthropology of Religious Charisma: Ecstasies and Institutions*, ed. Charles Lindholm, 117–43. New York: Palgrave Macmillan.

———. 2016. *Negotiating Respect: Pentecostalism, Masculinity, and the Politics of Spiritual Authority in the Dominican Republic*. Gainesville: University Press of Florida.

———. 2018a. "Victims of Illicit Desire: Pentecostal Men of God and the Specter of Sexual Temptation." *Anthropological Quarterly* 91(1): 133–71.

———. 2018b. "Ties that Bind: Pentecostal Churches, Youth Gangs, and the Management of Everyday Life in the Urban Barrio." *Religion* 48(4): 616–41.

UNPD (United Nations, Department of Economic and Social Affairs, Population Division). 2008. *World Marriage Data 2008* (POP/DB/Marr/Rev2008). Retrieved 9 September 2018 from http://www.un.org/esa/population/publications/WMD2008/Data/UNPD_WMD_2008_MARRIAGES.xls.

———. 2015. *World Population Prospects: The 2015 Revision*, Comprehensive Tables (ST/ESA/SER.A/379). Retrieved 9 September 2018 from https://population.un.org/wpp/Publications/Files/WPP2015_Volume-I_Comprehensive-Tables.pdf.

———. 2017. *World Marriage Data 2017* (POP/DB/Marr/Rev2017). Retrieved 9 September 2018 from http://www.un.org/en/development/desa/population/publications/dataset/marriage/data/UNPD_WMD_2017_MARITAL_STATUS.xlsx.

Wilson, Peter. 1969. "Reputation and Respectability: A Suggestion for Caribbean Ethnology." *Man* 4(1): 70–84.

———. 1971. "Caribbean Crews: Peer Groups and Male Society." *Caribbean Studies* 10(4): 18–34.

———. (1973) 1995. *Crab Antics: A Caribbean Case Study of the Conflict Between Reputation and Respectability*. Prospect Heights: Waveland Press.

Chapter 10

Between Cynicism and Idealism
Voluntary Waithood in Iran

Mehrdad Babadi

Introduction

Iranian society has undergone significant sociocultural, economic, educational, and technological transformations since the Islamic Revolution of 1979. The country has developed a solid middle class that includes bureaucrats, businesspeople, engineers, medical professionals, teachers, academic and religious scholars, entrepreneurs, and military officers (Bashirieh 1995). The educated adult population—those aged twenty-five or older with university degrees—reached 12.85 percent in 2010, making Iran the country with the second-highest educated adult population in the Middle East (Habibi 2015: 4). In addition, women's access to higher education, at both undergraduate and graduate levels, has increased dramatically (Shams 2016).[1] Furthermore, the government's population control program, implemented in the late 1980s, has been very successful, with fertility rates declining from 6 children per woman in the early 1980s to 1.9 in 2006 (Abbasi-Shavazi et al. 2009). More than 70 percent of the population is now urban (Census 2016), and despite attempts by the government to control electronic media, over 50 percent of the Iranian population have access to the internet and use online forums such as Instagram, Facebook, WhatsApp, and Telegram (ISNA 2018).[2]

When it comes to intimate life, Iran, like many other nations of the Global South, has experienced the emergence and even popularity of the ideals of romantic love and companionate marriage especially among urban middle-class youth. Janet Afary (2009: 8) observed the shift in the history of marriage in Iran. For centuries, Iranians had practiced arranged marriage known as *khāstegari* with significantly less normative weight given to the romantic aspect. During the Pahlavi era (1925–79) under fast-paced modernization, companionate marriage gradually found its place among the elite and the new urban middle class. However, "parents still played a key role in introducing prospective couples, approving marriages, and negotiating dowry and *mahriyeh (mahr)*." By the first decade of the twenty-first century, however, arranged marriages as well as endogamous ones[3]—in urban and even in some rural communities—have become less common (Afary 2009: 8). Today women, as well as men, expect intimacy and spontaneity as well as higher degrees of sexual and emotional closeness in their marriages. Although there are legal and religious prohibitions against the mingling of unrelated men and women enforced by "morality police" (*gasht-e ershād*) who control youth fashion and dress styles as well as opposite-sex interactions in the public domain, dating has become a common phenomenon, and young people interact and flirt with each other at parties, universities, shopping malls, and coffee shops and even in the streets. In addition, premarital sex, within the context of long-term relationships as well as casual hook-ups, has increased among youth (Azad-Armaki et al. 2011).

These transformations in marriage and related trends have created moral panic among religious and government officials. Governmental agencies and policy organizations are worried about the decline of morality and the collapse of traditional, religious, and familial values. Demographers are particularly concerned about the rise in the phenomenon of what is often referred to as "voluntary singlehood" (*tajarrod-e khod-khāsteh*) among Iranian youth and express anxiety over close to one million women who have now reached the age of "definite singlehood" (*tajarrod-e qat'i*), defined as age forty and above and never-married. A related concern has to do with the rising popularity of premarital sexual relationships. Mahmoud Golzari, deputy minister at the Ministry of Sports and Youth, has lamented that "intimate relationships between boys and girls have grown three times more common compared to thirty years ago. It starts in middle or high school now and its nature has turned from emotional into sexual. Furthermore, non-monogamous [sexual/romantic] relationships have increased too." Referring to the representative survey that he and his associates conducted among seven thousand high school students across the country, Golzari calls the data "disturbing" and adds that he is not willing to go into the details of those statistics. However, he warns that "we must educate teachers and parents about the students' sexual relationships and not close our eyes to the realities" (ISNA 2014).

In what follows, this chapter provides some statistics on marriage, divorce, and singlehood in Iran in order to present the overall picture and to demonstrate that the age of first marriage has increased significantly among both young men and women. Next, it focuses on "waithood" as a potential theoretical framework to explain some of the reasons behind the delay in marriage among youth in the Middle East. Based on the qualitative data that I have collected from educated middle-class young people, I argue that the nature of Iranian waithood is voluntary and that it is fueled more by psychological rather than economic reasons.

Youth and Waithood in Iran

Despite the historical centrality of marriage as the foundation of Iranian family and society, recent data show a decline in both the rate and the number of marriages taking place (Aghajanian et al. 2018). Since 2010, Iran has experienced a continuous decline in the number of officially registered marriages, while at the same time, the divorce rate is steadily rising[4] (see Figure 10.1).

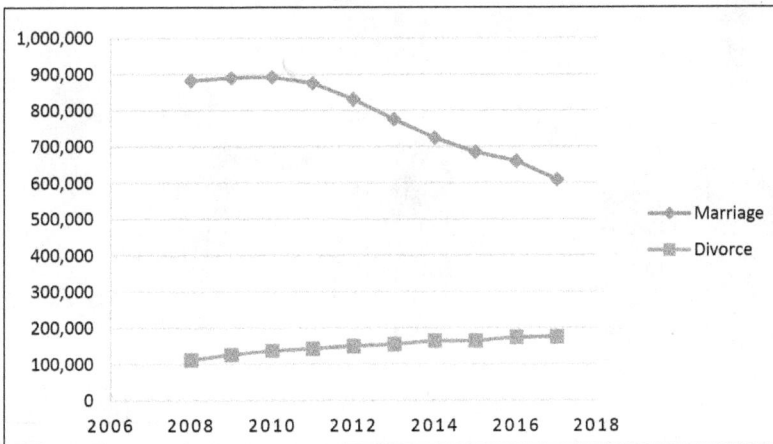

FIGURE 10.1. Statistics of Marriage and Divorce in Iran, 2008–17. Based on data from the Statistical Center of Iran (2018).

In addition, from 2005 to 2014 the percentage of unmarried men older than thirty-five increased from 6.7 percent to 10.2 percent while the percentage of unmarried women over thirty rose from 6.3 percent to 13.8 percent (*Al-Monitor* 2015).[5] According to the Iranian Census of 2016, there are three million households (out of 24 million) in which the status of the occupant(s) is single (ISNA 2017). Here "single" refers either to a person who has never been married, is divorced, or is cohabitating with their partner without being married. The latter phenomenon is known as "white marriage" in Iran.[6] The average age of first marriage has increased approximately from 24 for men and 20 for women in 1976 to 27.5 and 23 in 2016 (Fathi et al. 2017; see Figure 10.2). It is important to note that in 2016 the average age of first marriage for men and women in urban Tehran was 31.1 and 27.2 respectively (see Figure 10.2). This is a significantly higher average age of first marriage than that seen across the nation (YJC 2016). In other words, young people in Tehran (and perhaps other major cities) are marrying at considerably later ages than those in the provinces.

The phenomenon of delayed marriage is part of what is often referred to as "waithood"—an extended period of young adulthood in which marriage and childbearing are delayed. The framework, put forth initially by Diane Singerman (2007: 5–6, 7–9), refers to the prolonged period of stagnation in the life of young people in Egypt and the larger Middle East who have been disproportionately disadvantaged by neoliberal economic policies and a demographic

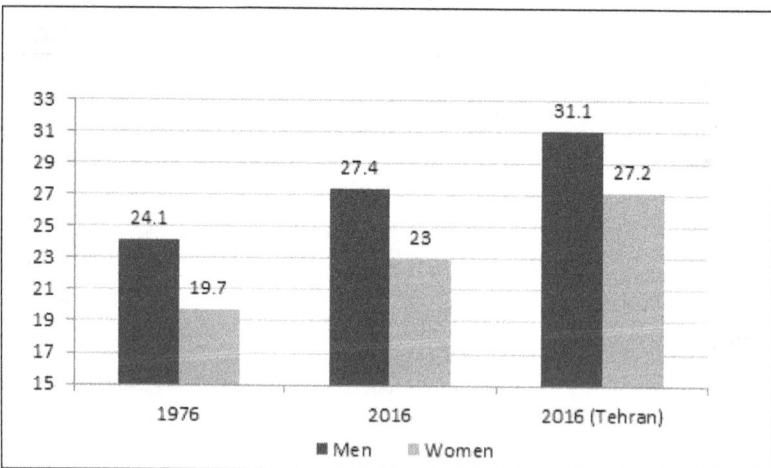

FIGURE 10.2. Average Age of First Marriage for Men and Women in Iran. Based on data from Fathi et al. (2017).

youth bulge. The youth in these countries have been economically excluded by high unemployment and the difficulty of securing what are considered to be good jobs in the public sector. Marriage and entry into adulthood are involuntarily delayed in part due to unemployment and the high cost of marriage. Waithood puts young people in an extended "liminal" situation where they are neither adolescents nor adults (Singerman 2013: 9–16).

When it comes to theorizing delayed marriage or waithood in Iran, leading economist Djavad Salehi-Isfahani has written extensively about Iranian youth and their transition from school to work and family formation and has focused on the economic difficulties facing Iranian youth (Egel and Salehi-Isfahani 2010; Salehi-Isfahani 2011; Salehi-Isfahani and Egel 2009). He observed that more than one-third of the country's population fall in the category of youth (born in the 1980s and 1990s). These young people are much better educated than the generation they are replacing, while accounting for more than two-thirds of the unemployed. Salehi-Isfahani argues that a larger cohort of youth is facing harsh labor market conditions because the supply of the workforce is growing faster than the demands of the market. For him, waithood essentially is a three-stage obstacle—competitive schools, inflexible labor markets, and a rigid marriage market—that contributes to "stalled transitions" filled with anxiety, unhappiness, and often depression (Salehi-Isfahani and Egel 2009: 60).

Young people also face a challenging marriage market "because of a gender imbalance caused by the fact that a larger cohort of women has reached marriage age several years ahead of the corresponding cohort of men" (Salehi-Isfahani 2011: 791). Thus, women born during the baby boom of 1979–84 face a 25 percent shortage of men when they reach the age of marriage, between twenty and twenty-four. Interestingly, Salehi-Isfahani argues that because of the fertility decline in the 1990s the situation will soon reverse: "the 20 percent shortage of men in 2010 is expected to change to a 40 percent shortage of women by 2020!" (Salehi-Isfahani 2011: 801).

In addition, Salehi-Isfahani mentions two other demographic factors, specifically women's lower fertility rates and higher levels of education, to explain the delays in marriage. The important question according to him is: how much of this increase in age of first marriage is voluntary and how much of it is caused by constraints imposed by the age imbalance and inefficient economic system? There is no doubt that the gender imbalance in the population has hurt young people's opportunities to meet and marry and therefore the delay in marriage is, in part, involuntary. However, evidence regarding the role of (un)employment (the economic factor) is mixed. In a piece based on the 2005 School to Work Transition Survey (SWTS), Egel and Salehi-Isfahani (2010) provide evidence that having a good job increases the probability of marriage for young men. Interestingly, employment for women has the opposite effect, reducing their probability of getting married.

One of the few qualitative studies that has attempted to address the reasons for delayed marriage is that of sociologist Manata Hashemi (2015). Hashemi's focus is on lower-class, disadvantaged youth and how they cope with precarious social and economic conditions. Building on Asef Bayat's (1997) work, *Street Politics*, she emphasizes the central role that cultural concepts such as "face-saving" (*aberu dāri*) and dignity-maintenance play in shaping lower-class youth efforts to obtain public goods and improve their living standards. Hashemi elaborates how, by following a strategy of four moral criteria—self-sufficiency, hard work, purity, and appearance—young people are able to accumulate moral capital, which allows them to win gradual gains in social and economic domains. She notes that the focus on hopelessness, marginalization, and exclusion of youth in many studies of waithood fails to notice how cultural practices such as face-saving create "moral status distinctions." These important moral status distinctions help these self-sufficient, pious, and hardworking youth to be perceived as reliable candidates for marriage or jobs offered by their networks of friends and neighbors in the community. Hashemi suggests a more nuanced analysis which limits itself to working-class and disadvantaged youth, not youth as a homogenous category. She includes both men and women in her data and elaborates some of the coping strategies and mechanisms of mobility, which inspire these youth to act with a degree of hope and optimism. Combining cultural variables with the economic, she allows for the recognition of human subjectivities and young people's existential struggles amid structural restrictions.

The hope and optimism reported in Hashemi's research with working-class and disadvantaged youth is confirmed by a report published by the conservative *Mehr News Agency* (2016). In its discussion of the declining rate of marriage in Iran, *Mehr News* notes that economic factors do not seem to be the main cause of marriage delays. In fact, the report points out that the annual number of registered marriages is higher in southern, less affluent, districts of Tehran compared to wealthy northern districts of the city. Moreover, age of first marriage is lower in the less economically developed provinces of the country compared to the more urbanized and developed parts (*Mehr News Agency* 2016). In other words, it is urban, educated, middle-class Iranian youth who have far fewer economic limitations to marriage who are waiting the longest to marry. By contrast, working-class youth from less economically developed areas of the country are getting married despite economic barriers.

Methodology

Beginning in the summer of 2015, but most intensively between 2017 and 2018, I conducted in-depth qualitative interviews with more than one hundred university-educated, middle-class Iranian youth with the aim of exploring the new patterns of youth intimacy and the reasons behind the widespread delays in marriage. Specifically, my interest was in exploring the question: Why are Iranian youth—especially middle-class, educated youth—so unsettled about settling down? In other words, why are they postponing their marriage to some unknown future?

My respondents were both females and males, between the ages of twenty and thirty-five, living in Tehran. They were college students, or more often, graduate students pursuing master's and doctoral degrees, as well as university graduates with or without permanent jobs. I knew some of these individuals personally and was introduced to the rest of them through my academic connections. Faculty members, research associates, and PhD students who were acting as teaching fellows from three major public universities in Tehran arranged my access to these young people. They connected me to their students and colleagues, and their students, in turn, put me in touch with the network of their friends (snowball sampling). I conducted the interviews fully in Persian and recorded them when permitted. I then transcribed and translated them into English. The interviews were semi-structured, with a good number of open-ended questions that allowed participants to elaborate on relevant issues, events, memories, opinions, and experiences. However, for the sake of precision, sometimes the interviews were conducted in a more structured manner with questions focused on specific topics. In order to protect the identity of research participants, I have used pseudonyms instead of their real names.

Interviews addressed topics such as marriage, love, romance, and the transformation of intimacy in contemporary urban Iran and lasted between one and three hours with some of the participants agreeing to follow-up sessions. My questions focused on the attitudes and opinions, practices, and lifestyles of young people regarding these topics, and the discussion of existing or emerging trends in broader society. The style of the interviews was to follow the narratives and life trajectories of the participants and to focus on specific relationships, persons, and events that the subjects perceived as significant and decisive in the evolution of their perspectives on relationships and marriage.

Cynical and Idealist Attitudes toward Marriage

The young people in my research are representative of urban, educated, middle-class Iranian youth. They are not the wealthy elites located in the rich districts of northern Tehran about which scholars like Pardis Mahdavi (2009) have written. They are instead the sons and daughters of middle-class professionals: engineers, doctors, lawyers, businesspeople, managers, teachers, artists, and owners of small private companies. For the most part, my respondents come from small families with an average of two children. The fact that many of their parents are university-educated and professionally active, and that they are from such small families, means that their parents have high expectations for their futures. They are willing to invest, financially as well as emotionally, in their children's education and personal development, not only through their twenties, but if necessary, even into their early and mid-thirties.[7]

The financial and moral support of parents has given the young people in my study the opportunity to explore life in its different dimensions: to pursue their studies in Iran as well as abroad, to travel, to follow their interests, to try out different types of internships and part-time jobs, and most importantly, to date and experience sexual and romantic relationships before marriage (Azad-Armaki et al. 2011). Drawing on the support of their parents, most of my respondents have at minimum a bachelor's degree; many have multiple postgraduate degrees, including PhDs. In the process of pursuing their educational and economic goals, they regularly come into contact with members of the opposite sex—at university, in the workplace, at parties, when they travel, and through their friends. Importantly, and contrary to the restrictive policies of the government on dating and the mingling of youth, parents, whether secular or religious, are tolerant of their children's social lives and their mixed-sex interactions. They state their support for their children's social experiences and in fact see such interactions as an important way to identify a future marriage partner; those from more religiously conservative backgrounds simply close their eyes to behaviors of which they disapprove.

It is important to point out that many parents of this generation were intensely involved in the Iranian Revolution of 1979. Many curtailed their educations in order to participate in demonstrations and political debates and to promote the revolution's ideals and values. Soon after the victory of the revolution, universities were closed. When they reopened a few years later, the new admissions process rejected many former and new students due to their political backgrounds. In addition, the ensuing Iran-Iraq War (1980–88) imposed an ascetic lifestyle on this earlier generation. The sacrifices they made in their youth along with their disappointments in the post-revolutionary sociopolitical and economic situation led them to hope for something very different for their own children (Khosravi 2017: 27–56).

Parents not only express their disappointment with the unfulfilled promises of the revolution, but they also recognize mistakes regarding their own intimate relationships. Many of them married young and hastily with minimum financial expectations in the heady atmosphere of revolutionary promise and quickly had children. The result is that a substantial portion of the parental generation is deeply unhappy with their unions. A significant number live together under the same roof in a state that has been described as "emotional divorce" (YJC 2017). Most of this generation have chosen not to divorce legally, clinging instead to a former ideal of respectability and commitment. The deeply felt flaws and failures of their own marriages, however, are behind their desire to see their own children marry more wisely and cautiously.

Fueled by their parents' economic and emotional support for their youthful plans and desires, many of the young people in my study express unrealistic idealism regarding their imagined futures, particularly when it comes to their envisioned marriage partner. At the same time and often reflecting on their own parents' marriages, they express considerable cynicism and doubt about the possibilities of achieving long-term marital happiness. Sara, one of my earliest contacts and among the most forthcoming, was especially harsh in her criticism of her own parents' marriage and determined not to make a similar mistake.

Sara

When I first met Sara, she was twenty-two years old and a senior
undergraduate student of Fine Arts at a top public university in Tehran. Our first meeting took place in a coffee shop around Vanak
Square in 2015, and we met for follow-up interviews repeatedly
over the next several years. Sara comes from a middle-class nuclear
family in Tehran, and her parents are both college-educated business
managers who work in private companies. At her first interview
with me when she was still in college, Sara expressed harshly cynical views about relationship and commitment—although she was
dating someone at the time. She said she thought that commitment
is never an authentic form of self-expression, and that "happy" romantic relationships are not lasting: "in my opinion, commitment
is a lie." She explained that nowadays dating and romance are very
common among Iranian youth, but since many young people also
believe in traditional and family values, they expect the relationship
to be meaningful and lasting: "They do not talk about marriage at
the beginning [of a relationship] but their intention is to stay together. Once a long-term prospect is guaranteed, then they are okay
to experience things together, even have sex together." She thought
that traditional values and romantic ideals blind young people from
seeing the "truth." The truth according to her could be reduced ba-
sically to two principles: first, that individuals are primarily selfish,
and second, that they change over time. These two qualities, according to Sara, make individuals incapable of committing to one person
exclusively and romantically over a long period of time.

I was curious about the roots of her cynical views about relationships. Certainly, families, the educational system, and religion all
promote commitment, so why did Sara think of commitment as a
lie? She explained that although her parents were together and not
divorced and did not constantly fight, they were nonetheless in a
state of "cold war." When she was a teenager, she thought the problem was unique to her family, but as she grew older she observed
that other families were similar. She concluded that the problem
comes from the institution of marriage itself. "All the [married] couples I saw were wrongly matched; they were together for the wrong
reasons." She wondered why they did not get divorced and then
added: "I did not see the beginning of these relationships, but from
the time I had the chance to observe them, they were nothing special or close to perfect. . . ."

Three years later, I interviewed Sara again to see if she had changed her perspective toward relationship, commitment, and marriage. She was about to turn twenty-six, had her college degree in hand, and was earning some money as a playwright for a theater company. The biggest change, according to Sara, was that she was less negative about the institution of marriage. Several of her acquaintances and relatives were in serious relationships or even engaged. "My friends and I are now between the ages of twenty-five and thirty, and we are expected to do something with our lives. The options are to continue studying, find a permanent job, emigrate somewhere, or get married." But for her, marriage was still a long way off. She noted:

> I still do not have a permanent job and sufficient salary. I am not sure if I want to stay in Iran or to go abroad, if I want to work in theater or some other field. When I do not know the answers to these questions, how can I think about marriage?! How can I even think about a serious long-term relationship?

In addition, the therapy sessions that she was attending convinced her to delay marriage.[8] She described them as an illuminating experience, and she told me that until she reaches a better understanding of herself and her past, she is not going to consider marriage or any serious relationship. "Knowing my problems and their roots are more important for me. That is why I do not want to let someone into my life now. When I can evaluate my life and reach a degree of peace with myself, then I can think about marriage."

When I asked Sara why she underwent therapy, she focused her harshest criticism on her parents as the reason for her negative attitude toward commitment. The disappointing nature of her parents' relationship fueled her pessimism toward marriage:

> For a long time, I was thinking that they were forced to be with each other. As a kid, I really wanted them to get divorced, but they did not, and that made me think there is a hidden reason behind it. Maybe it was because of my brother and me that they tolerated each other; maybe my mom would not be able to see us anymore if they got divorced. Now that I reflect on those memories in my therapy sessions, I see clearly that there was not any external pressure on them to make them remain together. My parents were both working and financially independent so they could divorce any minute, but they did not. They were nagging about their relationship in front of us all the time but never acted on it. The image of their marriage in my head

is extremely bitter. I guess the major reason that I am still terrified of commitment is their problematic relationship.

Sara may be the most outspoken of my respondents in her criticisms of her parents' relationship, but she is representative of a much larger group of young people in my study who describe their parents' marriages as "unfulfilled," "problematic," and "disappointing." The flip side to this cynicism regarding the institution of marriage and commitment is the strong idealism regarding an imagined marital partner.

Amir

Amir is exemplary of the young people in my study who express unrealistically high expectations of the perfect marriage partner. At the age of thirty-two, Amir is a postdoctoral researcher of political science at a research center affiliated with a top public university in Tehran. His family is originally from the city of Isfahan, but they moved to Tehran because his father was appointed as a professor of economics at a university when Amir was fourteen years old. His mother is a high school teacher of Persian literature, and his two younger siblings—one brother and one sister—are both engineers. Amir lives in a one-bedroom apartment independently of his family in Karim-Khan Street, a cultural district at the center of Tehran. We met there in a bookstore café.

Amir is single but actively dating and has had multiple long- and short-term relationships. His parents, especially his father, expect him to get married and even offered him their financial and moral support. They are open-minded about Amir's choice of partner, but at the same time, believe that marriage and family formation is a must. Amir feels pressured by their concerns and attempted to justify his singlehood to me, arguing that he is open to marriage when he meets the "right" person.

Amir told me that he has very high expectations for a partner, criteria that are not easily found all together in one person. "I am a picky guy when it comes to romantic partnership. I am not into compromising," He explained and then added: "It sounds conceited, but I know myself, and I know that when some qualities are missing in a partner, I am not going to stay in that relationship." I was curious to know what his criteria were. The ideal woman, he said, had to be beautiful, fit, educated, artsy, cultured, socially aware and politically progressive, flirtatious, sexy, and passionate in bed. The list was so long that he himself laughed and begged me not to judge him.

Interestingly, Amir had met his "ideal partner" in his first year at university. It was the first major relationship for both of them, their first encounter with sex and love. It lasted for three years. Like many other students of his generation, Amir thought that the next step, after falling in love was to think about marriage. However, when he discussed his idea with his girlfriend, Mina, and his own mother, both of them thought it was not a good idea. "Mina told me not to think about marriage and just enjoy the relationship while it lasted. She said we are both too young to think about marriage," Amir then added: "My mom did not like the idea either. She thought Mina was not a good fit for me because she and her family were more liberal and less religious than we were." Gradually Mina made plans to continue her education in the United Kingdom and told Amir that her affections for him were weakening. While this hurt him, Amir accepted her decision and they separated emotionally and geographically.

He believes that when he was younger and less experienced, he was more open and accepting toward marriage. But his many relationship experiences have made him both pickier and more cynical concerning lifetime commitment. He says:

> Ideally, I would like to have a long-term relationship if I could find a "suitable" partner but even then, marriage is not that central in my mind. I would marry only for legal purposes and social acceptability. What I care about most, is to find a woman with whom I can have deep sexual and intellectual connections.

Niloufar

Amir's idealism regarding a partner is shared by Niloufar, who labels herself a "fan" of marriage. Although she strongly believes in marriage and talks passionately about having children of her own, she remains single at the age of thirty-five. When I asked her why, she explained with a bitter smile: "White marriage and other new types of premarital relationships have ruined our chances of marriage." Niloufar has an MBA degree in financial management and has been working as a senior accountant at a private food company for eight years. Although financially independent, she still lives with her parents because as an only child, she does not want to leave them on their own. So, what has prevented her from getting married? We met on several occasions at V Café in Palestine Street in downtown Tehran to discuss her romantic trajectory. Niloufar explained:

> In a nutshell, I have not yet found the person I think I can marry. Some of my relationships have approached marriage, but when things were getting serious, I decided to terminate everything. Maybe because I am a perfectionist. I once compromised when I was selecting my college major [at the university entrance examination]. After that, I promised myself never to compromise on my dreams and ideals.

Every time Niloufar found herself close to marriage, she found something wrong with her partner at the time. She said she felt lucky for detecting those flaws before it was too late. Ideally, she wanted a cool and contemporary good-looking man, who at the same time is into marriage and more "conventional and meaningful" romantic relationships. "Someone who does not want to date several people at the same time. Someone thoughtful who puts less weight on sex and more on love, sentiments, and gentlemanliness." Niloufar believes her type of man is a dying breed:

> The urban contemporary man whom I prefer is incompatible with my moral standards. He would probably find me conservative. If I go his way, then I must sacrifice things that I care about. You see, maybe I am too hard on myself, maybe my criteria are wrong or paradoxical. Even maybe I make up these thoughts because I am scared to leave my secure and comfortable life alongside my parents for a relationship about which I am uncertain!

Niloufar is idealistic in her requirements for a partner and at the same time cynical about love and romance. She thinks men might be more romantic and idealist when they are younger and less experienced, but after a certain age, they are not that eager to get married because they can find sexual satisfaction with lesser costs. "Forget about marriage! It is difficult enough to find a boyfriend who cares about you and with whom you can have a healthy relationship. The majority of young people around me are looking for a hook-up, both boys and girls." In addition, decision-making becomes more difficult for men and women after a certain age. "It's very difficult for us, the middle class, to make our minds about marriage because we neither can make a life as good as what our parents are currently giving us, nor are we willing to start our life together modestly with basic means."

Middle-Class Youth and "Voluntary Waithood"

So far in this chapter, I have provided some statistics on the condition of marriage, divorce, and singlehood in contemporary Iran in order to illustrate the demographic landscape in which young people are living. In addition, I have drawn on ethnographic accounts to show why educated middle-class Iranian youth have delayed their marriage. Furthermore, I have engaged in discussions on waithood as a theoretical framework that explains the prolonged stagnation of the youth and their exclusion from the job market as well as their stalled entry into adulthood and marriage (Dhillon and Yousef 2009; Hashemi 2015; Salehi-Isfahani 2011; Singerman 2007, 2011, 2013).

According to Singerman (2013: 10), the phenomenon of delayed marriage in Egypt and several other countries in the Middle East and North Africa (MENA) is caused by youth unemployment and high costs of marriage. In other words, the delay in marriage among the youth is involuntary, fueled by economic barriers that block young people from obtaining good jobs and affording marriage costs. The unavailability of premarital sex and romance due to the strict moral standards of the Egyptian society, next to the impossibility of marriage due to high costs of living, causes young Egyptians to feel desperate and hopeless (Schielke 2009, 2015).

The young people in my study, however, provide different reasoning for delaying their marriage compared to the youth in Egypt and some other countries in the Middle East. In my reference group—middle-class educated youth—we find *voluntary waithood*, meaning that the motive behind their singlehood is psychological and not economic. My focus group is also different from the working-class youth described by Hashemi (2015). According to her, the working class youth from southern districts of Tehran are struggling to maintain their dignity (*aberu dāri*) and to gradually establish themselves economically through honest hard work and trust-building, so that their moral capital can be translated to economic capital by the support of their community and philanthropic entrepreneurs. Their reasons for delaying marriage are similar to the group of reasons put forward by Singerman in her study of youth in MENA societies. Their waithood, in other words, is *involuntary*. And yet, although they are marrying later, they have by no means rejected marriage as an important life stage and goal.

In contrast to the youth described by Hashemi, the educated, middle-class youth who are the focus of my project are delaying marriage for very different reasons. They come from small families.

The majority do not face serious economic barriers with regard to marriage. In fact, with the continued economic and emotional support of their parents these young people are enjoying their period of singlehood, engaging in self-exploration and identity formation by pursuing higher education, travelling, and working in part-time exploratory careers, and dating. Of course, their parents would like to see them marry, but also advise caution and suggest that their children enjoy and explore life before making a long-term commitment to marriage. They are stalled in their relationship commitments for psychological reasons. Their cynicism regarding marriage is linked, among other reasons, to their parents' problematic marital relationships as well as their own idealist requirements for the perfect partner. For these reasons, it is more appropriate to label their pattern of marriage delay as voluntary waithood.

Conclusion

This chapter argues that the phenomenon of delayed marriage, known as waithood, for educated middle-class Iranian youth is a voluntary decision, not an involuntary prolonged period of stagnation caused by youth unemployment and high costs of marriage. In other words, waithood, for this demographic, is primarily fueled by psychological factors, not economic barriers. The major psychological rubrics expressed by the respondents in qualitative interviews are cynicism and idealism. These two psychological regimes of thought may sound contradictory at first, but upon further probing, one can see that they are the two sides of the same coin. Together, they create a state of indetermination and inaction that cause the young people in my study to postpone marriage to an unknown future.

Idealism is a product of demographic change and higher levels of education and social freedom. The population control program that was implemented in the late 1980s has reduced the size of the Iranian family, and the average number of children per family is now below two. Among the middle class, where the size of the family is specifically small, parents who are university-educated, professionally active, and financially independent have high expectations for the future of their children. They invest in their children's education and personal development, financially as well as emotionally, all through their twenties and even thirties. The parental support gives the youth in my study the opportunity to explore life in its different dimensions—education, travel, work, internships, fun, and love. In addition, many parents support dating and the premarital romantic and/or sexual relationships of their children—implicitly or explicitly. These young people are following developmental paths, financially and morally supported by their parents, toward identity formation and self-actualization that have led to the rise of idealistic and individualistic attitudes among them. Many have unrealistically high expectations of their potential marriage partners.

The cynicism toward marriage among the young people in my study is rooted in two sources. First, they are suspicious, sometimes even disappointed, of the dysfunctional and broken marital relationships of their parents. Many parents married young and hastily with minimum financial expectations and little romantic experience in the heady atmosphere of revolutionary promise and quickly had children. They were clueless about what was expected of them in partnership, love, and sex. As a result, a substantial portion of the parental generation is deeply unhappy with their unions. A significant number live together under the same roof in a state that has been described as emotional divorce. They are not legally divorced but in the state of cold war and perpetual conflict, a situation that has intense negative consequences on the mental and emotional life of their children. Many of my respondents explained that their cynical views toward marriage come from what they have observed in the problematic marital life of their parents. The second source of cynicism in my study is closely related to the notion of idealism. The rise of expectations and ideals, if not satisfied with realistic and pragmatic solutions, can cause despair and disappointment. Many young people in my study express cynicism simply because they cannot find their ideal partner. In addition, some complain that the availability of options such as casual sex and short-term relationships has ruined the chances of finding healthy, stable, and lasting romance that can lead to marriage.

Mehrdad Babadi is a PhD candidate in the Department of Anthropology at Boston University. His dissertation explores the transformation of intimacy in contemporary Iran through studying the dating approaches, romantic lifestyles, and marriage decision-making of educated middle-class youth in three public universities in Tehran. A native of Iran, Babadi earned a BA in industrial management at Shahid Beheshti University, an MPhil in modern society at the University of Cambridge, and an MA in sociology at the University of Notre Dame.

Notes

1. According to a World Bank (2014) report, more than half of Iranian women of university age, attend a university. Women form over 60 percent of all university students in the undergraduate level in the last ten years, and in 2009, women comprised 43 percent of master's students and 33 percent of doctoral students. For further details, see Shams (2016).
2. For further information on the cultural politics of the internet in Iran, see Akhavan (2013).
3. By "endogamous" marriage, I am referring to marriages between parallel and cross-cousins. A traditional Iranian saying that "marriage between cousins is summoned in heaven" indicates the historical popularity of this practice.
4. For more information on statistics of marriage and divorce in Iran, check the websites of Statistical Center of Iran (www.amar.org.ir) and National Organization for Civil Registration (www.sabteahval.ir).
5. Also check Salehi-Isfahani and Egel (2009: 56–60).
6. White marriage *(ezdevāj-e sefid)* refers to the cohabitation of couples without any legal or religious contract and is illegal in Iran. For further reading on white marriage, see Azad-Aramaki et al. (2012).
7. On the rise of "developmental idealism" and the widespread tendencies toward individualism and self-actualization caused by the demographic change and the reduction of the size of the family in Iran, see Abbasi-Shavazi and Askari-Nodoushan (2012).
8. For the history and institutionalization of psychiatry in Iran as well as the emergence and popularity of psychiatric discourses and subjectivities among the post-revolutionary Iranian youth (1980s generation), see the excellent work of Behrouzan (2016).

References

Abbasi-Shavazi, Mohammad Jalal, and Abbas Askari-Nodoushan. 2012. "Family Life and Developmental Idealism in Yazd, Iran." *Demographic Research* 26: 207–38.

Abbasi-Shavazi, Mohammad Jalal, Peter McDonald, and Meimanat Hosseini-Chavoshi. 2009. *The Fertility Transition in Iran: Revolution and Reproduction.* New York: Springer.

Afary, Janet. 2009. "The Sexual Economy of the Islamic Republic." *Iranian Studies* 42(1): 5–26.

Aghajanian, Akbar, Sajede Vaezzade, Javad Afshar Kohan, and Vaida Thompson. 2018. "Recent Trends of Marriage in Iran." *The Open Family Studies Journal* 10(1): 1–8.

Akhavan, Niki. 2013. *Electronic Iran: The Cultural Politics of an Online Evolution.* New Brunswick: Rutgers University Press.

Al-Monitor. 2015. "Why Are Young Iranians Losing Interest in Marriage?" 2 June. Retrieved 16 April 2019 from http://www.al-monitor.com/pulse/originals/2015/06/iran-birth-rate-marriage-decline-divorce.html.

Azad-Armaki, Taghi, Amir-Hossein Sharifi, Maryam Isari, and Sahar Talebi. 2011. "Typology of Premarital Sexual Relationships in Iran." [In Persian.] *Cultural Sociology* 2(2): 1–34.

———. 2012. "Cohabitation: The Emergence of New Forms of Family in Tehran." [In Persian.] *Cultural Sociology* 3(1): 43–77.

Bashirieh, Hossein. 1995. *Political Sociology in Iran.* [In Persian.] Tehran: Nashr-e Ney.

Bayat, Asef. 1997. *Street Politics: Poor People's Movements in Iran.* New York: Columbia University Press.

Behrouzan, Orkideh. 2016. *Prozak Diaries: Psychiatry and Generational Memory in Iran.* Stanford: Stanford University Press.

Census. 2016. "Selected Findings of the 2016 National Population and Housing Census." [In Persian.] 1 August. Retrieved 16 April 2019 from https://www.amar.org.ir/Portals/1/census/2016/Census_2016_Selected _Findings.pdf.

Dhillon, Navtej, and Tarik Yousef, eds. 2009. *Generation in Waiting: The Unfulfilled Promise of Young People in the Middle East.* Washington DC: Brookings Institution Press.

Egel, Daniel, and Djavad Salehi-Isfahani. 2010. "Youth Transitions to Employment and Marriage in Iran: Evidence from the School to Work Transition Survey." *Middle East Development Journal* 2(1): 89–120.

Fathi, Elham, Mohammad Javid, Behnaz Sarkhil, Soudabeh Zebarjad. 2017. "Changes in the Average Age of Marriage in Iran." [In Persian.] *Statistics* 24: 8–12.

Habibi, Nader. 2015. "Iran's Over-education Crisis: Causes and Ramifications." *Middle East Brief Series,* Crown Center for Middle East Studies, Brandeis University 89: 1–7.

Hashemi, Manata. 2015. "Waithood and Face: Morality and Mobility among Lower-Class Youth in Iran." *Qualitative Sociology* 38(3): 261–83.

ISNA (Iranian Students' News Agency). 2014. "Intimate Relationships between Boys and Girls Has Grown Three Times Bigger." [In Persian.] 11 May. Retrieved 16 April 2019 from https://www.isna.ir/news/9302 2114123.

———. 2017. "Inclination toward 'Living Solo' is the Reason behind the Increase in the Number of Households." [In Persian.] 17 December. Retrieved 16 April 2019 from https://www.isna.ir/news/96062514302.

———. 2018. "What Percentage of Iranians do not Have Access to the Internet?" [In Persian.] 11 March. Retrieved 16 April 2019 from https://www.isna.ir/news/96121910674/.

Khosravi, Shahram. 2017. *Precarious Lives: Waiting and Hope in Iran.* Philadelphia: University of Pennsylvania Press.

Mahdavi, Pardis. 2009. *Passionate Uprisings: Iran's Sexual Revolution.* Stanford: Stanford University Press.

Mehr News Agency. 2016. "Decline in the Statistics of Marriage in the Fifth Consecutive Year." [In Persian.] 7 September. Retrieved 16 April 2019 from http://mehrnews.com/news/3762720.

Salehi-Isfahani, Djavad. 2011. "Iranian Youth in Times of Economic Crisis." *Iranian Studies* 44(6): 789–806.

Salehi-Isfahani, Djavad, and Daniel Egel. 2009. "Toward a New Social Contract for Iranian Youth." In *Generation in Waiting: The Unfulfilled Promise of Young People in the Middle East*, ed. Navtej Dhillon and Tarik Yousef, 39–66. Washington, DC: The Brookings Institution.

Schielke, Samuli. 2009. "Ambivalent Commitments: Troubles of Morality, Religiosity and Aspiration among Young Egyptians." *Journal of Religion in Africa* 39(2): 158–85.

———. 2015. *Egypt in the Future Tense: Hope, Frustration, and Ambivalence before and after 2011.* Bloomington: Indiana University Press.

Shams, Alex. 2016. "Revolutionary Religiosity and Women's Access to Higher Education in the Islamic Republic of Iran." *Journal of Middle East Women's Studies* 12(1): 126–38.

Singerman, Diane. 2007. "The Economic Imperatives of Marriage: Emerging Practices and Identities Among Youth in the Middle East." *Middle East Youth Initiative*, Working Paper No. 6, September, The Brookings Institution, Wolfensohn Center for Development, Washington, DC.

———. 2011. "The Negotiation of Waithood: The Political Economy of Delayed Marriage in Egypt." In *Arab Youth: Social Mobilisation in Times of Risk*, ed. Samir Khalaf and Roseanne Saad Khalaf, 85–108. London: Saqi Books.

———. 2013. "Youth, Gender, and Dignity in the Egyptian Uprising." *Journal of Middle East Women's Studies* 9(3): 1–27.

Statistical Center of Iran. 2018. "Statistical Tables: Registered Marriages and Divorces." [In Persian.] 26 September. Retrieved 16 April 2019 from www.amar.org.ir/طلاق-و-ازدواج/کار-نیروی-و-جمعیت/آماری-اطلاعات-و-دادهها.

World Bank. 2014. "School Enrollment, Tertiary (percent Gross)." Retrieved 16 April 2019 from https://data.worldbank.org/indicator/SE.TER.ENRR ?locations=IR.

YJC (Young Journalists Club). 2016. "Average Age of Marriage in Different Parts of the City of Tehran." [In Persian.] 18 May. Retrieved 16 April 2019 from https://www.yjc.ir/00NYN9.

———. 2017. "Emotional Divorce as a Dangerous and Important Problem to Iranian Families." [In Persian.] 28 July. Retrieved 16 April 2019 from https://www.yjc.ir/fa/news/6181325.

Chapter 11

REFUSING TO SETTLE

MIGRATION AMONG SINGLE PROFESSIONAL WOMEN IN JORDAN

Fida Adely

Introduction: The Story of Ibtisam

In 2008, several years after finishing her bachelor's degree, Ibtisam[1] moved to Amman from her village in Jordan to pursue a master's degree. She was working as a public-school teacher in her hometown but sought other professional opportunities in the capital city. She began by completing her master's degree and then switched careers to take advantage of more lucrative opportunities in the non-governmental organization sector. She never returned to live in her hometown, staying in Amman to build a career and eventually traveling abroad for more postgraduate education. In 2016, when she was in her early thirties, Ibtisam spoke with me about her migration to Amman and how, in her view, this experience had affected her marriage prospects:

> When I first came to Amman I thought, this is a city where I will meet like-minded people, but I was mistaken. I found that, despite the fact that they live in the city, men in the city are actually worse. City guys, they are really close to their mothers and so their mothers dictate their lives. Also, there is the class thing. People are like, "You are from a village" [so you are beneath us].

I met a lot of guys . . . online and offline. I was always looking, but I only had one romantic relationship. It was a very good relationship, but I was a bit older than he was, and he said his mother was not sure about us.

Amman is not a good place for a woman in her thirties. People have this pity for you and keep giving you suggestions for mingling to get married, but the end result is that you get more and more humiliated—through proposals from men who are old, married, or divorced, and God knows what problems they have. Everyone looks at you because you are in your thirties and you do not have the ring, and they look for reasons [to explain why you are still single]: "Oh, it's because she is from a village, or because she is short, or she laughs too much, or whatever."

Because you are single, people take advantage of you. One of my friends is having a terrible time. Some idiot she works with is making indecent proposals. Texting her and saying, "What are you doing now? What are you wearing?" This has happened to me too. Someone says, "Oh it's a pity you are not married. You are beautiful." They play on that—you are beautiful but unlucky—and [they] flirt with you.

Ibtisam's comments convey some of the issues faced by single women in Jordan today (and by single women in many other societies). Ibtisam argues that being single well into one's thirties can mark a woman for pity, for exploitation by coworkers, and for unsolicited comments about one's unmarried state. However, Ibtisam's labor migration to the capital city of Amman has also created new opportunities—for financial independence, further education, and greater mobility. In some respects, then, her migration and independent living have significantly changed the terms of being single. Ibtisam disclosed that she had many occasions to meet single men and that the anonymity of the city, and its spaces, have provided her with a degree of autonomy in pursuing these relationships that would not be possible in her hometown (Adely 2016; Kaya 2009). At the same time, she had to navigate tension with and pressure from family members to accept marriage partners she found less than suitable. While Ibtisam's experiences overlap with those of many single women in their thirties, her migration and the ways in which she is navigating the opportunities and challenges presented by her migration have in some respects provided new ways of being single.

In this chapter, drawing on several years of research, I examine the experiences of single women who migrated from their provincial homes to the capital city of Amman for professional opportunities. Specifically, I focus on women who lived on their own for as much as a decade and are beginning to reckon with the long-term possibilities of staying single. How should we think about their experiences in terms of "waithood" (Singerman 2007)? In many respects, the migration of these women was motivated by a refusal to wait—for professional opportunities, further education, or a marriage proposal. Believing that their home communities offer limited opportunities, these women leave their natal homes and move to the city in search of personal and professional possibilities. Nevertheless, as time passes, many are *refusing to settle*; these women are concerned about finding a suitable partner and marrying, but on their own terms. They insist on living a life of dignity (Singerman, Chapter 1, this volume).

Methodology

In 2011, while interviewing single Jordanian men and women about marriage, I met several single women living on their own in the capital city—in female student dormitories or apartments. While I knew of professional women moving to the capital for work, I was surprised by the large number because the prevailing norm is that single women do not live on their own, except in some cases when attending university.[2] Of course there were always exceptions to this norm, but rural to urban migration to Amman for jobs struck me as a relatively new phenomenon with important implications for women, men, and marriage.[3] Furthermore, in contrast to the bulk of the literature on rural to urban female labor migration, these women were not pursuing factory work or domestic service; rather, they were educated and seeking professional opportunities.

Over the course of four years, from 2012 to 2016, my research assistant and I interviewed forty-two women between the ages of twenty-three and forty-six, although the overwhelming majority of the women were between the ages of twenty-four and thirty-three when we first interviewed them. All of the interviews were conducted in Arabic and then translated into English by the author or a bilingual member of her research team. Of this initial sample, thirteen women participated in multiple follow-up interviews. Through snowball sampling, we identified women who had moved from towns, villages, and provincial cities all over the country to work in Amman. All were university graduates, and some had postgraduate degrees. In terms of their academic backgrounds and professional pursuits, about three-quarters of the women had degrees in what would be considered STEM (Science, Technology, Engineering, and Mathematics) fields, and the majority worked in the private sector in STEM-related jobs or for international organizations.[4] With respect to their family backgrounds, socioeconomic status, family size, and other demographic characteristics, the women we interviewed were quite diverse, and no discernable demographic pattern could explain their migration—other than being educated and being relatively successful in academic terms. Their academic successes put them in the position to take advantage of perceived opportunities in the capital city of Amman or motivated them to seek professional and academic experiences in the capital that they argued were unavailable in the provinces.

Fueled by stereotypes and journalistic accounts, some Jordanians with whom I spoke assumed that the migration of these women was necessarily exploitative, with their families pressuring them to work for financial reasons, taking their salaries, and preventing them from marrying for fear of losing their salaries. For example, *Ainnews*, an online media site, reported on three women who complained that their families prevented them from getting married because they wanted to continue to benefit from their salaries (Abutayeh 2013).[5] While I was skeptical of these assumptions, I wondered if their migration might complicate, if not hinder, the process of getting married, given that their migration to Amman represented a significant departure from the norm of living with family until one marries.[6] My own research did not corroborate the stories of family financial exploitation. While some women did help support their families (e.g., by supporting the education of younger siblings), this was not a given, nor was it a requirement of their migration except in very few cases. Some women could barely cover their own expenses and depended on the support of family or friends to stay in Amman. Only one of the women interviewed (out of forty-two) indicated that her family had pressured her to migrate and that her family's wishes interfered with her ability to marry. However, some wondered if they had put the interests of others before their own—delaying marriage unnecessarily and now facing the prospects of never marrying. At the same time, their experiences as single women living apart from their families had complicated their feelings about marriage, and altered their opportunities for finding life partners. Most significantly, these women argued that the experience of migration and living on their own had significantly changed what they wanted from a marriage, making it harder for them to "tie the knot." Their views on marriage, being single, and the characteristics of an appropriate spouse are the subject of this chapter.

The Demographic Context

According to Jude, a 34-year-old single woman living in Amman, "People like to call it a [marriage] crisis. The media considers it a crisis. They focus on spinsterhood. But maybe for those who are not married, it's not a crisis." Like many parts of the Arab world (Singerman 2007), the perception that the contemporary era is characterized by a "marriage crisis" has been circulating in the Jordanian press for at least three decades now. The crisis is typically framed in both economic and moral terms. Researchers and commentators frequently flag the costs of getting married and setting up a home as major obstacles. As early as the 1980s, kinship groups publicly released manifestos calling on families to scale back wedding celebrations that were making it difficult for young people to marry or forcing families into debt. The discourse surrounding the economics of getting married could also be gendered. In Jordan, it is customary for the costs of marriages to be borne by the groom and his family. While some women can and do contribute to household or wedding costs, the dominant expectation is that this is the male's responsibility. Part of the marriage crisis discourse is that the material expectations of women and their families are unreasonable, making it difficult for men to marry and leaving women vulnerable to "spinsterhood." Despite these perceptions, recent data reveal that the relative costs of marriage have decreased since the 1980s (Salem 2014). The widespread perception that divorces are on the rise has also contributed to the sense that there is a marriage crisis. While I do not have deep historical data, the available data do not indicate a steep upsurge in divorces.[7]

In this context, interventions by religious organizations, civil society groups, and the state work to prepare young men and women for marriage, to make marriage more affordable, and to educate the broader public about appropriate expectations surrounding marriage (Hasso 2010; Hughes 2017; Nahhas 2018). Despite these persistent concerns, most young men and women marry in Jordan. For example, in 2016, only 9 percent of women and 4.8 percent of men over the age of thirty-five were unmarried. While there has been a gradual increase in the numbers of unmarried men and women over the past decade, over 90 percent marry (See Figure 11.1).

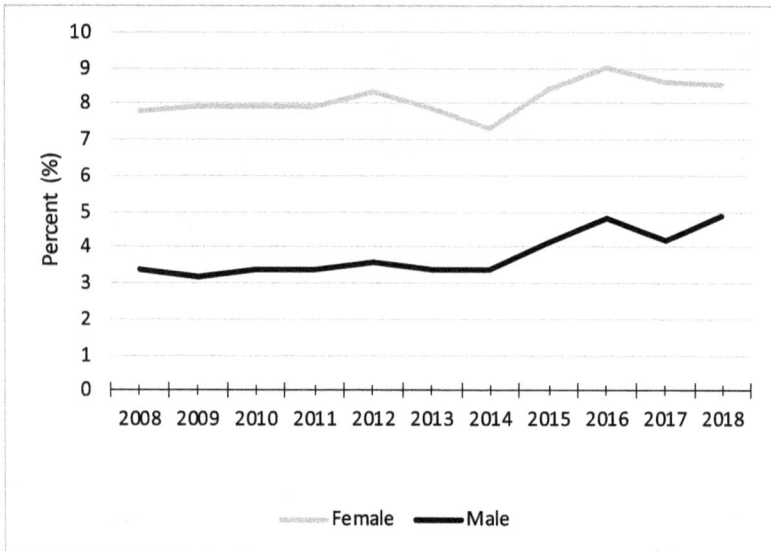

FIGURE 11.1. Single (Never-Married) Population Age 35 Years and Above in Jordan, 2008–18. Data retrieved from Jordan Department of Statistics: http://dosweb.dos.gov.jo/.

Furthermore, while the majority of women marry in their twenties, more women are marrying in their thirties today than ever before. For example, in 1970 only 3.5 percent of women married in their thirties while the number was closer to 10 percent in 2017 (Jordan Department of Statistics n.d.). Indeed, several of the women profiled here married in the course of our research project, some after lamenting the fact that they might never marry. Statistics for a slightly older age group (between forty-five and forty-nine years old) show an even lower number of singles in 2010 with 7 percent of females and 2 percent of males still single in their late forties (Salem 2014).[8] While the number of single women is lower than many people in Jordan assume, marriage age is later and as such women remain single for longer (Gebel and Heyne 2016). Furthermore, in the context of relatively low female labor force participation rates (13–15 percent), single university graduates are the females most likely to be working or actively seeking work (Assaad, Hendy, and Yassine 2014; Kawar 2000). As our research shows, not only are they the most likely to be working, but some single university graduates have become more mobile seeking labor in different locals. This chapter analyzes the experiences of some of these women.

Migration and Its Effects on Marriage Prospects

Ruweida was thirty years old and working for a public relations firm when I met her. She was living in an apartment on her own at the time of the interview, and, except for a brief period of unemployment when she went home to a town in the south, had been living in Amman since 2008. She said:

> Unfortunately, people's views toward girls who live on their own can be negative. If she lives on her own, in their perspective, this is a girl with too much freedom. This means she can express her opinion because she's open-minded and she knows her rights. This goes against the idea in our society that she should obey the man. She knows her rights, and so they say, "You can't have two roosters in one cage (*dikayyn fi qafas wahad*)" . . . A man may not have this view himself, but his family influences him because marriage is not a decision made by two people. It's made by the whole tribe. So it's not enough that he wants to marry you, but it's his father and mother and brother and brother's wife. They all give their opinions about the matter.
>
> Since I have lived a life where we [girls who have migrated] support ourselves financially, pay rent, water, and electricity, we do not need a man to take care of these things. . . Because we do everything by ourselves, a man is additional support in life no more and no less. And if he is not there, it does not mean we cannot go on. I will not be broken because I am able to stand on my own.

Ruweida's story captures some of the key themes that emerge about marriage and marriage prospects in the narratives of women who migrate. Women viewed their migration as a mixed bag in terms of their marriage prospects. Many shared her sentiment that people judged them or assumed the worst about them because they were living apart from their families. Ruweida argued that this criticism was directed specifically at her independence as a woman who had lived on her own for years. Others worried that their morality was being questioned. In this section, I discuss three main perspectives on migration and marriage: migration as liability, migration as opportunity, and migration as a complicating factor in finding a suitable marriage partner.

Like Ruweida, Salam, an educator from the south who was in her early thirties, complained that people judged her unfairly because she lived in a dormitory, questioning her intentions and morals. Salam reflected:

You always have to prove yourself to be a good person in an environment that sees you as a bad person. They always question why I came to work here far from my hometown. They always ask, "What brings you here? What's forcing you?" This is one of the challenges I face and now, because I am a little late in getting married, I am not viewed the same way as other girls.

When I interviewed Salam a second time, this concern about her reputation persisted. However, she also linked her continued single status to being far from her community: "Because I moved away from my community, people stopped knowing who I am." This final point can be understood only in a context where families still have a significant role in arranging marriages, and rates of consanguineous marriage are still relatively high, particularly in rural areas (Salem 2014). Thus, one's community and extended kin are often the source of potential marriage partners.

While families actively attempt to match up potential couples, this involvement can vary from arranging for a potential suitor to meet a potential bride in her parent's home (a visit that could lead to engagement shortly thereafter), to introducing a coworker to a relative looking to get married and facilitating an initial meeting in a public place without the involvement or supervision of the family. In reality, the scenarios for meeting, matchmaking, and dating are too varied to classify (Adely 2016).[9] Still, most marriages continue to be agreements between families in some respects.

When asked how she was meeting potential marriage partners, Muna, an engineer in her early forties, described a shifting degree of family involvement:

It depends really. Most of them come through colleagues, or relatives that hear someone is looking for a wife and they tell him about me. As for where I meet them—I went through several stages honestly. At first, I would always have to meet them at the house, and we would sit and talk for about a half hour then it would be like, "Ok well, decide." I didn't like that. The result of meeting in such a manner was that I would say no . . . Whenever a suitor came it would be like a state of emergency at home, a crisis, and this made me not like them (the suitors). Also, I was in love with someone else—a man I worked with—so I kept refusing, hoping it would work out, but he was more educated and his parents refused.[10]

Since I came to Amman there have been other options for meeting people. But, even then my parents initially insisted he must come meet me at our home. So he would have to travel from Amman to my hometown in order for me to meet with him. Then there was a time where I was engaged for a bit, but that did not work out. So the next stage became that I would meet the person at a relative's place in Amman. After that we moved on to meeting someone at a coffee shop, but I had to be with a friend; someone had to be with me. And finally, I was able to go sit with a person at a public space, or a coffee shop, on my own—then make a decision and let my parents know.

Muna's parents were initially strict about her interactions with men who were interested in meeting with her, and she consulted her parents about such meetings. Eventually, they agreed to let Muna meet men on her own. However, as she got older, the seriousness of proposals from men waned in her estimation:

When you grow older and you live with your parents, the situation is different than when you are living away from them. The only opportunity to change your situation is to get married. And people start saying, "Oh she's really desperate to get married." At first people [suitors and/or their family members] would not say this publicly, but after the first two or three meetings it would come out in an honest conversation. Guys would say, "If I'm going to marry you, you have to provide all these things in return because I am marrying you. You should be grateful that I am considering you at your age." And then there are the new offers that I have been getting lately: "Let's just date." They will say, "Oh I cannot get married but let's date, and I will get a studio and I'll spend [money] on you and get you gifts, etc."

Muna's situation was particularly challenging because she was relatively older than other women who had been interviewed (born in 1972) and because her family had been displaced by war, interrupting her education and delaying her professional career. When she finally had the opportunity to get a university degree, she was uninterested in proposals for marriage as she was determined to succeed and graduate quickly. Furthermore, health issues in her family and the death of one of her siblings meant that her family relied on her for emotional and financial support.

Nevertheless, migration to Amman significantly expands timeframes and spaces for meeting potential marriage partners. The proliferation of cafés and restaurants in the past two decades has provided acceptable spaces for men and women to meet (Adely 2016). In addition, the privacy afforded by technology and social media has expanded the space for dating. The sheer fact of being in Amman also gives women a degree of liberty (and relative anonymity) in these affairs, in some cases with the consent of families. In Muna's case it took some time before she was afforded that liberty—

and she, like many women, did not feel comfortable acting without the consent of her family. However, others saw the move to Amman as precisely that—the opportunity to independently date without consulting family members.

While not all of the women with whom I spoke felt comfortable meeting potential partners on their own or "dating," many believed that the move to Amman significantly expanded their marriage opportunities and increased the likelihood that they might meet someone "different"—unlike the men at home. However, in the opening pages of this chapter, Ibtisam argued that being from the provinces posed some challenges in meeting men because of class differences or perceived differences based on geography. Ammanites at times viewed those from the provinces as traditional and conservative peasants or "Bedouin,"[11] even if they came from large provincial cities. Nevertheless, the opportunities for meeting men were significantly expanded by their move, both because they were working and meeting people and by virtue of living in a large city with a more diverse population. Remaining at home unemployed would provide limited opportunities to meet men among a significantly smaller community. As I discuss in the next section, perhaps the greatest obstacle conveyed by the women we spoke with was their labor and migration and the expectations it had generated.

Being Single

Noor, an engineer in her late twenties, said:

> I don't let [marriage] worry me even if everyone pressures you to think about it. You see it in the eyes of your mother, and when she says, "*Ya rab tkooni fi baytik*" (Oh, God, may you be in your house [i.e., marital home]. I used to get annoyed but now I just smile and say, "*Inshallah*" (God willing).

Despite later ages at first marriage and a growing number of single women in the region, very little attention has been paid to single women as a category (Rashad 2015; Halabi 2007).[12] In this section, I share the perspective of women grappling with the likelihood they will stay single.[13] I discuss the intense pressures from family to marry that some women faced, the ways in which their experiences of migration ended up raising their expectations and decreasing their willingness to settle, and their long-term concerns about their futures as single women.

Family Pressures

Some young women faced active pressure from their families to marry. The story of Ferial indicates the lengths some parents would go to get their daughters married. I interviewed Ferial in 2011 when she was twenty-six years old. Ferial worked for a management-consulting firm and was from one of the northern provinces. She was one of the first women I knew who came from the provinces to live and work in Amman. Ferial told me her story:

> I was under a lot of pressure to marry. I had potential suitors coming to our home all the time. I would go home on the weekends to meet them, and my parents were pushing me to choose one. I had constant conflict with them. One suitor (Amjad) was particularly persistent. He had seen me at a wedding and my parents were pressuring me to take him seriously. I told my parents that I wanted to meet him outside the home, and they agreed. They told Amjad that he was free to go talk with me . . . Over a period of a few months, we saw each other a few times and my parents insisted that I needed to make a decision. They wanted me to get engaged.
>
> I got sick of the constant pressure and I began to approach the subject more practically. I decided, okay, he's from a good family, he has a good job, he is well off, and everyone speaks highly of him. Maybe I should give him a chance. I gave in and got engaged even though I was not sure.
>
> After the engagement, Amjad was in a rush to get married. I was still not feeling sure and I tried to get him to delay the wedding, but he insisted on setting a date soon and booked hotels and the like. But then he started acting weird, and he made me really uncomfortable. He was very pushy, and it made me worry about what was to come. It got to the point where I could not stand being around him, and I was becoming increasingly more disturbed about marrying this guy.
>
> I decided I could not go through with the marriage. I told my parents I did not love him and was not attracted to him. They refused to accept my decision, and I spent a month trying to convince them. They were furious and very tough on me. They said things like, "You just want to keep living on your own and having fun." They threatened me, telling me they would make me quit my job and go home. I told them, "Fine, I will quit my job and I will stay at home. But I will not marry him." Then I told them if they forced me, I would go through with the marriage, but they would be responsible for this decision. "If I'm miserable it will be your fault." Finally, they. . . relented.

After this incident, Ferial's parents eased up on the pressure to marry. Thereafter, Ferial insisted she would only meet with a potential suitor at her parent's home if she was 100 percent sure she wanted to marry him. She needed to get to know him before there was any discussion between families. Eventually, she met someone a family member introduced to her. She got to know him on her own terms and they eventually married; she was thirty-one years old at the time.

While all families hoped their daughters would marry, not all were as forceful in trying to get them married. Munira, a thirty-year-old engineer, had a different experience. Her family had been very supportive of her move to Amman in 2007 and did not express concern about her still being single. Of her family she said,

> They have always been flexible people, even when it came to marriage. A lot of my friends were pressured by their parents. They would say, "That's it. You have a good suitor. What's wrong with him? It's time to get married." I am not married, and we do not have this mentality in our house that you must get married . . . If it happens, it happens. It is fate (*nasib*). I have an unmarried sister at home, and no one pressures her.

Thus, families play different roles. For Ferial, and for other women who felt a great deal of pressure from families to marry, age matters. Families tended to exert a great deal of pressure as women reached "peak" marriage age, usually in their late twenties. However, women in their thirties felt less pressure from families. Perhaps this was because, as one woman put it, "They feel bad making an issue of it since they know we are past the point of likely getting married. They do not want to hurt our feelings." Many women acknowledged and appreciated that their parents worried about them and hated to see them alone. Their parents were worried about their futures.

I Won't Settle: Marriage Expectations

Nearly all of the women interviewed talked about refusing to marry just to marry. Maysoon, a 29-year-old working for an international organization relayed:

> Everyone assumes that you must be miserable, and if you are sad they assume it's because you are single. They also assume that you are trying to catch any available male around you . . . I will only marry if there is a good opportunity. I hear too many negative stories. At the same time, I cannot constantly be thinking about it. It is exhausting, especially because you have so little control over the matter.

Older women in particular argued that their life experiences made it difficult for them to settle for a suitor who could not offer them the quality of life they needed. Typically, this was not about material or financial needs, although there were some exceptions. Sumaya, for example, said she hoped to marry someone who was well-off enough that she would not have to keep working, and a few others shared this desire. For most, however, the key issue was finding a like-minded man who would respect their opinions and accomplishments in life. Some of this was colored by stories from their female friends who were in bad marriages. Maysoon, quoted above, told me about a friend who suffered domestic violence and a sister whose marriage had ended up in divorce.[14] Both served as lessons for her. A key sentiment conveyed by women was that the options available to them were just not satisfactory.

Tharwa, a 32-year-old engineer who had been living in Amman since 2006 expressed this sentiment in biting terms:

> The issue is not that I am working or living in a dormitory. I think the problem is with the men who are currently around us . . . I do not see myself as having a problem. I see women advancing and men not making half the effort. They are intimidated by you . . . I think they see you as competition more than anything. I would consider marrying if there was a suitable person, if I found a person who would support me. Why not? Meanwhile, all I see is men concerned with themselves. They want to remain in the spotlight and for you to become a new mom. I do not need money. I can take care of myself financially. I want someone to walk alongside me. I want someone who supports my ambitions.

Last I spoke with Tharwa in 2016, she told me about a few men whom she had met recently—either through family or on her own. According to Tharwa, none were particularly promising, except one with whom she was talking online. However, Tharwa seemed adamant as ever not to settle. In other dimensions of her life, things were going well. Her company, which had almost gone bankrupt (leaving her without a salary for months), was doing well, and her loyalty to the company had been rewarded. She was making a good salary and had bought a car. Also, her family with whom she had significant conflict over her refusal to come home to her town in the south, had finally come around to her living in Amman. She was looking for an apartment and contemplating pursuing another degree. In the meantime, she went out often and was open to meeting people but felt no pressure to marry.

Being Alone

Unlike Tharwa, some women were dissatisfied with their status as single women. As I was wrapping up my discussion with Salam, I said, "Thanks Salam. I think I'm done." She responded, "There are things you still need to know. You have not asked me if I am happy." I replied, "Are you happy?" Salam said:

> Sometimes I am, and sometimes I am not. When I am not, I try to tell myself, "Be quiet." I try to deflect the feelings of unhappiness. It's okay. Time will pass. Some days I am so tired from work I do not even have time to ask myself this question. But then I do, and I wonder, "What am I doing? Why am I here? Why [am I] here alone?"

Other women were concerned about the future. Part of the loneliness described by Salam had to do with dormitory living. Dormitories were officially student dormitories, although they might house women such as Salam. They ranged in quality and cost, and some were in much better physical shape than others. However, dormitory living was characterized by limited space and even less privacy, a difficult living arrangement for a thirty-year-old professional. In our larger sample, while almost all women lived in student dormitories when they first arrived in Amman (some after a brief stay with relatives), some eventually moved into apartments with other single women or alone. Apartment living was less expensive and provided more space. In addition, women who lived in apartments did not have to abide by a curfew (most dormitories shut their doors at 9:00 or 10:00 pm). Finally, as transportation was one of the biggest challenges in navigating the city, they could choose an apartment closer to their workplace. However, some families forbade their daughters from moving into apartments either out of fear for their safety (the assumption being that dormitories provided some security) or the moral implications of their daughters being completely unsupervised. For women in their thirties and forties, dormitory life was stifling.

Of all the women I spoke with, Amira was the one most concerned about her future. When I last met with her, in 2015, she was thirty-three years old and growing increasingly concerned about her future. She had been living in a dormitory since 2008 and wanted a home of her own. However, she did not think her family would allow her to leave the security and supervision of a dormitory. In addition to wanting a home of her own, she was also very concerned about the debt she had accumulated paying for her PhD, particularly given relatively low (relative to her education) wages she was earning in the public sector. Her sense of insecurity as a single woman was not strictly about her singlehood, but intimately linked to her family situation. Her parents had divorced when she was young, but many of the big decisions in her life required the cooperation of her male guardian—her father—who was generally absent or unwilling to facilitate any of her life projects. The last time we talked about the future she was discouraged. When I asked her if she ever thought about going back home to her village, she replied, "The problem is that I do not have a home."

Thus, the precarity of being single was tied to this family history, her relationship with her kin, and her challenging financial situation. Amira did not think living with relatives would be a good decision for her and very much wanted to get married. Given these dynamics, as well as her shy and somewhat reserved personality, she had also been reluctant to pursue or respond to several marriage proposals. In at least one case, conflict within the family derailed a potential suitor. In contrast to someone like Tharwa, she felt a great deal of insecurity as she looked to the future.

Women do not explicitly choose to stay single. While this path was appealing to some women in their twenties, it worried many in their early thirties. As we saw with Amira, this depended on the kind of singlehood they could imagine—the life they could lead. In many respects, being single is the result of a set of choices these women have made, but as we see from Inhorn (Chapter 15, this volume) and Vialle (Chapter 13, this volume), even in contexts where co-habitation is possible and forming relationships/marriages are largely the purview of the individuals, women faced difficulty finding compatible partners and/or partners willing to have a family. "Being alone" then is not a predetermined choice, but the outcome of a set of other choices and preferences.

While some women say they refuse to marry someone just to get married, this decision is always constrained and shaped by circumstances, as conveyed eloquently by Jihan, who had been living in Amman in a dormitory for more than ten years when I first met her. Jihan initially went to Amman as a university student, with a scholarship from the Jordanian army to study nursing. According to her, without the scholarship from the military, it would have been difficult to complete her university education at all:

> The situation in our house was such . . . my siblings were younger, and my father was sick. The credit hour at the university was 35JD. Can you imagine? There was no money, not even enough for everyday expenses. My mother said, "You have this other option (i.e., the military)." So you can say it was my decision, but it was shaped by very particular circumstances.

The decision at the age of eighteen to commit to a career as a military nurse far from her family had far-reaching implications for Jihan and her family. Jihan had great pride in her career; she had been promoted several times and was an excellent nurse. She was also proud of the opportunities she had been able to give her siblings, as she supported at least two of them in completing their educations. However, these decisions did not come without sacrifices on her part, and as Jihan entered her thirties, she reflected on the decisions she had made and the prospects of starting her own family:

> Sometimes I do feel some regret about the choices I made, especially when I see my girlfriends who have families—kids and a life partner who shares their concerns and feels what they are feeling. The feeling of stability is a beautiful feeling. I do not think about it a lot, but people keep reminding you: "You're still not married!" I regret not being more open to the options around me. There were many who were suitable. But I held onto this one relationship that did not work out, and then I had all these family responsibilities. If I regret anything, it is that I was not attuned enough to the need to balance my responsibilities to them with my responsibilities to myself. There are many days I feel lonely. But I am also at ease knowing that I accomplished a lot and that I took care of my family.

Jihan had a long-term relationship with a man that did not end up in marriage. At that point, according to Jihan, she had forfeited many opportunities. In 2015, Jihan was promoted to a job that brought her back to her hometown and enabled her to live at home. She, and another sister, had helped the family finance the building of a modest new home, enabling them to move out of the small apartment they had been renting for years. While she was home again, she regretted not having her own home and making the choices that led here there. At the same time, Jihan's regret was tempered by her sense that she had done right by her family.[15]

Conclusion

The internal labor migration of single women in Jordan has affected their marriage prospects in different ways. While migration provides many new opportunities—to meet people, to earn a salary and potentially gain financial independence, and to gain broader and more diverse social experiences—it also creates new responsibilities, challenges, and concerns for the future. What is clear is that being single in Jordan is still a challenging position to be in—if not materially, socially. As Ibtisam reflected after she married, "People speak to you differently when you are married. They treat you differently." Ibtisam's experiences, however, went beyond being single and were colored by the significant class bias she faced as a woman from the south in the capital. Her family also regularly complained about her single status. Thus, her social status as a single woman cannot be divorced from issues of class and geography and specific family dynamics. Nevertheless, Ibtisam was determined to pursue postgraduate education and seek new professional opportunities. She was also resolute in her conviction to marry someone who respected her accomplishments, as she did nearly ten years after leaving home.

Each of these women faced their own complications and navigated them toward a particular view of singlehood—some seemingly able to overcome the stigma and embrace a life on their own. Salam, who had initially lamented her single status, reflected on this last we met:

> Marriage is no longer a central thing for me. It is secondary. If I get married, I get married. If I don't, I don't. I have many accomplishments in my life. If marriage comes on its own, okay. I am not looking for it. I am working on my masters, my career, etc. It is not something that preoccupies me.

These comments may reflect the acceptance of a reality that is unlikely to change—being single. But Salam has also made a nice life for herself and seems increasingly at peace with it. Her successful career and supportive family of course help in shaping her views on being single.

Noor, a 27-year-old engineer, shares a similar perspective:

> Marriage is destiny (*nasib*). Whether I am here [in Amman] or on the moon or at my parents' home, if it is my destiny it will happen. But I am not going to marry just to marry, [only] if the right person comes along . . . Finding someone in Jordan will be difficult if not impossible, but I believe God will help me.

For each of these women, coming to terms with being single is a function of many factors, as they forge paths through this web.

Given that the overwhelming majority of young women eventually marry, one can hardly characterize the situation as a crisis of "singlehood." However, women (and men) are staying single longer, and single university women are the most economically active. As such, their experiences and views demand greater attention as they illuminate how young adults navigate socioeconomic shifts—not merely awaiting, but forging lives they deem valuable.

Acknowledgements

This research would not have been possible without my fabulous research assistant and collaborator Afaf Al Khoshman. Her life and career are a testament to the tenacity of the Jordanian women whom I have had the privilege to meet and befriend throughout my career. Afaf, you inspire me! Thank you to Marcia Inhorn and Nancy Smith-Hefner for their feedback and for bringing a diverse set of scholars together to think about ways of and reasons for waiting. This research was also made possible by a Senior Faculty Research Fellowship generously awarded by the Office of the Provost at Georgetown University.

Fida Adely is Associate Professor and the Clovis and Hala Salaam Maksoud Chair in Arab Studies at the Center for Contemporary Arab Studies in the School of Foreign Service at Georgetown University. An anthropologist, Adely explores education, labor, development, and gender in the Arab world. She is the author of *Gendered Paradoxes: Educating Jordanian Women in Nation, Faith, and Progress* (University of Chicago Press, 2012), in addition to numerous book chapters and journal articles. Adely received her PhD in comparative education and anthropology from Teacher's College, Columbia University.

Notes

1. All names have been changed to maintain the privacy of my interlocutors. In addition, given the personal nature of information shared, some details have been altered or withheld to maintain the privacy of individuals.
2. It is difficult to know how many women in Amman have migrated for work in specific or relative terms. I suspect that if they are counted in surveys, they are enumerated as members of their family's household.
3. Since as early as the 1980s, some female teachers migrated to the Arab Gulf countries, often through programs sponsored by the Ministry of Education (Shami and Taminian 1990). In addition, as a result of my

own research in Jordan since 2002, I know that there is a history of urban women migrating to rural or semi-rural areas as teachers.

4. As I discuss elsewhere (Adely 2012), the educational tracking system in Jordan is such that it encourages the strongest students to pursue a scientific track in high school. As a result, the number of women studying in STEM fields is relatively high (compared to that of the United States, for example).

5. In 2015, a female-run news media site called Hono al-Zarqa' or "Here is Zarqa'" (the name of a city in Jordan) (http://honazarqa.com/) ran a feature about fathers or guardians preventing their daughters from marrying for a variety of reasons, including wanting a daughter's salary. In the article, the author consults with a religious scholar about this phenomenon, who labels this practice *a'adil*, a pre-Islamic practice of preventing one's daughter from marrying.

6. Men also tend to live with their families until they marry unless they migrate for work. Were these women to be working in their hometowns, they would be living with their parents, as would their male peers.

7. The crude divorce rate for Jordan in 2003 was 1.7 (per thousand people) and 2.9 in 2013 (Jordan Department of Statistics 2013). Divorce as a percent of marriages in 2013 was 4.6 percent. In 2009 it was 4.5 percent. One important qualification to these statistics is that there are several different types of divorce, and in 2013 almost 75 percent of divorces happened after the signing of the marriage contract but before the consummation of the marriage (Jordan Supreme Justice Department 2013).

8. Another interesting point in the data is that rural women have higher rates of being single, and some of the provinces from which our respondents hail have a higher percentage of single women (Jordan Department of Statistics n.d.; Salem 2014).

9. Writing about shifts in marriage practices across generations in Saudi Arabia, Siham Alsuwaigh (1989) describes three types of marriage: pre-arranged, semi-arranged, and unarranged, which are helpful in thinking through the range of practices encompassed under the umbrella of arranged.

10. Muna went to university later in life, earning her Bachelor of Science when she was thirty-three years old.

11. In this context, calling someone a Bedouin is derogatory, implying backwardness and conservatism.

12. Between the years 2008 and 2015, the average age at first marriage has been around twenty-six for women and thirty for men (Jordan Department of Statistics n.d.).

13. Despite the concern expressed by those women older than thirty that they would never marry, several women did marry in their thirties.

14. Maysoon had gone through a broken engagement that was quite contentious. Her family had been supportive through it all; however, her

fiancé's family was furious and made her and her family's life difficult in the course of the breakup.

15. Just as I was submitting revisions for this chapter, I learned that Jihan had recently gotten engaged.

References

Abutayeh, Hala. 2013. "Coveting Their Salaries: Guardians Deprive their Daughters of their Right to Marriage." *Ainnews*, 28 February. Retrieved 10 April from http://ainnews.net/?p=229751#.W562QUxFw2x.

Adely, Fida. 2012. *Gendered Paradoxes: Educating Jordanian Women in Nation, Faith and Progress*. Chicago: University of Chicago Press.

———. 2016. "A Different Kind of Love: Compatibility (*Insijam*) and Marriage in Jordan." *Arab Studies Journal* 24(2): 102–27.

Alsuwaigh, Siham A. 1989. "Women in Transition: The Case of Saudi Arabia." *Journal of Comparative Family Studies* 20(1): 67–78.

Assaad, Ragui, Rana Hendy, and Chaimaa Yassine. 2014. "Gender and the Jordanian Labor Market." In *The Jordanian Labour Market in the New Millennium*, ed. Ragui Assaad, 105–43. Oxford: Oxford University Press.

Gebel, Michael, and Stefanie Heyne. 2016. "Delayed Transitions in Times of Increasing Uncertainty: School-to-work Transition and the Delay of First Marriage in Jordan." *Research in Social Stratification and Mobility* 46(A): 61–72.

Halabi, Hanan. 2007. "Profile of Single Women in Palestine." *Review of Women's Studies* 4: 27–46.

Hasso, Frances. 2010. *Consuming Desires: Family Crisis and the State in the Middle East*. Stanford: Stanford University Press.

Hughes, Geoffrey F. 2017. "The Chastity Society: Disciplining Muslim Men." *Journal of the Royal Anthropological Institute* 23(2): 267–84.

Jordan Department of Statistics. n.d. "Woman Statistics" Data Bank. Retrieved 5 August 2020 from http://dosweb.dos.gov.jo/population/woman-statistics/.

———. 2013. "Jordan Statistical Yearbook 2013." [In Arabic.] Retrieved 27 April 2019 from http://www.dos.gov.jo/dos_home_a/main/yearbook_2013.pdf.

Jordan Supreme Justice Department. 2013. "Annual Statistics Report." [In Arabic.] Retrieved 28 April 2019 from http://www.sjd.gov.jo/EchoBusV3.0/SystemAssets/PDFs/AR/Studies/2013.pdf.

Kawar, Mary. 2000. "Transitions and Boundaries: Research into the Impact of Paid Work on Young Women's Lives in Jordan." *Gender & Development* 8(2): 56–65.

Kaya, Laura. 2009. "Dating in a Sexually Segregated Society: Embodied Practices of Online Romance in Irbid, Jordan." *Anthropological Quarterly* 82(1): 251–78.

Nahhas, Roufan. 2018. "Jordan Introduces Free Pre-marriage Counselling to Lower Divorce Rates." *Arab Weekly*, 15 April. Retrieved 28 April 2019 from https://thearabweekly.com/jordan-introduces-free-pre-marr iage-counselling-lower-divorce-rates.

Rashad, Hoda. 2015. "The Tempo and Intensity of Marriage in the Arab Region: Key Challenges and their Implications." *DIFI Family Research and Proceedings* 25(1): 2.

Salem, Rania. 2014. "Trends and Differentials in Jordanian Marriage Behavior: Marriage Timing, Spousal Characteristics, Household Structure and Matrimonial Expenditures." In *The Jordanian Labor Market in the New Millennium*, ed. Ragui Assaad, 189–217. Oxford: Oxford University Press.

Shami, Seteney, and Lucine Taminian. 1990. "Women's Participation in the Jordanian Labour Force: A Comparison of Urban and Rural Patterns." In *Women in Arab Society: Work Patterns and Gender Relations in Egypt, Jordan and Sudan*, ed. Seteney Shami, Lucine Taminian, Soheir Morsy, Zainab El-Bakri, and E. M. Kameir, 132–55. Oxford: Berg Publishers Limited.

Singerman, Diane. 2007. "The Economic Imperatives of Marriage: Emerging Practices and Identities Among Youth in the Middle East." *Middle East Youth Initiative*, Working Paper No. 6, September, The Brookings Institution, Wolfensohn Center for Development, Washington, DC.

Chapter 12

NEVER-MARRIED WOMEN IN INDIA
GENDERED LIFE COURSES, DESIRES, AND IDENTITIES IN FLUX

Sarah Lamb

Introduction

India has witnessed significant changes in gendered norms over the past several decades, including increased opportunities for women to pursue education and work, and a growing sense that parents should not arrange their daughters' marriages before the ages of approximately eighteen to twenty-five (Fernandes 2006: 162–68; Radhakrishnan 2011; Sengupta 2007; Waldrop 2012). At the same time, the Indian news media has featured stories on singlehood as a trait of a fast-changing society—discussing rising divorce rates, increasing opportunities for unmarried professional women to work and live singly, and portraits of the new single women as "happy with their status and not wanting the burden of marriage on them" (Kuriakose 2014). "Brave New Woman," the 21 October 2019 cover story of *India Today*, explores the emergent reality of "the rise of the unattached, independent woman, who has rejected the socially sanctioned default setting of a married life" (Sinha 2019). She is "single by choice"— "answerable to no one but herself . . . armed with an education and a career and the empowering financial independence it brings" (Sinha 2019). "Why You Should Try Staying Single" underscores being "accountable to only one person—yourself," "discovering yourself," "building a career," and "taking decisions solely based on what *you* want from life" (Lawrence 2014, emphasis in original).

Such news stories tend to be strikingly upbeat, and perhaps they themselves contribute to the changing social norms they attempt to describe, by expressing viewpoints that lessen the social pressure to marry. However, readers get little sense of the complex social-cultural and political-economic contexts behind women's lives and decisions; neither does a celebratory notion of autonomous individuals making free choices to live singly capture the sense of ambivalence and constraint that single women highlight in their own narratives. One also gets little sense that single women are not limited to the new breed of younger cosmopolitan professionals. Such upbeat news stories in turn elide the extent to which marriage remains a powerful compulsory norm in India, particularly for women.

This chapter explores the stories of never-married single women across a range of social classes, living both in the urban metropolis of Kolkata and in smaller towns and villages of West Bengal, India, as a means to illuminate emerging possibilities and constraints of gender and the life course for women in contemporary India. I take off from the concept of "waithood," which scholars of the Middle East and Africa have developed to refer to a "prolonged and uncertain stage between childhood and adulthood" (Honwana 2012: 19)—experienced by youth who delay marriage as they engage in a protracted and uncertain quest for education and employment, pushing back their entry into normal social adulthood until well into their thirties or beyond (Dhillon and Yousef 2011; Dungey and Meinert 2017; Finn and Oldfield 2015; Gertel 2017; Hashemi 2015; Honwana 2012; McEvoy-Levy 2014; Singerman 2007, 2011). Diane Singerman (2007, 2011), first coining the waithood concept, gives primary attention to the experiences of young men in the Arab world, highlighting the role of governments and political economies in failing to provide sufficient employment and educational opportunities for their male youth, who find themselves unable to enter the labor market.

In India, too, waithood is a compelling and apt concept to describe the conditions especially of many young men. Male youth face an enormous lack of adequate employment opportunities, as they sit around idly and anxiously, seeking jobs in vain. Social expectations compel men to secure at least some financial security before marrying, even though sons often remain in their parents' multigenerational households, following virilocal residence patterns after marriage, unless jobs or desires take them farther away. To even hope to get one of the scarce government jobs that would come with a decent salary, employment stability, and old-age pension, my interlocutors tell me, one needs to offer up a bribe of around 100,000 to 500,000 INR, a formidable and even insurmountable expense for ordinary working-class and rural families.[1] So, parents worry and male youth wait.

Men in India do not age out of marriageability as quickly as women do, however, at least not until they are considerably older,[2] and unmarried men do not face as much precarity in their daily lives as single women do. Even when unmarried, adult Indian men, unlike women, retain a secure place in their natal home and community. Also, unlike women, unmarried men living singly apart from kin do not face overt discrimination when seeking housing. Single men are also not regarded as sexually dangerous and vulnerable in the way single women are.

For these reasons, I find the experiences of single women to be especially compelling. I explore what happens to women's gendered and sexual identities when they enter the labor market, giving work and/or education a higher priority than marriage, and eventually— due to deliberate choice, becoming "excessively" accomplished for their gender, and/or aging out—no longer finding marriage an option. In some ways, such delayed marriage trends for women in India are comparable to trends in China, where media attention has focused on the plight of highly educated, urban professional women who remain single into their late twenties or older. Called "leftover women" (*shengnü*), these women are characterized by state media campaigns and in public discourse as increasingly unmarriageable due to their advancing age, starting from their mid-twenties, and perceived unfeminine natures, as too educated, career-minded, selfish, and picky (Fincher 2014; Howlett, Chapter 7, this volume; Ji 2015; To 2013). To date, however, scholarship on "leftover women" has focused on younger women still expecting to marry, and statistical data reveal that few women in China are rejecting marriage altogether (Fincher 2014: 188).

I focus this chapter instead on single women above the age of thirty-five, generally the age beyond which women are regarded as unmarriable in India, and so on women who are no longer "waiting" to marry but who have decided, or have come to realize, that they will never marry. I shift the focus, then, from waithood to what might be termed *never-marriedness*. I have come to find that the condition of never having married puts never-married single women into a unique and anomalous social category, different from separated, divorced, and widowed women, as if the act of having once achieved marriage transfers one into (a comparatively) normal adult personhood, even without the man's current presence. I argue that, positioned outside the norm, never-married single women are able to see features of their society not easily recognized by others—systems of gender and sexuality, kinship and marriage, and social class—which they must both work within and strive to redefine as they endeavor to achieve forms of everyday well-being and belonging without being married.

As single women in India seek to actualize new ethical imaginaries of valued personhood beyond marriage, their narratives also challenge cosmopolitan, Western-centered liberal assumptions about the normalcy and value of the individual, independent subject. Even as they strive to craft meaningful lives outside of marriage, very few of the women I have come to know articulate their aspirations in terms of a drive for individual independence. As such, singlehood in India contrasts with the thrust of the US "epoch of single women" and "invention of independent female adulthood" that Rebecca Traister (2016: 7) depicts in *All the Single Ladies: Unmarried Women and the Rise of an Independent Nation*. What those crafting a single female life in India desire more than independence, I suggest, is belonging—to be someone who counts, is worthy of recognition, and is intimately connected with others as part of the social body. Tine Gammeltoft (2014: 231) highlights in her own work on selective reproduction in Vietnam a central aim of her book: "to point to the existential importance that communal belonging holds for people," calling on anthropologists "to pay closer attention to quests for human belonging" (9). Gammeltoft (2014: 13–14) critiques widespread liberal assumptions that posit ideals of autonomy and freedom as universal desires "outweighing other human needs such as the quest for companionship or the urge to belong and be taken care of" (cf. Kowalski 2016; Mahmood 2005).

Taking up insights from such scholarship, I explore single women's stories to help rethink the category of single—arguing that its conventional connotations of separateness, independence, autonomy, and living alone are conditions few unmarried Bengali women I have met actually live, and even fewer wish to live. The stories shared here beckon us to consider diverse ways of conceptualizing what it is to live well, as single women do the hard work of striving to redefine what is good and normal, aspiring to forge forms of recognition and belonging within the social body in ways not tied to marriage.

Methodology

In 2014, I began to focus my fieldwork in West Bengal, India, on the lives of never-married single women, to date making seven two-to-four-week fieldwork trips to Kolkata and nearby towns and villages for the project. I also draw on the narratives of single women gathered over years of ethnographic fieldwork conducted in the region since 1989. I combine formal, open-ended interviews with ethnographic research involving "hanging out" with women in daily-life contexts, in their homes and while going marketing, gathering with friends, talking over tea, dining out, seeing movies, attending single women's support group meetings, taking weekend getaways, and with some of the more English-speaking elite, engaging in dialogue over email, Facebook Messenger, and WhatsApp. I have often been accompanied by one of three research assistants during interviews and participant-observation research, choosing other Bengali women as assistants who are either single themselves or, in one case, living quite independently from her husband. The presence of other women researchers helps facilitate lively and intimate conversations and ensures that I do not miss the nuances of Bengali discussions. Most conversations took place in Bengali (except those with Indrani, who tends to use English with her friends and peers), although peppered with English terms as is common. I use single quotes to indicate English terms inserted into an otherwise Bengali conversation. Most single women I have encountered have been very interested in the project, as they feel under-represented and misunderstood in their wider societies and are eager to share their stories as part of their endeavors to "find a way to count in the social body" (Dickey 2013: 219). As of this writing, I have explored the stories of fifty-five women ranging in age from thirty-five to ninety-two.

On Single Women

Regarding terminology, "single" has been emerging as an emic, local category in India to refer to adult women and men who are not (yet) married, or who are divorced, separated, or widowed (e.g., Kundu 2018; Patel 2006). Naisargi Dave (2012: 107) examines Indian feminist and lesbian activists who, beginning around the 1990s, chose "single women" as a category both to informally organize around lesbianism, as well as to "address the widespread discrimination that all unmarried women face at the hands of family, society, and the state." A social movement called Ekal Nari Shakti Sangathan (ENSS), or "The Association of Strong Women Alone," has organized low-income "solo" (*ekal*) women in northwest India in a collective struggle for access to land, property, dignity, and "freedom from atrocities," including among widows, separated and abandoned women, and women over the age of thirty-five who have never married.[3]

Among my interlocutors in West Bengal, people use "single" in English, as well as "unmarried" in English,[4] and Bengali phrases such as *abibahita* (unmarried), and those who "did not marry" (*biye kore ni*) and whose marriage "had not happened" (*biye hae ni*), to refer to persons, men or women, who had not married.[5] Some Bengalis I would speak with about my project would query, "*Are* there unmarried women here [in West Bengal]?" or respond dismissively, as if there's nothing more to study, then: "If a woman remains unmarried, it is just that her parents failed to arrange her marriage." Others, however, helped me find single, never-married women, and soon I began to understand never-married women as a significant group illuminating important broader social trends.

The women I encountered during my fieldwork encompass a range of life experiences and perspectives, and no one is "typical." Some were highly educated urban professionals, while others were from rural villages, small towns, and the working classes. Some would be happy to find a male marriage partner if various insurmountable obstacles were not in the way; others had no interest in marriage and all its trappings of domesticity, although without defining themselves as non-heterosexual or queer; while others had taken on a lesbian identity—an identity that had become more available to women in India, although still hushed in most contexts, ever since the public discourse emerging around the film *Fire*. Deepa Mehta's (1996) film was released within India to much public controversy, the first mainstream Indian film to explicitly explore homosexual love, featuring two sisters-in-law who become lovers within a joint-family household. Dave (2011) discusses how the public dialogue surrounding the film led many women to embrace an "Indian and lesbian" identity; and each of the four self-identified lesbian women in my study also spoke of how *Fire* figured significantly in their realization of their lesbian identities (e.g., Lamb 2018: 56–58).

The never-married women in my study navigate a range of living situations: in private homes, with natal kin, with friends (though this option is rare for Bengalis of all social classes), in working women's hostels, and in old-age homes. A few had given birth to or adopted children and were raising their children as unwed mothers, which in India is generally a highly socially and often economically precarious situation. Many spoke at length of the hassles, dangers, and slander they face due to being regarded as sexually available and dangerous, as women unattached to husbands and to other protective male kin. Older single women tell of how women in their fifties and sixties are regarded as especially sexually voracious and bold at that mature age, so that surveillance, gossip, and sexual harassment do not subside until an unmarried woman reaches her seventies and beyond. Mindful of prevailing stereotypes and societal judgments, many single women foreground tales of carefully maintaining sexual propriety throughout life. The most elite women, travelling in global cosmopolitan circles at home and abroad, face fewer restrictions and stigmas in their own lives—while realizing their situations are unique in India. Some of these elite women even characterize it as "trendy" to be single in India today and tell of how they are enjoying their freedoms, possibilities for lovers, independence, and fulfilling work. Many narratives across social class also emphasize fulfillment and pride in one's strength, education, and/or career. Many women underscore critiques of society: "We have changed, but society has not caught up with us"; "Society has changed a lot, but not regarding marriage"; or "Ultimately, the final goal in our patriarchal society is that a woman will get married and have children; if she does not, she has no value—she is worthless."

Stories and Lives

All four of the following stories illuminate diverse experiences of never-marriedness in India. Each in some ways fits the profile of waithood, as the women initially delay marriage in pursuit of education or work. All four move beyond waiting, however, to craft lives as single women no longer expecting to marry. The first three featured are well-educated urban dwellers, but the fourth, a laborer from the countryside, demonstrates that never-married singlehood is not limited to the urban or middle classes.

Medha

Medha[6] is a professor of Bengali in a small city, exactly my age in her mid-fifties, living alone, and never married. When we met by chance in an outdoor Kolkata market purchasing tie-dyed housecoats, she eagerly volunteered, "You should study me!" Medha was born into a poor family of the mid-ranking Mahishya caste of farmers and raised in a remote village, eight kilometers from the nearest paved road. Her family often went hungry. Her mother sold vegetables on the foot path. Because of their lower-class status, they were forbidden to wear shoes when venturing near the local zamindar or landlord's home, lest this demonstrate her family's insubordination.[7] Yet Medha was the first girl in the village ever to complete secondary school. Her family did not have money for books, so from a young age Medha would read the shopping bags made from old newspapers, and would walk after school to a village library four or five kilometers away, returning in the evening carrying books through open fields as the sun set and her mother worried. After higher secondary school, Medha would trudge eight kilometers through knee-deep mud during the rainy season to get to the paved road where she could catch a bus to a provincial college, all the while struggling to pay the school fees and often going hungry. Medha is now a tenured college professor.

Originally, I assumed Medha had chosen to remain unmarried, but this interpretation is inaccurate. Medha emailed me the summer after we first met:

> Do you mind if I share some personal matters with you? In Bishnupur, as a small town of West Bengal, I've no opportunity to mix up with people from the same sphere of life. On the other side, the educated people of Kolkata are very snobbish about the small-town people . . . Again as an unmarried woman I have to obey some rules of the Indian morality. The result is very depressing. I am cornered, cornered seriously. It affects my life as well as my career.

One thought I had upon reading this email was that Medha might be alluding to being a lesbian (in her comment, "I have no opportunity to mix up with people from the same sphere of life"), but when I got the courage to ask her over email, while suggesting a lesbian support group I knew of in Kolkata, she replied, "I am not lesbian, I am a woman," and later confessed to how attracted she is to men, and how she would love to have a (male) lover, if not a husband.

Medha offers several reasons for why she is not married, one being that she had become too well-educated. She proclaims: "In Indian society, the groom must be superior to the bride in all ways, in *all* ways—except for looks!" In terms of looks, Medha describes herself as too "black" (*kalo*), short, and "ugly—with unusually high cheek bones and big teeth" to be a sought-after pick on the marriage market. When she was young, in addition, Medha did resist marriage. At one point after she had passed her tenth-grade exams, her

family arranged a marriage match for her, but she protested, saying,
"I will not marry—I will work." Medha continued:

> Other girls wanted to get married, dreamed of having husbands, hav-
> ing guests over, wearing jewelry. I never thought this way . . . Other
> people in the village would say to my older brother in front of me,
> "Why are you letting her study? What will she become? Why aren't
> you getting her married? What is she going to do—get a job?" After
> hearing all this, I would think, "Yes, I *will* get a job."

Later, when Medha finished her PhD and finally got work as a professor, she relates:

> I was thirty-plus. I could have easily gotten married. In Indian so-
> ciety, professors are valued . . . My brother would go around telling
> everyone, "My sister is a professor." . . . If there's a professor in the
> family, they have more family status. But when people spoke to him
> of eligible men, my brother would be quiet and not say anything . . .
> [My brother and his wife] didn't want me to get married because then
> they wouldn't have a way of getting money.

Benefitting from her generous professor's salary, Medha's natal family has now replaced their crumbling mud hut with a two-story brick
home with running water and electricity. Medha's brother's sons all
became well-educated and now have their own good jobs in the
city—"Due to me! Due to me!" Medha asserts. "Now my family has
money, education, status, jobs—because of me." Medha narrates:

> I finally advertised for my own marriage in the newspaper to see if
> I could get someone good, but I . . . just got a lot of weird and bad
> men . . . They all came because of my job—that I would work and
> bring them money. My brother, sister-in-law, and these men all
> wanted me for the job. They all wanted my money. I am not valued
> as a person—only my money is valued.

Now living alone, Medha finds the condition highly unfamiliar,
even unnerving. The most salient theme in Medha's life narrative is
that of not receiving love and companionship from natal kin, community, neighbors, and society. Medha reflects: "I have to fight with
hostility in every step in my life due to my not being [regarded as]
an ordinary person."

Indrani

Indrani returned to India to build an apartment and live above her
parents, after receiving a PhD in electrical engineering in the United

States and holding for several years a high-salaried job in New York City. She returned to Kolkata when her grandmother became ill, having had enough of US corporate life and wishing to be with her grandmother during her dying days. With a shipload of furnishings from the United States, Indrani created a lovely apartment with a roof garden above her parents, while securing another good job in Kolkata. She never gave too much thought to marriage while pursuing her education and career. But as she approached her forties, she began to long for a child.

Having trouble falling asleep one evening while in Kolkata, I rose from bed to check my email and came across this remarkable message:

> Just writing very quickly to say hello and that I am very much looking forward to seeing you again! I got your brief note from Kolkata [last year] just before you returned to the States, and there was a lot going on in my life at that time, and there was no short way of describing it to you. I had actually been in the queue for adoption for over three years and it was going nowhere. Although it is legal for single women to adopt in India (and has been so for at least a generation), there are a lot of biases, as I found out. Every step of the way I had to explain why I was not married, and I could not give any answer that was acceptable to them ... It all ended happily, eventually, and that allows me to look back and think of the horrendous experience as some kind of test I needed to pass. I can tell you more when we meet. But mainly I didn't/couldn't write back because there was so much uncertainty about the outcome, it was a bit like holding my breath for something and not being able to do or think of anything else. In the end [the adoption] happened just one day before I would have been legally outside the [45-year] age limit for this application!

When she and I met up, Indrani told me more: "My mother used to say that love can happen even at ninety-seven, but there is a time for having a child. I also very much longed for a child." Indrani and her parents passed through many adoption agencies over the three-year period. "Why aren't you married? Why didn't you get married?" the adoption agencies always asked. "'I was just studying all the time,'" Indrani reported replying. "You know, presenting myself as a real nerd. 'I was just studying all the time, and I didn't think of it, and then time passed.'" "'Well,' now glaring at my mother, 'a daughter may be able to forget such things as marriage, but a mother never should!'" Indrani said she would motion to her mother to not say anything, but just to sit there looking guilty.

In fact, Indrani's parents had tried for a short while to arrange her marriage when she was living in the United States. But Indrani describes contradictions in elite families like hers in the way girls are raised: On the one hand, daughters are taught to uphold Indian gendered conventions as "good girls," by not dating or having boyfriends. On the other hand, those in well-educated elite circles are beginning to find arranged marriages unfashionable. Indrani recalled:

> When Ma came to visit me in the United States, she asked, "Where's your boyfriend? Where are you hiding him?" "If I had a boyfriend," I said, "you would see him! I'm not hiding anything. And you *told* me not to get one!" "Yes, that is true," Ma said, "but I did not expect you to listen to me."

Her parents arranged a few meetings with potential grooms. Indrani tells of a few very awkward encounters:

> I had no way of evaluating them, whether they were good or not, a good match for me or not, never having really mixed much with men, never having dated, and having gone [when young] to an all-girls school. It was very awkward. I could not choose any of them for marriage. And that was that.

Some of the adoption-agency women interviewing Indrani over the years found her too pushy, not demure enough, or needing counseling. So Indrani went with her parents to several counseling sessions and returned to report that they had completed the counseling. Finally, Indrani with her parents was approved to adopt, with an agency in the neighboring state of Bihar—due to Indrani's good professional position and the fact that she lives with her parents. So, she is not really entirely "single"—singlehood makes it virtually impossible to be approved, as there is a strong sense that no one can raise a child alone, and that a child needs a family. But would there be an infant available before Indrani aged out? The last weeks were very stressful. Finally, just a day before her forty-fifth birthday, Indrani was given a six-week-old girl. They named her Nandini, "daughter who brings joy." Nandini has emerged into a beautiful, healthy, loving, and energetic little girl, beloved to both mother and grandparents. A photo album displays many happy, beaming photos of growing Nandini with her grandparents and with her mother, Indrani.

Indrani wonders how and what she will tell her daughter about her background. People ask continually, "Are you married?" "No," Indrani replies simply. Then they wait for an explanation. Indrani says little and just leaves them guessing. But she worries about when Nandini can understand more. Another problem is that Indian identification systems—for school identifications, high school exams, driver's licenses, passports—all require providing a father's name, in this patriarchal setting.

Indrani hints that she might still like to marry, if possible. She commented: "In the United States, nobody would think that a woman older than thirty-five would be unmarried forever. But here the pressure to marry stops after that age because people think you are old."

Sukhi-di

Sukhi-di,[8] now seventy-six, was born in a town on the outskirts of Kolkata to a family of modest means as the third-oldest sibling of twelve. She was a bright and industrious young woman, pursued a bachelor's degree, and quickly found ways to earn money to help support her natal household and contribute to the marriage dowries of the family's many other daughters. Her father, a film director, died when her youngest sister was just a baby. Sukhi-di proudly recollects how she graduated first out of two hundred in a telephone operator class, and later moved on to work for UNICEF and the Asiatic Society. Sukhi-di would travel around rural Bengal as the only woman with a team of researchers. Some of her male colleagues were shy about dressing and sleeping together in the same barracks, but Sukhi would matter-of-factly stretch a sari across the room as a barrier and was able to manage herself just fine. To one male co-worker she declared, "You are just like my little brother—and such a big bed, what will happen?" "I got into bed and slept just fine!" Sukhi recalled, laughing. "But he stayed in a chair all night long."

Sukhi-di loved her work and independence. "I lived in places all by myself," she recalled. "I was really brave and never scared! You constantly need to take precautions. When I lived alone, I always kept a knife under my pillow!" she laughed.

Thirty-five years ago when her jobs eventually brought her to Kolkata, Sukhi moved into the four-story Government of West Bengal Working Girls' Hostel, where working-class women, generally in their early twenties through their sixties, live two or three to a room paying just 150 INR (or a little over US $2) per month. In establishing the hostel, the state has assumed the role of paternalistic guardian of its city's unmarried working "girls" (as if being unmarried, the residents have not matured into adult womanhood), maintaining strict rules: a 9:00 pm curfew; no men, not even kin, allowed inside; and restricted visiting hours from 7:00–9:00 am and 6:00–7:00 pm.

When she was young, Sukhi-di never gave much thought to how she would care for herself in old age, but her situation is now precarious. She receives no pension after retiring several years back, and she depleted her savings on knee-replacement surgery when she was seventy-two. Her eight surviving siblings occasionally drop off a bit of money or a new sari.

My research assistant Anindita and I asked one evening during visiting hours, "When your brothers and sisters got married, and you made all the arrangements for their marriages, did you not ever think about your own marriage?" Sukhi-di replied vigorously, "That a female person would not think about marriage? That would never happen! She will *definitely* think about it!" Sukhi-di went on passionately, this conversation taking place after I had already known her quite well over five years, "That I wouldn't be aroused by 'sex'?" She used the English term. "'Sex' will of course be aroused!"

"Look," Sukhi-di continued:

> Within every person's life, whether beautiful or not, that person faces a moment when she stands in front of the mirror and says, "Well, today I am looking quite attractive!" This is a *rule* . . . Therefore, that my own 'sex' [sense of sexual desire] was not aroused, that is not the case! That no sexual arousal took place, and that I did not love anyone—I can't say that. *I* also fell in love! But, I did not bind him to me.

"Hmm, you had other attachments," I said softly, thinking of the deep responsibility she felt for all her siblings.

"Yes, I had other bindings," Sukhi-di agreed.

> I told him, that if you want to marry me, then you will have to wait for another ten to fifteen years. By then we will be an old man and old woman! What will be the use [she implies, of having sex] then? But at that time, it was *his* ripe age to get married! But he was saying, "No, I will not marry if not to you!" Finally, with coercion, he ran away from Kolkata, taking a job and moving to another place. Then later, he married. Why wouldn't he? All people should get married! I personally think so. Then why would have God created us that way, with different reproductive systems? Creation and recreation will not happen if no marriage.

Anindita asked, "Do you ever feel—?"

"Loneliness?" Sukhi-di interrupted:

> Yes! I feel lonely *very* often! This is the reason I say to everyone now that everyone needs one person. If you do not have a person beside you, it does not work. It is for that reason that marriage is necessary.

You would be living with each other! Not that it always happens well, but at times it does happen that you really like a person, isn't that so? Then even if he would have died after forty years of marriage, some memories would be there that one could live with. And his children would be there, and then the grandchildren. I could live with them all, and my days would pass nicely. But now, I am completely alone. If I look all around, it's like a desert. I am *completely* alone. No one at all.

"These kinds of hopes and memories," Sukhi-di reflected, "these days they come to me a little more often, now because I am old."

Subhagi

Subhagi, in her mid-fifties, works as a day laborer and feels fortunate to have lived her whole life in her natal village with her natal kin. Her exuberant glow makes it hard not to feel convinced that she is telling the truth that she chose not to marry, and in fact implored men not to take her in marriage, so that she could instead remain living with her own family to help care for them through her labor and love. "*This* is my fulfillment—that we are all together and having enough to eat," Subhagi declared.

Subhagi was born into a very poor family, members of the Lohar caste, one of West Bengal's officially designated "Scheduled Caste" groups of historically disadvantaged people. She was born in the middle of four sisters and one younger brother, and while the children were all still very young, both parents began to ail, her father with one hand paralyzed and her mother with cancer. They struggled for enough to eat. Subhagi worked hard to support the family— through caring for the village schoolmaster's young children, washing dishes and clothes in other people's homes, catching and selling fish, and working as a day laborer planting and cutting rice in the fields. "I was the one who worked so that they could eat," Subhagi recalled with pride. Subhagi also arranged her sisters' marriages, with her uncle's help, having horoscopes made for each of them and for herself, too. "Everyone came to look!" she recalled. "And my sisters were very attractive and fair-looking (*pariskar dekhte*). I would say, 'Whoever you like, you can choose and take away.'"

When asked if any suitors expressed interest in Subhagi, she exclaimed, "Yes! They did! But if I were to go, then my sisters and brother would have to go from house to house begging. *I* was the one feeding them by working! If I were to go away, what would people say?" Subhagi recalled, "I would tell [the men], 'Please forgive me, brother. Please forgive me,'" pressing her palms together in a prayer gesture. "'For these children, there is no one else to look after them.' I would say, 'Even if you take me without dowry, I will not go. I will not go.'" Subhagi affirmed, "So men did want to marry me, but if I went, who would look after my siblings and parents?" During the years while she was young and unmarried, Subhagi deliberately avoided appearing attractive to deter potential suitors. "Someone might have fallen for her!" women neighbors listening in exclaimed. "People might have looked at her, and something might have happened!"

Subhagi laughed with pride and said: "Still today, the entire village knows what I did for my siblings."

"With all this, I am happy, I am very happy. *This* is where I was born!" Subhagi exclaimed, experiencing a privilege usually reserved for men—to remain belonging to just one family and place. "Since I was young, we were all together here, so I am so attached to this place. I have never left this place since I was young—from here I have not gone *anywhere* else at all! And here there are grandchildren now," she said, hugging her brother's son's daughter to her chest as she spoke.

By now, Subhagi's parents have died and her sisters married off to other villages. She lives in her natal home with her brother and his family—his wife, son, son's wife, and grandchildren. Subhagi still works hard so they all can eat, describing serving her family as a moral-spiritual practice. She avowed, "Serving (*seva kora*) the people in this family, the happiness I receive is incomparable. Compared to serving a husband, and compared even to serving God, then serving one's family is the best!"

Opting Out of the Conventional Femininity of Marital Life

Key themes that emerge from these women's stories help explain the meanings of never-married singlehood, as well as illuminate broader operations of gender, sexuality, marriage, work, and social class in India today. Opting out of the conventional femininity of marital life as a choice is perhaps the most transparent theme in single women's narratives. Public media and discourse highlight this opting-out theme as well, crafting a vision of the new breed of modern, professional, independent-minded women with cosmopolitan aspirations and no need for marriage. At least in parts of their narratives, most of the single women with whom I have spoken express deliberately choosing not to marry—instead wishing to pursue educations and careers, to remain living with beloved natal kin as men are permitted to do, to pursue a treasured lesbian relationship (Lamb 2018: 56–58), or to shun the trappings of ordinary domesticity, particularly in its implications for women—where women are subservient to men and consumed by appearances, like wearing nice saris and jewelry, and by all the trivialities and bindings of family-domestic life.

Indrani, who had adopted her beautiful daughter the day before turning forty-five, sent this email:

> I hope you got home safely! It was lovely to hang out with you. I am sending you the quotation from the novel I mentioned to you: "I had chafed under the restraints and the ties which formed the common lot of women, and I longed for an opportunity to show that a woman is in no way inferior to a man. How hard it seemed to my mind that marriage should be the goal of woman's ambition, and that she should spend her days in the light trifles of a home life, live to dress, to look pretty, and never know the joy of independence and intellectual work!"[9]

A standard interpretive framework of choice and resistance to conventional femininity, however, does not capture the complexity of social forces women must negotiate, nor the precarity and social critique women face, as they strive to craft a life out of marriage. Pratima, a retired schoolteacher living wholly alone and feeling under the perpetual scrutiny of her watchful neighbors, reflected softly: "I would not advise my students now to be single—I tell them to think about it very carefully." When I told Indrani how 92-year-old Ena-di—who never on her own brought up the topic of marriage in a life narrative emphasizing education and work—had crinkled her nose dismissively when I asked if she had ever wished to marry or have children, Indrani reflected, "Well, she is likely telling you this because she does not want to evoke your pity. It is a story she now tells herself and others."

Ultimately, most of my interlocutors expressed ambivalence about their situation, whether as a central part of their narrative or as a subtle theme; few speak of being unmarried solely as a deliberate, simple choice. Especially for those who take roads less traveled, making a decision is not always straightforward, and often involves pain and loss. Tine Gammeltoft (2014: 15) writes of how "the concept of choice is, in many respects, empirically misleading; it tempts us to overemphasize people's freedom to shape their world as they want to." Choice, within constraints, is part of the story, for some an important part; but what else is shaping this phenomenon?

Work, Desires, Self, Kin

Increasing recognition of the value of educating women and acceptance of women's desires to work are two backbones of a silent revolution taking place around the world with regard to women and age
at marriage (e.g., Goldstein and Kenney 2001; Jones 2007; Mukhopadhyay, Chapnik, and Seymour 1994; Raymo and Iwasawa 2005;
Sabbah-Karkaby and Stier 2017). In particular, education (and for
Subhagi, work even without education) is strongly associated with
postponing and then foregoing marriage among the single Indian
women in my study.

There is ambivalence in wider society, however, as to how much
education and work are valuable for women. Many single women
tell of becoming too professionally high-powered for their female
gender, in society's eyes. Some education makes a woman more
valuable in the marriage market, but too much education and professional success lead to a dearth of eligible grooms. As Medha pronounced: "A man must be superior to his wife in all ways, in all
ways, except for looks." Author Bhaichand Patel (2006: xii) similarly articulates: "To put it crudely, men generally, and Indian men
especially, do not like to marry high achieving women. They become undesirable marriage partners." A joke in China pertaining to
"leftover women" resonates with perspectives in India: "There are
three genders in China: men, women, and women with Ph.D.'s"
(Fincher 2014: 43).

In a crowded ladies' compartment on a train heading into Kolkata, several of us got to talking about when our daughters might
marry and how much education they are pursuing. One woman's
daughters were still unmarried and studying, at ages twenty-two
and twenty-four. However, she reported that their (male) doctor
had recently cautioned that too much studying gives girls a hormonal imbalance. Girls and women are naturally soft and gentle
(*norom*), he had said, but too much education ruins that softness,
making marriage difficult. Medha described the history of women's
education in West Bengal: in the early twentieth century, those developing British-influenced middle-class *bhadrolok* ("gentleman")
lifestyles began to educate their women so they would make better wives and mothers for educated men and children. "And now
women have become *too* educated! That's it—nothing else!" and
laughed.

It is notable that Subhagi and Sukhi-di describe work even more
as a way to serve others in their families than as a means toward

individual self-cultivation. Both were proud of their work but narrate their central motivations as a way to serve (natal) kin. Women's passion for work represents for many, then, not only or primarily a profound shift in gender norms toward self-actualization and away from a primary focus on familial responsibility. Relatedly, many single working women express discomfort at the idea of spending their earnings on themselves and their own pleasures, pressed by their social communities to direct their income toward natal kin.

Middle-Class Aspirations and Gendered Mismatches of Class

Single women's narratives also illuminate how strongly class is tied to marriage and forms of belonging and how difficult it is to forge intimate social ties across class boundaries (Dickey 2016; Sayer 2005). In India's new economy, where educated women are finding increased opportunities for white-collar employment, employed married women can help propel aspiring marital families into the middle classes (Fernandes 2006; Radhakrishnan 2011; Vijayakumar 2013; Waldrop 2012: 603). Little scholarship has been conducted, however, on what happens to her marriage prospects if an unmarried woman—through education and/or employment—achieves an individual class status very different from that of her natal kin.

The class aspirations of their natal kin figure saliently in many single women's narratives. Medha describes how she and her natal kin, in less than one lifetime, transitioned from poor villagers with little to eat, wading through mud, to living in expensive homes, owning televisions and a car, and travelling abroad. Medha related:

> I am absolutely a farmer's daughter! A daughter of the earth! My mother sold vegetables from the field on the footpath. She was illiterate—'pure, pure illiterate'! . . . If they could see me now wearing pants,[10] they would go absolutely unconscious! . . . *Now* my family has money, education, status, jobs—because of *me*!

Sukhi-di, without bitterness, also acknowledged that her natal kin did not work to arrange her marriage because they needed her income: she was the brightest sibling and the first employed; her income supported the family and financed her younger sisters' weddings.

Single women's narratives also expose the problem of gendered mismatches of class. Marriage takes place not only between individuals but between families. If, through education and employment, a woman achieves a class status much higher than that of her family background, she becomes practically unmarriable. Medha explained, "I am a professor now with a good salary—but I do not belong to that kind of family that another professor could marry me . . . I also cannot marry a village boy from an uneducated family." Such instances of upward class mobility are less problematic for men: Since a man (and his family) is meant to be ranked higher than a bride (and her family), a man who has climbed social classes can offer a hypergamous marriage to a woman from his natal class, helping then to raise her status through marriage, while together producing higher-class children. Yet, a woman who rises in socioeconomic status both outside of marriage and outside of the natal family is inherently unable to marry. In an era of heightened middle-class aspirations, class change can seem achievable for a highly intelligent and industrious individual woman, but it can also make her marriage near impossible and steer her into a state of class and social limbo.

Conclusion

Medha, Indrani, Sukhi, Subhagi, and other never-married single women in India whose stories I have heard invite us to reflect on changing possibilities and identities for women in contemporary India. Positioned outside the norm, those who do not marry offer an insightful perspective on their society's values and institutions. Just as anthropologists argue that we can see the familiar more perceptively when we step outside to make it strange, those who depart from the conventional path of marriage in India are also situated outside of a familiar social identity, and from that position speak penetratingly about their society's social-cultural norms. Here, Lila Abu-Lughod's (1990) argument in "The Romance of Resistance" is useful to consider: examining resistance, such as to conventions of "normal" femininity and marriage, can illuminate or serve as a diagnostic of the hidden contours of power. Single women's stories help us recognize the workings of gender and sexuality, kinship and marriage, social class and personhood at the center of people's everyday lives—illuminating their tellers' intricate subjectivities as well as offering broader social-cultural critique.

New possibilities for education and work seem to be on many women's doorsteps. Indeed, each of the women featured here pursued work and/or education as a desired path toward both economic security and a prideful sense of self cultivation. Education and work give women opportunities to delay or forego marriage in a social setting that emphasizes the imperative to marry. At the same time, single Bengali women's stories complicate understandings of the autonomous individual at the heart of much public discourse on the rise of singlehood in modern societies (e.g., Klinenberg 2012; Traister 2016). The single women I have come to know in West Bengal seek not so much "the invention of independent female adulthood" (Traister 2016: 7) but rather new forms of recognition, belonging, and intimate sociality beyond the conventions of marriage. They do this through legitimizing the kinds of lifelong ties to natal kin their brothers have always enjoyed, finding ways to have children as unwed mothers, and cultivating social recognition and collegiality through meaningful work.

In these ways, never-married single women in India are striving to extend conventional expectations of what family, class, sexuality, and gendered personhood can entail, as they work to push beyond perceptions that the only way for a woman to count socially and to belong is through marriage. The stories shared here invite us to reflect on the ways people forge meaningful lives out of intersecting situations of possibility and constraint, as they also summon us to consider diverse ways of conceptualizing and working toward what it means to live well.

Acknowledgments

This chapter is adapted from my 2018 article, "Being Single in India: Gendered Identities, Class Mobilities, and Personhoods in Flux," published in *Ethos* 46(1): 49–69. I am indebted to the many single women in West Bengal who generously shared their stories, insight, and friendship with me over the years I have been pursuing this project. Research assistants Hena Basu, Anindita Chatterjee, and Madhabi Maity have also been enormously helpful and fun to work with. Research in India was supported by the Theodore and Jane Norman Fund for Faculty Research and a Provost Research Award at Brandeis University. The project has received approval from the Brandeis IRB (Protocol #15021, "Single Women in India"). Several colleagues and students, including Anindita Chatterjee, Elizabeth Ferry, Faris Khan, Clara Hwa Yeon Lee, Caitrin Lynch, Sasha Martin, and Diane Mines, offered extremely helpful suggestions on earlier drafts. I would also like to thank this volume's editors for their tremendously useful comments.

Sarah Lamb is Professor of Anthropology at Brandeis University. Her research explores aging, gender, families, and understandings of personhood in West Bengal, India, and the United States. Publications include *White Saris and Sweet Mangoes: Aging, Gender and Body in North India* (University of California Press, 2000); *Aging and the Indian Diaspora: Cosmopolitan Families in India and Abroad* (Indiana University Press, 2009); and *Successful Aging as a Contemporary Obsession* (Rutgers University Press, 2017). Her research has been recognized with major awards, including a 2019 Carnegie Fellowship. Lamb received a BA in religious studies from Brown University and a PhD in anthropology from the University of Chicago.

Notes

1. 100,000 INR (Indian Rupees) equals approximately US $1,400.
2. Expected age at marriage varies profoundly by social class and rural-urban contexts. In rural areas, parents tend to arrange their daughters' marriages between about the ages of fifteen and twenty-five, although India's Prohibition of Child Marriage Act, which not everyone follows, requires women to be at least eighteen years old and men twenty-one before marrying. Among more elite social classes and in urban contexts, young women pursuing educations or careers may marry between the ages of twenty-two and twenty-eight. Above the age of thirty, people begin to feel that the woman is getting too old for marriage, and it becomes highly unusual for a woman to marry after the age of thirty-five. In rural contexts, where the majority of Indians live, many start to worry about a girl if she is not married by the time she reaches eighteen or twenty. Grooms tend to be older than their wives by around two to twelve years, and many say that a man can marry at any age, although to marry at the age of thirty-five or forty is also getting old for a man, although this pressure is mitigated if he has a high-paying job. According to UNICEF, 47 percent of girls in India are married by eighteen years of age, and 18 percent are married by fifteen years of age (Times News Network 2018).
3. For more on The Association of Strong Women Alone, see Berry (2011) and http://www.strongwomenalone.org/, retrieved 25 February 2019.
4. The use of the English terms can signal the category's perceived foreignness and unfamiliarity, as well as (in some contexts) its relation to a cosmopolitan, global modernity. People also often feel more comfort-

able using English terms to discuss private or intimate matters regarding sexuality, as we see in Sukhi-di's story.
5. The passive "marriage has not happened to me" (*amar biye hae ni*) is used much more often to refer to women rather than men, but some of my women interlocutors assertively preferred the active *ami biye <u>kori</u> ni*, "I did not marry."
6. I use pseudonyms throughout and modify a few identifying details to protect anonymity. As Bengali names all have meanings, I select names that fit my sense of each person. Medha means "intellect" and is associated with the Goddess Saraswati, the Hindu goddess of knowledge, wisdom, and learning.
7. Note that class status trumps any concerns over caste here, as both Medha's and the zamindar's family were of the same Mahishya caste. Caste did not figure in the narratives of the next two women, but for readers who may wish to know, Indrani's caste is Brahman, and her family is well-to-do, while Sukhi-di is of the Bengali Kayastha caste, next in high rank to Brahman, and working middle class. Subhagi is of the Dalit or Scheduled caste and rural laboring class.
8. "Di," short for *didi* or "older sister," is a sign of both kin-like closeness and respect. Bengalis generally add kin terms to names when addressing persons senior to them. Sukhi, meaning "happy," is widely known for her up-beat and spunky personality.
9. Krupabai Satthianadhan's ([1894] 1998) autobiographical novel in English, *Saguna: A Story of Native Christian Life*.
10. Pants for women are a sign of modern, cosmopolitan female gender, almost completely unseen in West Bengali villages.

References

Abu-Lughod, Lila. 1990. "The Romance of Resistance: Tracing Transformations of Power through Bedouin Women." *American Ethnologist* 17(1): 41–55.

Berry, Kim. 2011. "Disowning Dependence: Single Women's Collective Struggle for Independence and Land Rights." *Feminist Review* 98: 136–52.

Dave, Naisargi N. 2011. "Indian and Lesbian and What Came Next: Affect, Commensuration, and Queer Emergences." *American Ethnologist* 38(4): 650–65.

———. 2012. *Queer Activism in India: A Story in the Anthropology of Ethics*. Durham: Duke University Press.

Dhillon, Navtej, and Tarik M. Yousef, eds. 2011. *Generation in Waiting: The Unfulfilled Promise of Young People in the Middle East*. Washington, DC: Brookings Institution Press.

Dickey, Sara. 2013. "Apprehensions: On Gaining Recognition as Middle-Class in Madurai." *Contributions to Indian Sociology* 47(2): 217–43.

————. 2016. *Living Class in Urban India*. New Brunswick: Rutgers University Press.

Dungey, Claire Elisabeth, and Lotte Meinert. 2017. "Learning to Wait: Schooling and the Instability of Adulthood for Young Men in Uganda." In *Elusive Adulthoods: The Anthropology of New Maturities*, ed. Deborah Durham and Jacqueline Solway, 83–104. Bloomington: Indiana University Press.

Fernandes, Leela. 2006. *India's New Middle Classes: Democratic Politics in an Era of Economic Reform*. Minneapolis: University of Minnesota Press.

Fincher, Leta Hong. 2014. *Leftover Women: The Resurgence of Gender Inequality in China*. New York: Zed.

Finn, Brandon, and Sophie Oldfield. 2015. "Straining: Young Men Working through Waithood in Freetown, Sierra Leone." *Africa Spectrum* 50(3): 29–48.

Gammeltoft, Tine M. 2014. *Haunting Images: A Cultural Account of Selective Reproduction in Vietnam*. Berkeley: University of California Press.

Gertel, Joerg. 2017. "Arab Youth: A Contained Youth?" *Middle East: Topics & Arguments* 9 (December): 25–33.

Goldstein, Joshua R., and Catherine T. Kenney. 2001. "Marriage Delayed or Marriage Forgone? New Cohort Forecasts of First Marriage for US Women." *American Sociological Review* 66(4): 506–19.

Hashemi, Manata. 2015. "Waithood and Face: Morality and Mobility among Lower-Class Youth in Iran." *Qualitative Sociology* 38(3): 261–83.

Honwana, Alcinda Manuel. 2012. *The Time of Youth: Work, Social Change, and Politics in Africa*. Sterling: Kumarian Press.

Ji, Yingchun. 2015. "Between Tradition and Modernity: 'Leftover' Women in Shanghai." *Journal of Marriage and Family* 77(5): 1057–73.

Jones, Gavin W. 2007. "Delayed Marriage and Very Low Fertility in Pacific Asia." *Population and Development Review* 33(3): 453–78.

Klinenberg, Eric. 2012. *Going Solo: The Extraordinary Rise and Surprising Appeal of Living Alone*. New York: Penguin.

Kowalski, Julia. 2016. "Ordering Dependence: Care, Disorder, and Kinship Ideology in North Indian Antiviolence Counseling." *American Ethnologist* 43(1): 63–75.

Kundu, Sreemoyee Piu. 2018. *Status Single: The Truth about Being a Single Woman in India*. New Delhi: Amaryllis.

Kuriakose, Simi. 2014. "Meet the 5 Kinds of Single Women." *Times of India*, 10 July. Retrieved 25 May 2017 from http://timesofindia.indiatimes.com/life-style/relationships/man-woman/Meet-the-5-kinds-of-single-women/articleshow/18848928.cms.

Lamb, Sarah. 2018. "Being Single in India: Gendered Identities, Class Mobilities, and Personhoods in Flux." *Ethos* 46(1): 49–69.

Lawrence, Ria. 2014. "Why You Should Try Staying Single." *The Times of India*, 21 July. Retrieved 5 February 2019 from http://timesofindia.indiatimes.com/life-style/relationships/man-woman/Why-you-should-try-staying-single/articleshow/35378495.cms.

Mahmood, Saba. 2005. *The Politics of Piety: The Islamic Revival and the Feminist Subject*. Princeton: Princeton University Press.

McEvoy-Levy, Siobhan. 2014. "Stuck in Circulation: Children, Waithood, and the Conflict Narratives of Israelis and Palestinians." *Children's Geographies* 12(3): 312–26.

Mehta, Deepa, director and writer. 1996. *Fire*. New Delhi: Kaleidoscope Entertainment.

Mukhopadhyay, Carol Chapnik, and Susan Seymour, eds. 1994. *Women, Education, and Family Structure in India*. Boulder: Westview Press.

Patel, Bhaichand, ed. 2006. *Chasing the Good Life: On Being Single*. New Delhi: Viking India.

Radhakrishnan, Smitha. 2011. *Appropriately Indian: Gender and Culture in a New Transnational Class*. Durham: Duke University Press.

Raymo, James M., and Miho Iwasawa. 2005. "Marriage Market Mismatches in Japan: An Alternative View of the Relationship between Women's Education and Marriage." *American Sociological Review* 70(5): 801–22.

Sabbah-Karkaby, Maha, and Haya Stier. 2017. "Links between Education and Age at Marriage among Palestinian Women in Israel: Changes Over Time." *Studies in Family Planning* 48(1): 23–38.

Satthianadhan, Krupabai. (1894) 1998. *Saguna: A Story of Native Christian Life*, edited by Chandani Lokuge. Delhi: Oxford University Press.

Sayer, Andrew. 2005. *The Moral Significance of Class*. New York: Cambridge University Press.

Sengupta, Somini. 2007. "Careers Give India's Women New Independence." *New York Times*, 23 November. Retrieved 27 July 2020 from https://www.nytimes.com/2007/11/23/world/asia/23india.html.

Singerman, Diane. 2007. "The Economic Imperatives of Marriage: Emerging Practices and Identities Among Youth in the Middle East." *Middle East Youth Initiative*, Working Paper No. 6, September, The Brookings Institution, Wolfensohn Center for Development, Washington, DC.

———. 2011. "The Negotiation of Waithood: The Political Economy of Delayed Marriage in Egypt." In *Arab Youth: Social Mobilisation in Times of Risk*, ed. Samir Khalaf and Roseanne Saad Khalaf, 85–108. London: Saqi.

Sinha, Chinki. 2019. "Brave New Woman." *India Today*, 21 October. Retrieved 2 February 2019 from https://www.indiatoday.in/magazine/cover-story/story/20191021-brave-new-woman-1607809-2019-10-11.

Times News Network. 2018. "Courts Still Confused about Legal Age of Marriage?" *Times of India*, 7 August. Retrieved 4 February 2019 from https://timesofindia.indiatimes.com/life-style/relationships/love-sex/Courts-still-confused-about-legal-age-of-marriage/articleshow/21333081.cms.

To, Sandy. 2013. "Understanding Sheng Nu ('Leftover Women'): The Phenomenon of Late Marriage among Chinese Professional Women." *Symbolic Interaction* 36(1): 1–20.

Traister, Rebecca. 2016. *All the Single Ladies: Unmarried Women and the Rise of an Independent Nation*. New York: Simon & Schuster.

Vijayakumar, Gowri. 2013. "'I'll Be Like Water': Gender, Class, and Flexible Aspirations at the Edge of India's Knowledge Economy." *Gender & Society* 27(6): 777–98.

Waldrop, Anne. 2012. "Grandmother, Mother and Daughter: Changing Agency of Indian, Middle-Class Women, 1908–2008." *Modern Asian Studies* 46(3): 601–38.

Part IV

DELAYED CHILDBEARING AND THE QUEST FOR MOTHERHOOD

Chapter 13

BLAMED FOR DELAY

FRENCH NORMS AND PRACTICES OF ART IN THE CONTEXT OF INCREASING AGE-RELATED FEMALE INFERTILITY

Manon Vialle

Introduction

Because women in Euro-American societies are deciding to postpone motherhood until later in life, more women in their forties are turning toward assisted reproductive technologies (ARTs) to help overcome age-related infertility (Friese, Becker, and Nachtigall 2006, 2008; Löwy 2009; Szewczuk 2012; Büchler and Parizer 2017). This trend is especially striking in France, where these new medical treatment demands are colliding with a stricter legal framework—in terms of ART—than those of other European countries.

In 1974, the average age of French women at their first pregnancy was 24, in 2010 it was 28, and in 2014, it had risen to 28.5 (Volant 2017). With increased age come changes in a woman's ovarian reserve that make it more difficult for her to become pregnant, a phenomenon that begins at age twenty-five and strongly increases after the age of thirty-five (Faddy and Gosden 1995; Fitzgerald, Zimon, and Jones 1998; Menken, Trussel, and Larsen 1986; Olafsdottir, Wikland, and Möller 2011; Sevon 2005; Szewczuk 2012).

While similar trends regarding pregnancy delays can be observed around the world, different countries respond in different ways

(Baldwin et al. 2014; Büchler and Parizer 2017; Friese et al. 2006, 2008; Löwy 2009; Olafsdottir et al. 2011; Sevon 2005; Szewczuk 2012). The comparison between France and Spain is particularly illuminating. In 2013, Spain was the most active in vitro fertilization (IVF) country in Europe, with more than 100,000 cycles. France, with 90,000 cycles, was close behind (ESHRE 2017). But France and Spain do not have the same ART policies. For example, the age limit for women to receive ART is fifty years old in Spain and forty-three in France (Büchler and Parizer 2017; Rozée 2011; Rozée and Tain 2010). Similarly, egg donation is allowed for every woman in Spain, but only under strict conditions in France. Moreover, egg donors are remunerated in Spain but not in France, where there are fewer donors and insufficient eggs to meet demand. Differences in systems of medical reimbursement, in understandings of the role of medicine in the fertility process, and in perceptions of the values of individual liberty and choice for women are found not just between France and Spain, but across Europe. As a result, women often cross state borders to receive ART services (Rozée 2011; Rozée and Tain 2010).

This chapter explores cases of French women who delay childbearing into their forties and then face difficulties in getting pregnant. I argue that, contrary to the popular assumption that French women are putting off childbirth for selfish reasons related to career and personal desires, there are multiple and complex reasons for their decisions to delay. First, I introduce the French ART framework, its policies, and the social discourses that blame women in their forties for waiting to pursue motherhood. Second, I present my research objectives and methodology. Third, I describe the profiles and sociodemographic characteristics of the women who were interviewed. Fourth, I explore their biographical trajectories, revealing different reasons for their decisions to delay motherhood past the age of forty. This research aims to highlight how postponing motherhood is the fruit of social evolution and not merely a marginal practice. In this way, I explore not only the personal feelings of my interlocutors but also the external environments that lead to this decision. The fifth part examines the representations of these temporal thresholds for reproduction and finds them profoundly out of step with those of social discourse and of the medical and legal establishment.

Ultimately, this chapter explores the phenomenon of "waithood" (Singerman 2011) and, in particular, "reproductive waithood" (Inhorn, Chapter 15, this volume), in the French context. Based on the empirical experiences of the interviewees, it highlights evolving tensions within French society that have led to new demands for ART treatment. Finally, it creates space to approach critically the legal, medical, and social visions concerning thresholds of ART and what I call *"female reproductive temporality,"* as women envisage a reproductive temporality that is based on physical, social, and relational factors.[1] In other words, women seek to satisfy a number of conditions that they deem necessary in order to welcome and raise children, within a temporality that they consider as socially and biologically appropriate.

French ART Framework

In France, unlike in Spain, ART is not considered a matter of individual choice and does not rely on market-based principles of supply and demand. Fully covered by the social security system, ART is considered within a strictly "therapeutic" framework (Théry 2011). Indeed, the public health regulations as set out in Article L2141-2, related to the Bioethics Law of 7 July 2011 assert that:

> The aim of assisted reproductive technologies is to rectify the infertility of a couple or to prevent the transmission to the child of a serious illness of one or the other of the couple. The pathological character of the infertility should be diagnosed medically. The man and woman who make up the couple should be living, of an age to procreate and able to consent in advance to the transfer of embryos or of the insemination . . .

As such, under the legal framework of France's Bioethical Law of 1994, subsequently revised under amendments of 2004 and 2011, ART is only intended to serve as a therapeutic response to a "pathological" problem. This legal framework rests on what it sees as a fundamental difference between "pathological" and "normal" infertility. While infertilities diagnosed as "pathological," thereby existing within a theoretically "natural" framework of reproduction (Fassin 2002; Löwy 2009), are considered legitimate for ART treatment, infertilities attributed to normal—that is, physiological—causes are not accepted. In other words, in order to access ART in France, it is necessary to be "at once, theoretically capable yet practically incapable of procreating" (Fassin 2002). People or couples considered "too old" to procreate, single women, and homosexual couples all fall within this category and are thus denied access to ART in France.[2]

Age Limits on Women

French law does not stipulate a precise age limit for women regarding access to ART, thus leaving doctors who specialize in reproductive technologies to establish these boundaries. For the most part, doctors refer to the age established by the social security system, which covers the cost of ART treatment for couples before the forty-third birthday of the woman partner. While doctors may treat patients older than forty-three, health insurance will not cover the cost of the procedure. An absolute cut-off date for women cannot be found anywhere (Vialle 2014). Around this 43-year-old marker, different options exist: some doctors refuse to treat any patients in their forties, while others will extend treatment to age forty-three, and others to age forty-five. Nevertheless, these decisions are all based on the same criteria: the ovarian reserve. Social security bases its decision to stop covering the cost of ART after the age of forty-three on a number of factors, including the diminished chances of women after the age of forty becoming pregnant via ART and the higher risk of medical complications for the mother and the baby due to the mother's age. Doctors can stop treatment for women younger than forty-three if they believe that age-induced changes to the ovarian reserve are too great. Egg donation is not proposed in such cases,[3] and IVF techniques using the gametes of the couple are unable to resolve this form of infertility. Beyond this forty-three-year threshold, doctors treat certain couples exceptionally, on the condition that the woman is still able to procreate, with the causes of infertility being, in these cases, either unknown or male. If the infertility is female, it is ascribed to the age of the woman and not considered pathological; accordingly, the request for treatment will be denied.

Age Limits on Men

Reproduction professionals do not apply the same age-related criteria to the male partner. The social security system does not limit reimbursement based on the age of the man. This is principally because reproductive medicine intervenes in the woman's body, where it is deemed that the risks outweigh the benefits. Professionals thus set a limit among themselves, based on shared understandings, which can vary but is generally placed around fifty-eight or fifty-nine years old. This limit is not related to natural infertility, physiology, or the number of pregnancies, as it is in the case for women. Rather, within the discourse of professionals, this limit is seen as related to caregiving capacities—that is, the ability of the man to be well enough to accompany the child until adulthood.

Thus, health professionals judge women differently than men. They are not evaluating the chances of men's fertility successes. Andropause (a hormonal reduction that affects procreativity in men between the ages of fifty and seventy years old) is not considered in the same way as menopause. As a result, men do not face the physiological limits of reproduction that women face. Moreover, it is well-known that, with technologies such as intracytoplasmic sperm injection (ICSI), many "infertile" men can envisage procreating if their partner has good quality oocytes (Friese et al. 2006, 2008; Inhorn and Birenbaum-Carmeli 2008). In contrast, according to French regulations, if the cause of infertility is attributed to poor quality oocytes, women must relinquish their aims of pregnancy (Löwy 2009).

Nevertheless, the progressive reduction in masculine fertility has begun to surface in some medical journals given that, as for women, there is a correlation between men's age and the rate of chromosomal abnormalities. Yet, in France in general, the fifteen-year gap between the limits imposed on men and women in accessing ART lifts pressure from men concerning (what nobody refers to as) their "biological clocks" (Vialle 2014).

"Blame" as a Social Discourse

The legal distinction in French law between "normal" and "pathological" infertility is accompanied by another—principally moral—distinction regarding, not women's health, but social conventions that govern ART in France. This distinction reinforces a strict binary between the two poles of legitimate ART, based on the need for a "treatment," and illegitimate ART, sometime couched in terms of "personal convenience," within the framework of requests for treatment for what is seen as "normal" infertility. This distinction structures not only the normative model for ART in France, but it legitimizes a social and medical discourse that faults women who rely on medical techniques to ameliorate female infertility associated with age. These women are blamed for not making the "right choices" at the "right moments" in life; they waited "too long" before deciding to have children. In other words, they "could" have or "should" have acted differently (Vialle 2014). This discourse resonates with an idea widely diffused within the medical world, and other strata of French society, that these women are above all "careerists," demanding their "rights to a child" too late. These women are accused of wanting to turn back their "biological clocks" and so bypass the "laws of nature" in order to satisfy their "personal convenience." Without a similar discourse concerning men, society intimates that these women should have procreated at a younger age. In this way, a tension exists within French society between, on the one hand, regulations governing access to ART based on a socially conservative discourse, and, on the other hand, new expectations concerning medical technologies linked to societal evolutions and the postponement of first pregnancies. This research examines this tension.

Research Framework, Objectives, and Methodology

In this context of critical discourse, this chapter studies those primarily affected by fertility norms and realities—that is, a group of women wanting to give birth over the age of forty using ART due to infertility ascribed to physiological aging of their ovarian reserve. It sheds light on the French bioethical model, especially the distinctions that comprise this system, including "normal" and "pathological" infertility, and "legitimate" and "illegitimate" ART.

Infertility progresses over time. According to doctors, ovarian capacity starts to decline from twenty-five years old and this phenomenon increases strongly from the age of thirty-five. The success rates of ART techniques, such as IVF, follow the same decrease as the egg quality declines (Belaisch-Allart et al. 2004; Szewczuk 2012). Moreover, this process progresses at different stages and ages, depending on the woman. As such, this form of infertility interrogates strongly the separation between what is considered normal and what is pathological. At what point does infertility become pathological and appear legitimate? At what age is it normal, and thus illegitimate?

The objectives of this research are to explore the biographical trajectories of these women and to understand why they considered childbirth after the age of forty. This research analyzes their discourses in order to understand their representations and experiences of infertility, related to the alterations of ovarian reserve, as well as questions of ART-assisted childbirth over the age of forty.

This study took place in 2014–15 and involved twenty-three women between the ages of forty and forty-three undergoing treatment within two French ART centers. Each woman participated in an in-depth qualitative interview lasting between one and a half and two and a half hours, either at their homes, their workplaces, the ART center, or my workplace. I conducted the interviews in French and translated them to English for this chapter. The interviews were structured around four major themes. The first was concerned with the personal and conjugal history of the interviewee, up to the moment when infertility was diagnosed; the second related to the way the ART process took place; the third considered the factor of age, in relation principally to the project of childbearing; and the last dealt with the women's views relative to the legislation that frames ART in France, notably in relation to the question of age-related thresholds.

The Study Population: Women in Their Forties Undergoing ART

The women interviewed within the framework of this study are all engaged in heterosexual relationships. In fact, ART centers in France are legally obligated to treat only heterosexual couples. For the same reason, no one was older than forty-three. Moreover, none of the twenty-three women interviewed were younger than forty, so that all would be concerned with the phenomenon of alteration to the ovarian reserve. Thus, because of their ages, they all faced a form of infertility linked to physical changes in ovarian reserve. Three of them had first been treated for another medical reason (male infertility, endometriosis, blocked fallopian tubes) and only later faced problems of changes to the ovarian reserve. These three interviewees were the only ones who had been registered for ART programs for more than three years; all the others had been involved in the program for less than two years, with half of them participating for less than one year. Among the women, four had already had a child, two of them from a previous relationship. The majority were undergoing ART for their first child.

The relationships of the interviewees were varied. The durations of the couples' relationships fluctuated between eighteen months and twenty-four years, the average being five years. That is to say, some were newer relationships, whereas others were long-term couples. Moreover, nine of the women were married, four were part of civil unions, and ten lived with partners without civil unions.

As for their social backgrounds, most interviewees came from a vast middle class. Their professions ranged from homecare assistant to physiotherapist. One woman belonged to what could be considered a higher social class, based on her profession as a human resources manager within a major company.

It is important to note that because these women were recruited directly from the ART centers, most of them were undergoing treatment when interviewed (twenty out of twenty-three). Among the three who had finished their treatments, two had just learned that they were pregnant, one had just concluded her fourth of four IVF treatments covered in France. As a result, for the majority, the outcome of the ART process was still uncertain. This uncertainty must be considered when reading their accounts. Their discourses relate to something being done—or undone—a story in progress with an unknown outcome: having a child and becoming a parent, or not having a child and having to renounce parenthood. This combination of known present and unknown future shaped the accounts that were collected. Indeed, "the narrative cannot avoid bringing into play the present, given that it is from the present of the person who speaks that this narrative is recomposed. It gives meaning to the present, and not only to what is finished" (Théry 1993: 259). The narratives of these women gave meaning to their struggles to successfully guide their own parenting projects (Vialle 2018).

While the social discourse presents these women monolithically as selfish and career-driven, their profiles reveal them as unique and with varied life experiences. These women offer a variety of reasons for pursuing their motherhood projects after the age of forty, even though, in many cases, they had been planning to procreate for many years. Their discourses bear witness to a diversity of pathways and allow us to see the plurality of reasons for deciding to pursue motherhood later in life. In what follows, these conditions are examined and analyzed via what I call the *feeling of unreadiness* for motherhood.

Feeling Unready to Mother

Women cite a diverse array of reasons for their feelings of unreadiness/unavailability[4] for motherhood. The examples they provide illustrate the importance of the feeling of readiness in deciding when to have a child. These situations fall into four broad categories of readiness/availability: partner, conjugal, material, and affective.

Partner Availability

Christina and her partner, both forty-two years old, have been living together for three years.[5] She is a secondary-school teacher, and he is an accountant. They began to consider having children after six to eight months as a couple and are currently undergoing ART treatment, waiting for the transfer of a frozen embryo after a second unsuccessful IVF. Christina reflected:

> I wanted children with the man I loved, and who loved me. Perhaps it is stupid—it seems very Walt Disney, fairy-tale like—but I really wanted to meet the father of my children. I didn't want a progenitor for my kids; I wanted the father of my children. And so, it is probably this decision that meant that it took me more time than others to find him, but then, that's the way it is. I had made that decision. I wanted a man I could grow old with, the man with whom I could form a family, the father of my children. I found him, and it's clear that we found each other at the age of thirty-eight and a half, nearly thirty-nine.

The question of the *partner availability* takes places within a context of growing social acceptance, in Western societies since the second part of the twentieth century, for couples to form and split more often. Being a couple is no longer necessarily a lifelong commitment, and periods of celibacy have become more frequent over the life course, at any age, now without social reprobation (Déchaux 2009; Giddens 2004; Prioux 2005). It is, consequently, more common for women between the ages of thirty and forty to delay childbearing because they are single. Within this study, the question of whether or not to have a child in the absence of a partner does not arise. Thus, the notion of *partner availability* is proposed here in order to illustrate the fact that feeling ready to procreate is related to the situation of the couple. The women interviewed attested to the fact that being part of a couple, and even more, being part of the "right" couple, was a necessary condition for feeling ready to start a family. In contrast, in the absence of a partner, or when not with the "right father," feelings of unreadiness prevail. Eleven of the twenty-three women who were interviewed postponed motherhood because of partner unavailability.

Conjugal Readiness

Françoise, a 41-year-old employment trainer, and her partner, a 38-year-old[6] sales agency manager, have been living together for five years. They have been attempting to have a child for four years, undergoing ICSI, while awaiting the first IVF round:

> Françoise: Well, after a year, I said to myself: It's really pretty good, as we have met each other. I was thirty-five years old, so I said that, after

all . . . it's getting old. So, after about a year, discussions, he didn't
want that. And so, well, discussion, discussion, he didn't want it . . .

Interviewer: He didn't want a child more broadly? Or not right then,
it wasn't the right time?

Françoise: It wasn't the time for him, so he didn't want that. Then
we split up because I wanted children, and then he came back . . . He
realized that perhaps it was the time, and since then we have been
trying, but it is not working.

Françoise was not ready to attempt motherhood until both she and
her partner were ready. For many women, if her partner was not
ready to procreate, she was also unready. In all of the observed cases,
the woman wanted to have a child while the partner preferred to
wait. The reverse was not observed. As a result, the woman delays
procreation and aligns herself with the temporality of her partner, or
the man brings forth his desire to have a child, aligning himself with
his partner's calendar, as is the case of Françoise. In both scenarios,
as the examples illustrate, this calendar adjustment does not take
place passively, but sometimes via stormy discussions and negotiations, or, ultimatums and separations (Bessin and Levilain 2004,
2012). Three of the women interviewed exhibited this scenario.

Material Readiness

Mounia, forty-two, and her partner, forty, both computer engineers,
have been living together for eleven years. They have been trying to
have a child for two years and are currently waiting for their fourth
and final round of IVF. Mounia describes:

When he moved into my house, I was living in a small student apartment . . . I was already working, of course, but I still lived in my small
student apartment, in a neighborhood that had a bit of a bad reputation . . . and so he moved in there. We were on top of each other with
his children, when he had them on weekends, and then we looked
for this house . . . All that took time, and that is why we didn't try to
have a child straightaway. Once we had finally been able to finance it,
find the house, when all the problems had been sorted out, we were
then faced with doing the place up.

Like Mounia, all of the interviewees who attributed postponing
childbearing to material reasons expressed a strong and long-felt
desire to have children. Whether this was because they were students, unemployed, irregularly employed, or living in small accommodations, they eschewed procreation for these reasons. Judging
their material conditions to be insufficient, they felt unready for a

parental project and sometimes underwent abortions during these periods. This issue of material inadequacy took different forms, including economic instability, as well as domestic discomfort. Women postponed parenthood in order to finish their studies, gain stable employment, or procure adequate accommodations. Many studies show the importance of these criteria when it comes to deciding when to have a child (Bessin, Levilain, and Régnier-Loilier. 2005; Bessin and Levilain 2012; Gonzalez and Jurado-Guerrero 2006; Mazuy 2009; Régnier-Loilier 2007; Régnier-Loilier and Solaz 2010; Régnier-Loilier and Vignoli 2011; Thompson 1997). This research also indicates that the importance given to these criteria varies according to gender, age, or social class. All of the women interviewed shared these concerns. Three of them were still deeply concerned, even after turning thirty-five years old.

Affective Readiness

Cécilia, forty-three years old and an information technology engineer, and her partner, a fifty-year-old network engineer, have lived together for fifteen years. They have been trying to have a child for two years. The couple is currently waiting for Cécilia's second and final IVF treatment, given her age. Below is a recount of our conversation:

Interviewer: Within your relationship, when did you start to broach the matter of having a child?

Cécilia: Very late. It was . . . it was when? Two or three years ago, not more. Not any earlier.

Interviewer: Prior to that, the question never came up?

Cécilia: No.

Interviewer: And when it did come up, how did that happen? Who raised the subject first?

Cécilia: It was me. It was me because I felt an emptiness in the house. The feeling of having built a nest with him over fifteen years but that there was nothing inside. Whereas before, the need, the desire had never made itself felt. Yes, but I had squashed this, telling myself that I already had something to do, I always had a professional project in progress, I had great vacations lined up . . . I always had something that had to come first . . . I had never imagined my ideal life with a family, children, a dog, and a house. It had never been that. I cannot even say if I had a vision of an ideal life, if it wasn't just that I wanted to be independent—there is no doubt about that. I did not want to depend on anyone and to be able to get by in any circumstances, and the idea of being a mother, I had the impression that it . . . would go against my independence.

Achieving personal goals, such as finding a partner or a stable job, does not necessarily lead to planning for the possibility of having a child. Focusing on living life as an economically independent person or as a couple before having children is an increasingly common, socially acceptable approach (Debest 2014; Mazuy 2009; Régnier-Loilier 2007). *Affective unreadiness* refers here to the sense of not being ready for motherhood as reflected in the idea that even the desire to have a child has not been manifested or expressed. Having a child is simply not on the agenda. This feeling is also relative, as it varies from one person to another, or within the same person according to different times in her life. Only one of the women interviewed was affected by this phenomenon.

The diverse paths of these women reveal a plurality of reasons for their maternal plans after the age of forty. Their biographical histories show that there are numerous conditions that are seen as necessary for the construction of a family. Whether it is a matter of partner availability (being in a couple), conjugal readiness (the parental project being shared within the couple), material readiness (professional and economic stability, comfort of accommodation), or affective readiness (desire for a child), the women interviewed presented all of these forms of readiness as required conditions for motherhood. These four forms of readiness for motherhood are not the only conditions required to have a child, nor are they exhaustive. Nevertheless, for these women, the presence of these factors contributed to their sense of not being ready for motherhood. This feeling, linked to conditions of the "reproductive norm" (to be at the right age, to be in a couple, to have a stable job, to be autonomous, etc.) (Bajos and Ferrand 2006), led to their inability to envisage the parental project before the age of thirty-five, and often later.

These observations indicate that, when it comes to the decision to become pregnant, the question of physiological readiness was not at the forefront of people's minds. This issue seemed secondary when it came to making decisions about motherhood. In a social context, when the number of children per family is decreasing, it is well known that the decision to become parents is deliberate. Having a child is, in effect, increasingly the result of a project. The moment of its fruition is considered in relation to a larger context in which the child will take its place, enabling the optimization of the conditions of its birth and development. This idea of the project emerges in the middle of multiple other personal objectives, such as those defined by the "reproductive norm." It is a matter, in other words, of what Luc Boltanski (2004) calls the "norm of engendering by project," which is evident here in the feeling of unreadiness. Yet, any reference to this social and relational context is missing from the social and medical discourse concerning childbearing over the age of forty, which refers only to the mother's "biological clock." And if this is not the case, women are accused of being "career-driven and selfish." However, this stereotype does not reflect the realities of the women interviewed, who share concerns about the circumstances of motherhood.

Even if the physiological dimension of reproduction was not central to their discourses, it is not absent from the biographical histories of the interviewees. Some women explained that the threat of the "biological clock" had sometimes transformed their feeling of unreadiness for motherhood, resigning them to their current situations (of being single, for example) and causing them to consider having a child in these circumstances. The biographical histories of these interviewees explain why many women decide to begin parental projects after the age of forty. Nevertheless, other factors must be considered. Their feeling of unreadiness for motherhood takes shape within a particular social context, with increased life expectancy and reorganization of age groups. Here, we see that their biographical pathways seem to match their feelings of youthfulness and the amount of time before them to procreate.

Reproductive Temporality

Prior to being between the ages of thirty-five to forty, the interviewed women never asked themselves whether they were at risk of not being able to have children because of their ages. This is partly because nothing, not even their bodies, revealed their increasing infertility. Their senses of self, of their bodies, and of their pathways were in accordance with their social milieu. Because of this, the news of their infertility was often surprising, and was perceived as being out of kilter with this feeling of otherwise being in line with the norm.

Feeling Young and Remaining Unaware of the Risk of Infertility

Mélanie, a 40-year-old architect, and her partner, a 48-year-old project manager, have been living together for eighteen months and planning to conceive for six. They have just begun the ART process and are waiting for the start of hormonal stimulation for their first round of IVF/ICSI. According to Mélanie:

Up to that point, I did not feel that I was growing old. As if, in fact, I don't know . . . life was going very, very quickly, but I mean really quickly, you know? As for me, I had the impression that I have not changed . . . that I am the same as when I was a student . . . I have a job that is not easy . . . and I spend my life doing that—it's true—and, all of a sudden, I did not see myself getting old.

Changes in fertility due to aging were often unthinkable for the interviewees, who characterized themselves as "feeling young." The phrase "feeling young" is employed to convey this perception that the women had of themselves physically, psychologically, and socially.

The majority of my interlocutors knew that fertility diminished with age, but they were nonetheless surprised by this phenomenon. Françoise represents many: "We know that as you get older you are less fertile, but I never thought it would get to this stage for me." Noëlle said, "I imagined that it was going to be complicated, but I never imagined having a level that was so low, in fact. And then, over a year, there was the fatal blow."

Whether or not these interviewees had been informed about the risks of infertility when they were younger had no effect on their awareness or internalization of these risks later in life. The women featured in this study felt young, and, because of this, they felt they had enough time ahead of them to carry out their parental projects. It was not until they found out about changes to the ovarian reserve that they were confronted with this "illusion of youth." This illusion is based on the fact that, because they still felt young as they approached the age of forty, they felt that they were able to procreate. Consequently, they dedicated themselves to studying, advancing professionally, moving houses, looking for partners, and so on. They did not appreciate, in any real sense, the approaching risk of becoming infertile because of their age.

Feeling Young and Increasing Life Expectancy

According to Mélanie, her parents reinforced this lack of urgency to have a child:

I think that my parents are not aware either of my age, so they still see me as someone . . . who is fully . . . [able] to have children . . . I think that . . . the fact that I was treated like a child quite late, that means that you do not really plan. You see, they never made me see that I did not have the time, that I should go for it. Over the last few years they have always pretty much told me that . . . I had the time, that it was not very serious.

Mélanie's parents' attitude reflects changing attitudes in French society. During the interviews, women referred to societal evolutions that have affected women over the course of the second half of the twentieth century and the beginning of the twenty-first: the growing number of women in higher education and professional positions, increasing equality between the sexes, acceptance of multiple, or short-lived, romantic relationships, and increasing life expectancy overall. These trends foster an environment that encourages women to procreate later in life.

It is important to clarify that the phenomenon of increasing life expectancy does not translate to prolonged old age. Rather, it redeploys across age groups, leaving people to feel younger overall (Théry 1998; Vialle 2014). Thus, within this context of rejuvenation, "feeling young" and the pathways it yields would seem in harmony with sociodemographic norms.

As a result, society encouraged these women to approach procreation differently, as Mélanie's example indicates. While gynecologists share this knowledge, these warnings are not always sufficient to convince women, especially single women. Awareness of the physical depletion of the ovarian reserve does not seem to be a determining factor. Undoubtedly, some interviewees regretted not having more information, but others, who had been informed, still did not advance their parental plans. Either their situations led them to feel unready (mainly because of the lack of partner or lack of conjugal readiness), or there existed a large gap between intellectual knowledge about infertility and the internal consciousness of this phenomenon. Feeling young and remaining unaware of physical changes to their bodies, particularly their reproductive bodies, they rarely felt affected by age-related infertility. Within the context of increasing life expectancy and the redeployment of age groups, the trajectories of these women bear witness to an evolution of norms concerning age and reproduction.

Feeling Young Despite Reproductive Aging

Émilie, a 41-year-old musical programming assistant, and her partner, a 30-year-old graphic designer, have been living together for five years and planning to have children for three years. They are currently waiting for their fourth and final round of IVF and, in case of failure, have made plans to access donated oocytes from Spain. According to Émilie:

> Women, it is true that, in my case for example, we are "old young," in fact. And, all of a sudden, I have found myself thinking about my

age every day for the last three years. I feel old because my oocytes do not work anymore, and I feel like I am almost seventy years old. For the last two years, I have not thought of anything else . . . I have the impression that suddenly my life flipped, from being a young girl, an adult, and now a pensioner.

While the women in the study all sought medical advice (gynecology, general medicine), given their age, they were quickly directed toward ART centers, where they were immediately treated by professionals who started a "race against the clock," or indeed against "the biological clock" (Vialle 2014). All became aware of the changes in ovarian reserve and thus of their infertility. This news was often a surprise for them. Moreover, the awareness of changes to their fertility levels sometimes affected their perceptions of themselves. As Émilie illustrates, these women felt not only a loss of confidence regarding their parental projects but a lack of harmony within their own bodies.

This chapter proposes an interpretative hypothesis for this feeling, based on the difference between ovarian capacity and gestational capacity, which is played out within these women's bodies. While ovarian capacity refers to the state of the ovarian reserve—that is, the production of oocytes in sufficient quantity and quality—gestational capacity refers to the ability to carry a pregnancy to term—that is, the possibility that an embryo will develop in utero until childbirth. This difference is made particularly visible via ART treatments, which rely on the distinction between these two elements within the reproductive process. Many anthropological studies that explore surrogacy underline these distinctions in discussions of genetic motherhood, gestational motherhood, and, sometimes, social motherhood (Delaisi de Parseval and Collard 2007; Martin 1987; Mehl 2011; Ragoné 1996; Weber 2013). The surrogacy process clarifies the difference between ovarian and gestational capacity, as it becomes embodied by different protagonists (the intentional mother, who may or may not be the same as the oocyte donor, and the gestational carrier). Regardless, within the context of a study of intra-conjugal ART, this distinction helps explain the experiences of these women.

Interviewees describe a tension between their perceptions of their youthful bodies and social lives and their experiences with age-related infertility. While these women feel young enough to carry, birth, and raise children, they find themselves too old to produce oocytes of sufficient quality to lead to pregnancy. In other words, they are not faced with complete infertility but an impediment to just one part of their physiological reproductive capacity: their ovarian capacity diminishes, while their gestational capacity remains. This dual capacity corresponds with a dual temporality: gestational capacity outlasts ovarian capacity. This duality yields new expectations regarding ART treatment, which is seen as a solution for women with reduced ovarian capacity.

Nevertheless, the rules governing ART in France base the timeframe for female reproduction on just one biological condition: ovarian capacity. The data presented here show, however, that this should not be the sole consideration, nor should it be applied rigidly to women confronted with age-related infertility (Vialle 2018). The study shows that many women in France are determined to resist these changes through ART treatment and, in case of failure, through seeking egg donors from abroad (five of the eleven women who had reached the end of the process were considering this). This determination to continue the parental project can be explained by their "feeling young," despite their diminished ovarian capacities. These women recognized that, although they were partially infertile, they were still able to carry and birth children. Their fight against the changes in their ovarian capacities made sense because of their confidence in their gestational capacities and their confidence in their maternal capabilities.

Conclusion

The data presented here highlight the gap between the empirical pathways of the women interviewed and the social discourses concerning age-related female infertility. Two major points emerge. First, the trajectories of these women do not match the stereotypical representation of the "egotistical careerwomen" who delay motherhood solely for "selfish personal convenience." Second, these women envisage a reproductive temporality based on physical, social, and relational factors, and they therefore seek to satisfy a number of conditions that they deem necessary in order to welcome and raise children. This analysis thus reveals that the ways in which these women consider the thresholds of reproduction is profoundly out of step with the simplistic distinction between the "normal" and "pathological" categories of infertility that structure the French bioethical model. The latter fails to account for the pluridimensional aspects of the female reproductive temporality and (in)fertility, which are not only biological, but also social, relational, and temporal.

We can therefore question the basis of the moral discourse that challenges these women. Acknowledging this more complex view of (in)fertility and reproductive female temporality reveals the disconnect between these categories of infertility and women's experience of age-related infertility. Without concrete consistency in practice, this legal opposition cannot constitute the foundation of the social and moral discourse on what would be legitimate or illegitimate access to ART. Instead, French society perpetuates a moral vision reinforced by biological/social, nature/culture, and female/male binaries, which precludes access to ART, justified by this distinction between "normal" and "pathological" infertility. For decades, feminist anthropologists have criticized the distinction between female/nature and male/culture to explain gender inequality in Western societies (Guillaumin 1992; Inhorn 2017; Mathieu 1973; Ortner 1974). In their wake, and because this issue always appears to be important in the context of this research, it seems necessary to examine this issue critically and to eliminate moralizing and paternalistic remarks, in particular toward women, so that ART techniques can be envisioned for all as a means to access greater freedom and equality in reproduction, especially in terms of reproductive temporality.

Manon Vialle is a postdoctoral fellow at the Nobert Elias Center in France, where she is researching infertility through issues of kinship, age, gender, and biographical temporality. She also teaches in the Department of Sociology at Aix-Marseille University. Vialle's work focuses on representations, treatments, and experiences of infertility in France. She has published numerous articles in French and received several grants to conduct her doctoral research. She holds a PhD in sociology from the École des Hautes Études en Sciences Sociales.

Notes

1. The concept of "female reproductive temporality" and the data presented here were analyzed in a previous French-language publication (Vialle 2018).
2. It should be noted that during the year 2020, French bioethics laws were subject to a new revision. It is highly probable that the legal framework presented here will ultimately be modified, in particular concerning access to ART for lesbian couples and single women. However, no change is expected regarding the age limits for ART treatment and, more

broadly, representations of the thresholds for female procreation. The analysis remains current, at least until final revision of French bioethics laws.

3. Both because of the shortage of egg donation and because of the legal framework granting only people with "pathological" infertility access to ART treatment, most women in their forties with age-related infertility do not receive egg donation.

4. The French phrase is "sentiment de disponibilité." In English, this translates to "feeling of unavailability" or "feeling of unreadiness." In this case, both translations apply; I want to refer not only to the personal feelings of whether the interviewees feel ready to have a child, but also to their different situations, which can be considered outside their will. Most of these women have wanted to have a child for many years but thought that they could not because of their situations.

5. All names have been changed to preserve the anonymity of the respondents.

6. The age difference within the couple could explain why the man did not feel ready to procreate when the woman did. But that does not fully explain this misunderstanding. For other couples in this situation of conjugal unreadiness, the man was not younger than the woman. And in the cases of couples with younger men, this misunderstanding about the right moment to have children has not yet appeared.

References

Bajos, Nathalie, and Michèle Ferrand. 2006. "L'Interruption Volontaire de Grossesse et la Recomposition de la Norme Procréative" [Voluntary interruption of pregnancy and recomposition of the procreative norm]. *Sociétés Contemporaines* 61: 91–117.

Baldwin, Kylie, Lorraine Culley, Nicky Hudson, and Helene Mitchell. 2014. "Reproductive Technology and the Life Course: Current Debates and Research in Social Egg Freezing." *Human Fertility* 17(3): 170–79.

Belaisch-Allart, Joëlle, Aviva Devaux, Jean-Philipe Ayel, and Jacques de Mouzon. 2004. "La Femme de 40 Ans et Plus en FIV et en ICSI: Données FIVNAT" [Women aged 40 and over in IVF and ICSI: FIVNAT data]. *Gynécologie Obstétrique Fertilité* 32(9): 730–36.

Bessin, Marc, and Hervé Levilain. 2004. "Pères sur le Tard: Logiques Temporelles et Négociations Conjugales" [Late fathers: temporal logics and conjugal negotiations]. *Recherches et Prévisions* 76: 23–38.

———. 2012. *Parents Après 40 Ans* [Parents after the age of 40]. Paris: Autrement.

Bessin, Marc, Hervé Levilain, and Arnaud Régnier-Loilier. 2005. "La Parenté Tardive: Logiques Biographiques et Pratiques Éducatives" [Late kinship: biographical logics and educational practices]. *Allocations Familiales, Dossiers d'Étude* 67.

Boltanski, Luc. 2004. *La Condition Fœtale: Une Sociologie de l'Engendrement et de l'Avortement* [The fetal condition: a sociology of childbirth and abortion]. Paris: Gallimard, Collection NRF Essais.

Büchler, Andrea, and Karène Parizer. 2017. "Maternal Age in the Regulation of Reproductive Medicine: A Comparative Study." *International Journal of Law, Policy and the Family* 31(3): 269–90.

Debest, Charlotte. 2014. *Le Choix d'Une vie sans Enfant* [The choice of a childless life]. Rennes: Presses Universitaires de Rennes.

Déchaux, Jean-Hugues. 2009. *Sociologie de la famille* [Family sociology]. Paris: La Découverte, Collection Repères.

Delaisi de Parseval, Geneviève, and Chantal Collard. 2007. "La Gestation pour Autrui: Un Bricolage des Représentations de la Paternité et de la Maternité Euro-Américaines" [Surrogate motherhood: a tinkering with the representations of European-American fatherhood and motherhood]. *L'Homme* 183: 29–53.

ESHRE (European Society of Human Reproduction and Embryology). 2017. "Cross Border Reproductive Care." ESHRE Fact Sheets, 1 January. Retrieved 9 April 2019 from https://www.eshre.eu/~/media/sitecore-files/Press-room/Resources/1-CBRC.pdf?la=en.

Faddy, Malcolm J., and Roger G. Gosden. 1995. "A Mathematical Model of Follicle Dynamics in the Human Ovary." *Human Reproduction* 10(4): 770–75.

Fassin, Éric. 2002. "La Nature de la Maternité: Pour une Anthropologie de la Reproduction" [The nature of motherhood: for an anthropology of reproduction]. *Journal des Anthropologues* 88–89: 103–22.

Fitzgerald, Cheryl, Alison E. Zimon, and Ervin E. Jones. 1998. "Aging and Reproductive Potential in Women." *Yale Journal of Biology and Medicine* 71(5): 367–81.

Friese, Carrie, Gay Becker, and Robert D. Nachtigall. 2006. "Rethinking the Biological Clock: Eleventh-Hour Moms, Miracle Moms and Meanings of Age-related Infertility." *Social Science Medicine* 63(6): 1550–60.

———. 2008. "Older Motherhood and the Changing Life Course in the Era of Assisted Reproductive Technologies." *Journal of Aging Studies* 22(1): 65–73.

Giddens, Anthony. 2004. *La Transformation de l'Intimité: Sexualité, Amour et Érotisme dans les Sociétés Modernes* [The transformation of intimacy: sexuality, love and eroticism in modern societies]. Le Rouergue: Chambon.

Gonzalez, Maria-José, and Teresa Jurado-Guerrero. 2006. "Remaining Childless in Affluent Economies: A Comparison of France, West Germany, Italy and Spain, 1994–2001." *European Journal of Population* 22: 317–52.

Guillaumin, Colette. 1992. *Sexe, Race et Pratique du Pouvoir: L'Idée de Nature* [Gender, race and power practice: the idea of nature]. Paris: Côté-femmes.

Inhorn, Marcia C. 2017. "The Egg Freezing Revolution? Gender, Technology, and Fertility Preservation in the Twenty-First Century." In *Emerging Trends in the Social and Behavioral Sciences*, ed. Robert Scott and Marlis Buchmann, 1–14. New York: Wiley.

Inhorn, Marcia C., and Daphna Birenbaum-Carmeli. 2008. "Assisted Reproductive Technologies and Culture Change." *Annual Review of Anthropology* 37: 177–96.

Löwy, Ilana. 2009. "L'Âge Limite de la Maternité: Corps, Biomedicine et Politique" [The age limit for maternity: body, biomedicine and politics]. *Mouvements* 59: 102–12.

Martin, Emily. 1987. *The Woman in the Body: A Cultural Analysis of Reproduction.* Boston: Beacon Press.

Mathieu, Nicole-Claude. 1973. "Homme-culture et Femme-nature?" [Male-culture and female-nature?]. *L'Homme* 13(3): 101–13.

Mazuy, Magali. 2009. "Avoir un Enfant: Être Prêts Ensemble?" [Having a child: being ready together?]. *Revue des Sciences Sociales* 41: 30–41.

Mehl, Dominique. 2011. *Les Lois de l'Enfantement: Procréation et Politique en France (1982–2011)* [The laws of childbirth: reproduction and politics in France (1982–2011)]. Paris: SciencesPo, Les Presses.

Menken, Jane, James Trussel, and Ulla Larsen. 1986. "Age and Infertility." *Science* 233(4771): 1389–94.

Olafsdottir, Helga Sol, Matts Wikland, and Anders Möller. 2011. "Reasoning about Timing of Wanting a Child: A Qualitative Study of Nordic Couples from Fertility Clinics." *Journal of Reproductive and Infant Psychology* 5: 493–505.

Ortner, Sherry B. 1974. "Is Female to Male as Nature Is to Culture?" In *Women, Culture, and Society*, ed. Michele Zimbalist Rosaldo and Louise Lamphere, 68–87. Stanford: Stanford University Press.

Prioux, France. 2005. "Mariage, Vie en Couple et Rupture d'Union" [Marriage, relationship and break-up]. *Informations Sociales* 122(2): 38–50.

Ragoné, Helena. 1996. "Chasing the Blood Tie: Surrogate Mothers, Adoptive Mothers, and Fathers." *American Ethnologist* 23(2): 352–65.

Régnier-Loilier, Arnaud. 2007. *Avoir des Enfants en France: Désirs et Réalités* [To have children in France: desires and realities]. Paris: INED, Collection Cahiers.

Régnier-Loilier, Arnaud, and Anne Solaz. 2010. "La Décision d'Avoir un Enfant: Une Liberté sous Contraintes" [The decision to have a child: a constrained freedom]. *Politiques Sociales et Familiales* 100: 61–77.

Régnier-Loilier, Arnaud, and Danièle Vignoli. 2011. "Intentions de Fécondité et Obstacles à leur Réalisation en France et en Italie" [Fertility intentions and obstacles to their realization in France and Italy]. *Population* 66(2): 401–31.

Rozée, Virginie. 2011. "L'AMP sans Frontière [ART without borders]." *Bulletin Épidémiologique Hebdomadaire* 23–24: 270–73.

Rozée, Virginie, and Laurence Tain. 2010. "Le Recours aux Techniques Procréatives: Des Disparités Nationales aux Circuits Transnationaux" [The use of reproductive technologies: from national disparities to transnational channels]. In *Santé et Mondialisation (Actes du Colloque International du 12–13 Mars 2009)*, ed. Virginie Chasles, 297–314. Université Jean Moulin–Lyon 3.

Sevon, Eija. 2005. "Timing Motherhood: Experiencing and Narrating the Choice to become a Mother." *Feminism and Psychology* 15: 461–82.

Singerman, Diane. 2011. "The Negotiation of Waithood: The Political Economy of Delayed Marriage in Egypt." In *Arab Youth Social Mobilisation in Times of Risk*, ed. Samir Khalaf and Roseanne Saad Khalaf, 85–108. London: Saqi.

Szewczuk, Elizabeth. 2012. "Age-related Infertility: A Tale of Two Technologies." *Sociology of Health and Illness* 34(3): 429–43.

Théry, Irène. 1993. *Le Démariage* [The Unmarriage]. Paris: Odile Jacob.

———. 1998. *Couple, Filiation et Parenté Aujourd'hui, le Droit Face aux Mutations de la Famille et de la Vie Privée* [Couple, filiation and kinship today: law in the face of changes in the family and private life]. Paris: La Documentation française/Odile Jacob.

———. 2011. *Des Humains comme les Autres: Bioéthique, Anonymat et Genre du Don* [Humans like any other: bioethics, anonymity and gender of the gift]. Paris: EHESS.

Thompson, Elizabeth. 1997. "Couple Childbearing Desires, Intentions, and Births." *Demography* 34(3): 343–54.

Vialle, Manon. 2014. "L'Horloge Biologique des Femmes: Un Modèle Naturaliste en Question, Les Normes et Pratiques Françaises Face à la Croissance de l'Infertilité Liée à l'Âge" [Women's "biological clock": a naturalistic model in question, French norms and practices in the face of the growth of age-related infertility]. *Enfances, Familles, Générations* 21: 1–23.

———. 2018. "L'Expériences des Femmes Quadragénaires en AMP: Les Seuils de la Temporalité Procréative, de la Fertilité et de l'Infertilité en Question" [The experiences of forty-year-old women in ART: the thresholds of reproductive temporality, fertility and infertility in question]. *Enfances, Familles, Générations* 29. Retrieved 18 January 2020 from http://journals.openedition.org/efg/2161.

Volant, Sabrina. 2017. "Un Premier Enfant à 28,5 Ans en 2015: 4,5 ans Plus Tard qu'en 1974" [A first child at 28.5 years old in 2015: 4.5 years later than in 1974]. *Insee Première* 1642. Retrieved 18 January 2020 from https://www.insee.fr/fr/statistiques/2668280.

Weber, Florence. 2013. *Penser la Parenté Aujourd'hui* [Thinking about kinship today]. Paris: Éditions Rue d'Ulm.

Chapter 14

WAITING TOO LONG TO MOTHER

INVOLUNTARY CHILDLESSNESS AND ASSISTED REPRODUCTION IN CONTEMPORARY SPAIN

Beatriz San Román

Introduction

In March 2012, then-Spanish Minister of Justice Alberto Ruiz-Gallardón proposed a restrictive reform of the current abortion law (approved in 2010), which was intended to eliminate the voluntary termination of pregnancy during the first trimester and limit the right to abortion to cases of rape or serious danger to the woman's health. In the Chamber of Deputies, Ruiz-Gallardón declared that the new law aimed "to increase the protection of [a] woman's right par excellence: the right to motherhood" (Espinosa 2012). Answering a question from a socialist deputy about whether his government maintained its intention to "cut back women's sexual and reproductive rights," the minister stated that motherhood "is what makes women authentically women" (Martín 2012). His assertions were met with strong opposition, from even inside his own political party, the Partido Popular (Manetto 2014). Eventually, he was forced to resign, and the law proposal was withdrawn, even though the Partido Popular had absolute majority. Despite the fact that Ruiz-

Gallardón's words sounded old-fashioned, they resounded repeatedly in my conversations with women facing involuntary childlessness. His assertions can be read as an update of Franco's dictatorship
discourse, which confined women to the domestic sphere by exalt-
ing and imposing the mother's role. What was considered a duty
in the past was now presented as a right. In both cases, the underlying idea is that a woman is not complete (is not "authentically a
woman") without motherhood.

Other works in this volume point out the delay in the age people get married (Adely, Chapter 11; Masquelier, Chapter 3; Mc-
Lean, Chapter 5; Smith-Hefner, Chapter 8) and the postponement
of motherhood (Berry, Chapter 4; Vialle, Chapter 13) as significant
elements of what has been referred to as "waithood" (Singerman
2007), which is understood as a liminal status of those who are
no longer adolescents but have not reached adulthood or, at least,
achieved the markers of adulthood. In contemporary Spain, despite
a 10 percent rise in its population, the number of marriages has decreased by 20 percent in the last two decades and 47 percent of all
births take place outside marriage (INE 2019). Therefore, getting
married is no longer considered the gateway to adulthood (Benedicto 2016; Imaz 2001). On the other hand, following the arrival of
democracy in 1975, motherhood seems to have changed from an
inescapable fate to a choice, while the postponement of childbearing has led to a large number of involuntarily childless women. To
become mothers, many of these women resort to the use of eggs
provided by other women, usually younger women who choose
to "donate" the eggs to earn money, despite the associated inva-
sive procedures and health issues (Marre, San Román, and Guerra
2018; San Román, Guerra and Marre, forthcoming). Their stories
reveal how the social mandate of motherhood and the precarious-
ness faced by a significant portion of Spanish youth who struggle to
become independent adults close a circle of needs, constraints, and
violence against female bodies and lives. In both cases, though, the
individual and social narratives usually revolve around choice and
decision.

Since the 1990s, the anthropology of kinship has produced a significant body of literature revolving around the idea that choice
and desire were central in contemporary kinship. In fact, a number
of works—such as those by Jane Mattes (1994), John A. Robertson (1994), Rickie Solinger (2001), and Kath Weston (1997)—used
the notion of choice in their titles. As Joan Bestard (2009) notes, it
seemed that the desire for parenthood was the constituent element

of filiation in contemporary kinship, at least in developed countries. Other works analyzed how the politics of reproduction in contemporary societies has led to the stratification of reproduction, where both children and cells (particularly eggs) circulate between countries and classes (Inhorn 2015; Inhorn and Patrizio 2009; Nahman 2006; Whittaker and Speier 2010), and where women's reproductive choices are constrained by intersecting factors such as gender, race, and class (Briggs 2012; Pande 2011; Thompson 2005). In this context, while adoption can be read as "a national and international system whereby the children of impoverished or otherwise disenfranchised mothers are transferred to middle-class, wealthy mothers (and fathers)" (Briggs 2012: 4), the use of assisted reproductive technologies (ARTs) has been seen as an option restricted to global elites (Inhorn and Birenbaum-Carmeli 2008). Thus, a central concern of the research on different forms of third-party reproduction has been the power asymmetries that privilege some reproductive desires and choices while denigrating others (Ginsburg and Rapp 1995; Inhorn and Birenbaum-Carmeli 2008).

A notable number of works focus on the constraints and limitations that shape women's reproductive decisions (and desires) and how norms, beliefs, and ideologies model both desires and choices (see Bennett and Kok 2018; Hochschild 1990; Mishtal 2014). Drawing on Michel Foucault's ([1976] 1990) conceptualization of governance through biopower, Lynn Morgan and Elizabeth Roberts (2012) developed the notion of "reproductive governance." They highlight how the

> different historical configurations of actors—such as state, religious, and international financial institutions, NGOs, and social movements—use legislative controls, economic inducements, moral injunctions, direct coercion, and ethical incitements to produce, monitor, and control reproductive behaviors and population practices. (Morgan and Roberts 2012: 243)

This chapter analyzes the tensions between the notions of duty and choice with respect to women's reproductive choices in contemporary Spain. To do so, it first presents an overview of the changes affecting women's lives (and their reproductive decisions) with the arrival of democracy in 1975 and then the reproduction strategies they employ when struggling with fertility issues. The results of the Fertility Survey by the Spanish National Institute of Statistics (INE 2018a)—the largest study on the issue in the last two decades—are then examined, with special attention to the results that portray the reasons why Spanish women decide not to have children or to delay childbearing. Finally, drawing upon the fieldwork carried out on ART at different times between 2014 and 2018, this chapter analyzes the experiences and narratives of infertile women. The results point out that, even if the Spanish feminist movement aimed to legitimize (and even promote) the option of not having children as a means for women's emancipation (Alborch 1999), many women feel that they are not "complete" without motherhood. This development might indicate that motherhood is still a marker of adulthood since childlessness impedes the "achievement of full adult personhood" (Inhorn 2015: 1). However, today motherhood is not outlined as a duty, but as a desire whose non-fulfillment incites guilt and extreme distress. As Byung-Chul Han ([2014] 2017: 1) notices, "the freedom of *Can* generates even more coercion than the disciplinarian *Should*." In fact, most women participating in the study waited to become mothers not because of material constraints. Their narratives suggest that delaying childbearing was not an inevitable outcome, but a personal choice fueled by the belief that they could procreate later, after doing other things that they also wanted to do (such as travelling or "enjoying life"). Theirs was what I call a "*waithood choice*"—one that did not prevent them from feeling completely adult. However, when they finally decided it was "the right time," they found out that as time had passed, their opportunities to reproduce "naturally" had diminished.

Methodology

The quantitative data used in this chapter come from the most recent edition of the Fertility Survey (there were three previous surveys, in 1977, 1985 and 1999), published by the Spanish National Statistics Institute (INE) at the end of 2018. The study used a random stratified sampling to select 14,446 women (ages eighteen to fifty-five) who completed a questionnaire during the first half of 2018. The survey's objective was "to identify the determinants of current and recent fertility" (INE 2018c: 5).

Qualitative data come from fieldwork conducted between 2016 and 2018. It included twenty months of participant observation in fertility clinics in Barcelona (one day a week) where I was allowed to attend first visits and counseling sessions with those patients who accepted and signed an informed consent form to be part of the research. In addition, interviews with forty women who were using or had used ART to achieve a pregnancy—recruited at clinics, in an association of intended parents via surrogacy, and through a snowball technique—were conducted. Thirty-three patients had stable partners who were also involved in their efforts to become parents. In approximately half of these cases, their partners were also present and participated in the interviews, which were conducted in Spanish or Catalan, according to the paticipants' preference. (All quotes used in this chapter have been translated into English.) To ensure anonymity, pseudonyms have been used for all participants.

The Decline of Fertility in Spain after the Dictatorship

The Franco regime (1939–75) implied a huge setback in the rights of women in Spain. According to National Catholicism—the regime's ideological base—women were the moral foundation of the Spanish family and were expected to dedicate their lives to their family's care and well-being. The reform of the education system in 1938 made compulsory for females what were called "home subjects" (*materias del hogar*), which included cooking, home economics, and needlework (Agulló Díaz 1999). Women's confinement to the private space of the home was driven by a legal system that not only encouraged them (through a state dowry) to quit the labor market once married but also forbade their access to most higher public administration jobs, such as judge, prosecutor, diplomat, property registrar, notary, and labor inspector (De Riquer 2010). Women lost most of their rights in the public sphere and became subordinate to their husbands, who signed contracts on their behalf and administered their savings. Even during late Francoism (1960–75), when important economic and social changes took place and there was an increasing need to incorporate women into the labor force, they still required the authorization of their husbands to be employed.

In 1975, Franco died. Despite the gender-based inequities that remain, the arrival of democracy opened up new horizons for Spanish women. Contraception was legalized in 1978 and divorce in 1981. In 1982, the Socialist Party won the national elections for the first time, and it was under President Felipe González's mandate that abortion was decriminalized (1985) and the first law on ART was approved in 1988. In 1976, women represented 36 percent of university students; by 1997, they already accounted for 53 percent (López de la Cruz 2002). During that period (1976–97), the number of men studying at the post-secondary level doubled and the number of female students quadrupled, while the rate of women in formal employment rose from 28 percent to 35 percent.

As the participation of women in the labor market and the public sphere increased, natality and fertility indexes experienced a notable fall. In 1975, the Spanish total fertility rate (TFR) was one of the highest in Europe at 2.8 children/woman; by 1993, it was 1.3. Thus, Spain had shifted from being among those European countries with the highest rates of fertility to being, along with Italy, the first European country to reach what Hans-Peter Kohler, Francesco C. Billari, and José Antonio Ortega (2002) called "lowest low fertility levels"— that is, TFR at or below 1.3, far below replacement rate. From that point on, the Spanish TFR has remained extremely low, peaking at 1.4 in the period 2006–10 (INE 2018a). With these figures, the sharp decrease in Spanish natality could be read as a waning desire for children. However, Spain also has one of the largest "child gaps"— the average difference between the desired and actual number of children—in the European Union (Bernardi 2005).

This scarcity of children has been related to delayed childbearing (Delgado, Zamora López, and Barrios 2006; Kohler et al. 2002), as is the case in other contexts since the 1970s, particularly in the United States, Europe, East/Southeast Asia, and the Middle East (Anderson and Kohler 2013; Budds, Locke, and Burr 2013; Frejka, Jones, and Sardon 2010; Romeu Gordo 2009; Singerman 2007). While Spanish mothers' mean age at first birth was 25.2 years in 1975, it was already 28.4 in 1995 and reached 30.1 in 2017 (INE 2018b), which makes it one of the highest in Europe (Eurostat 2016). In addition to more widely available contraception and educational opportunities, other factors have been highlighted as contributing to the postponement of motherhood and the increase in the use of ART in Spain, such as unfavorable working hours, low wages, job instability, lack of effective policies to support working mothers, and men's limited participation in family and domestic work (Alvarez 2017, Comas d'Argemir, Marre, and San Román 2016; Marre et al. 2018).

"Outsourcing Reproduction": From Transnational Adoption to Egg "Donation"

Since the 1990s, other ways of constituting a family after a certain age have become possible in Spain, not only because of the development of ART, but also as a consequence of social and economic inequalities that provide gamete "donors"[1] and surrogates, as well as children through transnational adoption (Briggs and Marre 2009; Downie and Baylis 2013; Fonseca, Marre, and San Román 2015; Marre et al. 2018; Pande 2014). Following the sharp decrease in birth rates at the end of the twentieth century, Spain went from being a place where foreign couples came to adopt a child to being one of the main adoption receiving countries in the world. By 2004, Spain became the second country (only behind the United States) in the number of children adopted abroad (Selman 2009). Until the end of the twentieth century, adoption was a last resort for Spanish couples unable to procreate (Berástegui 2010), an embarrassing fact that became a taboo surrounded by secrecy (García Villaluenga and Linacero de la Fuente 2006). The spectacular growth of transnational adoptions (most of which were also transracial) entailed a visibility of adoption and a substantial change in its social consideration. A family with an adopted child became a desirable and normative family, as well as a visible sign of the great humanity of the adoptive parents (Berástegui 2010).

In 2004, transnational adoption reached its peak, both in Spain and at the global level. During the following years, though, it experienced a sharp decline, mainly attributed to the scarcity of young healthy children to be adopted in those countries that had been the main "sources" in previous years (IRC/ISS 2014; Selman 2012). At the same time, the use of third-party oocytes in assisted reproduction treatments increased dramatically. According to the official statistics of the Catalan Government (Catalonia is the only region in Spain that gathers complete data on the subject), transfers with donated ova grew 772 percent between 2003 and 2013 (Servei d'Informació i Estudis 2007, 2017). In the same period, the number of children arriving in Spain annually via transnational adoption decreased by 70 percent.

According to the European Society for Human Reproduction and Embryology (ESHRE), at the present time Spain is, by far, the European country where the most fertility treatments take place, including more than 100,000 in vitro fertilization (IVF) cycles in 2014 (ESHRE 2018). Even if we did not consider the 8.5 percent of treatments that correspond to foreign residents (ESHRE 2017), Spain would be still ahead of the second country, France with 90,000 cycles (ESHRE 2018). Despite the substantial differences among the Spanish regions, the fact that more than 5 percent of all children in Catalonia in 2014 were born through ART (Servei d'Informació i Estudis 2017) gives us a sense of the growing numbers. More than half the transfers in Catalonia use donated eggs, which is related to

346 Beatriz San Román

the age of the recipients: 82 percent are more than thirty-four years old and 50 percent are more than thirty-nine years old (Servei d'Informació i Estudis 2017), statistics that highlight the effects of the postponement of motherhood.

The popularity of egg donation in Spain is also related to its legal frame, which is one of the most inclusive in Europe. Any woman, regardless of her marital status or sexual orientation, is allowed to use ART, and lesbian couples have access to the Reception of Oocytes from the Partner, which has become very popular in recent years. Although public health services include both artificial insemination and IVF for women younger than forty, most of them end up in a private clinic. The long waits to receive treatment through the public service vary from region to region, but in many cases are more than two years. Furthermore, according to the principle of affording every woman at least one chance, if the first cycle is not successful, she is once again placed at the end of the list.

The Fertility Survey: Reasons for Childlessness and the ART Turn

According to the data gathered by the Spanish National Institute of Statistics, the percentage of childless Spanish women has increased by 8 percent in less than twenty years. The difference is especially notable for those older than thirty (see Figure 14.1), which reflects the delay in the age Spanish women bear children. Those who continue studying after finishing mandatory education are more likely not to have children. The childlessness rate of those who went for vocational education and those who accessed higher education is very similar: 43 percent and 46 percent respectively versus 23 percent of those who did not continue studying. The income level also seems relevant: 50 percent of all women with no income are childless, in contrast with only 26 percent of those earning between 2,000 and 3,000 euros per month. However, the percentage of childless women who earn more than 3,000 euros increases to 32 percent.

Following the publication of the Fertility Survey, the media echoed the press release (INE 2018c) that highlighted both the fact that a majority of Spanish women desire two or more children, and the increase in the use of ART (Martín Plaza 2018; Sosa Troya 2018). Given that the high cost of ART is only accessible for a certain segment of the population, the figures are particularly striking: in the

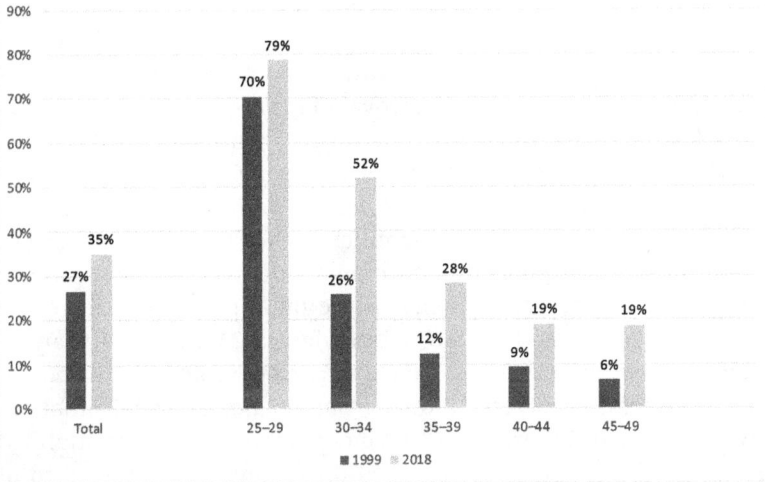

FIGURE 14.1. Spanish Childless Women by Age in 1999 and 2018. Based on data provided by the Spanish National Institute of Statistics (Instituto Nacional de Estadística).

two clinics where I conducted fieldwork, one round of IVF costs approximately 5,000 euros, which is a notable amount in a country where the median annual salary is 19,432 euros and 46 percent of all salaries are below 18,345 euros (Calvo 2018). As shown in Figure 14.2, the percentage of women who reported having undergone or who were undergoing fertility treatments ranges from 0.8 per-

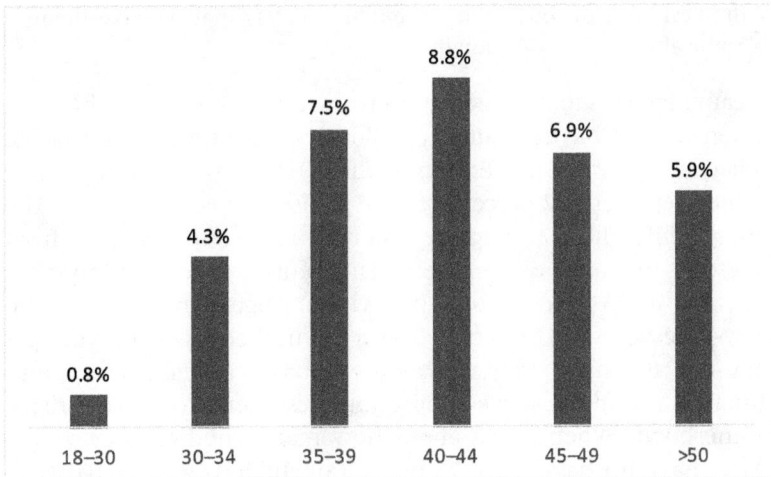

FIGURE 14.2. Spanish Women's Use of ART by Age. Based on data provided by the Spanish National Institute of Statistics (Instituto Nacional de Estadística).

cent of those younger than thirty years old to 8.8 percent for those aged forty to forty-four. According to a psychologist working in a fertility clinic in Barcelona, the latter percentage can only be explained by the impact of the approval of same-sex marriage in 2005 (Law 13/2005): "Nowadays no lesbian goes without a child."

While the increase of lesbian couples using ART to become parents is well known in the Spanish fertility industry, the percentage among wealthy women may be much higher than the 8.8 percent found in the survey for the entire population (neither income nor class were included as variables in the published results in regard to ART treatments). In 2018, I interviewed Marta, a 39-year-old woman, who was expecting a child after undergoing IVF. Although I never asked her directly about income or her financial situation, several pieces of information that emerged in our conversation led me to think she came from a well-off family: she had studied at an expensive private school; her father, her uncle, and one of her brothers were doctors; and I became aware that she was going to New York to go Christmas shopping during an exchange of mails to set up an appointment. At some point during the interview she told me:

> I have become a fertility expert [laugh]. It is not only our own process . . . I had a group of six friends . . . We have been very close since school, and we meet at least once a month for lunch. Four of them have already had their children through IVF, and another one is now thinking about it. And then there is Laura. She says she will become the best aunt for our children, but she prefers that we take them home after a while [laughing].

Laura belongs to the category of women who assert that the main reason for not having had any children is that they do not desire to become mothers. According to the 2018 Fertility Survey, these women represent 12 percent of the Spanish female population. The notable differences among the different age groups (ranging from 8 percent for those women between twenty-five and twenty-nine years old to 23 percent for those who are between forty-five and forty-nine years old) might reflect a cultural change (the younger they are, the more they see motherhood as a desirable option). Other data from the survey point out a resurgence of the desire for motherhood. When asked about how many children they would like to have (or have had), 75 percent of childless women between the ages of thirty-five and thirty-nine declared at least one. The percentage drops as age increases: only 59 percent of those between the ages of forty and forty-four, and 54 percent of those between the ages of forty-five and forty-nine wished that they had had at least one child. But, as Bernardi, Mynarska, and Rossier (2015) pointed out regarding pregnancy intentions, it could also be the case that childlessness is explained differently "before" (when there is still time to change one's mind) than "after" (when you realize that it might be too late).

The Fertility Survey asked childless women for their main reason for not having children. This specific question provides interesting information about the postponement of motherhood, even if the quantitative data do not show a clearly predominant cause. For one out of five women, between the ages of thirty-five and forty-nine, the main reason for childlessness was not having found the right partner. A similar proportion of women over the age of forty selected the option, "I do not want to become a mother," which was only chosen by 9 percent of women between the ages of thirty and thirty-four (and 13 percent in the range of women between the ages of thirty-five and thirty-nine). Contrasting with much of the literature on the issue, structural factors do not show a much higher weight: while in previous edition of the survey in 1999, 31 percent of women said that they had had fewer children than desired due to financial reasons,[2] in 2018 only 9 percent chose this reason (and an additional 10.7 percent referred to difficulties in life-work balance). However, specifically for those in the ranges between thirty and thirty-four and between thirty-five and thirty-nine, the combination of financial reasons and work-life balance increases to 35 percent and 28 percent, respectively. One possible explanation for this is the global financial crisis that started in 2008, at a time when it might have deterred women from childbearing.

The figures also suggest that nearly nine out of ten childless women in their thirties would like to have offspring but have not due to different reasons. According to the quantitative data of the Fertility Survey, the reasons appear to be heterogeneous. Thus, only one of the options given as the "main reason" for childlessness, that of "not having had the right partner," reached more than 20 percent, with 20 percent of those between the ages of thirty and thirty-four and 22 percent of those between the ages of thirty-five and thirty-nine selecting it. It could also be the case that the questionnaire design failed to account for social and lifestyle changes and that more qualitative research is needed to understand the phenomenon.

Women in ART Treatments

Motherhood: A (Postponed) Desire

As contraception allowed women to gain control over their bodies
and their reproductive capacities, having a child has shifted from a
phenomenon intrinsic to a woman's lifecycle to a deliberate decision
(Del Fresno García 2011). In her research with working mothers,
Alvarez (2017) suggested that there are two main approaches to this
issue: for some women, especially those living in rural areas, becoming a parent is simply what follows marriage; for others, becoming a
parent is related to a lifestyle option, something upon which women
decide either on their own or as part of a couple.

In most interviews with women undergoing fertility treatments,
motherhood did not appear to be a conscious choice. Women stated
they "have always wanted to become mothers," so that the decision
was about timing. While waiting for the right partner to embark on
parenthood together emerged as a theme with five out of seven participants facing motherhood alone, it was not the case for those with
stable relationships. The latter referred to "the right time," with only
a few cases having to do with what Vialle (Chapter 13, this volume)
calls "material readiness." This was the case of Marta, a 39-year-old
graphic designer married to a lawyer:

> We have been living together for nine years now. Five years ago, we
> decided to get married. It's not that it was very important [to be mar-
> ried] for him... and it was not either for me, but I wanted to have a
> wedding party. I love weddings! . . . We talked about having kids at
> the beginning of our relationship. Both of us come from large fami-
> lies, and we agreed we would have children someday. But it was not
> until we bought a house that we started to seriously think about it. I
> think . . . it was probably related to having certain stability, in terms
> of jobs and so on.

In most cases, "the right time" was in relation to other factors,
such as traveling or "enjoying life." As Jennifer S. Barber (2001)
pointed out, these "competing alternatives" may be more explica-
tive of reproductive behavior (and the postponement of motherhood) than attitudes toward childbearing. Sofia, who works in the
financial department of a multinational company, expressed:

> Both Carlos [her husband] and I were sure we wanted to have a family
> [*tener familia*], but we were not in a hurry. We both enjoy traveling and
> have been to many, many places, from New York to New Delhi. And
> when we decided the time had come and we got down to it . . . noth-

ing, no . . . We had tests done, and they told us everything was fine . . . but nothing. And then we started with the treatments. [I asked, "How old were you then?"] I was thirty-eight, and Carlos was forty-three.

These kinds of "hedonist" motivations to delay childbearing did not appear as answer options in the Fertility Survey, but they seem to have been better identified by those marketing experts working to promote egg freezing (Inhorn, Chapter 15). In 2018, a fertility clinic located in Barcelona launched an advertising campaign that points in this direction. It showed two contrasting images: a presumably attractive stereotypical "bad boy" and a sweet little baby. The text reads, "Fall in love one thousand times . . . before falling in love forever." Another piece from the same campaign depicts two different images: a young woman wearing jeans, sneakers, and sunglasses, pushing a luggage trolley facing another young woman wearing a dress and high heels, pushing a baby carriage. The text reads, "Go around the world . . . before you start the biggest journey of your life."

Other works in different contexts note the impact of economic uncertainties in the postponement of motherhood (Adsera 2005; Sobotka, Skirbekk, and Philipov 2011). For most of those women in ART treatments, this does not seem to be a determining factor. They express motherhood as a desire ("I desperately want to become a mother"; "we wanted to have a family") that they postponed mainly because they were doing other things they also wanted to do. But as shown in the next section, when faced with infertility, these women feel guilty, which suggests that motherhood remains a priority in order to feel complete.

The Infertility Shock

Struggling to become pregnant is not only a common experience among women who decide to reproduce in their late thirties or early forties but also an unexpected one. For most of the women I interviewed, knowing that they would not achieve pregnancy with their own eggs was a surprising disappointment. Ironically, the achievements of ART (and their reflection in late motherhoods of celebrities in the media) contributed to this disappointment. Marta, forty-one years old, had already been through three IVF cycles when her doctor told her it was pointless to try another one unless they used donor eggs:

It was a real shock. I never thought I could not . . . I mean, I feel young; I am young. I had seen Ana Rosa Quintana [a television host who gave birth in her late forties] and her twins . . . I never thought I wouldn't be able to have my *own children*. I feel so guilty. ["Guilty?" I asked]. Yes, guilty, for having waited for so long . . . and for not being able to give my parents a grandchild.

Both the guilt and the "shock" (of learning that their eggs are unable to produce children) were present in many interviews. On one hand, these women feel guilty for "being late" and, in some cases, for failing to transmit the family lineage—which, according to the classic Euro-American paradigm, is related to genetics (Schneider 1980). On the other hand, according to their narratives, nobody had ever told them that conceiving with their own genetic material would become more and more difficult as years passed. Carolina, forty years old, commented on this by referring to interactions with her gynecologist: "I had my ovarian reserve checked every year, and my doctor always told me that I had time, that there was nothing to worry about."

Feeling or being young was a recurring subject in interviews with women in ART treatments (see also Vialle, Chapter 13), as was the sorrow related both to the grief for not having a genetic child and the repeated failures to achieve a pregnancy. Anna, thirty-seven years old, explained to the psychologist in the fertility clinic her feelings after the third unsuccessful embryo transfer:

> I am more . . . irritable, but above all, I am sad. I found myself crying nearly every day. It is difficult to concentrate on anything else; my mind always goes back to the treatments . . . I have problems falling asleep. I go to bed and I start thinking, "Why me? What if it doesn't work?" I think I can't imagine myself not as a mother.

While doing fieldwork in one of the clinics, I met Carla, twenty-nine years old, with whom I had worked in the past. She explained that she had decided to "freeze" her eggs and, during the process of doing so, discovered that her ovaries were unable to produce viable oocytes. As a result, she had been on medical leave for depression for six weeks. Her narrative encompassed the void and feeling of incompleteness I encountered in many other women struggling with infertility. For her, as for many others, being unable to conceive is experienced as an invisible disability (Clark, Martin-Matthews, and Matthews 2008; Inhorn 2015; Miall 1985). As Carla said:

> I am still on medical leave, and I can't even think of getting back to work. It's hard even to leave the bed in the morning . . . My girlfriends call me to go out, but . . . how could I? . . . I feel I am less than any other woman. If I go out, and I meet a man I like, I have to tell

him I can't have children. Nobody would want to be with me. I can't have children. I am . . . defective.

Anna's and Carla's reflections reinforce the idea that "reproductive disappointments" (Bennett and de Kok 2018) seem to convert what previously was a non-urgent desire into a source of extreme distress and even a threat to one's sense of self. The widespread access to contraception and the broader opportunities of women in the public sphere—both in terms of work or professional careers and consumption—made delaying childbearing seem like a rational choice. However, without accurate knowledge about the lifespan of women's fertility, this waithood choice can result in unexpected fertility struggles. Most participants were unaware of the likelihood of these potential struggles; information about infertility related to age has only recently started to appear in mass media through its link to a new service: oocyte vitrification, or egg freezing (Armora 2018; García 2018; Vázquez Lodeiro 2018). Moreover, after delaying motherhood, most of these women are unable to utilize ART due to financial constraints, and they will probably remain childless against their will.

Conclusion

Following the arrival of democracy and the availability of contraception, birth control became a default option in Spain, as in other "advanced societies" (Balbo, Billari, and Mills 2013: 1). These developments facilitated what is called "the emergence of a culture of childlessness" (Bernardi et al. 2015: 132), where childbearing becomes a choice based on notions of personal fulfillment. In the Spanish context, in the last decades of the twentieth century, the feminist movement did its best to dissociate motherhood from womanhood (Alborch 1999; Valiente 2003). Nonetheless, most Spanish women still want to bear children. What has changed, as noticed by Bernardi et al. (2015), is the way they explain their desire or intention to have offspring. What in the past was simply considered a *natural* progression into adulthood, "a normative rite of passage" (Del Fresno García 2011), is now explained in terms of choice and desire.

In other European countries, such as Poland (Mynarska 2010) and France (Letablier 2013), the dominant "moral regimes" (Morgan and Roberts 2012) reinforce parenthood as inevitable and intrinsic to adulthood. In Spain, while it is politically incorrect to express that women should become mothers, the failure to achieve a pregnancy is accompanied by strong distress and a sense of incompleteness. Thus, motherhood can be seen as an example of the new mechanisms developed by power in neoliberalism, where "achievement-subjects" have replaced "obedience-subjects" (Han [2010] 2015: 8) and where the control of the psyche has replaced the control of the body (Han [2014] 2017). In what Han calls societies of burnout, "prohibitions, commandments, and the law are replaced by projects, initiatives, and motivation" (Han [2010] 2015: 9), resulting in "a more efficient kind of subjectivation and subjugation" (Han [2014] 2017: 1). Thus, those women who fail to achieve the pregnancy they desire see themselves as responsible and feel guilty, instead of questioning a system that led them to postpone childbearing.

According to the narratives of those women using ART at a later age, postponing childbearing was not the product of structural constraints, but a "waithood choice." This choice seems to then be the answer to the combination of cultural expectations of what Hays called "ideology of intensive mothering"—according to which motherhood is "child-centered, expert-guided, emotionally absorbing, labor intensive, and financially expensive" (Hays 1996: 8)—and the contemporary belief that being a mother is one of the most fulfilling stages of a woman's life course (Faircloth 2013). Delaying motherhood is thought to allow women to have it all: a childless stage where they can achieve other goals, followed by a meaningful experience of motherhood. While quantitative studies, such as the Spanish Fertility Survey, consider important structural factors, such as labor market conditions, they fail to reflect this "waithood choice." In order to understand these fertility rates, and also the phenomenon of involuntary childlessness more fully, these types of studies would benefit from increased qualitative research.

Acknowledgments

This research was funded by MINECO/FEDER, UE through the R+D Project CSO2015-64551-C3-1-R, *From Birth Control to Demographic Anxiety: Disclosure, Secrecy and Anonymity in the Reproductive Technologies of XXI Century.*

Beatriz San Román is Lecturer at the Department of Social Psychology at the Autonomous University of Barcelona. Her research interests include issues of choice, justice, and power relations in situations of third-party assisted reproduction technologies, as well as family diversity, family relations, and children's rights. San Román is the author of several articles, chapters, and books, as well as co-director of *AFIN Magazine*. Currently, she is the coordinator of BRIGHTER FUTURE, a European project focused on the school inclusion of children in foster or adoptive care.

Notes

1. The use of the word "donors" to name egg providers in assisted reproduction techniques is controversial among feminist scholars (Beeson, Darnovsky, and Lippman 2015; Deomampo 2016; Downie and Baylis 2013; Nahman 2008). Considering the provision of eggs as a gift rather than a form of labor "is often simply a way to expropriate donors and deny them rights over their bodily material" (Waldby and Cooper 2008: 67). Nevertheless, this text uses "egg donors" and "donation" for expositive clarity and because these are the terms used in the Spanish legal and social context.
2. Both the questionnaire and the sample design varied from one edition to another. The first notable difference is the age of the respondents: while in 1999 the survey was addressed to women between the ages of fifteen and forty-nine, the last edition chose to interview those between the ages of eighteen and fifty-five. This change acknowledges the extension of women's fertility life.

References

Adsera, Alicia. 2005. "Vanishing Children: From High Unemployment to Low Fertility in Developed Countries." *American Economic Review* 95(2): 189–93.

Agulló Díaz, María del Carmen. 1999. "Azul y Rosa: Franquismo y Educación Femenina" [Blue and pink: Francoism and female education]. In *Estudios sobre la política educativa durante el franquismo*, ed. A. Mayordomo, 264–65. Valencia: Valencia University.

Alborch, Carmen. 1999. *Solas*. Barcelona: Planeta.

Alvarez, Bruna. 2017. "Las (Ir)racionalidades de la Maternidad en España: Influencias del Mercado Laboral y las Relaciones de Género en las Decisiones Reproductivas" [(Ir)rationalities of motherhood in Spain: Influences of the labor market and gender relations in reproductive decisions]. PhD dissertation. Barcelona, Spain: Autonomous University of Barcelona.

Anderson, Thomas, and Hans-Peter Kohler. 2013. "Education Fever and the East Asian Fertility Puzzle: A Case Study of Low Fertility in South Korea." *Asian Population Studies* 9(2): 196–215.

Armora, Esther. 2018. "Cuarenta Años del Primer 'Bebé Probeta' del Mundo: Del Debate Científico al Ético" [Forty years of the world's first "test tube baby": From the scientific debate to the ethical one]. *ABC*, 15 July.

Balbo, Nicoletta, Francesco C. Billari, and Melinda Mills. 2013. "Fertility in Advanced Societies: A Review of Research." *European Journal of Population* 29(1): 1–38.

Barber, Jennifer S. 2001. "Ideational Influences on the Transition to Parenthood: Attitudes toward Childbearing and Competing Alternatives." *Social Psychology Quarterly* 64(2): 101–27.

Beeson, Diane, Marcy Darnovsky, and Abby Lippman. 2015. "What's in a Name? Variations in Terminology of Third-Party Reproduction." *Reproductive Biomedicine Online* 31(6): 805–14.

Benedicto, Jorge, dir. 2016. *Informe Juventud en España 2016* [Youth in Spain Report 2016]. Madrid: Instituto de la Juventud.

Bennett, Linda Rae, and Bregje de Kok. 2018. "Reproductive Desires and Disappointments." *Medical Anthropology* 37(2): 91–100.

Berástegui, Ana. 2010. "Adopción Internacional: Solidaridad con la Infancia o Reproducción Asistida?" [International adoption: solidarity with children or assisted reproduction?]. *Aloma, Revista de Psicologia, Ciències de l'Educació i de l'Esport* 27: 15–38.

Bernardi, Fabrizio. 2005. "Public Policies and Low Fertility: Rationales for Public Intervention and a Diagnosis for the Spanish Case." *Journal of European Social Policy* 15(2): 123–38.

Bernardi, Laura, Monika Mynarska, and Clémentine Rossier. 2015. "Uncertain, Changing and Situated Fertility Intentions: A Qualitative Analysis." In *Reproductive Decision-Making in a Macro-Micro Perspective*, ed. Dimiter Philipov, Aart C. Liefbroer, and Jane Klobas, 113–39. New York: Springer.

Bestard, Joan. 2009. "Lo Dado y lo Construido en las Relaciones de Parentesco" [The given and the constructed in kinship relations]. *Revista de Antropología Social* 18: 83–95.

Briggs, Laura. 2012. *Somebody's Children: The Politics of Transracial and Transnational Adoption*. Durham: Duke University Press.

Briggs, Laura, and Diana Marre. 2009. "Introduction: The Circulation of Children." In *International Adoption: Global Inequalities and the Circulation of Children*, ed. Diana Marre and Laura Briggs, 1–19. New York: New York University Press.

Budds, Kirsty, Abigail Locke, and Vivien Burr. 2013. "Risky Business: Constructing the Choice to Delay Motherhood in the British Press." *Feminist Media Studies* 13(1): 132–47.

Calvo, Javier. 2018. "Análisis de los Salarios en España: El Sueldo más Frecuente cae Hasta los 16.497 Euros" [Analysis of wages in Spain: the median salary falls to 16,497 euros]. *Eleconomista.es*, 29 May. Retrieved 24 April 2019 from https://www.eleconomista.es/economia/noticias/91

69491/05/18/Analisis-de-los-salarios-en-Espana-la-remuneracion-mas-frecuente-cae-hasta-los-16497-euros.html.

Clarke, Laura Hurd, Anne Martin-Matthews, and Ralph Matthews. 2008. "The Continuity and Discontinuity of the Embodied Self in Infertility." *Canadian Review of Sociology/Revue Canadienne de Sociologie* 43(1): 95–113.

Comas d'Argemir, Dolors, Diana Marre, and Beatriz San Román. 2016. "La Regulación Política de la Familia: Ideología, Desigualdad y Género en el Plan Integral de Apoyo a la Familia" [The political regulation of the family: ideology, inequality and gender in the Comprehensive Family Support Plan]. *Política y Sociedad* 53(3): 853–77.

Del Fresno García, Miguel. 2011. "Familia y Crisis del Matrimonio en España" [Family and crisis of marriage in Spain]. *Studia Europaea Gnesnensia* 3: 79–94.

Delgado, Margarita, Francisco Zamora López, and Laura Barrios. 2006. "Déficit de Fecundidad en España: Factores Demográficos que Operan Sobre una Tasa muy Inferior al Nivel de Reemplazo" [Fertility deficit in Spain: demographic factors that operate on a rate much lower than the replacement level]. *Revista Española De Investigaciones Sociológicas (REIS)* 115(1): 197–222.

Deomampo, Daisy. 2016. "Race, Nation, and the Production of Intimacy: Transnational Ova Donation in India." *Positions: East Asia Cultures Critique* 24(1): 303–32.

De Riquer, Borja. 2010. *Historia de España (IX): La Dictadura de Franco* [History of Spain (IX): Franco's dictatorship]. Barcelona: Crítica.

Downie, Jocelyn, and Françoise Baylis. 2013. "Transnational Trade in Human Eggs: Law, Policy, and (In)action in Canada." *The Journal of Law, Medicine and Ethics* 41(1): 224–39.

ESHRE (European Society for Human Reproduction and Embryology). 2017. "Cross Border Reproductive Care." *ESHRE Fact Sheets I*, January. Retrieved 4 April 2019 from https://www.eshre.eu/~/media/sitecore-files/Press-room/Resources/1-CBRC.pdf?la=en.

———. 2018. "ART Fact Sheet." ESHRE Press Information, 18 February. Retrieved 4 April 2019 from https://www.eshre.eu/~/media/sitecore-files/Guidelines/ART-fact-sheet_vFebr18_VG.pdf?la=en. Last accessed 28 August 2018.

Espinosa, Juan M. "Gallardón, sobre el Aborto" [Gallardón on abortion]. 2012. *20 Minutes*, 7 March. Retrieved 24 April from https://www.20minutos.es/noticia/1330629/0/gallardon/derecho-mujeres/maternidad.

Eurostat. 2016. "Fertility Statistics: Eurostat Statistics Explained." Retrieved 4 April 2019 from http://ec.europa.eu/eurostat/statistics-explained/index.php/Fertility_statistics.

Faircloth, Charlotte. 2013. *Militant Lactivism? Attachment Parenting and Intensive Motherhood in the UK and France*. New York: Berghahn Books.

Fonseca, Claudia, Diana Marre, and Beatriz San Román. 2015. "Child Circulation in a Globalized Era: Anthropological Reflections." In *The Inter-*

country Adoption Debate: Dialogues Across Disciplines, ed. Robert L. Ballard, Nsomi H. Goodno, Jr., Robert F. Cochran, and Jay A. Milbrandt, 157–93. Newcastle upon Tyne: Cambridge Scholars Publishing.

Foucault, Michel. (1976) 1990. *The History of Sexuality, Vol. 1: An Introduction.* New York: Vintage Books.

Frejka, Tomas, Gavin W. Jones, and Jean-Paul Sardon. 2010. "East Asian Childbearing Patterns and Policy Developments." *Population and Development Review* 36(3): 579–606.

García, Carolina. 2018. "Madre a los 40, Sí, pero Sabiendo a lo que se Enfrenta" [Mother at forty, yes, but knowing what she's up against]. El País, 29 June.

García Villaluenga, Leticia, and María Linacero de la Fuente. 2006. El Derecho del Adoptado a Conocer sus Orígenes en España y en el Derecho Comparado [The right of adoptees to know their origins in Spain and in comparative law]. Madrid: Ministry of Labour, Migrations and Social Security.

Ginsburg, Faye D., and Rayna Rapp. 1995. "Introduction." In *Conceiving the New World Order: The Global Politics of Reproduction*, ed. Faye D. Ginsburg and Rayna Rapp, 1–17. Berkeley: University of California Press.

Han, Byung-Chul. (2010) 2015. *The Burnout Society*. Stanford: Stanford University Press.

———. (2014) 2017. *Psychopolitics: Neoliberalism and New Technologies of Power*. London: Verso.

Hays, Sharon. 1996. *The Cultural Contradictions of Motherhood*. New Haven: Yale University Press.

Hochschild, Arlie Russell. 1990. "Ideology and Emotion Management: A Perspective and Path for Future Research." In *Research Agendas in the Sociology of Emotions*, ed. Theodore D. Kemper, 117–42. Albany: State University of New York Press.

Imaz, Miren Elixabete. 2001. "Mujeres Gestantes, Madres en Gestación: Metáforas de un Cuerpo Fronterizo" [Pregnant women, mothers in gestation: metaphors of a border body]. *Política y Sociedad* 36: 97–112.

INE (Instituto Nacional de Estadística). 2018a. *Encuesta de Fecundidad 2018* [Fertility survey 2018]. Madrid: Instituto Nacional de Estadística. Retrieved 4 April 2019 from https://www.ine.es/dyngs/INEbase/es/operacion.htm?c=Estadistica_C&cid=1254736177006&menu=resultados&idp=1254735573002.

———. 2018b. *Indicadores de Fecundidad* [Fertility indicators]. Retrieved 4 April 2019 from https://www.ine.es/jaxiT3/Tabla.htm?t=1579&L=0.

———. 2018c. *Encuesta de Fecundidad Año 2018. Datos Avance* [Fertility survey 2018 data preview] Madrid: Instituto Nacional de Estadística. Retrieved 4 April 2019 from https://www.ine.es/prensa/ef_2018_a.pdf.

———. 2019. *Demografía y Población: Fenómenos Demográficos* [Demography and population: demographic phenomena]. Retrieved 4 April 2019 from https://www.ine.es/dyngs/INEbase/es/categoria.htm?c=Estadistica_P&cid=1254734710984.

Inhorn, Marcia C. 2015. *Cosmopolitan Conceptions: IVF Sojourns in Global Dubai.* Durham: Duke University Press.

Inhorn, Marcia C., and Daphna Birenbaum-Carmeli. 2008. "Assisted Reproductive Technologies and Culture Change." *Annual Review of Anthropology* 37: 177–96.

Inhorn, Marcia C., and Pasquale Patrizio. 2009. "Rethinking Reproductive 'Tourism' as Reproductive 'Exile.'" *Fertility and Sterility* 92: 904–6.

IRC/ISS (International Reference Center for the Rights of the Children Deprived of their Family/International Social Services). 2014. "2013 Statistics: Few Changes." *Monthly Review* 186: 1–3.

Kohler, Hans-Peter, Francesco C. Billari, and José Antonio Ortega. 2002. "The Emergence of Lowest-Low Fertility in Europe during the 1990s." *Population and Development Review* 284: 641–80.

Letablier, Marie-Thérèse. 2013. "The Politics of Parenting: The Meaning of Children, the Meaning of Work." In *The Social Meaning of Children and Fertility Change in Europe*, ed. by Anne Lisa Ellingsaeter, An-Magritt Jensen, and Merete Lie, 12–30. London: Routledge.

López de la Cruz, Laura. 2002. "La Presencia de la Mujer en la Universidad Española" [The presence of women in Spanish universities]. *Revista Historia de la Educación Latinoamericana* 4: 291–99.

Manetto, Francesco. 2014. "Monago lleva su Rebelión Contra la ley del Aborto al Parlamento Extremeño" [Monago takes his rebellion against the abortion law to the Extremaduran Parliament]. *El País*, 15 January.

Marre, Diana, Beatriz San Román, and Diana Guerra. 2018. "On Reproductive Work in Spain: Transnational Adoption, Egg Donation, Surrogacy." *Medical Anthropology* 37(2): 158–73.

Martín, Patricia. 2012. "Gallardón: 'La Maternidad Hace a la Mujer Auténticamente Mujer'" [Gallardón: "Motherhood makes women authentically women"]. El Periódico, 28 March. Retrieved 24 April from https://www.elperiodico.com/es/sociedad/20120328/gallardon-la-maternidad-hace-a-la-mujer-autenticamente-mujer-1596041.

Martín Plaza, Ana. 2018. "Las Españolas Tienen Menos hijos de los que Desearían por Razones Económicas y por Falta de Conciliación" [Spanish women have fewer children than they would like for economic reasons and lack of conciliation]. 2018. RTVE, 28 November. Retrieved 24 April from http://www.rtve.es/noticias/20181128/mujeres-espanolas-tienen-menos-hijos-desearian-razones-laborales-economicas-conciliacion/1845001.shtml.

Mattes, Jane. 1994. *Single Mothers by Choice.* New York: Times Books.

Miall, Charlene E. 1985. "Perceptions of Informal Sanctioning and the Stigma of Involuntary Childlessness." *Deviant Behavior* 6: 383–403.

Mishtal, Joanna. 2014. "Reproductive Governance in the New Europe: Competing Visions of Morality, Sovereignty and Supranational Policy." *Anthropological Journal of European Cultures* 23(1).

Morgan, Lynn Marie, and Elizabeth F. S. Roberts. 2012. "Reproductive Governance in Latin America." *Anthropology and Medicine* 19(2): 241–54.

Mynarska, Monika. 2010. "Deadline for Parenthood: Fertility Postponement and Age Norms in Poland." *European Journal of Population/Revue Européenne de Démographie* 26(3): 351–73.

Nahman, Michal. 2006. "Materializing Israeliness: Difference and Mixture in Transnational Ova Donation." *Science as Culture* 15: 199–213.

———. 2008. "Nodes of Desire: Romanian Egg Sellers, 'Dignity' and Feminist Alliances in Transnational Ova Exchanges." *European Journal of Women's Studies* 15(2): 65–82.

Pande, Amrita. 2011. "Transnational Commercial Surrogacy in India: Gifts for Global Sisters?" *Reproductive BioMedicine Online* 23(5): 618–25.

———. 2014. *Wombs in Labor: Transnational Commercial Surrogacy in India.* New York: Columbia University Press.

Robertson, John A. 1994. *Children of Choice: Freedom and the New Reproductive Technologies.* Princeton: Princeton University Press.

Romeu Gordo, Laura. 2009. "Why Are Women Delaying Motherhood in Germany?" Feminist Economics 15(4): 57–75.

San Román, Beatriz, Diana Guerra, and Diana Marre. Forthcoming. "Egg Providers in Spain: Sociodemographic Characteristics and Motivations."

Schneider, David M. 1980. *American Kinship: A Cultural Account.* Chicago: University of Chicago Press.

Selman, Peter. 2009. "The Rise and Fall of Intercountry Adoption in the 21st Century." *International Social Work* 52: 575–94.

———. 2012. "The Global Decline of Intercountry Adoption: What Lies Ahead?" *Social Policy and Society* 11(3): 381–97.

Servei d'Informació i Estudis: FIVCAT.NET. 2007. *FIVCAT.NET: Sistema d'Informació Sobre Reproducció Humana Assistida Catalunya 2004* [IVCAT.NET: Information system on assisted human reproduction Catalonia 2004]. Barcelona: Departament de Salut, Generalitat de Catalunya.

———. 2017. Estadística de la Reproducció Humana Assistida a Catalunya 2014 [Statistics of human assisted reproduction in Catalonia]. Barcelona: Departament de Salut, Generalitat de Catalunya.

Singerman, Diane. 2007. "The Economic Imperatives of Marriage: Emerging Practices and Identities Among Youth in the Middle East." *Middle East Youth Initiative*, Working Paper No. 6, September, The Brookings Institution, Wolfensohn Center for Development, Washington, DC.

Sobotka, Tomáš, Vegard Skirbekk, and Dimiter Philipov. 2011. "Economic Recession and Fertility in the Developed World." *Population and Development Review* 37(2): 267–306.

Solinger, Rickie. 2001. *Beggars and Choosers: How the Politics of Choice Shapes Adoption, Abortion, and Welfare in the United States.* New York: Hill and Wang.

Sosa Troya, María. 2018. "Más de la Mitad de Españolas de 45 a 49 Años sin Hijos Habría Querido Tenerlos" [More than half of Spanish women between forty-five and forty-nine years old without children would have liked to have them]. 2018. *El País*, 29 November. Retrieved 24

April from https://elpais.com/sociedad/2018/11/28/actualidad/1543401
111_002007.html.

Thompson, Charis M. 2005. *Making Parents: The Ontological Choreography of Reproductive Technologies*. Cambridge: MIT Press.

Valiente, Celia. 2003. "Central State Child Care Policies in Postauthoritarian Spain: Implications for Gender and Carework Arrangements." *Gender & Society* 17(2): 287–92.

Vázquez Lodeiro, Domingo. 2018. "Congelar Óvulos Antes de los 35 Años Reduce el Riesgo de Necesitar Donante en una Maternidad Tardía" [Freezing eggs before the age of 35 reduces the risk of needing a donor in a late motherhood]. 2018. *Farodevigo*, 3 October. Retrieved 24 April from https://www.farodevigo.es/empresas-en-vigo/2018/10/03/congel ar-ovulos-35-anos-reduce/1973026.html.

Waldby, Catherine, and Melinda Cooper. 2008. "The Biopolitics of Reproduction: Post-Fordist Biotechnology and Women's Clinical Labour." *Australian Feminist Studies* 23(55): 57–73.

Weston, Kath. 1997. *Families We Choose: Lesbians, Gays, Kinship*. New York: Columbia University Press.

Whittaker, Andrea, and Amy Speier. 2010. "'Cycling Overseas': Care, Commodification, and Stratification in Cross-Border Reproductive Travel." *Medical Anthropology* 29(4): 363–83.

Chapter 15

THE EGG FREEZING REVOLUTION?
GENDER, EDUCATION, AND REPRODUCTIVE WAITHOOD IN THE UNITED STATES

Marcia C. Inhorn

Introduction

Around the world today, healthy women of reproductive age are increasingly turning to a technology called oocyte cryopreservation, or egg freezing, as a form of fertility preservation—one that allows their eggs to be successfully stored in egg banks for future use. Egg freezing is being heralded as a "reproductive backstop," a "fertility insurance policy," an "egg savings account," and particularly as a way for thirty-something career women to "rewind the biological clock" (Goold and Savulescu 2009; Hughes 2012; Wyndham, Figueira, and Patrizio 2012). Younger women in their twenties are increasingly being encouraged to consider egg freezing as a way to "put their fertility on hold," "slow down their biological clocks," and "postpone motherhood" in order to have time to achieve their educational and career goals (Lockwood 2011; Shkedi-Rafid and Hashiloni-Dolev 2012). Indeed, the planned postponement of women's fertility through egg freezing has been heralded as a "reproductive revolution," equivalent to the introduction of the birth control pill in the early 1960s (ASRM 2018; Gibbs 2010; McDonald et al. 2011).

Yet, the development of egg freezing was not straightforward. As with many other low-temperature technologies used in biomedicine to "hold still" life processes, the freezing and thawing of human eggs proved technologically difficult. Although cryopreservation of human eggs was first tried in the early 1980s, and the first reported frozen egg baby was born in 1986 (Lockwood 2011), the methods of slow freezing being used at that time led to low oocyte survival, chromosomal defects, poor embryo development, and overall low birth rates (De Melo-Martin and Cholst 2008).

However, in the new millennium, a novel method called vitrification, which involves "flash-freezing" of human eggs, was introduced (Mertes and Pennings 2012). Despite initial caution, vitrification was proven to lead to excellent clinical success rates—an outcome that encouraged some governments, such as Israel, to authorize and begin using egg freezing in in vitro fertilization (IVF) clinics as early as 2011 (García-Velasco et al. 2013; Inhorn et al. 2018a, 2018b; Lockwood 2011).

Although vitrification remained experimental in the United States and most of Europe, the American Society for Reproductive Medicine (ASRM) lifted the experimental ban on 19 October 2012, with the European Society for Human Reproduction and Embryology (ESHRE) soon to follow. While not enthusiastically endorsing egg freezing as in Israel (Shkedi-Rafid and Hashiloni-Dolev 2012), the ASRM allowed egg freezing to be performed in the United States for a variety of medical and "social" reasons (ASRM 2012). Still, the ASRM urged caution—stopping short of recommending egg freezing to postpone childbearing. As it pointed out, there were insufficient data on safety, success rates, cost effectiveness, and physical and emotional risks to women, who might be lulled into a false sense of security. Furthermore, reliable data on the ultimate success of egg freezing were not readily available, as so few women had returned to use their frozen eggs. In other words, according to the ASRM, the viability of egg freezing and what it would ultimately mean for American women and their future children remained highly uncertain.

Having said this, IVF clinics on both the east and west coasts and in many American cities began by late 2012 to create their own egg freezing programs, with several commercial egg banks also launched at that time. The response on the part of American women was almost immediate. Approximately five thousand egg freezing cycles were undertaken in the United States within the first year of the technology's approval, according to the Society for Assisted Reproductive Technology (SART). However, according to SART, that number more than doubled to nearly eleven thousand cycles five years later, with that figure expected to rise steadily.

Egg freezing also received major media attention during this period. For example, a 2012 cover story in *The New York Times* explained that parents were offering to subsidize egg freezing for their single, "thirty-something" daughters in the hopes of future grandchildren (Gootman 2012). Five years later, *The New York Times* reported on the "aggressive" marketing of egg freezing to younger millennial women by clinics that "really, really, really want to freeze your eggs" (La Ferla 2018). Although stand-alone egg freezing clinics are promoting egg freezing to younger and younger women, the reality is that this technology is expensive—at a minimum of about $10,000 per cycle with accompanying hormonal medications. Thus, at the present time, egg freezing is a technology of limited access, available only to those who can afford it.

Most of the media coverage, as well as scholarly reviews on the subject, seems to suggest that women are undertaking egg freezing intentionally to "delay," "defer," or "postpone" their fertility for educational and career purposes, thereby achieving reproductive autonomy (Goldman and Grifo 2016) and forestalling age-related fertility decline (Argyle, Harper, and Davies 2016; Cobo and García-Velasco 2016; Donnez and Dolmans 2017; Gunnala and Schattman 2017). However, without empirical evidence, it is unclear whether the postponement of fertility through egg freezing is intentional and planned, and whether the achievement of education and career advancement are women's primary goals. Similarly, whether women are pursuing egg freezing on the path to "reproductive autonomy"— either from men or from reproduction itself—is highly uncertain.

As early as 2013, Belgian ethicist Heidi Mertes (2013) worried that common media and scholarly portrayals of egg freezing might "oversimplify" women's motivations and circumstances. She pointed to the three distinct ways in which women seeking egg freezing were commonly portrayed: 1) "selfish career-pursuing women," 2) "victims of a male-oriented society that makes it difficult for women to combine motherhood with a good education or professional responsibilities," or 3) "wise, proactive women who will not have to depend on oocyte donors should they suffer from age-related infertility" (Mertes 2013: 141). Mertes questioned whether these portrayals were accurate and suggested that the absence of a male partner might, in fact, be the most common reason for women's adoption of egg freezing as a form of fertility preservation.

Emerging survey data among women who have completed egg freezing in the United States (Greenwood et al. 2018; Hodes-Wertz et al. 2013), Belgium (Stoop et al. 2015), Australia (Hammarberg et al. 2017; Pritchard et al. 2017), the Netherlands (Balkenende et al. 2018), Korea (Kim et al. 2018), and the United Kingdom (Gürtin et al. 2019) seem to support Mertes's suggestion. In most of these reports, women specifically listed "lack of a partner" as their primary reason for undergoing egg freezing. In the Australian study in particular, women were contacted by mail up to fifteen years after completing egg freezing; 90 percent of women had yet to use their stored oocytes. Most reported that they were still hoping to find a partner, thereby avoiding single parenthood (Hammarberg et al. 2017). In one of the US studies undertaken in the San Francisco Bay Area, women who had undergone egg freezing on average two years before completing an anonymous survey reported significant anxiety, depression, loneliness, and hopelessness about their reproductive futures in the absence of a current male partner (Greenwood et al. 2018). One in six women also experienced regret for having undertaken egg freezing, for reasons that remained unclear in the study.

A number of small-scale, interview-based studies in the United Kingdom (Baldwin 2019; Waldby 2015, 2019), United States (Carroll and Kroløkke 2018), and Turkey (Göçmen and Kılıç 2017; Kılıç and Göçmen 2018) explored women's egg freezing motivations and experiences directly. For example, a study by Baldwin and colleagues (Baldwin 2017, 2018, 2019; Baldwin et al. 2015, 2018), focusing primarily on twenty-three British women who had completed at least one cycle of egg freezing, found women to be highly educated professionals (68 percent with postgraduate degrees or other professional qualifications), who were mostly working in managerial roles (74 percent). Although all the women hoped to be in a committed heterosexual relationship, 84 percent were single at the time of egg freezing, despite their "readiness" for motherhood. As the authors stated, "For most women, this 'readiness' consisted primarily of being in a stable relationship with a partner who they felt was committed to having a child" (Baldwin et al. 2015: 243). Similarly, an interview-based study of twenty-one Turkish women who were in the process of egg freezing or had completed a cycle within the previous year found these women to be highly educated professionals, with a median age of forty, all of whom were unmarried and six of whom had never had sexual intercourse (Göçmen and Kılıç 2017; Kılıç and Göçmen 2018).

In the United States, sociologists Brown and Patrick (2018) interviewed thirty women who had frozen their eggs, nineteen who were considering it, as well as three who had decided against it. As in the qualitative studies from Britain and Turkey, most of the participants in the American study were single and looking for a long-term reproductive partner; only seven women brought up career factors as the main reason for freezing their eggs. As Brown and Patrick (2018: 967) note, "worries about their romantic lives" drove most women in this study to freeze their eggs, with egg freezing being seen as a way to "temporarily disentangl[e] the project of finding a partner from the project of having children."

Given this emerging evidence that highly educated professional women may be preserving their fertility due to lack of suitable partners—rather than intentionally postponing their fertility due to educational or career planning—it is important to clarify whether egg freezing is being used primarily for planned *fertility postponement* (i.e., in achieving educational or career goals during one's twenties or early thirties), or whether it is being used primarily for *fertility preservation* in the absence of a committed reproductive partner (i.e., in the mid- to late thirties and early forties).

This chapter attempts to answer this question definitively through evidence provided by the first large-scale, ethnographic, interview-based study of more than one hundred American women who have completed at least one cycle of egg freezing. The focus here is on *waiting*: Namely, were these women waiting to become mothers on their paths to professional fulfilment? Or were they unable to become mothers because they were waiting for a reproductive partner? These questions of *"reproductive waithood,"* as I call it here, are of a fundamentally different order and kind.

A positive response to the first question would suggest that women are pursuing egg freezing for reproductive autonomy, to potentially "liberate" themselves from the biological "time clock"—and from men—in order to pursue reproduction on their own terms and at their own pace. Such intentional reproductive waithood bespeaks the revolutionary potential of this technology to decouple women's motherhood from the constraints of reproductive timing. It also suggests that women are using egg freezing in an emancipatory capacity to decouple their reproduction from their professional attainments.

A positive answer to the second question suggests fundamentally different life circumstances for women. If women are employing egg freezing as a stop-gap measure while waiting to find a suitable partner, then egg freezing becomes a *technological concession* to unintentional reproductive waithood beyond a woman's individual control. Waiting for a man in order to become a mother is a quite different reproductive scenario, one that does not bespeak a "reproductive revolution" facilitated by this new technology. Rather, this interpretation of reproductive waithood suggests that liberal feminist readings of egg freezing are fundamentally misguided.

Following a brief description of the study's methodology, this chapter first examines the detailed sociodemographic characteristics of the women in the study, then the reasons they cite for undertaking egg freezing, as well as their own reflections on the broader societal issues underlying this phenomenon. The final section of this chapter provides compelling evidence that reproductive waithood is intimately tied to gender, education, and delays in marriage, which, in the United States, are underlain by growing, but little discussed, gender-based disparities in men's and women's educational achievements. These disparities in education are also globally present, suggesting that reproductive waithood may become a widespread global phenomenon in the twenty-first century.

The Ethnographic Study

This study of egg freezing was designed to assess the motivations and experiences of women who had completed at least one egg freezing cycle. Between June 2014 and August 2016, the author recruited women from four IVF clinics (two academic, two private), three of which were located on the East Coast corridor (New Haven, Connecticut; New York, New York; and the Washington, DC/Baltimore, MD, area) and one in the San Francisco Bay/Silicon Valley area. Women were contacted primarily by email from the four participating clinics, or they were given flyers directly by their clinicians during appointments.

In total, 114 women who had undertaken at least one egg freezing cycle volunteered to participate in the study, along with twelve other women who were either in the process of egg freezing, or had not completed a cycle for a variety of reasons.[1] All women who volunteered for the study signed written informed consent forms, agreeing to a confidential, audio-recorded interview in a private setting. Interviews were undertaken in women's offices and homes, in the author's office, in IVF clinic settings, or in restaurants, bars, and cafés. Most of the interviews were undertaken by the author in person with women who were living in the New Haven or New York City areas. However, because women from Boston, Baltimore, Washington, DC, San Francisco, and the Silicon Valley area also volunteered for the study, most of those interviews took place by Skype or telephone. Some women contacted by the clinics had also moved to other cities, such as Chicago, Seattle, St. Louis, or Los Angeles, and were interviewed by the author by Skype or telephone.

Interviews always began with a brief series of sociodemographic questions (i.e., age, place of birth, current residence, education completed, current employment, marital status, ethnicity, religion), as well as relevant details of reproductive history (i.e., age at menarche, contraceptive use, any known reproductive problems). Following these semi-structured questions, the author asked women to describe their life circumstances at the time of egg freezing, and their primary motivations for pursuing fertility preservation. Women often "led" the interviews, describing their egg freezing "stories" and their decision-making processes in detail. Conversations usually lasted about one hour but ranged in length from one-half to more than two hours.

Completed interviews were then transcribed verbatim by two research assistants at Yale University. All interview transcripts were uploaded into a qualitative data analysis software program (Dedoose) for thematic content analysis, and detailed interview synopses were written and summarized by the author. Sociodemographic information was transferred into Excel files by a third research assistant for descriptive statistical analysis. The research protocol was approved by the Yale Institutional Review Board and by the ethics committees of all the collaborating IVF clinic sites. The study was generously funded by the US National Science Foundation's Cultural Anthropology and Science and Technology Studies programs.

Egg Freezing: A Sociodemographic Profile

As noted above, basic sociodemographic information was collected from all of the women in this study. Thus, a sociodemographic profile of the women who had pursued egg freezing could be constructed. As shown in Table 15.1, "A Profile of Study Participants and Their Egg Freezing Cycles," about three-quarters (73 percent) of the women froze their eggs in their late thirties (ages thirty-five to thirty-nine), with the remainder in their early thirties (17 percent) or early forties (10 percent). The average age at egg freezing was 36.6. Only one woman in the study had frozen her eggs before age thirty (at age twenty-nine, as encouraged by her IVF physician father).

More than half of the women (57 percent) undertook only one egg freezing cycle, and one-third (31 percent) undertook two cycles. A minority of women undertook a third (9 percent) or higher-order

TABLE 15.1. A Profile of Study Participants and
Their Egg Freezing Cycles.

Characteristics	n	%
Age at Egg Freezing		
25–29	1	<1
30–34	19	17
35–39	83	73
>40	11	10
Total	*114*	*100*
No. of Egg Freezing Cycles		
1	65	57
2	35	31
3	10	9
<3	4	3
Total	*114*	*100*
Total No. of Eggs Stored		
<5	7	6
5–10	25	22
11–15	20	17
16–20	25	22
21–25	18	16
26–30	7	6
31–35	6	5
36–40	3	3
>40	3	3
Total	*114*	*100*

cycle (3 percent). On average, nearly eighteen eggs per woman were retrieved and frozen by the women in this study.

As shown in Table 15.2, "Educational Achievement and Ethnicity of Study Participants," women who froze their eggs were of many different ethnic backgrounds but were almost uniformly highly educated. Two-thirds (69 percent) of the women were white, nearly one-fifth (18 percent) were Asian American, and women of African American, Latinx, mixed-race, and Middle Eastern heritage were also represented in the study (13 percent overall). In terms of ed-

TABLE 15.2. Educational Achievement and Ethnicity
of Study Participants.

	n	%
Highest Degree		
Associates Degree (2-Year)	1	1
Professional Arts Performance	2	2
Bachelors	23	20
Masters	52	45
MD	16	14
PhD	11	10
JD	8	7
MD-PhD	1	1
Total N	*114*	*100*
Ethnicity		
White	79	69
Asian American	20	18
African American	5	4
Latinx	4	3.5
Mixed Race	4	3.5
Middle Eastern Heritage	2	2
Total N	*114*	*100*

ucation, only three women had not graduated from college due to
their successful careers in the performing arts or military. The rest
of the women had considerable educational achievements. Twenty
percent of the women had completed bachelors' degrees, but the
rest—nearly 80 percent—had earned advanced degrees, including
master's degrees (45 percent), medical degrees (14 percent), doctoral degrees (10 percent), and law degrees (7 percent). More than
10 percent of the women had done dual graduate degrees (e.g., MD-
PhD, MD-MPH, MPP-PhD). Interestingly, among these highly educated American women, thirty-six women (32 percent) had attended
Ivy League institutions, and another thirty women (26 percent)
had attended highly ranked public (e.g., University of California-
Berkeley) or private (e.g., Georgetown) universities. In other words,
well over half (58 percent) of these American women had attended
so-called elite US academic institutions.

Given these women's high levels of education, it is not surprising that all were gainfully employed in professional fields, including, among others, health care, basic and applied sciences, government and law, diplomacy and foreign service, academia, business management, information and technology, entrepreneurship, media and communications, human resources, the arts, the military, and beyond. However, only one woman—who, at age thirty, was the second youngest woman in the study—had explicitly used egg freezing to postpone her fertility "en route" to becoming a successful entrepreneur. Another woman, age thirty-three, had passed the difficult Foreign Service exam and froze her eggs in order to pursue her new career in Latin America. But with the exception of these two women, the rest of the women did not pursue egg freezing for career-related purposes.

Rather, as shown in Table 15.3, "Relationship Status and Reproductive Outcomes Following Egg Freezing (EF)," the highly educated professional women in this study were freezing their eggs primarily because they lacked partners. Exactly 82 percent were single at the time of egg freezing, either because they had no partner, were divorced, or had recently broken up from long-term relationships. Among the 18 percent of women who were partnered at the time of egg freezing, half of these relationships were unstable for the reasons outlined in Table 15.3. Only ten women in the study (9 percent) were stably partnered at the time of egg freezing with men who eventually hoped to have children with them.

Table 15.3 also describes the post–egg freezing life circumstances of women at the time of their interviews. More than three-quarters of women (78 percent) were still single, while 22 percent were partnered (with either the same or a new partner). Seven percent of the partnered women had gone onto marry. However, there were often significant differences in age, education, and reproductive history among women and their partners (e.g., a 38-year-old woman with a 55-year-old divorced man with children, or a female emergency room physician with a high-school–educated paramedic). Only five percent of women described themselves as being in "equal" partnerships in terms of their partners' education, age, and reproductive history (i.e., no children from a prior relationship).

As also shown in Table 15.3, some women, whether partnered or not, decided to have children, with or without their frozen eggs. Ten women in the study had born children and three were currently pregnant at the time of their interviews. Few of these women had relied on their frozen eggs to become pregnant. Only ten of the 114 women

TABLE 15.3. Relationship Status and Reproductive Outcomes Following Egg Freezing (EF).

Years Elapsed Since EF Undertaken	n	%
Same year	40	35
1 year	28	25
2 years	21	18
3 years	12	11
4 years	7	6
5 or more years (5–11)	6	5
Total	*114*	*100*

Relationship Status at Time of EF	n	%
Single		
Being Single	59	51
Divorced or Divorcing	19	17
Broken Up	16	14
Total Single	*94*	*82*
Partnered (Unstable)		
Relationship Too New or Uncertain	6	5
Partner Refuses to Have Children	2	2
Partner Has Multiple Partners	2	2
Total Unstable Partnerships	*10*	*9*
Partnered (Stable)		
Partner Not Ready to Have Children	10	9
Total Stable Partnerships	*10*	*9*

Relationship Status Following EF (at Time of Interview)	n	%
Still Single	89	78
Partnered	17	15
Married	8	7
Total	*114*	*100*

TABLE 15.3. (*continued*)

Status of Those Women Partnered/Married		
Equal Partnership (Education, Age, No Children from Prior Relationship)	6	5
Partner Divorced without Children	1	1
Partner Divorced with Children	7	6
Partner Significantly Younger	3	3
Partner Significantly Older/Retired	2	2
Partner Significantly Less Educated	1	1
Partner Significantly Less Educated/Divorced	1	1
Partner Significantly Less Educated/Divorced with Children	1	1
Partner Significantly Less Educated/Younger	1	1
Partner with Alcohol or Legal Issues	2	2
Total and Percent of Total N	25	22

Pregnancy and Live Birth Outcomes Post-EF (at Time of Interview)		
Child Born from Frozen Oocyte Conception	1	1
Child Born from Natural Conception (No Frozen Oocytes Used)	3	2
Child Born from Donor Sperm (Single Mother by Choice, No Frozen Oocytes Used)	2	2
Child Born from IUI, IVF or Surrogacy (No Donor Sperm, No Frozen Oocytes Used)	4	3
Currently Pregnant from Frozen Oocyte	1	1
Currently Pregnant from Natural Conception	2	2
Total and Percent of Total N	13	11

Women Who Had Used Frozen Oocytes (by Time of Interview)		
All Oocytes Thawed, One Live Birth, One Blastocyst Remaining	1	1
All Oocytes Thawed, Currently Pregnant, 24 Embryos Remaining	1	1
All Oocytes Thawed, No Fertilization	8	7
Total and Percent of Total N	10	9

interviewed (9 percent) had pursued reproduction using frozen oocytes. Eight women had thawed all of their eggs in an attempt to become pregnant, but only one had delivered a child, while another learned that she was pregnant at the time of the interview. The overall usage of frozen eggs remained low, as did the rate of frozen-egg conceptions.

In summary, the overall sociodemographic profile of the women in this study clearly suggests that the lack of a stable partnership is the primary motivation for egg freezing among these highly educated American professional women. Throughout their educational and career-building years, women in this study had attempted to find compatible male partners, with whom they could build families. But when they were unable to find suitable partners, they had pursued egg freezing, usually in their mid- to late thirties, but sometimes in their early forties, in an effort to preserve their remaining reproductive potential. In short, the widely circulated notion that women are pursuing egg freezing primarily for career advancement is inaccurate, at least at the present time. As shown in this study, few women were "postponing" their fertility for the sake of their careers. Already well established in careers they loved, most women did not view their jobs as a major reproductive obstacle, nor the reason that they had pursued egg freezing. In this study, career planning had little if anything to do with egg freezing, although this may change over time as younger women become more familiar with the technology (Kirkby 2018; La Ferla 2018).

Reproductive Waithood: Women's Perspectives

Given the overwhelming evidence that egg freezing is about partnership problems, not career planning, it is not surprising that women in this study expressed significant frustration over their inability to find partners. Most could only speculate as to why stable relationships with reproductively committed men were so difficult to achieve. Many women experienced this partnership-related reproductive waithood as a significant source of anguish. As one woman, an academic physician in her mid-thirties, put it,

> If I found a man, I'd move to Alaska! But most men don't want relationships. They just want to meet and date. And most women won't go out with the [uneducated] check-stand dude, but men will. So, I think I have about a 0.9 percent chance of meeting someone. And meanwhile, I was feeling like, "OMG [oh my god!], my biological

clock, it's ticking, it's ticking, it's ticking," you know? So, even though I'm 1,000 percent happy I did it [egg freezing], it felt somewhat like a defeat. I felt like I gave up, because I couldn't find a man.

During ethnographic interviews, women offered a variety of perspectives on reproductive waithood amid the absence of men, not only in their own lives, but in the lives of educated women more generally. Women's assessments could be summarized in four main ways: women's higher expectations, men's lower commitments, skewed gender demography, and self-blame.

Women's Higher Expectations

Women in this study described how their parents, especially mothers, had encouraged them to "have it all," and that they are now part of the generation of women "leaning in" to their careers (Sandberg 2013). These American women had been raised to believe in gender equality and egalitarian relationships at home and at work. Thus, they hoped not to "settle" for a man who was less educated, less professionally accomplished, or less committed to similar interests and life goals. Many women said that they were still hoping to find the "right" person—the "soulmate" with whom they were "meant" to be. Searching for this egalitarian relationship took time and commitment but could prevent the fearful outcome of "settling" into a "bad marriage." Women in this study were generally still "searching" for these partnerships, but argued that such men were hard to find, rarer even than "unicorns."

Furthermore, women often described their difficulties in "dating down" to less educated or less successful men. They characterized such relationships as fraught with "intimidation" on the part of men, who were generally emasculated by a woman's superior professional status, living situation, or earnings. Gail, a filmmaker who froze her eggs at thirty-five years old, had this to say about her relationship expectations and experiences:

> I just recently came to realize, okay, now that I'm thirty-six, that I am now one of those people that I looked at in my twenties and wondered, "What's wrong with them? Why don't they have a partner?" And I'm now thinking that my perception of what's out there is so different. I just want to have a rich partnership with someone who's intellectually and personally and physically stimulating. And I don't meet them very often. I do meet plenty of options, but I mean, yeah, I have a very limited pool of what I'm looking for. I want someone who wants to have a family now. Someone who's driven and successful and has their priorities together in terms of their career, but also

someone who's not intimidated by the fact that I'm the same. And I don't blame them for feeling that way, because we give them the royal "we." We put out a very conflicting message, which is: "I am a strong woman, I can do everything for myself, and I don't need a partner." But I *do* want a partner, and I *do* want a fulfilling relationship and partnership that lasts and a family. I'm not super vulnerable, you know, on the surface, when it comes to connecting with men. So, I don't think they know what to do with us! [laughing] I mean, I don't get hit on very often any more, and the funny thing is, it's only by not-so-bright men [who do so]. But for men of the same educational/professional level? Yeah, it's almost never.

Men's Lower Commitments

Indeed, women in this study were skeptical about American men of their generation, and whether these men shared the same desires and life goals. Women pointed out that men were not necessarily socialized in the same way to want egalitarian relationships with professional women, with whom they could balance the burdens and responsibilities of family life. Women in this study described men's increasing "commitment phobia," particularly men who were the "children of divorce" and were not sanguine about the virtues of either marriage or fatherhood. Furthermore, women on the West Coast often described the "Peter Pan" syndrome—i.e., boys (in men's bodies) who never grow up. These "man-children" were either described as wealthy venture capitalist types who wanted to delay marriage indefinitely while "playing the field" and never committing, or they were described as men unwilling or unable to hold steady jobs, sometimes living with their parents (or being subsidized by them or trust funds), and unable to fulfill the roles assumed by adult men in society. Furthermore, in the San Francisco Bay Area and other "progressive" cities, women described the growing phenomenon of "polyamory"—namely, millennial-generation men's desires to have multiple, open relationships with "primary," "secondary," and even "tertiary" female partners.

In short, women in this study described men's lowered commitments to fidelity, marriage, and parenthood—the trifecta often expected within traditional, heteronormative family structures. Eleanor, a journalist who had frozen her eggs at age thirty-five, had much to say on this subject:

> Of the people lately that I've met, who I've wanted to be in a relationship with, they haven't wanted to be in a relationship with anybody. Like, they just want to not have that kind of obligation. So, I think it's

like they don't want to be emotionally responsible for another person. That's what I find to be the particular challenge—that there *are* men out there, you know, but the ones who are single in my age group don't want a relationship. And there are ones who do, but the ones that I've met lately don't. It's really interesting. I mean, I was talking about this with some of my cousins recently, and all of us are thinking about our fathers and how there are so many things that are different today. Like, tons of things that are different today. But one of them is that for our fathers, being a father and having a family was huge, you know. And I don't think they imagined anything else. But I think that a lot of men today—and I can tell you, like I've met *many* of them, and some of them are my friends, too, who are in their mid-thirties, late thirties, early forties—like they just, they don't have that same sense that they need to be a father or they need to have a partner in order to fulfill whatever dreams they have or, you know, to be who they want to be.

Skewed Gender Demography

Beyond changing gender expectations on the part of both women and men, my female interlocutors acknowledged that men of similar backgrounds—namely, single, college-educated, professionals, often with advanced degrees and high earnings—were simply hard to find. As one woman explained it succinctly, "the caliber of women is just higher than the caliber of guys." This lament was especially true among women on the East Coast, and particularly in New York City and Washington, DC, metropolitan areas that are known (via media reports) to have higher percentages of educated women than men. Women in those cities often complained about the dearth of "available" (and heterosexual) male partners in the skewed gender landscapes in which they were living. This predicament was clearly expressed by Alice, a scientist who was working for the federal government in Washington:

> You know, it's funny. I'm living in DC, and we joke about this in Washington. It's like I know a lot of really brilliant, amazing women. The friends of mine who do have partners did not meet their partners here. They met them in graduate school, and they married them like right after grad school, and then they moved here. Because when you read the statistics on DC, there are, you know, like 60 percent women and 40 percent men and all this horrible stuff. And I know *lots* of amazing women scientists. Literally, [where I work] I can point out, like, all of our names are on the website. I mean we're all on there, right? And I can point out to you how many of them are single and amazing and are in their thirties, right, and are single, and have prob-

ably been single for a long time, actually, or have dated for a while
and then broken up or whatever. And that's just how DC is. It's not
uncommon. Like, a very close friend of mine who got her PhD from
Harvard and is doing something amazing here in DC, you know, she
just had a kid on her own. And she just kind of, she just got a sperm
donor and just did the whole thing and just had her kid last year. And
that's actually, I think, something that I had thought about doing.
But the egg freezing was a pathway that I was willing to go down, I'll
say, because then I could continue to date and still hope that I find
someone.

For women like Alice—already at the highest levels of educational and professional achievement—"finding someone" was inherently problematic on many levels. Because women in the United
States have traditionally been told to marry "up" (hypergamy) while
men marry "down" (hypogamy) in terms of age, class, education,
salary, and so on, trying to reverse this entrenched gender norm was
difficult, especially for women already "at the top." Furthermore, according to most women in this study, men could be very "ageist"—
preferring to marry "down" to younger women, rather than women
in their late thirties or early forties who might place immediate "pressure" on a partner to have children. Women in this study said that
they found few single men of their own age who were eager to partner and have children. Men who were available were often older, divorced, and, if they had children, were often reluctant to have more.
Or they were incompatible in other ways, often based on differences
in educational background. Angela, a New York City-based architect,
described her troubled dating life with both pathos and humor:

> The last thing I want to do is, like, drop my work and go out to a bar
> and hope I meet somebody. You know, prioritizing meeting people
> feels so inauthentic when you're just going to a place because you
> hope maybe you're going to find your husband there. And when you
> get there and it's all girls, you're like, ugh! I don't like that experi-
> ence. It feels like I'm not really present. Now I am scratching up the
> dregs, savoring them, while I wait for the divorcées to release some
> decent men so I can have a turn. But the pickings are slim! I've gone
> on a couple dates recently, and you know, this guy smoked two packs
> of cigarettes a day for twenty years, quit a couple years ago, is now
> sober for eight years, and he's a rock and roll star, or a rock and roll
> singer. And he sends me all these intense, heavy metal-y tracks. Like,
> really? This is what I have? If I could teach a daughter one thing, it
> would be: "Snatch up one of those uninjured, healthy, ambitious
> college boys! And save a couple hundred thousand dollars—have ba-
> bies pronto!"

Self-Blame

Like Angela, women who found themselves in this position—namely, with no prospects of a viable partner in their mid- to late thirties— sometimes posed the question, "Why me?" Often with sadness, women expressed their amazement and disbelief that they had somehow "ended up" this way. Yet, they often added that they knew (many) other professional women in this situation. Women sometimes blamed themselves for not finding a partner, criticizing themselves for being too "picky," only attracted to "alpha males," or that they had let a "good one" get away, were not attractive enough to men, or had not put enough "energy" into dating (especially on-line dating, which was ubiquitous in the study population). Further-more, women worried about being typecast as desperate, somehow turning off men by their perceived need to reproduce in a hurry. As Jessica, a physician who had undertaken egg freezing at age thirty-seven, explained,

> It's easy to start feeling a little humiliated sometimes, just because you know, you don't want to be like so many of the portrayals of the "cougars," the desperateness. They're always high strung and kind of bossy and Type A. They're always running around trying to catch the man. You know? It's this neurotic kind of crazy person. And so you know, it is scary initially, to feel like you might be typecast like that. Like what's wrong with me? But at least at [the egg freezing clinic] the nurses were so nice, the doctors were so nice. They never for a split second made me feel like I was doing something odd or crazy or out of the norm. It really relaxed me about the whole thing.

Indeed, as seen in Jessica's case, egg freezing is becoming the "new normal" for American professional women who find them-selves in a situation of unintended reproductive waithood due to the dearth of available male partners. Such normalization may even-tually serve to mitigate women's feelings of self-blame—a negative discourse that author Sarah Eckel (2014) has questioned in her book *It's Not You: 27 (Wrong) Reasons You're Single*.

Reproductive Waithood: Educational Disparities and the "Man Deficit"

These American professional women's turn to egg freezing begs two important questions: first, where are all the "missing men," who should presumably want to couple with these accomplished American women? Second, should lack of a partner be taken for granted as a "natural fact" of educated women's reproductive lives?

To answer these questions about "missing men," it is useful to turn to the work of Jon Birger (2015), a business journalist and author who has analyzed US census and World Bank data to understand what he calls the "man deficit." Using US census data, Birger showed in 2015 that there were 5.5 million university-educated women in their twenties (ages twenty-two to twenty-nine) in the United States for only 4.1 million university-educated men. This is a ratio of 4:3. Between the ages of thirty and thirty-nine—when women start freezing their eggs—there were 7.4 million university-educated American women for only 6 million university-educated American men. This is a ratio of 5:4. Adding the two groups together, there were nearly 3 million more university-educated women than university-educated men in women's prime reproductive years in the United States. To quote Birger (2015: 3), "These lopsided gender ratios may add up to a sexual nirvana for heterosexual men, but for heterosexual women—especially those who put a high priority on getting married and having children in wedlock—they represent a demographic time bomb."

What Birger calls a "massive undersupply" of university-educated men in the United States: 1) is growing over time as young women enter universities at much higher rates; 2) has reached a new high of 37 percent more American women than men in higher education, according to the most recent census data; 3) makes the long-term prospects for millennial-generation women decidedly worse; and 4) is particularly acute in major US cities such as Washington, DC, New York, and Miami, where university-educated women tend to cluster, but now outnumber university-educated men by the hundreds of thousands (Birger 2015).

Beyond the United States, this "man deficit" appears to be emerging around the world. As seen in Table 15.4, "Countries Where

TABLE 15.4. Countries Where Women Significantly Outnumber Men in Higher Education.

Country	F/M Ratio	% More Women than Men in Higher Education
Albania	1.39865994	40%
Algeria	1.55961001	56%
Argentina	1.61947	62%
Armenia	1.12863004	13%

TABLE 15.4. *(continued)*

Country	F/M Ratio	% More Women than Men in Higher Education
Aruba	2.26302004	126%
Australia	1.40989006	41%
Austria	1.20158994	20%
Bahrain	1.92068005	92%
Belarus	1.32676005	33%
Belgium	1.31350005	31%
Belize	1.60633004	61%
Bermuda	2.31813002	132%
Botswana	1.43773997	44%
Brazil	1.39809	40%
Canada	1.29524887	30%
Chile	1.13678002	14%
China	1.18620002	19%
Colombia	1.16246998	16%
Costa Rica	1.30727994	31%
Croatia	1.35680997	36%
Cuba	1.42532003	43%
Czech Republic	1.40742004	41%
Estonia	1.53139997	53%
Finland	1.20589006	21%
France	1.22571003	23%
Georgia	1.21904004	22%
Guyana	2.03288007	103%
Hong Kong SAR, China	1.16025996	16%
Hungary	1.25191998	25%
Iceland	1.71160996	71%
Indonesia	1.1243	12%
Ireland	1.09338999	9%
Israel	1.3829	38%
Italy	1.35718	36%
Jamaica	1.72571003	73%
Jordan	1.11230004	11%
Kazakhstan	1.23714995	24%
Kuwait	1.61944997	62%
Latvia	1.42805004	43%

(continued)

TABLE 15.4. *(continued)*

Country	F/M Ratio	% More Women than Men in Higher Education
Lebanon	1.15689003	16%
Lithuania	1.46904004	47%
Luxembourg	1.13515997	14%
Macao SAR, China	1.32536995	33%
Macedonia, FYR	1.24822998	25%
Malaysia	1.52705002	53%
Malta	1.37038004	37%
Mongolia	1.38279998	38%
Myanmar	1.22817004	23%
Netherlands	1.10478997	10%
New Zealand	1.35090995	35%
Norway	1.45779002	46%
Palau	1.54859996	55%
Panama	1.49242997	49%
Philippines	1.28163004	28%
Poland	1.52178001	52%
Portugal	1.13217998	13%
Puerto Rico	1.40998995	41%
Romania	1.23240995	23%
Russian Federation	1.21165001	21%
Serbia	1.33327997	33%
Slovak Republic	1.54595995	55%
Slovenia	1.44420004	44%
South Africa	1.48450994	48%
Spain	1.17773998	18%
Sri Lanka	1.53942001	54%
St. Lucia	1.90204	90%
Sweden	1.52547002	53%
Syrian Arab Republic	1.13739002	14%
Thailand	1.41378999	41%
Tunisia	1.65129006	65%
Ukraine	1.15558004	16%
United Kingdom	1.30744004	31%
United States	1.36754	37%

Women Significantly Outnumber Men in Higher Education,"[2] World Bank data from 2012 to 2016 show that women significantly outstrip men in higher education in more than seventy countries where data are available (World Bank 2018).[3] This includes, for example, Australia, where there are 41 percent more women than men in higher education, as well as Belgium (31 percent), France (23 percent), Italy (36 percent), New Zealand (35 percent), Norway (46 percent), Sweden (53 percent), and the United Kingdom (31 percent). In many non-Western countries as well, these educational disparities are emerging, including in Argentina (62 percent), China (19 percent), Cuba (43 percent), Lebanon (16 percent), Malaysia (53 percent), Panama (49 percent), South Africa (48 percent), Thailand (41 percent), and Tunisia (65 percent), to name only a few.

This study on egg freezing reflects these growing educational disparities between men and women. Table 15.3 depicts how some women decided to make "unequal" alliances with older, younger, or divorced men, including men with children from previous relationships, and often men with significantly less education. As women continue to rise educationally around the globe, and men no longer keep pace, such decisions among educated professional women to marry lesser-educated men may become more and more frequent. Birger (2015), for one, calls these unequal partnerships "mixed-collar marriages," where educated women are beginning to marry "down" (hypogamy), reversing traditional patterns of both male hypogamy and female hypergamy.

Reproductive Waithood:
The "Men as Partners" Problem

What we see, then, are the difficult choices currently facing educated women in the United States, and potentially many other Western and non-Western societies, in terms of partnership and family formation. Clearly in this study, a variety of "partnership problems" emerged as the key factor in women's decisions to pursue egg freezing. Both with and without partners, women in this study were being forced into an indefinite period of "reproductive waithood" because men were either absent or uncommitted to reproduction, now or in the future.

Indeed, this "men as partners" problem has been identified since the early 2000s in international reproductive health circles (Wentzell and Inhorn 2014). Reproductive health scholars and policy

makers have recognized that: 1) reproduction is inherently relational, 2) both men and women are involved in reproduction, and
hence 3) men must be included in reproductive health policies and
programs, given their potential importance in enhancing women's
reproductive health and rights.

However, this "men as partners" problem is rarely articulated in
assisted reproduction scholarship, even though it is the main reason
why American women are freezing their eggs. Through listening
carefully to more than one hundred women's egg freezing stories, it
was clear in this study that the "men as partners" problem in these
professional women's lives is both overwhelming and distressing.
Indeed, these highly educated, successful women were experiencing
their own reproductive lives as being in jeopardy.

Virtually all of the women in this study (except two) were heterosexual, and most were explicit that they were looking for marriage
to a man they loved. They hoped to achieve equal partnerships with
committed men who would participate with them in parenthood
within heteronormative family structures. Although few women in
this study had been able to find a reproductively committed partner, most were not willing to condemn all men as callous "jerks."
Indeed, the clear majority of women in this study were intent on
dating, still hoping to find "Mr. Right." In struggling with what to
do in the absence of equal partnerships, some women in this study
had "dated down," entering relationships with men who were less
educated, less successful, and often younger (or substantially older)
than themselves. Others had given up on partnerships altogether,
pursuing egg freezing on their way to becoming "single mothers by
choice" (Bock 2000; Hertz 2008; Potter and Knaub 1988).

As seen in their interviews, many women realized that their inability to find stable reproductive partnerships was not necessarily
their fault. Rather, they spoke of shifting gender norms, including women's higher expectations for egalitarian relationships with
men who are not intimidated by them. Furthermore, some women
were aware of the skewed gender ratios in their urban areas (e.g.,
Washington, DC), due to media reportage on this subject. However, knowledge of the educational gender gap, whereby educated
women significantly outnumber educated men, is still not widespread in the United States.

As argued in this chapter, however, educational disparities between
men and women are growing ever wider, making it increasingly difficult for educated women to find partners. Amid this educated man
deficit, "to freeze or not to freeze" has become the leading question

among some of the most educated American women (Greenwood et al. 2018). Egg freezing is not about women who are intentionally "delaying" childbearing or "planning" to "postpone" their fertility—even though the American Society for Reproductive Medicine (2018) has recently characterized the technology in this way. Rather, egg freezing appears to be a stop-gap fertility "preservation" measure among highly educated women, who are forced to grapple with partnership-related reproductive waithood well beyond their individual control.

Conclusion: The Egg Freezing Revolution?

As this chapter shows, the men as partners problem is leading highly educated American women to pursue egg freezing. Moreover, the sadness of partner-related reproductive waithood reverberates through the stories and the lives of the highly educated women in this study. Instead of achieving motherhood, this cohort of exceptionally well-educated, thirty-something American women finds themselves in what author Melanie Notkin (2014) calls "otherhood"—single and approaching the end of their fertility, but still hedging their bets as to whether they can find a loving partner willing to commit to marriage and family life.

Amid this "otherhood-not-motherhood," reproductive waithood seems here to stay. Although egg freezing holds out hope for fertility preservation during this waithood period, it cannot begin to address the educational disparities that underlie the waithood problem in the United States and beyond. That reproductively committed and equally educated men are now "missing" is a major societal trend that must be addressed. This study speaks to the need for future global research to address why men are falling behind on their educational paths, while women are rapidly moving forward. In addition, ethnographic research on educated heterosexual men must be conducted, to get a sense of why many of them are now waiting to marry and become fathers, or are opting out of these pathways altogether.

In addition, research on highly educated women around the globe must be conducted, as they begin to pursue egg freezing in the diverse national settings in which this technology is now becoming available (Allahbadia 2016; Santo et al. 2017). Further global research of this kind will help to determine whether reproductive waithood via lack of male partners is the leading cause of egg freezing elsewhere, or whether education and careers themselves are leading women to wait on marriage and motherhood.

Given the overwhelming ethnographic evidence about reproductive waithood presented in this chapter, it seems important to end by answering the chapter's main question. Is egg freezing heralding a new "reproductive revolution"? This ethnographic study suggests that—at least for now—probably not. The technology is too costly and the results too uncertain to declare a reproductive revolution at the present time. But as egg freezing becomes increasingly globalized and normalized in educated women's circles, and made more accessible over time in larger numbers of clinics at reduced costs, this technology may come to represent the future of reproduction for educated women without partners. Only time will tell.

Marcia C. Inhorn is the William K. Lanman, Jr. Professor of Anthropology and International Affairs in the Department of Anthropology and MacMillan Center for International and Area Studies at Yale University, where she serves as Chair of the Council on Middle East Studies. A specialist on Middle Eastern gender, religion, and health, Inhorn is the author of six award-winning books, including *America's Arab Refugees: Vulnerability and Health on the Margins* (Stanford University Press, 2018). She is (co)editor of ten books, founding editor of the *Journal of Middle East Women's Studies* (*JMEWS*), and coeditor of Berghahn's "Fertility, Reproduction, and Sexuality" book series. Inhorn holds a PhD in anthropology and an MPH in epidemiology from the University of California, Berkeley.

Notes

1. In addition, thirty-four women with serious medical diagnoses, especially cancer, were pursuing "medical" fertility preservation and were included in the larger study, along with the wives of two infertile husbands and one transgender man who had frozen his eggs. Eleven clinicians were also interviewed around the country, to get a sense of the regional distribution and uptake of egg freezing. Two other individuals with knowledge of infertility and egg freezing also took part, for a total of 176 interviews in the United States.
2. Gratitude goes to Jon Birger, who compiled this table from World Bank data. It can be found in Inhorn et al. 2018a.
3. This table is based on the most recent World Bank data available from 2012 to 2016, as collected by the United Nations Educational, Scien-

tific, and Cultural Organization (UNESCO) Institute for Statistics: https://
data.worldbank.org/indicator/SE.ENR.TERT.FM.ZS?end=2011&name_
desc=false&start=1970. The data for Canada are available at http://www
.statcan.gc.ca/tables-tableaux/sum-som/101/cst01/educ7lb-eng.htm.

References

Allahbadia, Gautam N. 2016. "Social Egg Freezing: Developing Countries are not Exempt." *Journal of Obstetrics and Gynecology India* 66: 213–17.

Argyle, C. E., Joyce C. Harper, and M. C. Davies. 2016. "Oocyte Cryopreservation: Where are We Now?" *Human Reproduction Update* 22: 440–49.

ASRM (American Society for Reproductive Medicine). 2012. "Mature Oocyte Cryopreservation: A Guideline." Retrieved 22 April 2019 from https://www.asrm.org/uploadedFiles/ASRM_Content/News_and_Publi cations/Practice_Guidelines/Committee_Opinions/Ovarian_tissue_and_ oocyte(1).pdf.

———. 2018. "Planned Oocyte Cryopreservation for Women Seeking to Preserve Future Reproductive Potential: An Ethics Committee Opinion." *Fertility and Sterility* 110(6): 1022–28.

Baldwin, Kylie. 2017. "'I Suppose I Think to Myself, That's the Best Way to be a Mother': How Ideologies of Parenthood Shape Women's Use for Social Egg Freezing Technology." *Sociology Research Online* 22: 2–15.

———. 2018. "Conceptualising Women's Motivations for Social Egg Freezing and Experience of Reproductive Delay." *Sociology of Health and Illness* 40(5): 859–73.

———. 2019. *Egg Freezing, Fertility and Reproductive Choice: Negotiating Responsibility, Hope and Modern Motherhood.* Bingley, UK: Emerald Publishing.

Baldwin, Kylie, Lorraine A. Culley, Nicky Hudson, and Helene L. Mitchell. 2018. "Running Out of Time: Exploring Women's Motivations for Social Egg Freezing." *Journal of Psychosomatic Obstetrics and Gynecology* 40(2): 166–73.

Baldwin, Kylie, Lorraine A. Culley, Nicky Hudson, Helene L. Mitchell, and Stuart Lavery. 2015. "Oocyte Cryopreservation for Social Reasons: Demographic Profile and Disposal Intentions of UK Users." *Reproductive BioMedicine Online* 31(2): 239–45.

Balkenende, E. M., T. Dahhan, F. van der Veen, S. Repping, and M. Goddijn. 2018. "Reproductive Outcomes after Oocyte Banking for Fertility Preservation." *Reproductive BioMedicine Online* 37(4): 425–33.

Birger, Jon. 2015. *Date-onomics: How Dating Became a Lopsided Numbers Game.* New York: Workman Publishing.

Bock, Jane D. 2000. "Doing the Right Thing? Single Motherhood by Choice and the Struggle for Legitimacy." *Gender and Society* 14: 62–86.

Brown, Eliza, and Mary Patrick. 2018. "Time, Anticipation, and the Life Course: Egg Freezing as Temporarily Disentangling Romance and Reproduction." *American Sociological Review* 83(5): 959–82.

Carroll, Katherine, and Charlotte Kr">kke. 2018. "Freezing for Love: En-
acting 'Responsible' Reproductive Citizenship through Egg Freezing."
Culture, Health & Sexuality 20(9): 992–1005.

Cobo, Ana, and Juan Antonio García-Velasco. 2016. "Why All Women
Should Freeze their Eggs." *Clinical Obstetrics and Gynecology* 28(3): 206–10.

De Melo-Martin, Inmaculata, and Ina N. Cholst. 2008. "Researching Human Oocyte Cryopreservation: Ethical Issues." *Fertility and Sterility* 89(3):
523–28.

Donnez, Jacques, and Marie-Madeleine Dolmans. 2017. "Fertility Preservation in Women." *New England Journal of Medicine* 377: 1657–65.

Eckel, Sara. 2014. *It's Not You: 27 (Wrong) Reasons You're Single.* New York:
Penguin.

García-Velasco, Juan Antonio, Javier Domingo, Ana Cobo, Maria Martinez,
Luis Carmona, and Antonio Pellicer. 2013. "Five Years' Experience Us-
ing Oocyte Vitrification to Preserve Fertility for Medical and Nonmedical
Indications." *Fertility and Sterility* 99(7): 1994–99.

Gibbs, Nancy. 2010. "The Pill: So Small. So Powerful. And so Misunderstood." *Time*, 3 May. Retrieved 9 August 2020 from http://content.time
.com/time/magazine/0,9263,7601100503,00.html.

Göçmen, İpek, and Azer Kılıç. 2017. "Egg Freezing Experiences of Women in
Turkey: From the Social Context to the Narratives of Reproductive Ageing
and Empowerment." *European Journal of Women's Studies* 25(2): 168–82.

Goldman, Kara N., and Jamie A. Grifo. 2016. "Elective Oocyte Cryopreservation for Deferred Childbearing." *Clinical Obstetrics and Gynecology* 23(6):
458–64.

Goold, Imogen, and Julian Savulescu. 2009. "In Favour of Freezing Eggs for
Non-medical Reasons." *Bioethics* 23(1): 47–58.

Gootman, Elissa. 2012. "So Eager for Grandchildren, They're Paying the
Egg-freezing Clinic." *The New York Times*, 14 May, A1.

Greenwood, Eleni A., Laurie A. Pasch, Jordan Hastie, Marcelle I. Cedars,
and Heather G. Huddleston. 2018. "To Freeze or Not to Freeze: Decision
Regret and Satisfaction Following Elective Oocyte Cryopreservation."
Fertility and Stertility 109(6): 1097–1104.

Gunnala, Vinay, and Glenn Schattman. 2017. "Oocyte Vitrification for Elective Fertility Preservation: The Past, Present, and Future." *Clinical Obstetrics and Gynecology* 29(1): 59–63.

Gürtin, Zeynep B., Trina Shah, Jinjun Wang, and Kamal Ahuja. 2019. "Reconceiving Egg Freezing: Insights from an Analysis of 5 Years of Data
from a UK Clinic." *Reproductive BioMedicine Online* 38(2): 272–82.

Hammarberg, Karin, Maggie Kirkman, Natasha Pritchard, Martha Hickey,
Michelle Peate, John C. McBain, Franca Agresta, Chris Bayly, and Jane
Fisher. 2017. "Reproductive Experiences of Women Who Cryopreserved
Oocytes for Non-Medical Reasons." *Human Reproduction* 32(3): 575–81.

Hertz, Rosanna. 2008. *Single by Chance, Mothers by Choice: How Women are
Choosing Parenthood without Marriage and Creating the New American Family.*
Oxford: Oxford University Press.

Hodes-Wertz, Brooke, Sara Druckenmiller, Meghan Smith, and Nicole Noyes. 2013. "What Do Reproductive-Age Women Who Undergo Oocyte Cryopreservation Think about the Process as a Means to Preserve Fertility?" *Fertility and Sterility* 100(5): 1343–49.

Hughes, Virginia. 2012. "Frozen in Time." *New Scientist* 214: 40–43.

Inhorn, Marcia C., Daphna Birenbaum-Carmeli, Jon Birger, Lynn Marie Westphal, Joseph O. Doyle, Norbert N. Gleicher, Dror Meirow, Martha Dirnfeld, Daniel S. Seidman, Arik Kahane, and Pasquale Patrizio. 2018a. "Elective Egg Freezing and its Underlying Socio-Demography: A Binational Analysis with Global Implications." *Reproductive Biology and Endocrinology* 16: 70.

Inhorn, Marcia C., Daphna Birenbaum-Carmeli, Lynn Marie Westphal, Joseph O. Doyle, Norbert N. Gleicher, Dror Meirow, Martha Dirnfeld, Daniel S. Seidman, Arik Kahane, and Pasquale Patrizio. 2018b. "Ten Pathways to Elective Egg Freezing: A Binational Analysis." *Journal of Assisted Reproduction and Genetics* 35(11): 2003–11.

Kılıç, Azer, and İpek Göçmen. 2018. "Fate, Morals and Rational Calculations: Freezing Eggs for Non-Medical Reasons in Turkey." *Social Science & Medicine* 203: 19–27.

Kim, Ran, Tae Ki Yoon, Inn Soo Kang, Mi Kyoung Koong, Yoo Shin Kim, Myung Joo Kim, Yubin Lee, and Jayeon Kim. 2018. "Decision Making Processes of Women Who Seek Elective Oocyte Cryopreservation." *Journal of Assisted Reproduction and Genetics* 35(9): 1623–30.

Kirkby, Rhiane. 2018. "This is Why More Women Than Ever Are Freezing their Eggs." *Stylist*, 21 April. Retrieved 9 August 2020 from https://www.stylist.co.uk/long-reads/fertility-clinic-london-uk-test-ivf-egg-freezing-motherhood-baby-research-opinion/202508.

La Ferla, Ruth. 2018. "These Companies Really, Really, Really Want to Freeze Your Eggs." *The New York Times*, 29 August. Retrieved 9 August 2020 from https://www.nytimes.com/2018/08/29/style/egg-freezing-fertility-millennials.html.

Lockwood, Gillian M. 2011. "Social Egg Freezing: The Prospect of Reproductive 'Immortality' or a Dangerous Delusion?" *Reproductive BioMedicine Online* 23(3): 334–40.

McDonald, Casey A., Lora Valluzo, Leslie Chuang, Flora Poleschchuk, Alan B. Copperman, and Jason Barritt. 2011. "Nitrogen Vapor Shipment of Vitrified Oocytes: Time for Caution." *Fertility and Sterility* 95(8): 2628–30.

Mertes, Heidi. 2013. "The Portrayal of Healthy Women Requesting Oocyte Cryopreservation." *Facts, Views, and Visions in Obstetrics & Gynaecology* 5(2): 141–46.

Mertes, Heidi, and Guido Pennings. 2012. "Elective Oocyte Cryopreservation: Who Should Pay?" *Human Reproduction* 27(1): 9–13.

Notkin, Melanie. 2014. *Otherhood: Modern Women Finding a New Kind of Happiness*. Berkeley: Seal Press.

Potter, Ann E., and Patricia Knaub. 1988. "Single Motherhood by Choice: A Parenting Alternative." *Journal of Family Economic Issues* 9(3): 240–49.

Pritchard, Natasha, Maggie Kirkman, Karin Hammarberg, John C. McBain, Franca Agresta, Christine Bayly, Martha Hickey, Michelle Peate, and Jane Fisher. 2017. "Characteristics and Circumstances of Women in Australia who Cryopreserved their Oocytes for Non-medical Indications." *Journal of Reproductive and Infant Psychology* 35(2): 108–18.

Sandberg, Sheryl. 2013. *Lean In: Women, Work, and the Will to Lead.* New York: Alfred A. Knopf.

Santo, Elisangela V. Espirito, Felipe Dieamant, Claudia G. Petersen, Ana L. Mauri, Laura D. Vagnini, Adriana Renzi, Camila Zamara, João Batista A. Oliveira, Ricardo L. R. Baruffi, and José G. Franco, Jr. 2017. "Social Oocyte Cryopreservation: A Portrayal of Brazilian Women." *Journal of Brazilian Assisted Reproduction* 21(2): 101–4.

Shkedi-Rafid, Shiri, and Yael Hashiloni-Dolev. 2012. "Egg Freezing for Non-Medical Uses: The Lack of a Relational Approach to Autonomy in the New Israeli Policy and in Academic Discussion." *Journal of Medical Ethics* 38(3): 154–57.

Stoop, Dominic, E. Maes, Nikolaos Polyzos, Greta Verheyen, Herman Tournaye, and Julie Nekkebroeck. 2015. "Does Oocyte Banking for Anticipated Gamete Exhaustion Influence Future Relational and Reproductive Choices? A Follow-up of Bankers and Non-bankers." *Human Reproduction* 30(2): 338–44.

Waldby, Catherine. 2015. "'Banking Time': Egg Freezing and the Negotiation of Future Fertility." *Culture, Health & Sexuality* 17(4): 470–82.

———. 2019. *The Oocyte Economy: The Changing Meaning of Human Eggs.* Durham: Duke University Press.

Wentzell, Emily A., and Marcia C. Inhorn. 2014. "Reconceiving Masculinity and 'Men as Partners' for ICPD Beyond 2014: Insights from a Mexican HPV Study." *Global Public Health* 9(6): 651–75.

World Bank. 2018. "School Enrollment, Tertiary (Gross), Gender Parity Index (GPI)." Retrieved 3 April 2019 from https://data.worldbank.org/indicator/SE.ENR.TERT.FM.ZS?end=2011&name_desc=false&start=1970.

Wyndham, Nichole, Paula Gabriela Marin Figueira, and Pasquale Patrizio. 2012. "A Persistent Misperception: Assisted Reproductive Technology can Reverse the 'Aged Biological Clock.'" *Fertility and Sterility* 97(5): 1044–47.

Conclusion

WAITHOOD IN
THE TWENTY-FIRST CENTURY

Marcia C. Inhorn and Nancy J. Smith-Hefner

In the twenty-first century, waithood is a growing global phenomenon, with young people waiting to marry and have children, and, in the process, extending their period of young adulthood. In this volume, research by fifteen scholars—including fourteen anthropologists and one political scientist—demonstrate *why* waithood is occurring with increasing frequency, and *how* it is being experienced by young people around the world. Overall, these chapters reveal two broad forms of waithood, both of which pivot around the notion of *intentionality*. These forms might best be described as *unintentional waithood* and *intentional waithood*.

Unintentional waithood reflects the original meaning of the term, which was introduced by political scientist Diane Singerman in 2007. In her research on education and marriage in the Middle East, Singerman used the term "waithood" to refer to a pattern of widespread marriage delay among educated youth in Egypt and in other resource-poor countries across the region (Singerman 2007). As Singerman showed, young people were obtaining higher levels of education than ever before, but their education was not leading to employment. In her work, Singerman gave primacy to the experiences of young men, so as to highlight the role of governments in failing to supply sufficient remunerative employment opportunities and the failure of educational systems to adequately prepare young men for the jobs that existed.

In this setting, young people were forced to wait—for jobs, for housing, for marriage, for sex, and for families of their own. Thwarted by high marriage and housing costs—in a cultural setting where young men were expected to pay for both—waithood was both undesired and unintended by the men caught in this situation, as well as by the young women who were waiting for them as marriage partners. For both parties, extended unmarried singlehood led to a period of prolonged dependence on parents, as young people were expected to live at home and remain celibate until marriage. Such unintended waithood ultimately translated into delayed adulthood, given that marriage and childbearing were the ultimate markers of full adult status.

A decade later, in the aftermath of the tumultuous 2011 Arab uprisings, Singerman has updated her original waithood research for the purposes of this volume. Utilizing a variety of quantitative and qualitative date, Singerman underscores the fact that unintentional waithood has become widespread across the Middle Eastern region, especially for youth in resource-poor societies such as Egypt, Jordan, Morocco, and Tunisia. Caused by corrupt and callous governments incapable of insuring economic and social justice for their citizens, this unintentional youth waithood was a major precipitating factor in the Arab Spring, as well as in more recent protests in places like Lebanon and Iraq. Singerman thus extends her analysis in this volume to focus on what she calls the "politics of waithood," in which the state bears major responsibility for the crisis underlying young people's waithood plight.

The plight of young people experiencing unintentional waithood elsewhere is further developed in several other chapters in this volume, particularly those that focus on young men in sub-Saharan Africa. As in the Middle East, increasing numbers of young men living in resource-poor African countries are being forced to delay marriage and family formation, with consequences for their gender identity and social welfare. As seen in this book, even highly educated African young men face difficulties and frustrations, given that government jobs are scarce, formal employment formidable, and the required money and goods necessary for securing a marriage and establishing a household beyond reach. These young men are being "forced to wait" against their will, leading in some cases to out-of-wedlock fatherhood without the culturally sanctioned benefits of marriage. However, even in situations of enforced waiting, these "youthmen," as they are called in some societies, demonstrate what might be called "agency in waiting." In most cases, men strive for education and employment against all odds, sometimes developing social networks dedicated to helping one another.

Waithood takes a different form in societies where economic and political constraints are not so pronounced and stressful for young people. Indeed, the majority of chapters in this volume demonstrate emergent forms of *intentional waithood*, in societies ranging from Asia to Europe to Latin America. Intentional waithood signals agency and aspiration, as young people pursue education and new forms of skilled employment, explore opportunities for travel and self-development, and identify appropriate partners for modern, companionate marriage. Intentional waithood plays out in different ways, but the phenomenon is significantly gendered.

To wit, for women around the world, the basic trend is one where, as educational and employment opportunities become more widely available, young women take advantage of those opportunities and postpone marriage and childbearing by choice. Education in particular is becoming women's aspiration, with women now outstripping men in higher education in more than one-third of the world's nations. Women's pursuit of education in their twenties and thirties offers an important space of discovery and freedom, one that was largely unavailable in their mothers' generation. This twenty-first-century shift toward education and intentional waithood on the part of women involves several forms of social recognition: first, the value of women's education; second, women's desires to work and pursue professional careers; third, women's rights to personal development and self-actualization; fourth, new gender norms and sexual identities; and finally, new enactments of courtship, dating, and practices of intimacy.

For young women, but also for young men, intentional waithood and the prolongation of unmarried singlehood has led to new configurations of romance and partnership beyond the bounds of marriage. This can be seen in the growth of online dating services, young people's pursuit of multiple romantic and sexual partners over time, increases in non-married cohabitation, and the emerging acceptance in some societies of childbearing without marriage. These changes have often been viewed as a cause for alarm on the part of the older generation, with well-established religious and moral authorities sometimes warning of a "marriage crisis."

Over time, however, these transformations toward intentional waithood and new forms of gendered intimacy have led to powerful shifts in social values in many societies, with young people becoming much freer to choose among a variety of pathways to partnership and parenthood. But perhaps the most striking social consequence of all in this ongoing social transformation is the global rise in age at first marriage—and, even more consequentially, the global declines in marriage as some people choose to never marry at all. Today, nearly 90 percent of the world's population lives in a country with falling marriage rates. Several chapters in this volume focus on this trend, showing the ways in which women are "opting out" of marriage, either through specific "tactics" of marriage delay, or simply by inertia as they follow their educations and careers into permanent states of singleness.

Having said this, it is important to note that in the majority of cultural contexts, including those presented in this volume, (a) marriage is still a given, (b) childbearing is still expected within the bounds of marriage, and (c) both are closely linked to the achievement of social adulthood. Non-marriage, especially for women, is viewed as a personal failure, as seen in some chapters where unmarried women may face derision, scorn, and social, economic, and physical vulnerabilities. While opting out of marriage may be acceptable in an increasing number of Western societies, it is typically *not* experienced as something desired or planned in other places, especially by women. Rather, non-marriage—and consequent lack of childbearing—may be an unintended consequence of simply "waiting too long."

Indeed, as shown in the final section of this volume, intentional waithood may have *unintended consequences,* particularly for women. For one, educated women are now surpassing the educational achievements of young men around the globe. But they are then faced with a smaller pool of equally well-educated men to marry. These gender-based educational disparities are leading to a "man deficit" and "leftover women," as highly educated women are unable to find marriage partners. For those educated women who do go on to marry, the common pattern of hypergamy (or women marrying "up") is being challenged by a pattern of hypogamy (or women marrying "down"). In other words, an educated woman who wants to marry may be forced to choose a man who has less education, is younger, is economically less secure, or comes from a different ethnic, racial, religious or class background.

Highly educated women around the globe who are unable to find marriage partners are increasingly turning to egg freezing as a way to preserve what's left of their fertility. For women, age-related fertility decline begins in the early thirties, but is significantly amplified in the late thirties and early forties. As several of the chapters in this volume show, waiting *too long* to reproduce—because of extended educational or career opportunities, inability to find a committed reproductive partner, anxiety over one's financial ability to raise a child, feeling fit and healthy and unaware of the inner "biological clock," and any number of other factors—may result in women's inability to achieve desired reproductive goals. Age-related infertility cannot necessarily be overcome, even with resort to costly assisted reproductive technologies. Particularly in parts of Europe, significantly increased rates of age-related infertility among women, resulting from prolonged states of waithood in the reproductive-aged population, are turning some societies into so-called "barren states," where populations are no longer replacing themselves.

In Europe and beyond, approximately half the world's population now lives in societies where total fertility rates are below replacement level. Particularly in East Asia, the term "ultra-low" is being used to describe total fertility rates well below two children per couple. In Japan, for example, the overall reluctance of young people to *ever* marry or *ever* have sex for the purposes of procreation is leading to a demographic crisis that no amount of egg freezing or assisted reproduction can solve—despite the country's commitment to in vitro fertilization, with the second highest number of IVF clinics (nearly 600) in the world.

Thus, what waithood will mean for the twenty-first century remains to be seen. Will young people around the world increasingly delay marriage and childbearing, or forego it altogether as in Japan? Will societies around the world follow the "ultra low" fertility patterns now common in East Asia? Will young people's reproductive waithood effectively reverse normal population pyramids? Will marriage rates continue to plummet as the costs of marriage continue to increase? Will marriage no longer be a marker of adult identity, and childbearing be accepted outside the bounds of marriage? Will remaining single become a socially accepted lifestyle choice? And will new forms of sociality emerge for people who decide to have children on their own, with or without technological assistance?

All of these questions are inextricably linked to the theme of waithood, with answers likely to emerge over the course of the twenty-first century. Yet, two broad patterns of waithood are already clear, as seen in this prescient volume. Thus, the task for future anthropologists, political scientists, demographers, and others interested in gender, education, marriage, and childbearing will be to "wait and see" how waithood unfolds.

Marcia C. Inhorn is the William K. Lanman, Jr. Professor of Anthropology and International Affairs in the Department of Anthropology and MacMillan Center for International and Area Studies at Yale University, where she serves as Chair of the Council on Middle East Studies. A specialist on Middle Eastern gender, religion, and health, Inhorn is the author of six award-winning books, including *America's Arab Refugees: Vulnerability and Health on the Margins* (Stanford University Press, 2018). She is (co)editor of ten books, founding editor of the *Journal of Middle East Women's Studies* (*JMEWS*), and coeditor of Berghahn's "Fertility, Reproduction, and Sexuality" book series. Inhorn holds a PhD in anthropology and an MPH in epidemiology from the University of California, Berkeley.

Nancy J. Smith-Hefner is Professor of Anthropology and Chair of the Department of Anthropology at Boston University. A specialist of Southeast Asia, gender, and Islam, she is author of *Khmer American: Identity and Moral Education in a Diasporic Community* (University of California Press, 1999) as well as numerous book chapters and journal articles. Her recent book, *Islamizing Intimacies: Youth, Sexuality, and Gender in Contemporary Indonesia* (University of Hawaii Press, 2019), is a study of the changing personal lives and sexual attitudes of educated, Muslim Javanese youth against the backdrop of a resurgent interest in more normative forms of Islam. Smith-Hefner received her BA, MA, and PhD from the University of Michigan.

INDEX

Powell, Dorian, 233
power of choice, 193
pregnancies, 23; age-related female
  infertility, 317 (*see also* infertility);
  intentions of, 349; in Sierra
  Leone, 139; trends, 317, 318. *See*
  also childbearing
premarital sex in Iran, 250, 263. *See*
  also sex
pressure to marry (in India), 300,
  301
privilege, male, 61
process interviews (ARTs), 323–24
production, 116. *See also*
  reproduction
professional women, 269–71;
  being single in Jordan, 278–84;
  demographies, 273–74; egg
  freezing and, 377–78 (*see also* egg
  freezing); migration and effects
  on marriage prospects, 275–78.
  See also refusing to settle; women
prophylactics, 210
Protestant churches, 64, 229. *See*
  also Christianity
protests, 47, 48. *See also* Arab Spring
providers, concept of, 74
public health regulations (France),
  319
purposeful waiting, 15

QQ, 189
queer-identified individuals, 180,
  295, 305, 346, 348. *See also*
  lesbian identity

Rahman, Abdul, 80, 81
al-Razzaz, Omar, 50
real-life responsibilities, 166, 168,
  170
recent graduates (*jeunes diplômés*), 89
refusing to settle, 11t, 22, 269–71;
  being single in Jordan, 278–84;
  demographies, 273–74; migration
  and effects on marriage
  prospects, 275–78; overview of,
  271–73

regulations, public health (France),
  319
relationships: compassion in
  (Indonesia), 218; egg freezing,
  372t–373t; long-term, 166;
  non-monogamous, 250. *See also*
  courtships; dating; marriage
religion: in the Caribbean, 226;
  and Muslims, 15. *See also* specific
  religions
reproduction, 116–18; autonomy,
  366; in the Caribbean, 233–35;
  governance, 341; incentives
  shaping, 123–26; and Indigenous
  Peoples, 118; outsourcing, 344–
  46; revolution (1960s), 362
reproductive temporality, 9t,
  329–33
reproductive waithood, 11t, 25;
  educational disparities, 379–83;
  ethnographic study, 367–68;
  egg freezing, 362–67; men as
  partners, 383–85; from women's
  perspective, 374–79
reputations in the Caribbean, 235
resources, non-governmental
  organizations (NGOs), 121
respectability in the Caribbean, 235
retirement, 292
Revolutionary United Front
  (ROOF), 137
risks of infertility, 329–30
Robertson, John A., 340
romance, 393; in Iran, 255;
  modernization of, 201, 210–11;
  tea circles (*fadas*), 103–6. *See also*
  marriage; sex
romantic companions (Caribbean),
  228
rotating credit association (*tontine*),
  100
Ruiz-Gallardón, Alberto, 339, 340
rural-to-urban migration, 177–81,
  187, 188, 271. *See also* China
Rusagara, John, 156
Rwanda, 17; care for elders,
  164; demographies (women),

www.ingramcontent.com/pod-product-compliance
Lightning Source LLC
Chambersburg PA
CBHW062107040426
42336CB00042B/2260

* 9 7 8 1 8 0 0 7 3 6 2 9 0 *